# LOYAL TO THE END

# LOYAL TO THE END

**Author's section crossing the river and the River is called Chior
on a suspect raft, that was later ambushed.
(See page 143)**

By
*Frederick William Hudson*
CREMER PRESS

First Published in Great Britain in 2006 by
Frederick William Hudson
C/0 Cremer Press, Blackburn. BB2 2JE.

## ISBN 1 898722 59 5
## 978 1 898722 59 5

Printed in Great Britain in 2006 by
**Edmund Mercer,** Cremer Press,
45 Harrison Street, Blackburn. Lancs. BB2 2JE.

This book is dedicated to the following

## The Somme Training Platoon 1957
All Malayan Veterans 1948-1960

## All Soldiers Past and Present
Especially Granddad, James Hudson

From
'The Proudest of Regiments'

# The Loyal Regiment
NORTH LANCASHIRE

AND

## The Queen's Lancashire Regiment
'LOYALLY I SERVE'

## And to the two-thousand
NATIONAL SERVICEMEN
1948 TO 1962

Who failed to return home to their 'Loved Ones'

# 'In the Peacetime'

**Which made their loss more poignant
and their sacrifice**
## More Easily Forgotten

# FOREWORD

National service is still a contentious subject and can generate much heated debate. In *'Loyal to the End'*, Fred Hudson has taken a hard and honest look at the subject. Through the eyes of one who experienced national service first hand, you follow Fred from leaving home, through his vigorous army training, then on to combat in the steamy jungles of Malaya.

This is not just a story of an individual soldier however, it is also the story of his friends and comrades in the 1st Battalion of the Loyal Regiment (North Lancashire), or the Loyals as they were nicknamed. A typical Lancashire infantry regiment, the Loyals recruited many soldiers from around the North-West of England, but specifically Preston and Bolton.

As infantry they were the backbone of the British Army, and it is a constant truth throughout history, that success or failure on any battlefield, will ultimately depend upon the fighting spirit of the infantry soldier. As a result the infantry will always endure the greatest hardships and suffer the greatest casualties. The men of Lancashire have always been recognised as some of the best, and today the Queen's Lancashire Regiment, maintains the spirit and traditions of the Loyals.

In Malaya the British Army got it right, and through the dedicated service of Fred Hudson and his fellow national servicemen, Malaya did not fall to the evils of Communist terrorism.

Usually war stories are told from the perspective of a senior officer, but the strength of this book is that we follow the story from the point of view of the man on the ground. As such, this full account is a valuable insight into the role of an ordinary Lancashire soldier from a county regiment, in this country's fight against terrorism in the 1950's. It has great merit, both for its factual and often frank accounts of the war in the jungles of Malaya.

Fred's enthusiasm for the subject comes across strongly, and in addition to his enlightening account, he has also used his energy to establish a Malayan archive in the museum of the Queen's Lancashire Regiment, which is located at the old Loyals Depot at Fulwood Barracks in Preston. It is hoped the reunion of Malayan Veterans, that took place in February 2003, will result in the formation of a Loyals Malayan Veteran's Association within the existing Regimental Association.

National service was, and remains, a controversial subject, and the utility of the national serviceman is often questioned today. Nevertheless, the events in Malaya proved that properly trained and motivated national servicemen, well led by Regimental Officers', were a force to be reckoned with.

Loyally I Serve


Lt Col. *Mike Glover* MA, AMA.

# PREFACE

When I visited the Loyals Regimental Museum at Fulwood Barracks in Preston for the first time at the request of David, one of my younger brothers, I wondered if we would see anything of interest from my time as a national serviceman when I spent time serving with the Loyals and pursuing the Communist terrorists in the Malayan jungle.

I had not realised prior to that visit, that David, who was only a young child at the time, remembered vividly my marriage to Betty five days before my two year's enlistment into the army, and my return from Malaya two years later, as a so called jungle fighter and war veteran!

As we wandered through the museum I was beginning to feel somewhat disappointed, as I had seen nothing relative to my time with the Loyals. I had almost reached the end of the exhibition when I came upon a display case that contained some Malayan campaign artefacts.

As I was studying the display with great interest, David called me back to a corner of the room, "Do you know anyone on this photograph?"

The large photograph was displayed at ceiling height and had been missed by myself as I passed by it. When I looked up I was in for a real shock because the photograph was of my section. I should say here that I was a section commander with 4 Platoon for most of my time in Malaya.

David repeated his question impatiently. "Do you know anyone in the photograph?"

As I replied, "I know all of them; it was my section," a member of the museum's staff happened to be walking past.

He stopped and came towards us, directing an inquiring gaze at me. "Can you actually put names to the lads in the photograph, as nobody here knows who they were."

"I'll be more than pleased to do that," I said out loud, thinking at the same time, "That's the least I can do for my lads, my old comrades."

The staff member now introduced himself to us saying that his name was Mark, and in turn we told him our names.

"Are there any other displays on Malaya apart from the small display?" I asked him eagerly. ("I later found out, to my surprise, that this display had been provided by Major Maher, one of my old comrades in 'B' Company.")

Mark replied that there wasn't, which we all found disappointing, but he said that he would ask Gary Smith, the Assistant Curator at the Museum to come down and have a chat with us.

Two minutes later I was asking Gary what artefacts they were holding on Malaya?

His reply was that they had very little, but they did have some photographs. Unfortunately, with many of the photographs, no one knew where they were taken, or who the lads were in them. He asked if I would be interested in coming into the museum at some time, to put names to some of the faces, if I was able to do so?

As I was now retired and had time on my hands, I eagerly told him, "I'll be only too pleased to look at the pictures, and help out the museum if I'm able."

My brother and I left the museum with our spirits very much uplifted, and I eagerly looked forward to going back again.

As usual one thing led to another, and some time later I was asked if I would like to do a sound recording for the North-West Sound Archives about the Loyals in Malaya. Amazingly that lasted for seven and a half-hours, and was two days in the making. After doing the recordings, I told Gary Smith that there were still parts of the Malayan story untold, he suggested that I should write a book about my experiences.

That was the idea that started me working on this book. The following pages contain a tiny part of the Loyals history and a large part of mine; I hope that you find it to be of some interest.

*Frederick William Hudson*

**Author's Footnote:-**
Between completing writing 'Loyal to The End' and my work being published, the Queen's Lancashire Regiment was reformed along with the King's Own Royal Border Regiment and the King's Regiment into **The Duke of Lancaster's Regiment.** All dedication and acknowledgements within this book also apply to the new Regiment.

# CONTENTS

# ACKNOWLEDGEMENTS

The author would like to thank the following:-

## Kirkham Grammar School
For teaching me the important 3 R's.

RESPECT
RESPONSIBILITY
RECTITUDE

## Mum, Dad and Annie
For teaching me the importance of helping others.

## Doreen Manley, Rob Povall, Dean and Stella Hudson,
For ensuring that the text is legible.

## Lt Col. J. P. Cross. OBE. FABI. MIL. BA.
For his proof reading, editing and encouragement.

My Courageous Editor
**Madeleine Fish**

**All the staff** at the Regimental Museum,
Fulwood Barracks, Preston,
For all their help, interest and kindness.

# INTRODUCTION

The first National Service Act of Parliament was passed during the Second World War to cover the war and the consequences of the war. The National Service Act of Parliament 1948 brought about the modern concept of Army, Navy, and Air Force National Service. That came into force and was effective from January 1st 1949 and the call-up continued until the 31st of December 1960. The last national serviceman, 23819209 Private Fred Turner was discharged on the 7th of May 1963.

In the beginning national service was for a fixed period of eighteen months with four years in the reserves, but in the early 1950's, due mainly to the Korean War and the on-going Malayan Campaign, this was changed to a two-year period with three and a half years in the reserves.

By Acts of Parliament, national service was for the period 1948 to 1960.
The Malayan Conflict lasted for the period 1948 to 1960.
More than any other, Malaya was the national serviceman's campaign.

The Malayan Campaign saw, for the first time in the world, helicopters being used as part of the military action, to both ferry troops in and out of the jungle areas quickly, and also to evacuate casualties directly from the conflict to the hospitals.

It was also the military campaign that prevented the much feared, and so-called domino effect, to the far Eastern Countries, where one country falls to the Communists and then the next country and so on, like falling dominoes throughout the Continent.

The most important fact, and the greatest tribute to the national serviceman, is that it is the only conflict in which the Democratic Western World has been engaged against a Communist Army, on grounds of their choosing, and emerge triumphant.

In May 1948 a secret meeting of the Malayan Communist Party Politburo was held inside the jungle, near to Raub in the State of Pahang. At the meeting the new leader of the Party, Chin Peng, revealed his plans to switch from achieving their objectives by peaceful political means, to a military armed conflict based on a Communist army operating from within the jungle, and supported by civilian members living within the community at large.

Less than a month later the opening shots of the protracted Twelve-year's War were fired in the State of Perak, near to Sungi Siput, when three unsuspecting British rubber planters were assassinated on their plantations.

As one would expect, the enemy was brutal to the extreme, and any British soldiers who were wounded or captured could expect little mercy at their hands, and would be tortured and then killed. This was in spite of the fact that it was the British who had befriended them, and had been their allies in Malaya during the conflict against the Japanese during the Second World War. The British were also responsible to a large extent for their training, and providing the arms that were now being used *against* them.

The Malayan civilians who failed to co-operate suffered badly at the hands of the Communists, especially those who lived in the countryside and worked on the cultivation and plantations. Any failure to provide supplies to the Communists when requested would result in torture or death.

The Great Malayan Communist Army quickly became known as the Communist Terrorists, to the security forces they were the CT's, to the national serviceman they were referred to as 'Charlie'.

# INTRODUCTION

## 'THE ENEMY'

### 'The Malayan Alamo'

## BUKIT KEPONG POLICE STATION

Anyone who served in Malaya heard the story about the Police Station at Bukit Kepong. It was built on a bend about forty miles inland on the River Muar in the State of Johore. The Station was staffed with nineteen Malayan policemen and three local Home Guard. Also in the police compound were the living quarters, which housed twelve wives and their children.

In the early morning darkness on the 23rd of February 1950, the Fourth Independent Company of the Malayan Communist Army, consisting of about two-hundred men, attacked the police compound.

Several attacks by the CT's were beaten back by the defenders, who were continually weakened by each attack, until they were finally overpowered five hours after the initial attack. In the course of the attacks, the living quarters had been set on fire whilst women and children were still inside. After the final attack, any wounded and children that were left, were brutally thrown alive into the flames of the burning quarters.

Such was the barbarous enemy that we were fighting and totally committed to eliminating!

After this attack, Mat Indra, the leader of the raid on the police station, declared that the Malayan Communist Liberation Army had dealt a glorious defeat on the

Imperialists and had struck a blow for the oppressed peoples of Malaya.

Under British Rule, and then Independence in 1957, the Malayans had the freedom, and all the time required for them to make their own mind up on that one.

Mat Indra was dealt his glorious defeat some time later when he walked into an ambush.

I personally spoke to dozens of Malays and Chinese during my time in Malaya, and the message that I was nearly always given, was that under the Japanese they had already experienced rule by masters, who would beat or kill them if they didn't do what was required, and sometimes beat and kill them even when they did!

# NOTE FROM THE AUTHOR

Loyal to the end is my autobiography. It tells of my personal experiences as a national serviceman with the 1$^{st}$ Battalion, Loyal North Lancashire Regiment, in Malaya.

It is a personal and factual account of some of the experiences encountered within my two year's enlistment as a national serviceman. All the incidents within the book did occur to me, and are recounted from memory, with the help of personal notes, letters, photographs and artefacts from that period of time.

Many of the chapters are accompanied by supporting photographs which I personally took at the time of the events covered within the book.

I have written the book from a personal level, and in an attempt to appeal to readers of all types and ages, rather than just military personnel. I believe that I have been successful in doing this, and I hope that you enjoy reading the book, maybe just as much as I have enjoyed 'Laying the ghosts of the past'.

*Frederick William Hudson*

# THE MORNING PERIMETER STAND TO

Flickering eyelids challenging the impenetrable blackness.
The mind probing the senses as to awake or in a dream.
A slow stirring to the lasting darkness of the jungle night.


The dawn chorus reverberation from the jungle canopy above.
Apprehensive mortals below dwelling in an unfamiliar land.
English sounds unknown there in the strange surroundings.


Monkeys chattering in the canopy above the jungle darkness.
Birds singing their opening call to the pale morning light.
The jungle darkness below not yet touched by the dawn.


Friend and foe awaking to another day of survival.
Each bonded to the other by the dark jungle and belief in
duty.
The hunter and the hunted but which.


The sun rises above the far distant mountain ridge.
Its radiance brightly illuminating the jungle below.
Its warm bright rays piercing the canopy like magic lanterns.


Another new day with its unknown challenges.
A silent prayer kept secret within one's turbulent thoughts.
Then to pursue the destiny still hidden within the new day.


*Frederick William Hudson*
MALAYA JUNGLE (1959)

# LIST OF BRITISH ARMY INFANTRY RANKS WITH ABBREVIATIONS
### (For reference use throughout the story as needed)

| Rank | Abbreviation |
|------|--------------|

**Rank**     **Abbreviation**

**Private**     **Pte**

**Lance Corporal**     **LCpl**
(Probably second in command of a Platoon Section
  2.1 C.Section)

**Corporal**     **Cpl**
(Probably Platoon Section Commander   1.C. Section))

**Sergeant**     **Sgt**
(Probably Platoon Sergeant)

**Colour Sergeant**     **C/Sgt**
(Probably Company Quarter Master   Q.M.)

**Company Sergeant Major**     **C.S.M.**

**Regimental Sergeant Major**     **R.S.M.**

**Warrant Officer**     **W.O.**
(Probably, possibly R.S.M.)

**Second Lieutenant**     **S/Lt**
(Probably, possibly Platoon Officer   I.C. Platoon

**First Lieutenant**     **Lt**
(Probably, possibly Platoon Officer   I.C. Platoon)

## Captain                                                    Capt
(Possibly Company Commander I. C. Company or could be
Company 2. I.C.

## Major                                                      Maj
(Probably, possibly Company Commander I.C. Company or could be
Battalion 2.I.C.)

## Lieutenant Colonel                                         Lt Col
(Probably, possibly The Battalion Commander Officer   The C.O.

## Colonel                                                    Col
(Probably, possibly The Battalion Commander Officer   The C.O.

## Brigadier General                                          Brig
(Probably, possibly The Commanding Officer of the Regiment

## Major General

## Lieutenant General

## General

## Field Marshal

# CHAPTER ONE
## Call Up and Basic Infantry Training

It's now over forty years since the last call-up for national service, and since I was personally called to do my duty for Queen and Country!

In the 1950's *'Your Country Needs You'*, was one of the wind-up sayings from friends and acquaintances when they knew that you were nearing the age for enlistment. That could have been from when you turned eighteen up to twenty-one years of age. The modern concept of national service commenced in January 1949 and lasted for fourteen years before being abandoned.

I know that forty years is a long time to wait before writing about one's army experiences, but as to why I did not do this before, well I cannot really answer that. Whilst I have often considered writing about my time with the Loyals, and my wife has suggested many times that I should put pen to paper after relating this or that story about Malaya; most of the time I was just too busy working and trying to run a business, any spare time that I had was used up serving the people of Lancashire and wearing various hats.

In the early days after I had returned from Malaya I was just too frightened of stirring up too many painful memories. For years afterwards I was still trying to get my mind back together following those days. But I believe that having left it for so long, the writing of this book now will make it so much the better, the small irrelevant memories and all the clutter that was important to me then, for whatever reason, have gone. The only memories that are now left are the **important** ones, those with the details that are burnt into one's mind forever, and therefore still seem to be as clear as if it all happened yesterday.

It's impossible to put onto paper the feelings and fears from that time so long ago, and all the anguish, pain and humiliations that one had to endure during the two years national service, ranging from big-mouthed sergeants and corporals on frozen parade grounds in the UK, to big-mouthed tigers, leeches and 'Charlie' shooting at you in the steaming hot jungles of Malaya!

Looking back now it would appear that because so much happened in such a short time, a lifetime had somehow become crammed into that two-year period.

Like all other boys and young men in the 1940's and 50's I grew up fearful of having to possibly do national service. We had all heard the tales that were told by the ex-soldiers who had been and done it; although we knew that many of them had in truth never left the shores of the UK. It must be remembered that everyone of our age spent their childhood and youth growing up in the middle of the Second World War, and of course following that there were Palestine, Egypt, Kenya, Cyprus and Korea to name just a few places in the world where British soldiers were being killed, and of course Malaya.

It also didn't help our fears knowing that a lot of what the old soldiers were saying was being embellished or invented, simply to make us feel worse at the prospect of being called up. I am sure we did the same after we had done our 'bit' for Queen and Country.

I wasn't all that unduly worried myself, because my doctor had been telling me for years that because of a perforated eardrum I would be classed as Grade 4 at my army medical, and so deemed not eligible for national service.

In fact I had damaged my left ear badly when I was just a one-year old child by pushing a sharp pencil into it. By the time that I was eight-year's old I loved, and was heavily involved with swimming, and had to visit my doctor on a regular basis due to water continually penetrating and infecting my ear. Perhaps it was foolish not to keep out of the water, but I was the 1952 Northern Counties 50-metre schoolboy free-style champion, and addressed as a possible member of the future Olympic Team. I was also for many years, a member of the British Life-Saving Society and a lifeguard on Blackpool beach.

One autumn Saturday evening in 1955 at the Winter Gardens, Blackpool, I was destined to meet the girl who was to become my wife, and immediately swimming was no longer the most important aspect in my life. Betty didn't swim, so within two or three weeks of meeting her I had given up competitive swimming, and I must say here that I have never regretted that decision.

Fortunately, or unfortunately, when I was called up for my military medical check-up two years later, my eardrum had healed, or so they made out, and I was passed A1 grade. I have been told since that once my ear was damaged, it was damaged for life, and I therefore should not have been passed A1, but then, as now, *they* could do whatever they wanted, and if they had failed me, then you would not be reading this or what's to come later, and I would have missed out on the greatest adventure in my life.

A week or two after the medical at Cop lane, Penwortham I received notice I was A1 and that I had to report to Ladysmith Barracks in Ashton-under-Lyne. Betty and I had already decided that if I was called up, we would get married before I went in. This was in case of anything happening to either of us, then she would have been recognised by the army to be my next of kin and treated accordingly, no matter where in the world I happened to be.

At that moment in time I had no idea that I would be sent to Malaya. I knew the Loyals were out there, but I had been called up into the Manchester Regiment, much to my disgust. I do not wish to offend anyone who knew the Manchesters for they were a good regiment, but I had personally selected the Loyals as my first choice.

My choice was coloured for me by my Grandfather, for he had been in the Loyals during the First World War. He was wounded, gassed, and was the sole survivor of his platoon on more than one occasion. He died in 1946 from war wounds that he received in the 1914-18 World War. To me he was a great and loving man, and as a child I could never understand anyone wanting to hurt him, nor him wishing to hurt another human being; he really was such a gentle man. I do know that he was proud to have served with the men of the Loyals, his gallant comrades!

However my desire to be with the Loyals was not *just* down to my Grandfather's service, but also because I was in the Loyal Cadets for three years, while studying at Kirkham Grammar School.

In the 1940's and 50's military life was a part of life, especially after this country had been caught out unaware twice, and had become involved in two World Wars, because they were unprepared. It was the country's decision that this was never going to happen again. Where this leaves us as a Nation today I shudder to think, as we are in all probability more unprepared now than we have ever been!

After I left the grammar school in 1952 I was asked to join the Kirkham Home Guard by Major Lawson, who was an old farmer in Weeton, as well as the Home Guard Commander at Kirkham. This came about because he knew I was a good shot with a rifle, and Kirkham Home Guard had a good rifle team that tended to win all the shooting competitions.

The Home Guard unit was a detachment of the Loyal Regiment, so I was with the Loyals again. I joined the Home Guard at the indoor rifle range on the Kirkham RAF camp at 20:30 one dark and wet autumn evening, and the following morning at 07:00 it was announced that the Home Guard was being disbanded with immediate effect.

I believe that with the Home Guard being disbanded in the early 1950's the way it had been, would make me the last person to have joined. I must have upset someone with something that I said. After all I have always had a real talent for doing that!

The old RAF camp is now Kirkham Prison, I suppose that some of the national servicemen who served there would say that it hasn't changed a bit. The Home Guard had been stood down from a war footing in 1942 after the first Americans started arriving in the UK. I do know that I really enjoy watching and get a special kick out of the television programme 'Dads Army'.

So obviously with the Loyals being my first choice of Regiment, and my strong connection with them, I was upset at not being called into the Loyal Regiment; but that was all to change later.

Betty and I were married at St. Nicholas Church in Wrea Green on the Saturday afternoon of the 20th July 1957. It was a beautiful warm English summer day, and the birds were singing beautiful choral refrains in the trees all around the church.

All our families were there, along with those of our friends who were able to make it. Some of my friends were in the forces doing their national service, so obviously they could not be there, but that's the way it was in those days; people made the best of things when they were together, because no one knew what was waiting around the corner.

When my lovely bride and I passed through the church doors having been married for just a few minutes, the traditional English summertime countryside way of life opened up before us. The lych-gate to the church was surrounded with old school friends and acquaintances; the sun was shining and the birds were still singing.

From the village green opposite, came the sound of leather hitting willow, as the men in their white shirts and pants were playing cricket. One or two who would say, "hello" when we passed them in the village, turned at the sound of the church bells ringing and waved to us. It was not only a cherished wonderful moment in time, but for Betty and myself it was a traditional English way of life, something that we had grown up to love and to believe in, and at that moment we thought it would last forever.

Five days later on Thursday the 25th July at 10:30, I walked through the gates of Ladysmith Barracks to begin my army national service, and although none of us realised it then, the traditional English way of life that we all loved had gone forever.

To me now, it seems sometimes as though all of one's life is preordained and that someone is watching over you, making sure you don't stray from the chosen path.

There are some quite amazing coincidences in this book, and this is the first one. On the 25th July 2001 at 10:30, exactly forty-four years to the minute, after walking through the gates of Ladysmith Barracks to start my national service, I walked through the gates of Fulwood Barracks in Preston to give a 'sound' interview about national service in Malaya for the North-West Sound Archives. Later on there are even more amazing coincidences in this book, all of which I promise are absolutely true and were never planned.

I entered Ladysmith Barracks with a great amount of trepidation; all the horror stories that I had been told came flooding to the front of my mind, and they were most definitely not helping me in any way at that moment in time.

It was one of those mornings in which the weather was in the same mood as myself, one of those oppressive summer days that needed a good downpour to clear the air. A Lance Corporal (LCpl) stood just through the gates directing everyone to a large barrack room to the side of the square. To put it politely he was a big nasty-natured type of a person. He was there as our first culture shock, and the first of many.

Behind the Lance Corporal was an area that I was to get to know well - the parade ground, or 'The Dreaded Square'. It was about the size of two football pitches joined together side by side. The centre was all tarmac, and surrounded by a border built from two rows of kerbstones, set two feet apart, with soil in the middle. I don't remember any small flowers growing but they were probably there, or maybe they just didn't dare!

The entrances to the square were just as the pockets on a billiard table, one in each corner and one in the middle each side, plus an extra one opposite the main gate. There was a large old stone building at the top of the square, with a flagpole complete with a Union Jack.

This building turned out to be the Officers' Mess, which probably explained why that area had trees and shrubs. Down each side of the square to the left and the right were old-fashioned stone-built barrack blocks. The ones to the right were the living quarters, while the ones on the left were offices, Quartermaster's stores, the Armoury and such like rooms.

Behind that block were lecture rooms, an indoor rifle range and the dreaded barbers. I think the barber was a national service (NS) man awaiting demob, because you most certainly didn't need training to do those haircuts. It's no wonder crew cuts became the fashion!

Behind the barrack blocks on the right were the cookhouse and dining-room, and just behind them, but nearer to the guardroom was the gymnasium. Between the gym and the guardhouse were the NAAFI and the NAAFI shop. To the right of the Officers' Mess were the medical centre and hospital with about twelve beds. Behind the mess and the medical centre was the football field, and behind that was a large and new brick-built building that housed the Army Pay Corps.

I was to find out four week's later that one of my best friends was in there, Gordon Harris. We were on a night out together when I met Betty at the Winter Gardens, and Gordon went out with Betty's friend Pat, for a couple of months. Gordon was one of the friends already in the army when Betty and I got married.

When my friend Gordon came to visit me after I had been in Ladysmith for a few weeks, he was already a Corporal (Cpl), and you will not believe it now, but I was even frightened of him; that's what the terrifying infantry training did to you.

The physical side I could manage, having been a non-smoking ex-sportsman, but the psychological games that were played on us took over our minds and our thinking. They really did dehumanise a person.

The barrack room that I was directed to was over on the left. When I got into the large barrack room I saw a long line of frightened white-faced newcomers waiting their turn to be interviewed by two sergeants (Sgts). As I made my way slowly to the table, the line lengthened behind me, with more new entrants still arriving. It turned out that there were sixty-seven new entrants on that intake, who, when they were sorted, made up three training platoons.

When it came my turn to be interviewed, or should that be interrogated, as anyone who has done national service will know what I mean, I took my heart in my hands and did something that surely very few N.S. men have ever done. I asked the sergeants if there was a leave pass waiting for me?

I am not totally sure of the colour that they turned, but I think that you would have to call it a very bright red. It was the only time in my army service that I saw two sergeants speechless. Naturally it didn't last.

No, I am not that brave so I had better explain about the leave pass that I had requested. The week before, my father had telephoned Ladysmith Barracks and had spoken to the Commanding Officer (CO) explaining that I was being married on the Saturday, just five days prior to joining the army. He asked if it would be possible to defer my joining for a few days on compassionate grounds? The CO sent his best regards, and said that he would consider the request and let me know, but I had heard nothing. So fingers crossed I asked about the leave pass and said that the CO had been considering it. At the mention of the Commanding Officer the sergeants returned to their normal colour.

With an almost normal voice one of them ordered me, "Go to the Orderly Office to check about a leave pass."

I could almost feel the looks of envy from the other lads that someone could be in with a chance of escaping this demented madhouse, created especially for people who had done nothing apart from being born and coming of age. I wasn't that convinced, and fully expected having to return in ten minutes time to the even greater delight of the NCOs.

Somehow I managed to find my way to the Orderly Room, which was situated over the guardroom by the main gate. With my heart in my mouth, I tapped on the office window.

A private soldier opened the window and amazingly he was quite normal, and asked how he could help me?

My spirits began to lift, because I realised that the whole place wasn't a madhouse after all, and there where normal people about, soldiers maybe, but normal.

The Orderly Room Sergeant came to the window and listened to what I had to say. He then told me that the CO was busy that day but it was normal to allow a week's leave, if one had just got married, so he would make one out for me, which he did.

I could not believe my luck, for two minutes later I was walking out of the barrack gates. I could have made it in one minute, and I could have been running, but I didn't want to push my luck, so I walked carefully out. I stood at the bus stop opposite the barracks expecting at any moment that someone would come out to me to say that it was a mistake. However the bus arrived first and I climbed on board with a great feeling of relief.

Betty was obviously pleased to have me back home for another week, but it did mean that by the end of that week I would only have one hundred and three weeks left to do, but as sure as night follows day, the end of the week came, and the time for me to face it all again.

Once more the gates to Ladysmith Barracks were beckoning me. I walked through them and to the guardroom.

I was greeted with, "Ah the missing link returns, aren't they going to have some fun with you!"

However this time it did not seem quite as bad, though it could have been the friendly knowing smile and wink from a soldier in the background that put me more at ease. Anyone who's been in the forces knows that the longer you are 'in', the more you realise that service life is a series of wind-ups, some true, most not; but the send-ups do seem to have a way of somehow keeping everything and everyone normal in times of stress.

I didn't see this facet of life in other nationals that I met. In fact, they could not even begin to understand that side of British humour, if you can call it humour. I believe that it is one of the reasons why the British Army is, like for like, so special when the going gets tough. I can actually remember out in Malaya giving a small nervous chuckle when the shooting started.

This was because someone in the background distinctly said, "They are winding me up!"

But that's a story for later.

At Ladysmith's one hour later, things improved even more, if that was possible. When I was being fitted out in the Quartermaster's stores, I was given a Loyals cap badge, and told that we had been rebadged to the Loyals. This was especially great news for me.

When I was young everyone had members of their family who had been with a certain Army Regiment, in the Navy or RAF, and it had become more or less traditional over the years to follow into one's older family member's service; and of course most Regiments were drawn from certain areas of the country, so you also tended to be with people from your own locality and background. A modern comparison would be that if your family and yourself support Preston North End Football Club, then you would not go around wearing a Manchester City shirt.

Over the next day or two I found out that the rest of the intake weren't as pleased as I was. Some of them wanted to be in the Manchesters or other Regiments, just as I wanted to be in the Loyals. There was also the fact that the Loyals were fighting out in Malaya, so no one was keen to be out there.

Now I had finally joined my training platoon, which was called the Somme Platoon. I hadn't really missed much in the week that I had been off, for the platoon had been run ragged just to show them that they were in the army, and they would do exactly as they were told, whether they liked it or not.

On the parade ground half the platoon didn't know how to march, let alone 'About-Turn', or 'Slope Arms', or obey all the other marching commands. Luckily all of these presented no problem at all for me. I was fortunate to have already mastered this previously, due to enjoying three years in the Army Cadets. Sergeant Beckingham, the Somme Platoon

Sergeant, soon spotted that I knew the ropes and stopped climbing all over my back.

Now I am not going to write about each and every day in training, all I intend to do is to give the general highlights, so that way we will get to the exciting recollections quicker. More importantly I will not break out in a cold sweat, or have a nervous breakdown, thinking about the time that has led to me spending over forty years of my life trying to forget. I have no problems now in telling you all about Malaya and the shooting, ambushing, spiders, snakes, hornets, heat, or all of the hundreds of horrible things that were really nasty, for they were nothing compared to the training. The training NCOs' were always telling us that if we survived their training, then we would survive Malaya.

It's difficult, if not impossible, to put pen to paper, and convey the fears that all NS men who were engaged in infantry training felt. The punishment for refusing to obey an order, running away, or refusing to serve was at least JAIL.

We were continually told that we would suffer if we or our parents wrote to our MP, because word would soon get back to them. The MP for Liverpool, Bessie Braddock, was always being mentioned by the NCOs, because she was always in the news along with other MP's complaining about the treatment dished out to NS men. You have to realise that a lot of NS men died in training due to the treatment they received.

One of *our* intake, I think he was a twenty-one year old lad from Liverpool, died after about seven weeks into training. I cannot tell you much about him because he was not in our platoon, and so I did not know him personally, but as I remember he was well-liked and quite obviously his parents were devastated by his death.

I am trying to do the almost impossible here, to get across and to make it clear, so that you are able to feel what training was like both physically and mentally for the NS man. I have to say now, that it is an experience that obviously and fortunately, you will probably never have to endure, for one really has to go through the experience to know how one was both exhausted physically, and torn apart mentally by it.

You may have seen on your TV, the programmes on the training courses for the SAS, the Paratroopers, the Marines and even the Officers'. Believe me those training courses are nothing to what the NS men were put through. Remember also that those people on TV are free agents; they choose of their own free will to be there. In the first weeks they can just freely walk away, and after that they can still buy themselves out, so the initial psychological pressures that one encounters when they begin training, is reduced to almost zero.

I would agree fully though that all those men, and now women, that you seen on the TV programmes are pushed to the very edge of endurance, and I would be the last person in the world to deride their endeavours, having been through intensive training myself. I am using no artistic licence in writing this account to try to tell exactly what it was like. Infantry NS men were pushed to the very edge of endurance all through training, and many times they were pushed well over the edge both physically, and what to me was far worse, mentally.

We had with us in training three or four Manchester Regiment recruits. They had signed on as regular soldiers to join the Manchester Regiment, so they were not rebadged to the Loyals as the NS men were. It was always noticeable that when anything nasty was coming up, they would be on a lecture or assessment course for the Manchester Regiment.

Regular army recruits at that time could freely leave in the first six weeks of training, and buy themselves out after that time. so regulars, no matter what they say, were treated with kid gloves, unlike NS men whose only other option was a jail sentence and a criminal record. Don't forget that compounding all this treatment was the fact that all the training staff were regular soldiers, whilst **we** were just civilian soldiers, *their* playthings, and we were not even part of the Manchester Regiment and not ever seen as good enough for the Manchesters. We were only fit to join the Loyals in Malaya and be buried in the jungle.

One of the first things we did after I had joined my training platoon was to go to the main rifle range, which was situated up on Saddleworth Moor. We had three days there spending two nights sleeping on a wooden cabin floor. There were one or two highlights for me there. The range was set well up a valley on the moor which I thought was really beautiful, but it became obvious to me that a lot of the lads were not happy out in the countryside. They were what country folk call 'townies', and it made me wonder then how they would react to the jungle, but I thoroughly enjoyed the moors.

Nearly all the lads finished up with bruised shoulders through not keeping the .303 rifle pulled well into their shoulders when firing. They had not realised what a kick the rifle gave out when fired. I was fortunately experienced with both a 12-bore shotgun that had quite a kick, and I had fired a .303 on several occasions in the cadets when I was younger and smaller. The .303 had an even greater kick than a 12 bore shotgun, so I knew from personal experience to keep the butt of the rifle pulled well in to my shoulder.

The first thing that we did was to sight our rifles, which now were our own personal weapons until we had finished our training. The Armourer came up from the barracks each day to carry out any work required on the rifles. We all had to fire at a target 25 yards away, and we were told to try and fire at the same spot each time on the target.

There were twenty firing points along the range and the first action was to get everyone to lie down correctly. This involved a lot of leg and foot kicking by the NCOs, but because I had done it before I had no problem; although everyone had to have a kick (I got the feeling that it was mandatory).

We all fired five rounds and then we had to go and stand by our targets while the Regimental Sergeant Major (RSM) came along to inspect everyone's target and tell the Armourer what setting to put on the rifle sights. I found out later that he always came to the range when it was in use because he loved shooting. Not only was he a good shot, but he really was the best I have seen.

Now the first two targets he checked had the five shots scattered all over the target. Most of the targets only had four shots or even less put into them. One or two had no hits.

When he came to my target he asked, "Whose is this target?"

"Mine Sir," I answered.

"You have shot before lad," he said.

"Yes sir," I replied proudly.

He was actually getting excited, and got a penny out of his pocket. He put the penny over the five holes in the target and all the holes disappeared beneath it. He searched his pockets and then asked if anyone had a halfpenny?

Someone had one and gave it to him.

He put it over the holes and said, "That was close."

Half of one of the holes was showing from under the halfpenny.

He turned to me and said that it was superb shooting, and that it was the nearest he had seen for five shots from a trainee to fit under a halfpenny coin. He also said that if it wasn't a fluke I would be in his rifle team.

I realised there and then how thankful I was for my time spent on the Altcar Ranges, firing the same British Army weapons, during which time I had been fortunate enough to develop my shooting skills.

After three enjoyable days on the range, we returned to the nightmare of Ladysmith's and the horrendous training waiting there for us.

Training! Yes! Well, as I said earlier only the general highlights. I want to try to place you in some of these situations in your mind's eye. I am not going to take you into when we were getting all our injections for this, that and the other: two at a time, two a day, too many that's for sure. I will skip over the mention of blunt needles, with lads fainting around us; nor the visit to the barber's twice a week; nor voluntarily giving a blood donation, stood with your back up against the wall with anyone who does not want to voluntarily give a pint asked to take an impossible step back. Nor will I enlarge on the Asian 'flu' epidemic that in 1957 put down half the nation and half of my platoon; nor the cross-country runs, the gym and the boxing, in which everyone had to fight (covered by the local newspaper reporter), nor the forced marches in full packs and rifles; nor the running to the rifle range three miles away in full gear, with target shooting as soon as you got there, lying down in the cold and wet winter mud; nor the guard duty, marching up and down outside the main gate day and night.

Just in passing, and to lighten this moment, Betty and I recently visited Ladysmith Barracks. All the barrack buildings had gone, and in their place new housing has been built, the stone walls and gun emplacements that surrounded the barracks are still there, as is the main gate structure where so many soldiers for well over one hundred years have paced up and down while on the dreaded guard duty. I felt as though a part of my life had been ripped away when I saw that most of the barracks had gone.

But back now to the realities of 1957, not to mention the lectures and films and bayonet practice and indoor rifle range and church parade on Sundays; nor the square bashing (drill), nor the litter pickets and fire pickets and boiler house pickets and cookhouse pickets, nor the weapons instructions, laundry parades, pay parades, morning parades, be on parade to find something wrong parades.

Then there were the parades when the Company Sergeant Major (C.S.M.) would go round on inspection and push the ends of his pace stick up your nose to push your head back, one point up each nostril saying, "Get your chin up boy."

Who could forget rifle drill when your fingers were frozen in the cold. It all appeared to go on forever, or so it seemed to us then.

I have not mentioned the 'bull,' which was all day every day; everything and everywhere was cleaned, pressed and polished, every day and every spare minute. I will just give you two examples on the bull, to demonstrate what it was like when applied to everything else that we had to do.

The Officer of the day or the C.S.M. would come around the barracks each day. He would be wearing clean white gloves and would then run his hands on any surface that may be hiding dirt; on the floor, the top of a door, locker or windowsill, anywhere he thought there might be dust. If he found any dirt on his gloves when he had finished there'd be trouble.

Naturally we got wiser and smarter with each passing week. We would make sure that the floor and the tops of everything within reach were given a quick wipe two minutes before the inspection, but of course he had been doing it for years, so he would come in and not bother with the cupboards or the more obvious things. He would just wipe his hand on the large heating pipes. We hadn't thought of that so we were in trouble again. Next time the hand went behind the radiators, where dust was found again and so it went on week in and week out.

"Stand by your beds," became another order to fear, another chance to be caught out again, and have the dreaded 'Jankers' loaded on your back, on top of everything else that you had to do. Don't get the impression that it was just 'inside' your barrack room, for the cleaning had to be done absolutely everywhere. The toilets, corridors, stairs and every single place and thing outside the barrack block had to sparkle and gleam as well. It was another continuing impossible nightmare.

The second item I will tell you about has to be army boots. Let's face it the army is famed for the 'bull' to the boots or should I say 'was'. The boots that we were issued with were just common-or-garden leather boots; the ones where the leather had the little lumps all over. We had to turn them into patent leather boots within two weeks, then keep them like that no matter what. To turn them shiny you had to put black shoe polish on with the handle of a spoon heated over a candle, and then spit and polish them for days, or should I say nights, without end.

One trick with the boots was to unscrew the metal heel plate slightly so that when you were marching together as a platoon, there was a double crack, as all the heels went down together onto the square, and it sounded very effective when we were on parade. Another thing that we had to do was to iron the cotton bootlaces so that they were flat, and when you laced up the boots, the laces had to be absolutely flat to the boot. Thank goodness all that mind-bending rubbish ended when we got to Malaya.

When we had been in the army, and of course training for six weeks, we were considered to be near enough soldiers to be allowed out of Ladysmith Barracks for the first time since starting our training. The barracks had an Open Day on the Saturday for the public, which in reality was meant for family members and friends. Betty, together with her mother and mine, came on the train to Ashton-under-Lyne and Ladysmith. After six weeks it was really wonderful to see them, and at that time I remember wondering how on earth am I going to manage not seeing them for nearly two years when I go to Malaya?

I showed them around the barracks and introduced them to my comrades (closer than friends). We had a coffee in the NAAFI, and then we left the barracks and went into Ashton-under-Lyne. It felt really great to be out and in the *real* world. We did some shopping during the afternoon, and I remember being very down after I had waved goodbye to them at the railway station, but it had been a very pleasant day and a reminder that God willing, there would be more pleasant days to come.

Unfortunately, I knew that they would also be accompanied with the downers and goodbyes. There is one item of note that I must mention, something that Betty and my mother have never forgotten. We had lunch in a café in the town centre. We all started with soup then we had the main course. I had steak and chips and then we all had a sweet.

Everyone was full except me, and I said that I could manage the same again. Betty and both our mothers could not believe it because I had never been a big eater. In fact, they always tried to get me to eat more, 'Would not feed a sparrow', is the phrase that seems to spring to mind.

However in the café they all said, "If you can manage it then you have it."

The waitress could not believe it when I said that I would have the same again starting with the soup and right through to the sweet, but I managed to eat every bit of it, and I myself still cannot believe that I did that.

I must say at this point that whereas a lot of the lads lost weight in training I put on nearly two and a half stones. Before you start to relate that if the training was so hard how come I put weight on, remember I worked for my father which was hard work, and I did say that it was the psychology battle that I found the most difficult.

Another drill that I haven't mentioned yet is the arm's drill on the square. I quite enjoyed arm's drill as I had already done all the different drills whilst in the cadets. Here though there was always the regime of terror that really was unrelenting. Late on into the training the weather had turned cold and each morning the square would be covered in ice for the first parade.

One particular morning we were all marched onto the square in the top corner. When the sergeant shouted, "Halt!" half of the platoon went down on the ice.

We all got back up quickly with the help of the Sergeant's mouth. He could have been singing the latest pop song. I wouldn't put money on it though, but he was high-pitched. We completed forty-five minutes arm's drill with all the, 'Slope arms', 'Shoulder arms', 'Present arms', and other orders. Of course the rifles were the standard British Lee-Enfield of the time and they were certainly not light.

When we got off the square after the arm's drill, with most of us bruised from the fall, one of the lads was in real pain; his arm was already swelling up and beginning to go black. We persuaded him to go and see the Medical Officer (MO) and it turned out that he had badly broken his arm. We were told that the MO went mad that the lad had been expected to do anything with that arm, never mind arm's drill. But that was the fear at the time. You cannot imagine that happening today can you? That lad suffered absolute agony for three quarters of an hour, but he was more prepared to stand the pain than suffer the wrath of the sergeant. If you are thinking that was just a one-off, don't, because that was normal!

Let's have a look at the assault course; I haven't told you about that yet have I? When you came out of the barrack main gates the assault course was over the other side of the road and about half a mile up to the left. The course was based on an old council rubbish tip, and the start to the assault course was to the side of the entrance to the tip where it went steeply down hill into the base of a valley where a stream was running. The hill was about one hundred yards long. Unfortunately, for us that is, the hillside had been the tipping spot for all the glass bottles. In those days there were no plastic bottles and everything was in a glass jar or bottle, and from the Ashton-under-Lyne area they all finished up on our assault course, at least the NS man's assault course.

Can you imagine going down this hillside of broken glass bottles? It was too steep for a person to go down slowly, and of course the glass itself was always slipping and sliding. I don't mind admitting that it scared me something terrible; it was a miracle that no one got very badly injured. The rest of the assault course was just the normal army nasty of the day, so I shall not bother telling you about that.

However I will tell you of another nasty trick that was played on us. We also used the assault course for battle training, we used blank ammunition with the rifles, and the NCOs used to throw thunder-flash grenades. These were just like a large banger firework, but very dangerous. If you held one in your hand and it went off, it would easily blow your hand off.

None of the lads in my platoon had seen them before, but I was used to them because they were used regularly both inside and outside the RAF camp in Kirkham. We had also used them in the cadets, so I knew of them and had been instructed as to the dangers of a thunder-flash.

In the army the NCOs used to throw them from a good distance away, and attempt to get them to land between your legs; they did manage to scorch one or two uniforms, which meant more trouble. After I had warned the lads of the dangers, they always used to roll away, much to the annoyance of the NCOs but we got the impression that they knew they were pushing their luck when civilians walked past, who were obviously ex-soldiers. They used to tell the NCOs off for being childish.

I had a look at the assault course while I was there last year. It's overgrown now and well filled in, but I could still recognise it. I am not going to tell you any more about the three month's training at Ladysmith's. By now I have told you enough for you to realise that the training was an absolute nightmare that stayed with me, and I know with others, for years, with thoughts of it still lingering to this day.

At the end of the twelve week's training there was a Passing Out Day. It had been a peculiar feeling for many of us over the last few days to be actually looking forward to a day at Ladysmith's. Could that really be possible?

The dawn was bright and sunny and for October it turned out to be a lovely Saturday morning. The square was surrounded with seating, and everyone as far as I know had friends and family coming for the Passing Out Parade.

My wife came along with her mother, my father who was driving the car and dear old George Edwards, who lived next door to my mum, dad and family in Kirkham. Juddy, as he was known had come along to tell my father which way to go, because he knew the Manchester area very well, as he had been in charge of all the parks and gardens in and around the Manchester area. That day was very special and we had been practising all week for the Passing Out Parade.

It would be the first time that all three training platoons had marched together to the sound of the Army Band. All we had in the past was a sole drummer to give the beat during the practice. The drummer was also the bugler at Ladysmith's and used to wake us up at 06:00 each morning, including every Sunday for Church Parade.

We were dressed in our best uniform; boots highly polished and heel plates loosened. In the barrack room our bags were all packed, because after the Passing Out we were off on three week's pre-Malayan embarkation leave. All our gear and bedding had been handed in to the stores, we were nearly there. Already members of the public, our friends and relatives were arriving, and the seats around the Parade Ground began to fill.

The flags were flying; the sun was shining and the order came to, "Fall In On Parade."

This was it, our big day. We formed up behind the barrack block with our rifles, and out of sight of our friends and relatives. Our platoon was going to be the last one out onto the square, which was great for me because I could see everything happening in front of us.

Then the order finally came, "Attention, Shoulder Arms, Left Turn, and By the Left, in columns of three, Quick March!"

The band struck up at the same time and there we were, around the end of the barrack block and onto the square, three platoons of real soldiers with marching lines, which were as straight as a ruler, and perfectly in step to the last man. It was impossible to be better. We were as good as ... no, we were even better than, any Guards' Regiment I have ever seen, and that's the truth.

The parade went just as planned; the Quick March, the Slow March, the Queen's Salute, all were absolutely perfect. When it came to the march past and off the square and then finish, I thought to myself, we are soldiers now, the best, and for the unnecessary cruelty that you gave to us, you, the NCOs' and Officers of the Manchester Regiment around the square have had to watch the smartest intake you have ever had on your square, the most venerated area of the Manchesters and the heart of the Regiment. and we, the LOYALS, are marching right across it, just as we had said to you, we would be the best, and with every step the heels dug down into the square, altogether in a split second perfection of time.

**Special Note:**

While researching facts of verification for this work, I found that the history books state that the Home Guard was completely disbanded a long time before I joined the Kirkham detachment. What I have written about the Home Guard in the early 50's and at the beginning of this chapter, is exactly as it happened.

I can only assume now that throughout the country some of the units continued together more as a social gathering of comrades. What I always regarded as their termination in the early 50's was possibly the withdrawal of permission to use MOD buildings, arms and equipment.

# CHAPTER TWO
## *More Training in Chichester and then Singapore*

Well all good things do come to an end; as I walked back through the barrack gates at Ladysmith, it felt as though I had only just left the place, for the three week's embarkation leave had not seemed to have lasted three minutes. I went to the guardroom to book back in.

There were a couple of our lads already in the guardroom talking to the staff and it seemed unusual to be having a normal conversation with the Manchester Regiment guys. They were having to do their own guard duty now as the Loyals were no longer doing it as we were out of training, and were leaving for Malaya within a few hours anyway. The words 'Still arrogant after the Passing Out' were mentioned, and so the message had gone home with them after all, which made me and everyone else feel a lot better.

I supposed it was because old habits die hard, that we all drifted back to our old barrack rooms. It gave me a queer feeling to see them empty and dusty. One would have expected the barracks to be filled with a new training intake. The Manchester lads said that they were expecting notification anytime as to the next intake. They also told us that all our training NCOs were away on leave and they were conspicuous by their absence. It was probably a diplomatic move for them not to be there, and just as well; as there were a few of the 'hard nuts' who had been intent on settling scores before we left for Malaya.

We had been hanging around for a couple of hours waiting for the orders to be posted on the notice-board to tell us at what time we were leaving, and also how exactly we would be travelling to Malaya. We had spent some of the time in the NAAFI drinking tea and coffee, talking about our leave and what we had been doing, wondering about Malaya and what it was going to be like; how hot was it going to be, all that sort of thing. Of course, we had all the rumours and wind-ups; we were all going to be rebadged into this, that and the other. The boat had broken down and we were all going to get another week's leave, and so it went on, although we did not know it then, this was our first proper taste of that part of army life, spending your time waiting for orders and listening to wind-ups. At least in Malaya we were doing a real soldier's job, and the only waiting time was in ambush, waiting for the CTs.

All the lads had arrived back in camp, and everyone was milling about in the old barrack rooms and corridors, or in the NAAFI. Suddenly we could hear a commotion outside, someone in the corridor said that the orders had been posted so we all dashed to the door and looked down the corridor.

"Well I am definitely not battling through that lot," I thought, because the end of the corridor was packed with bodies trying to get to the notice-board. "What's the point? We are all going to the same place together, so we will find out soon enough what's happening."

Sure enough within a few seconds one of our lads came in with the news. We still regarded our old training platoons as *ours* but they did not exist anymore; now we were just one Embarkation Company. We were due to have a meal at 13:30, and then on to the three-ton trucks for transportation to the railway station and the train down to Southampton.

We were all sat down and just had a laugh thinking about this and that, when just at that moment one of the lads came in and spoke to me.

"You lucky sod, you're not going."

I really did not believe him, and put it down to another wind-up, but he kept insisting that it was true and that I was going on a course. In the end I went to look at the notice-board and sure enough it was true, I was going down to the South coast and the Army Administration Training Centre. It was absolutely the last thing that I had expected.

I stood in front of the notice-board and kept on reading the news before it disappeared; vanished like magic before my eyes; all the possibilities flashed across my mind and I worked out that I would be home for Christmas. Great, this really was unbelievable.

I had to report to the orderly room for further orders with immediate effect. Once again I was outside the orderly room office window and feeling decidedly good. I tapped on the window and the same lad who I had first seen answered it. I started to explain but he was ahead of me. He gave me an order sheet with all the details and told me where I was sleeping that night which happened to be in the barrack room belonging to the Ladysmith's office staff. I felt quite honoured, for this area was out of bounds to the training company which had been us.

I went back to our old barrack room and collected all my kit. The lads were genuinely pleased for me and wished me all the best. I told them that I would see them all in the dining-room in twenty minutes after I had dropped my kit off in my new and temporary barrack room.

I found my new spot with no trouble, there was even the bedding stacked on the bed ready for me. This was too good to be true, and I made a mental note to check everything carefully when I got back, just in case the Manchester's were playing tricks. I put all my kit into the locker, closed it, then went down to find the lads in the dining-room.

On second thoughts I went to the public telephone in the NAAFI and rang my parents to let them know the news. I was one of the lucky ones whose family had a telephone at home, for very few had in those days, and one or two of the lads had never even used a phone. How times have changed.

Fortunately I managed to catch dad at home, and he said that he would call in to see Betty in Kirkham and give her the good news.

Feeling more at ease now I went to the dining-room. The lads were in there and they had saved my seat at our table. All were still sat at the same table where we had always sat throughout our training. I should have realised that this was going to be the last time in our lives that we would all sit down and eat together.

I knew that they were all off to Malaya in just over an hour's time. I told them that tomorrow I was going on a clerk's course, down to Chichester near Portsmouth for four weeks. All the swear words relating to me being a lucky 'what have you', came out, and even more so when I pointed out that I would be home for Christmas.

We enjoyed that meal including all the customary banter that went with it, but all too soon it was over and suddenly they were all climbing onto the backs of three-ton trucks with their kit. Seeing them all climbing on board was like being at the cinema watching a war film. Typical of the army's lack of sentiment, as soon as the last man was on board, the five trucks were driven away. As they turned through the main gates I could not help but come to attention and salute them.

I could still hear the trucks going down the road towards Ashton-under-Lyne when I realised that I was on my own, with nobody around, no leg pulling, no wind-ups. I made my way up to the room where my kit was, but there was still no one about, and I was beginning to feel very lonely. I set to and made my bed up; with everything tucked in, neatly folded and so tight that a coin would bounce on it when dropped from shoulder height.

Then I thought, "Why am I bothering, there is no one coming round to inspect it?"

I got a book out of my kit and lay on the bed reading it. The author, Ian Fleming, was a good writer. This was the second James Bond book that I had bought, and was finding it to be just as good as the first one. It's amazing how many books you read in the army; everyone was always lending and borrowing them.

I looked at my watch, and as it was nearly 16:00 I decided to go down to the NAAFI for a coffee, where I could watch the TV for a while, because the television programmes would be starting soon. That was providing that the TV transmitters weren't broken down again; television in those days was not on for long and was very unreliable.

I finished my coffee and because the TV was rubbish, I decided to go back up to the room and read my book until it was time for tea, but firstly I called into the NAAFI shop and bought a four ounce bar of Cadbury's dairy milk chocolate. It still seemed strange to me to be able to buy chocolate and sweets without needing ration coupons. I thought, "Thank God those days of rationing are over, maybe one day they will stop national service."

When I got back up to my room there were two Manchester Regiment lads in there who introduced themselves. They knew who I was due to both of them working in the Orderly room. One of them had brought more paperwork for me, including my travel warrants and train times. They were both NS men with about half their time left, and they asked if I would like to join them for tea in the dining-room? They said that they were going to the cinema in Ashton that night and I was welcome to join them.

This is another army lesson, even if you wanted to be on your own and lonely, you would never manage it. Over tea they told me all about Chichester as they had both been there and on the same course to which I had been assigned. Just in passing, one of the lads was from Preston and called George Weston. I met up with him again by chance some years after I returned from Malaya and we worked together, on and off, for quite a few years after that meeting.

The following morning I was going through the main gate at Ladysmith's, once again bound for somewhere other than home. I felt that I was getting used to doing this and it did not fill me with the customary apprehension. Of course all my friends and comrades were now already many miles away, so I had fewer reasons for wanting to stay at Ladysmith's.

I was looking forward to the rail journey to Chichester which would be something different. The train journey down through London and on to the South coast was uneventful and I spent most of the journey reading but as the train started nearing our destination I began to worry about getting to the barracks. Did I have to catch a bus or were the barracks near enough so that I could walk?

I decided that when I got off the platform I would have to ask someone and then make my mind up as to what I should do. In the event it did not matter because outside of the station was a one-ton army truck waiting for anyone coming off the train and bound for the barracks. I threw my kit up, climbed aboard and off we went.

The barracks weren't far away, maybe a mile, and it was still within the boundaries of the city. Just near to the station was a small market square with an old and small covered structure set in the middle. It was if I remember correctly, called 'the old cross'. The city was very pleasant-looking and obviously very old, but there were signs of some of the wartime bombing damage still awaiting repair. I remember a level crossing and a cinema in, or near the centre of town, and a really good fish and chip shop on the way to the barracks. I cannot remember much more about the place, due to working hard on the course, and with it being December, never seeing the city in the daylight. But I do remember especially that the people of Chichester were friendly and very nice, as most people were to servicemen in those days.

I remember the kindness to the servicemen of that time by a particular company based in Chichester; they were called Shippam's and are famous for producing the first sandwich spreads. Their works were close to the barracks and the Company held a regular social evening for their employees, to which servicemen were always invited and made welcome, but we were warned at the barracks to be on our best behaviour. We all enjoyed and appreciated the free spread that they provided.

In those days there were very few people who didn't have a father, husband or brother serving in the British forces somewhere, and most of them not by choice. I have never been back to Chichester after leaving at the end of the course in December 1957, but Betty and I are hoping to spend a week sometime in the future, travelling along the South coast. I would imagine that there have been many changes to the place. I would think that the barracks have long gone, as they were out of date when I was there with our accommodation and workrooms being in the old type corrugated metal Nissen huts.

As it was late in the day when we arrived I was shown straight to the Nissen hut that was to be my home for the next three weeks. Bedding was piled onto several empty beds so I chose one in the corner. I made the bed, stored my kit away in the locker, wrote a letter to Betty and went in search of the post-box and the NAAFI.

Our first parade was at 09:00 the following day. It was a dull morning but dry, and there was no ice about. It's always warmer on the South coast, and it certainly felt warmer to me that morning. Surprisingly there were quite a few people around watching our parade, although I shouldn't have been surprised considering the number of different Regiments on parade. There were all of the Guards, the Black Watch, the Paras, Infantry and Light Infantry, and Artillery, in fact a full mix of the British Regiments, and of course all the various uniforms including the different kilts. It certainly made for quite a spectacle for the onlookers.

We were all aware of the spectators, so when the order came to "Quick March!" we were all intent on putting our best foot forward, which we did, to the delight and howls of laughter from the assembled spectators who had obviously been there and seen it all before, and had come back for another look!

Here I should explain that every Regiment in the British Army marched at a different pace; some slow, some fast and some very fast, so when the order "Quick March!" came, everyone set off at their Regimental pace and collided with everyone else. There were bodies falling about all over the place and the two Durham Light Infantry lads were already halfway up the road.

We could not but help joining in the laughter as we were reassembled on parade and just given a "Fall Out" order. To me on reflection, it had all been deliberately engineered with the customary British intelligence, not just to give us all a laugh which it did, but to get home the message that, although we were all from different Regiments, each with its own individual ways, here we were one unit together, and from that moment we were.

We were told that first morning that the course was normally a four week's course, but it was being condensed into three weeks with the Christmas leave coming up. A little cheer was raised at this point.

But it would mean doing some studying in the evenings and the classrooms would be left open all night for anyone who wanted to carry on working. This information was followed by a little booing. However nobody really minded with Christmas leave on the horizon.

One small point of interest while I was at Chichester, was that the famous Vulcan Jet Delta-winged A-Bombers were based near to the town and used to take off over our camp on a regular daily basis with a tremendous roar.

Our course covered everything connected with running an office in the army, from the orderly room (main office), to Company offices and front line combat offices. We were taught the phonetic alphabet, that's the A for Apple, B for Baker, C for Charlie system. We were also taught how to abbreviate a message into its simplest form, so it would be quicker to send and easier to read. This book would have been condensed into a couple of pages using the army way without photographs and very boring, but then army signals weren't sent just to stop you being bored. We were taught how to type, and had to be able to complete so many words in a minute, obviously without mistakes. We also learnt about part one, two and three orders. In short, anything and everything that had to do with the office side of running the army was covered by the course. As this course was normally for four full weeks with a lot of ground to cover, we really had to concentrate to pass the course in just three weeks, but I think that everyone worked extra hard and passed.

Some of the lads did some work over the two weekends that we were there, but I was lucky enough to have my older sister June living in South London, so both weekends I got a leave pass and travel warrant and left the camp on the Friday evening and returned on the Sunday night having spent the weekend with her and my brother-in-law Ray.

Two points of interest occurred on my weekends at my sister's. On the first trip to her home I passed the Lewisham train disaster, which had happened that day. This had involved three passenger trains colliding under a bridge, which then collapsed onto the trains killing many of the passengers who where returning home after Christmas shopping in London. It upset me very much at the time, seeing the rescue teams pouring over the wreckage reminded me of thirteen years earlier when I was eight-year's old and watching the American rescue teams pouring over the school in Freckleton after the plane crash which killed so many innocent children.

Many years later I worked in London for two and a half years and I would travel regularly past that very bridge. The other point of interest on these weekends was that on a Sunday morning, Ray and myself would walk up the hill to the Crystal Palace Park and then back home to where my sister June would have prepared the Sunday lunch. On the way back we would stop at Ray's local for a pint. He was always amazed at the number of old men that having seen my cap badge and Loyals' flash on my shoulder, would come up to me, offer to buy me a pint and start talking about the North Lancashire Loyals on the Somme during the First World War, saying what a good Regiment the Loyals had been. It really did give me a big thrill, and I can't tell you just how proud it made me feel, especially with my Granddad having been there, which I obviously told them about.

Most young lads of today will probably never have the experience of anything like that, the pride of belonging to a group, that was so easily recognisable and that others were proud to have known. It happened regularly that people would come up and introduce themselves, but as I said earlier, it really was a different nation in those days and I have to say, then it was a very proud Nation.

Well the end of the course came and I had managed to pass. The last day was very relaxed, all the work was done and we had all packed away the kit that we were not going to need. That evening Christmas dinner was served and enjoyed in the dining-room. The next morning we all received our leave passes and travel warrants and left Chichester for home and a fortnight's leave.

I arrived back home in Wrea Green late that evening. It was great to be back and quite unexpected, because when I left nearly four week's earlier I wasn't expecting being on leave until the year after next, but it really was great to be home that Christmas. I felt lucky and glad to be there and even more so the following year because, while I was in Malaya, Uncle Percy died.

Percy was Betty's uncle and because Betty's father, Arthur, had died when she was young, Uncle Percy, as the father figure, gave her away on our wedding day. He was a farmer in Wrea Green and that Christmas, Auntie Annie and Uncle Percy had a party for us all at Brown's farm in Wrea Green. It was an old-fashioned get together and I took great pleasure from the evening then, and it is now extra special to me because it was to be the last time that I would see Uncle Percy with him passing away the following year while I was in Malaya.

Christmas and New Year had become a memory and once again I was returning back through the main gate at Ladysmith's. I reported to the guardroom and was directed to the Orderly room. There was a lot more activity in the barracks, which obviously meant that the new intake had arrived. It was immediately clear to me from the language on the square that they were not being treated as harshly as we had been. I went up to the Orderly room office and knocked on the window.

Once again the same lad as before opened it. He smiled and told me to go around to the door, which he opened for me. The two lads I had tea with before I left congratulated me on passing the course, so I knew the barracks had been notified of the results. The Sergeant who had given me my first week's leave came over and introduced himself. He told me that I would be working in the office with them until my posting for Malaya came through. I must admit that I was a bit worried that I might be rebadged back to the Manchesters but thank goodness that was not to be and I was a Loyal to the end.

The Sergeant gave me the morning off to get organised and I finished up with the same bed that I had before I went down to Chichester, only this time I had to go and get my own bedding from the stores. I reported to the office after lunch and immediately my job seemed to be attending to the part two and three orders. The orders were basically concerned with the daily running of the barracks and the men based there. My job was to collate the information, type it all out so it made sense, transfer all the information onto a printing skin, get the skin signed by the Adjutant, print out fifteen copies, then deliver them to where they belonged. The first copy had to be posted on the training company office notice-board at 16:00, and then followed with the rest delivered around the barracks, the last copy going to the museum. The worst part was trying to find the Adjutant who could be anywhere, but they had to be signed. I must say that I found office work a nightmare. Being in the same place all the time was not for me; my mind was already made up as to what I was going to do in Malaya.

I had been working in the office for about three weeks when my name came up for part three orders. I was leaving for Malaya in just over a week's time, so with quick thinking I worked out that I should have two weekends at home before I left. The orderly room sergeant came over when he knew that I had seen my name appear.

He said to me what I was already thinking. "Well, Fred, you had better make the best of your weekends left at home. Try and go to the Winter Gardens on Saturday night, it's going to be your last chance for a year or two."

"I know Sarge;" I replied, "I just hope that I can get home."

"Oh you'll get home alright," he said. "Here is a leave pass for nine days starting at 16:30 today and a travel warrant home, so you had better go and get your kit together now, then hand all your bedding into the stores, because you are not coming back here. You are going straight to London from home, and whatever you do, don't go without coming here for your documentation to Malaya. By the way you are flying out there."

I could not believe it. Here I was going on leave, and in just over a week's time I would be flying to Malaya. Now that was something I had always wanted to do, not the Malaya bit; the flying bit. All my kit was packed, all my bedding handed in and I was ready again for the off.

I went to the orderly room but I didn't need to knock this time because I had been a part of the team. The Sergeant came across and gave me a large envelope that carried all the details that I required. He told me not to lose it and to read it carefully when I got home. I thanked him for all he had done for me and all the leaves he had got for me from the first day to the last at Ladysmith's. I said my goodbyes to everyone there, and that was it, I was off.

I went down the stairs from the office and out of the door, and there facing me was the square. On the parade ground was a training platoon of Manchesters being put through their paces, but not with the same passionate hatred that the Loyals had been subjected to, which was probably why they were nowhere near as good as we had been. I walked to the main gate, stopped and took one last look around. It was the last time in my life that I would see Ladysmith barracks, and it was to be many years before I returned to Ashton-under-Lyne.

I had not time to let anyone at home know that I was coming on leave, so Betty was surprised when I walked in again. Pleasantly surprised I might add. We especially enjoyed that week together for we knew for certain this time that it was the last week we would spend together for a year or two. We lived with Betty's mother Annie, who was a wonderful person, and kind beyond belief. Tragically she died just two week's before Tony, the first of our four children, was born. While I was in training Annie had bought a TV so that Betty would have something to do while I was away, and I know that this helped enormously.

But once again all good things come to an end, and once more it was time to go. We were doing things differently this time because Betty and my sister Barbara came with me to the railway station in Manchester, so that Betty and I could be together for as long as possible. I think that particular railway station is now an Exhibition Centre. Most things change with time.

We said our goodbyes, then the train was easing away from the station platform and on its way to London. It was a big steam locomotive pulling us, for of course in those days there were no electric or diesel trains, everything was pulled by steam. So here I was in uniform and heading towards London again. It was a grey and dark wintry day with the occasional rain shower that at times beat heavily on the carriage windows.

I tried to cheer myself up by thinking, "Well I am heading towards a hot sunny climate, so there won't be any of this sort of weather out there."

But that didn't help too much and the joints in the rails seemed to be continually saying, Clickety-clack, clickety-clack."

In my mind that sound soon turned into, "You're not coming back, you're not coming back."

I couldn't stand it any longer so I stood up and went out into the corridor, and walked towards the engine end of the train just to stretch my legs. In the second carriage down was a soldier looking out of the window, so I stopped for a chat as soldiers did, and I suppose still do. I cannot remember his regiment, but the amazing thing was that he was on his way to Chichester on a clerk's course.

I spent some time telling him all about it and that there would be transport waiting at the station. I told him all about what he would be studying and that all the NCOs were great, and nothing like the training platoon that he had just left. I didn't tell him about the first parade though, it just didn't seem right to do that and spoil everyone's fun, nor to diminish his future memories. I looked at my watch and realised that I had been talking to him for well over an hour, so I said that I may see him later but if he thought of anything that he would like to know about Chichester, I was only a couple of carriages down.

I got back to my seat feeling a little better; I got my book out and read that until we reached London. The next move was to Woolwich Arsenal barracks, which was on the South side of the river and meant taking the tube. That presented no problems to me as I was fully conversant with the mapping for the tube, having used the underground on several occasions in the past. In just over half an hour I was walking into the barracks.

They were quite modern; the place was actually a transit barracks and only used for troops passing through. I was directed to my barrack room where I chose a convenient bed with bedding already stacked on it. The barracks being designed just for passing through was obvious; it's the only time that I have ever seen three-tiered bunk-beds.

Everyone who had just arrived at the barracks decided to go for a meal. They were all saying that there had just been several write-ups in the newspapers about this place, and apparently the dining-room had gone self-service with six of everything to choose from. When we got into the dining-room it was unbelievable but true, even down to choices of ice-cream, and the food really was first class. What was the British Army coming to? Mind you someone did say that they were only doing this because we were going overseas, and they wanted us to feel even more homesick. I must say that I enjoyed the two meals that I had there, dinner, and breakfast the following morning. I also had a meal at supper time because the dining-room stayed open until 22:00, and you really could just help yourself. It was just like a modern motorway services cafeteria without the cash till at the end. I have often wondered how long the experiment lasted; maybe they still do that because it certainly was a good idea.

The following morning we had to hand in all our UK battledress uniforms. We kept our boots, berets, cap badge, underwear and socks, and packed these into our kit bag which was due to be stowed in the aircraft hold, so would not be seen by us again until we reached Singapore.

We had changed into our civilian clothes as we had to wear them until we reached the Loyals in Malaya, as apparently some of the countries we would be landing in were not keen on British troops being on their soil.

So here we were again ready for the off. It was about 11:00 and rather cold as we got on the coach that was to take us to the airport. The sky was clear blue and I hoped that I would have a window-seat on the aeroplane, because the view would be superb. We left Woolwich Arsenal Barracks and headed through London.

I was surprised at the direction we were taking, because I thought that we would be flying from Croydon and we were heading the other way. This was in the days long before Heathrow and Gatwick terminals. Before long we were going under the Blackwall Road Tunnel which brought back memories for me of five years earlier.

When I was sixteen Gordon Harris (that's the friend who visited me during training at Ladysmith's) and I, hitchhiked to France. We crossed the River Thames by walking through the tunnel at about 02.00, but I knew that I was definitely going further abroad this time. As we kept heading North I hadn't a clue which airport we were going to until I saw a sign that rung a bell in my mind, Stanstead. That was the place that we had been heading for since we left the barracks.

There wasn't much in those days to an airport, at least compared to now; they were in reality the remains of the RAF wartime bomber airfields. We turned through the airfield gates and drove up to a group of large round corrugated steel wartime Nissen huts which were serving as the airport main buildings, and were just about the only buildings on the airfield apart from one or two large wartime aircraft hangers on the other side of the airfield.

We collected our kit from the coach and went into the reception lounge, where the staff immediately set to weighing and labelling everyone's luggage before placing all our baggage onto a trolley. We were taken to the dining-room for a meal before the flight that was due to take off later at 16:00.

I was really hungry, as I always seemed to be in my army days, but I was now losing some of the weight that I had put on since joining. Some of the civilians and lads who were flying to Singapore decided not to bother, because they were not hungry, while one or two of the others only wanted a cup of tea. I didn't realise at the time, but they were terrified of flying.

We finished the meal about 15:00 and everyone moved back to the lounge. There didn't seem to be any sense of urgency, then someone said that there was a delay. I think that they were waiting for the airmail for Singapore, but it could have been anything. Of more interest to me was the plane which was being loaded up with the baggage. It stood on the concrete runway about fifty yards from the airport buildings, which is very close by today's standards.

It's very unlikely that you've heard of this type of aeroplane, but it was a four-engine airliner; the engines were piston-driven with massive propellers fitted to the front. Jet planes were just in their infancy then, and the world's first passenger jet plane, the Comet, had only just started flying. At the back of the plane were three tail fins, which was unusual, and it also had a tricycle undercarriage which again was unusual in the 50s. However it was a graceful-looking aircraft, and I was looking forward to flying in her.

At 16:45 we were requested to go out to the aircraft ready to board, once more it was nothing like it is today. There was no speaker announcement, someone just came round and asked us to board the aircraft. We had to walk out across the tarmac to the plane, then climb the steps to get to the door of the plane. Everyone had a boarding card, which was handed to the stewards at the bottom of the steps.

Up I went and into the plane, which held about forty-five passengers. I was in real luck, because I got a window-seat on the far side of the aircraft just level with the leading edge of the wing. I kept that seat all the way to Malaya. The only disappointment was that it was now nearly dark, and all the lights were coming on in the buildings that we could see. Within five minutes the outer door was closed and locked on the inside. Shortly after that the voice of the plane's Captain came over the loudspeaker giving all the normal procedures, then we were moving to the northern end of the runway.

We sat at the end of the runway for probably two minutes before the engines increased in power, the brakes snapped off, then we were rolling down the runway with the speed picking up every second. I had a great view of all the lights around the airfield and the runway lights alongside of us. We were really shooting past them now, and then with no other sensation they just started going farther and farther away and we were up and flying. As we got higher I could see lights from miles away, and all the lights of the cars motoring along the roads beneath us. Within a few minutes we were flying over London. It was quite easy to make out the different landmarks around the capital. The Captain put the engines into cruise run making it comfortably quiet on board, with the only sense of movement being the lights on the ground that were slipping past below us.

Unlike the modern jets this plane really flew. On take-off you didn't know when you had left the ground, whilst the landing was just as smooth, so it really was a pleasure to fly in. Of course the down side of this smooth and quiet flying was that it was very slow, plus the fact that in those days a plane didn't fly very far on a tankful of fuel, so we had to keep landing to refuel.

It's hard to believe it now, but it took us nearly a week to fly to Singapore from London, and we landed in quite a few cities along the way. I think that the most noticeable points of the journey were how it was obviously warmer each time we landed, and the changes in the food that we were given at each stop and on the plane after a stop. Also the standard of the airport buildings was unbelievable at some of the stops. In Rangoon, Burma, it was just a small wooden cabin at the side of the runway. Some of the stops we made were overnight, this gave us a chance to sleep. On the overnight stops a coach would pick us up at the airport and take us to a nearby hotel, and of course back to the airport in the morning. I had realised by this time that quite a few of the passengers were terrified of flying. I suppose that I had been lucky to have been looking forward to flying for the first time, and when we became airborne and over London, that was an absolutely magical moment for me.

The stops we made from the first one to the last were, Brindisi in Italy, Istanbul in Turkey, Ankara also in Turkey, Baghdad in Iraq, Karachi in Pakistan, New Delhi in India, Calcutta, also in India, Rangoon in Burma, Bangkok in Thailand, and Singapore itself.

Yes, finally we had reached Singapore, and my first feeling was that I would never ever get used to that heat, to me then it was unbelievable. When we got off the plane at Singapore we had to wait in the reception lounge until the plane had been unloaded, which didn't take too long, but it was always the same, when you were in the army and with British administration, you were not kept waiting, especially when you were urgently needed elsewhere.

My luggage arrived on a baggage trolley, which I retrieved and put straight onto the army truck that was waiting to take us to the transit camp. There were only five other plane passengers who were going to the same transit camp as myself. That place was for any army personnel going up country the following morning, of which I was one.

The transit camp wasn't too bad, much better than I had expected, so it didn't take too long to get organised with basically just a bed and bedding to sort out. Over my bed was another new experience for me, that was the mosquito net, which was hanging on cords that came down from the roof of the hut. During the day the net was rolled up and tied above the top of the bed then untied when you retired at night. When you untied the net you draped it so it was hanging all around the bed, and most people tucked it under the mattress at the top, bottom and the opposite side to which you got into bed. That wasn't done especially to keep the mosquitoes out, but rather some of the other creepy-crawlies that were about like spiders, scorpions and snakes. None of us wanted any of those in bed with us when we woke up in the morning, like I later and many times found, to my horror in the jungle.

Another habit that I picked up that day was to always shake out my footwear before putting them on, and that's another little habit that's still with me to this day. I bet that nearly everyone who was out there still does that without realising that they are still doing it. To the lads who were out there and now reading this, do you remember within the first two or three months of getting back home, what you did when a car backfired? Yes, old habits die hard don't they, especially so when your life depended upon them. Isn't it noticeable that cars never backfire nowadays?

One of the good things about army life was that no lad would ever leave you to find out the hard way what you should do to avoid trouble, and that includes lads who were complete strangers. You always, from the beginning of your service to the end, watched each other's backs, and always without fail!

I made my bed and stored what bit of kit I had in the locker. I was still in civilian clothes, we had been told when we arrived that we would be kitted out when we reached our Regiments, which for me was the Loyals. I still wasn't certain what Regiments everyone belonged to because we had no uniforms. We were advised before we left London not to ask because some of them could have been on special missions.

I decided that while I was waiting for teatime I would take a walk around the camp perimeter. I had a lot of friends and workmates back home who were in Singapore during the war and became Japanese prisoners of war. All of them were older than me of course, and some of them used to tell me about Singapore under the 'Japs' and how cruel they had been. Some would not talk about it, just wanting to forget the cruelty, and I certainly could understand that. So as I walked slowly around the camp, I thought about them, and the fact that it had only been twelve years before then that the horror for them came to an end. I wondered where Changi Jail was from this spot, as it was there where many of them were imprisoned for years.

After my walk around the camp I felt a little better, at least we hadn't got hoards of 'Japs' bearing down on us, and in that mood I went to the dining-room for tea. If I remember rightly the only real meal that was on the menu was curry and rice, and as I had never in my life tasted curry, and was not about to start, the tea was a complete disaster.

There was a small cinema in the camp so that evening after the failure of teatime I decided to go. It did help to relax me somewhat, and after the film I went to the NAAFI for a drink. The NAAFI had my favourite drink, Mackeson stout, so I bought a can and enjoyed a taste from home. I did not know it then, but apparently Mackeson is the only drink that tastes the same wherever you are in the world, which was lucky for me as that was my first choice drink. These were ice cold, so I had another. That night, despite the unaccustomed and unbearable heat, I slept like a log.

I was up early the following morning as we had to be on the transport at 08:45 to get to the railway station and catch the train up to Ipoh. It appeared that there were four of us going up country to join the Loyals, with another three going to Ipoh to join other units. There were also another three who were going with us on the train up to Kuala Lumpur, which is the capital of Malaya, and just over half the distance to Ipoh. We all loaded our kit onto the truck, then we had to report to the armoury where the others and I got the realisation shock, of this is really it, and we have definitely arrived. We were all issued with a Lee-Enfield rifle and a full clip of .303 ammunition for travelling on the train up to Ipoh.

I felt sure that each of us was thinking, "What on earth have I got involved with?"

In one minute I went from looking forward to the train journey, to being full of apprehension at the prospect of a trip into the unknown. With those thoughts I climbed aboard the truck, and we were away bound for the railway station. It was most peculiar walking through the station to get to the right platform for our train. Remember we were still in civilian clothes, yet there we were, each with a loaded rifle over our shoulder, but I must say that although I felt as if I stuck out considerably, nobody seemed at all bothered; it was obviously quite normal to them, and within ten minutes it was normal to me. How quickly one's accepted attitude to a satisfactory civilised way of life changes, and the abnormal suddenly becomes the norm.

The train for Ipoh was standing at the platform. We were walking up towards the engine when a British soldier whistled to us from an open window and waved us over.

"Get in here," he urged, "you don't want to go up to that end. If the CTs' blow the track, it's that end of the train that gets it."

We didn't need telling twice and quickly found seats in that carriage. There was nearly half an hour before we were due to pull out of the station so I asked the lads to watch my kit. I picked up my rifle and had a walk up to have a look at the steam engine. It was a modern steam train which seemed big and impressive. It also had a cowcatcher fitted to the front, just like the ones you see in the Western movies. Just in front of our train was another engine with just one small carriage. Both the engine and carriage were armoured and I had never seen anything like them. There were a couple of soldiers stood looking and one of them asked me if I had just arrived.

"Yes I am just out from the UK."

I asked about the armoured train, and they explained that it ran about quarter of a mile in front of the main train as protection.

My mind worked overtime on hearing their reply, and with a great deal of trepidation I asked when was the last time a train was attacked?

They answered, "Oh it was a year or so back."

I felt a little better with that reply and the chance of it happening today had suddenly reduced. "Right," I said, "might see you later." I then turned and made my way back to my carriage and within a few minutes the train was underway.

I was leaning out of the window, and as we rounded a bend in the track I could see that there was only one set of rails, so we were travelling on a single-track railway system, which was a surprise to me. Apparently the railway at that time was single track throughout the whole of Malaya.

Ten minutes later we were heading over the Johore Causeway that joins Singapore to Malaya. The causeway wasn't very wide, but was just able to carry the various pipelines, the road and by its side the railway. There were no trees or bushes, and apart from the telephone and electric poles it was completely barren. The sun was beating down, it was already very hot and still only mid-morning. As I looked along the causeway towards Malaya, the coastline was just a mass of dark green trees, and when I looked back towards Singapore the view was very much the same. Out over the waters to each side of the causeway there were a multitude of small boats. Farther out towards the horizon you could see large ocean-going vessels at anchor, and the water sparkling brightly with the movement of the small boats in the dazzling morning sunshine.

Suddenly the train left the causeway and crossed the threshold onto the mainland of Malaya. Like a curtain had been pulled across the window, the panorama was gone. All I could see now were trees and the road with a few cars and old lorries that were loaded to overflowing. Along the road where the occasional brick-built building and a lot of corrugated steel huts. Around them and behind was a never-ending blanket of palm trees and cultivated fields. As we moved farther inland I could see in the distance the rolling jungle, a seemingly never-ending mass of greens with a feint wisp of mist rising out of the treetops, to be immediately swallowed up by the rays of the hot morning sun. The feeling I had looking at a jungle for the first time in my life was a strange desire to be exploring beneath that dark green canopy. I say a *strange* desire because I knew that under the treetops were Communist Terrorists intent on killing, but from that first moment I knew that the jungle itself would hold no undue fears for me, provided I could get in there; but first I had to get out of the office job that awaited me in Ipoh with the Loyals.

There was nothing eventful during the train journey to Ipoh apart from the stop at Kuala Lumpur. The railway platform was a tremendous length, someone said it's the longest platform in the world. I don't really know for sure, but I would not be surprised if it was. The single track railway system was double track in the station, so that two trains could pass each other. We were told that we had a half-hour wait for a train that was coming the other way.

Most people got off the train to buy food or drinks including myself, but I avoided the ice-cream and iced-drinks having been warned of the dangers of disease due to polluted water being used in their production. We finally arrived in Ipoh at about 18:30. The other three lads and I who were due for the Loyals got off the train with our kit. I looked around and immediately spotted a Loyals' cap badge at the back of the station.

We walked over to him, and thank goodness, for it turned out that he was our driver, and he was there to meet us and take us to Colombo Camp and the battalion, at last!

# CHAPTER THREE
## *Malaya, the Battalion and Jungle Training*

We left the station and drove through Ipoh in a north-easterly direction. After a few minutes we were driving through the suburbs and along a tree-lined road with scattered housing.

As the lorry rounded a bend in the road someone said, "That's the camp."

This was the first sighting of what was to be my home for the next year and a half, and what I could see was a collection of huts about three-hundred yards away on the top of a low hill. On the right-hand side of the hilltop was a large group of parked army vehicles.

We crossed over a small bridge under which a stream was running around the bottom end of Colombo Camp. To the right, and about fifty yards upstream from us, was a narrow metal footbridge with metal tube sides about one foot high spanning the water. Built on the low ground, and between the footbridge and the main camp, was a silver-painted corrugated metal Nissen hut with a red door and no windows.

Walking round the hut was an armed guard, who was carrying a peculiar looking rifle. I assumed correctly that this must be the ammunition dump, and that what the guard was carrying was one of the new-type rifles that we had heard about in the UK.

The army three-ton Bedford climbed up the short hill onto the level ground where the main camp was situated. It was just a normal narrow Malayan road that we were on, but it appeared to run right though the centre of the camp with a six-foot high barbed wire fence to each side of the road.

My first gut reaction was that the camp was just a collection of both corrugated iron and grass huts, and although I did not know exactly what to expect, I must say that I had not expected this. The camp looked more native Malay than anything that I had seen on the way up from Singapore.

On the journey through Ipoh, the cinemas, petrol stations and the like were all very much up to date, with very modern buildings, so it was a surprise after these, to find the camp looking the way it did.

We pulled up on the motor transport park and were directed by the driver to the bottom end of the camp. The training company office appeared to be a small grass hut. Although on closer inspection it wasn't grass, but long dried leaves, which I later found out were called attap leaves.

As we walked down to the office and passed the lines of huts, it was noticeable that there weren't many lads about the place for the amount of accommodation that we could see. Of course we should have realised that most of the platoons were on operations out there in the jungle. The lads who we did pass were all wearing nothing more than jungle green shorts with flip-flops on their feet.

They all seemed very relaxed and friendly, and even pleased to see us, at least I think that is what they meant by, "You'll be sorry."

The friendly Lancashire accents and smiles said it all, and they knew, even better than we did, just how much that meant to us at that moment in time.

We booked in at the company office, handed in our rifles at the Training Company Arm's Cote, then were shown to our accommodation. This turned out to be a tent, well a tent roof actually, because there weren't any tent walls, but that did mean that it was cool for us at night. When we'd been shown the ropes, if you'll excuse the pun, we were told that there was a meal waiting for us in the cookhouse and we would be kitted out the following morning.

I didn't sleep too well that night; I knew that I had finally arrived in Malaya and would be there for some time to come; I also knew that I had to be ready to come to terms with whatever my time there was going to throw at me.

We were all up bright and early the following morning, and by lunch time we had all been kitted out. There was a far more relaxed attitude here, which was completely different to training and attitudes in Blighty. That afternoon the Training Sergeant and the two Corporals showed us around the camp, explaining everything about the place, and what we would be doing in training.

Later the Sergeant spoke to me personally, "You won't be completing the full course; you're due to go into one of the offices."

When I said that I wanted to go into the jungle and not into an office, they all thought that I had gone completely mad. They tried to talk me out of it by relating all the horror stories about the Malayan jungle; stories that were as much for everyone else's benefit as mine, but my mind was already made up, and I would not be swayed.

The following morning I was on Company Orders and questioned as to why I wanted to go into the jungle and not into the office?

The reason that was worrying me with regards to having my request turned down was first given, and that was the cost of training me for the office, then the cost of then having to fly me out to Malaya. The fact that my request was unusual was underlined by the statement that they had dozens of requests and reasons for *not* going in, or for coming *out* of the jungle, which should say *something* to me, but to turn down a HQ post to go *into* the jungle was unheard of.

I had my say on the matter, then it was left that I would complete the jungle training course in full, which included three days in an operational area of the jungle at the end of the course. If at the end of this I still wanted to go on operations and into the jungle, then my request would be granted.

Their final comment was, "At least now we can always say that we have men who *want* to go into the jungle."

I came out of the Company Office feeling much better, knowing that the choice was up to me after first having the chance to assess what it was like in the jungle. With all the disturbing comments and remarks from the people who had been in there, I did wonder if my choice was likely to change?

Training was certainly not intense; I think that the steady pace of everything at that time was also to give us time to become accustomed to the unbelievable heat.

With so many people now going there on holiday, I often wonder how they can enjoy it, because it takes about six weeks for the initial acclimatisation, and a full year before you really get used to it. Of course the holiday-makers who have been, when I have spoken to them say that everything and everywhere is air-conditioned, and it's too hot to spend too long outside. So really they never do become conditioned to the climate.

When I was there in the beginning, the only place that was air-conditioned was the American-owned cinema in Ipoh, which was down to, I believe approximately 75°F. I went there twice during my time in Malaya, but wore my blazer the second time because it felt so cold.

The heat was such in Malaya that for the first few weeks I was unable to walk properly, as the skin on the back of my legs was stretched so tightly that I was unable to straighten them properly. In those days we didn't have air-conditioning as we know it today, but of course we did have the next best thing, tents without walls, which was Army-style air-conditioning. I can guarantee that this works, because only one year later we were playing football in the middle of the afternoon. That's what I call conditioning, and we were the Englishmen who were chasing the mad dogs out in the midday sun.

Anyone who has been on holiday to the South of Malaya or Singapore, or up to the North of Ipoh and Penang Island, will perhaps agree that it was hot, but not to the extremes I am speaking of. I can only state that they probably never spent any of their time in Ipoh. Those other areas are cooled all the time by the sea breezes, that's why I used to go to Penang on leave. But Ipoh and the Loyals were in the Perak valley.

I will tell you why it was so hot in our area. The valley was about forty miles in length and narrow, varying between five and ten miles in width. It was rich in tin ore and very rich in iron ore. In fact it was so rich, that on the main rifle range and also the jungle range, when it rained the ground would turn red with rust, and our uniforms would be covered with the red dust. The ore would draw the sun, then hold the heat overnight. The mountains that formed the valley sides also held the heat in the valley, preventing any cooling winds from reaching us. Compounding all of this was the fact that the valley ran exactly North to South, thus catching the sun from sunrise to sunset. We were situated just over three-hundred miles North of the equator, so no wonder it was so hot there.

At first as you might expect, we were covering the differences between European and jungle warfare. We would go to the North-East of the camp into the small rubber plantation, and the thin jungle-type scrub that was next to it. There we would sit in the shade and discuss what we could see and what we would or should not do in different situations?

One thing we did watch were all the different ants. There always seemed to be a long column of ants coming from nowhere and going to nowhere; they were guarded by the massive soldier ants running up and down the outsides of the columns. The ants were about the size of a peanut, whilst the soldier ants were about the size of a large walnut. Then there were the tailor ants. We would watch them pulling leaves together, then stitching them to make a nest, but we didn't get too close because they really nipped if they got on you. It was far worse than a wasp sting I can tell you.

The Ibans used them to stitch up body wounds by nipping the heads off the ant when the pinchers had closed over the cut. This was a training lesson for the jungle I think, along with the need to always carry a razor blade for snakebite poison, or cutting out the ticks. During training we seemed to come across all the things we might encounter on a daily basis in the jungle, and by now I was definitely thinking seriously about that office job.

Another section we covered were the weapons that we had used back in Blighty and the jungle weapons that were especially for Malaya. I say *especially* for Malaya, because some of these weapons would have been illegal in other theatres of war. The first thing was the difference in standard weapons and special weapons, and then the new weapons that we had only heard rumours about in the UK.

The first different weapon that we came across was the Mk5 Lee-Enfield rifle. It was just the same as the standard UK Lee-Enfield rifle, except the barrel was a lot shorter, making it easier to carry and use in the jungle. Also there was a flash eliminator fit in the form of a funnel about three inches long on the end of the barrel. One weapon we used in Malaya was also one of the standard UK weapons of that time, and for many years before then, the ubiquitous Bren gun. I must say I could never understand the logic of carrying a Bren in the jungle; it really was too clumsy and heavy for those conditions.

One of the differences with the Bren gun in Malaya was a pistol-type handgrip fitted to the front of the Bren near to its legs. I know that anyone who has ever used a Bren gun in Europe won't believe it, but we used to fire it from the shoulder as with a rifle; the only difference being that the butt of the Bren rested *on* the shoulder, rather than up against it. The Bren guns were also used on top of the scout cars in pairs, and could be fired by remote control from within the vehicle.

Another weapon that was used in Europe, but used to different ends in Malaya was the two-inch mortar. This was only used to fire parachute flares when on night ambushing in the plantations. Other standard European weapons in use were the Smith and Wesson and the Browning handguns, which were used by some of the Officers, radio operators and the dog handlers. Mills hand-grenades were used on some of the jungle edge and plantation patrols, but **never** in the jungle. Smoke grenades and flare guns where used for the re-supply airdrops inside the jungle.

The special weapons for the Malayan jungle were the Remington and the Winchester five-shot repeater twelve-bore shotguns, which were devastating at close range. Leading scouts, some officers and certain NCOs used these.

The main weapon used by the majority of the lads in the Loyals was the new FN-SLR, the Fabrique National self-loading rifle. Jungle training was the first time that I had seen or used one, as both the FN and the Patchet sub-machine-gun were on field trial with the Loyals in Malaya. The FN was an excellent weapon, and easy to use with a magazine that, if I remember correctly, held twenty rounds. I am not sure, because it was never my personal weapon.

My choice of weapon was the Patchet. It was convenient for me as an NCO because it had a shoulder-strap, so I could hang it around my neck while I studied the map and compass, which was always a two-handed job. It was also convenient, in so much as you could fold the handle under the barrel, to make a very short weapon. The hitting power wasn't brilliant, but the magazine held thirty rounds of ammunition. We only used twenty-eight rounds to try and save the life of the spring inside the magazine, though at a push you could squeeze in thirty-two rounds.

One interesting adaptation tried was a torch fastened to the barrel of a rifle to act as an aiming beam in a night ambush. We tried it in the training section, but I never came across the idea again with the platoons, but it did come back to me years later when I saw the first laser sight on a television programme. Could that idea have been a first for the Loyals? I really don't know!

Well the training period had slipped nicely by; we were beginning to get used to the heat, as well as getting a suntan, so we didn't stand out that much from the old sweats, (Experienced jungle soldiers).

This also meant that we didn't get as much ribbing with, "Hey whitey straight from Blighty, get some in."

But finally we had come to the point of the jungle initiation, which for me personally meant the moment of truth. We had all been briefed on what to expect, and what to do when we were in the jungle, and at 05:00 the following day we were going to be on our way.

We spent the afternoon packing everything we would need into our backpacks and side-packs. We were going in for three days; so every single thing that we would need for those days had to be packed and carried. The first job was to unpack the food boxes with which we had been issued. There were three food boxes, one for each day in the jungle, and like everyone else I emptied all my boxes onto my bed with a great deal of interest in what I might find inside.

Each day in Malaya you had to take a tablet to prevent malaria. It was called a Paludrine tablet, so the first thing in each food pack was this tablet. Then there were toilet paper, a small fold flat tin opener, a bag of twelve barley sugar sweets, a packet of chewing gum, one Oxo cube, a packet of sugar, two tubes of condensed milk, a packet of tea leaves, one small tin of cheese, three hard biscuits, a small box of nuts and raisins, one tin of Heinz baked beans and pork sausages, a large tin of Swifts steak and onions, one small packet of curry powder and a bag of rice.

Of course each food box varied slightly, so if you got something you didn't like, you would swap with someone else for something that they didn't like. We would get a tin of frankfurter sausages, which I couldn't stand, but everyone else seemed to love, so if I got one of those, I always had an easy swap for something that I liked. Another thing that we got was a small fold-up metal cooking stove, together with a pack of twelve Hexamine (Examethylenetetramine) blocks inside, and a tin of sterilising tablets for our drinking water.

So I had all this gear on my bed ready for packing, plus two boxes of matches for lighting the blocks on the cooking stove, and a book to read in the quiet moments, if there were any. Also I had to pack my mess tins to cook in, and my eating irons (knife, fork and spoon) would have to be squeezed in before we set off after I had finished eating in Colombo Camp.

My cup was in the bottom of the pouch that carried my water bottle, which fitted inside the cup. Both the cup and bottle were made of alloy, the pouch was green canvas, which clipped onto my jungle belt. The bottle held two pints of water. There was also my machete, which was a very sharp jungle knife about eighteen inches long. We all carried a small sharpening stone for keeping the blade razor sharp.

Another thing that we had to pack was our water bag. This again was jungle green and about the size of a pillowcase. It was made out of a rubberised material. In the jungle you would fill it at the water point, then carry it to your basha and tie it to a convenient tree. When filled the bag would keep you supplied with your water needs for a couple of days.

I put all the clothes that I thought I would need onto the bed, including a thin blanket and my poncho, which was a waterproof cape used for the roof of the basha under which you lived and slept.

In the middle of the tents was a table that was loaded with equipment that had to be shared out amongst everyone. There were three spades that folded up to be shorter than normal spades (tools entrenching), eight large batteries for the radio, four water bottles full of 100% pure grog (Navy rum), ammunition magazines for the Bren guns, which had to be picked up in the morning from the Armoury. Then there were parts for the radio, a medical bag, plus a tin of salt tablets. All of this gear had to be carried along with your own personal equipment, plus of course your rifle and ammunition.

My allocation of extra equipment for packing was a radio battery and a spade. I tried to pack everything, but it just wouldn't go into the packs, and I was used to camping back in Blighty. One of the Corporals was checking everyone, and telling them how to pack the gear away. It turned out that I wasn't too bad really. The poncho went over the top on the outside of the pack, with the thin blanket wrapped inside to keep it dry, whilst the spade went on the back. The batteries went one to each small pack and that was more or less it. I tried the belt and the packs on; I could not believe the weight that we were expected to carry into the jungle.

Then someone said, "Don't forget that you also have a rifle and ammo."

My thoughts were that we would never manage to carry all that weight. We were going to be uphill and down dale in well over 100°F and we were talking of the need to carry around one-hundred pounds or more. I can tell you that at times carrying well over that weight on the long and deep jungle operations was absolute torture.

I was fit and reasonably strong, having had a physical job, and also having been a sportsman for many years, so how some of the lads got through it I really don't know. There were many times when we just had to help each other, or we never would have got up the hills that we had to climb. We always operated as a tightly-knit unit, but first we had to find all this out in training.

That night we all went down to the NAAFI for a drink or two, then turned in early. I found it difficult to get to sleep knowing that the following day was going to be so important, different and daunting. For some reason I kept thinking about Tarzan in a film I had seen in the main hall at Kirkham Grammar School one Saturday night. I finally dropped off to sleep, to seemingly be awoken immediately. It was 03:30. I had a queer dry taste in my throat that I could not place and it lasted most of that day. Strange as it may seem, and without fail, I always got that taste and feeling before every jungle operation that I went on. I never had it before Malaya, and I have never had it since. I can only put it down to nerves.

We set off dressed in our jungle greens, loaded up with our packs, our belts loaded down with everything that was hung onto them. On the way to the motor transport park we called at the Arm's Cote to draw out our weapons and three full magazines of ammo. Then we went on to the MT Park where we threw up our gear, then climbed onto one of the three-tonners that were standing waiting for us.

As soon as everyone was on board we were off, heading North into the dark night beneath a sky filled with a multitude of bright stars and the wonderful Malayan moon. The only sounds and movement were from the army lorries on which we were travelling, and the constant buzz and humming from a whole host of insects that were carried by the wind, or resided on the ground.

There was a strict curfew in force, which meant that nothing else moved, so the only signs of life were the occasional light from one of the native huts that we passed, or the police checkpoints on the road; the personnel of which would now and again wave to us.

This was a completely new experience for all of us because it was the first time that we were out of Colombo Camp at night, and the first time that any of us had experienced a curfew. After coming from a free and democratic homeland, it just didn't seem right that *we* were out here on the road and entitled to be driving around, whilst the people whose country it was, who were born and lived here, were inside the darkened huts, or behind the occasional chink of light from a window, but not allowed out on pain of death.

It was a situation that constantly troubled me, but I also knew that they had lived with this fear for many years both under the Japanese, and after that with the Communist Terrorists, both of whom could, and did, carry out the most horrendous atrocities against the civilian population. I knew that we would never treat them that way, and before long these people would be free to go when and where they wanted, at whatever time of day or night without fear.

Some of the lads at the front of the lorry were talking about the terrible plane crash that had just happened, in which so many Manchester United football players had been killed and injured. I couldn't believe it when I first heard the news, which spread like wildfire throughout Colombo Camp. I also couldn't believe the number of lads who stood and cried on hearing this news. I think now that a lot of it was due to the fact that they were so far away from home, and not part of what was happening back there. There stood old sweats with a tear in their eye, but believe me they were real men that's for sure!

We had gone about fifteen miles and were on a lonely road, and what seemed to me completely in the middle of nowhere, when suddenly the trucks slowed down then stopped. We all climbed down off the trucks and someone passed down all the kit.

I squeezed my backpack on, then tightened up my belt, which felt like a Christmas tree with all the gear hanging from it. I looked around and could see everyone quite clearly in the light created by the false dawn. Everything happens faster on the Equator, and in ten minutes it would be just about full daylight.

Suddenly there was a sharp crash from the lorry next to us. For a fraction of a second all the buzz and humming of the insect world around us stopped, then restarted. It was just as though someone had quickly turned a light off and then back on. The noise was due to someone from the next lorry dropping their rifle onto the road. It got our adrenalin pumping, and certainly put one's senses on edge.

The lorries pulled away down the road as we started towards the jungle up the track next to where we had been dropped off. It was now full daylight; I could see that we were heading through some tapioca plantations and up into a valley. Farther on up the valley I could see the jungle which was about a mile away. On each side of us, and up the valley sides, the jungle was only about five-hundred yards away, and of course the farther up the valley we went, the nearer we got to it.

I looked at the strung-out line of men up in front of me; they all seemed to be trying to make their kit more comfortable, as carrying all that weight was very unpleasant for us all. The packs on everyone's back looked like small rubber dinghies strapped on; for some reason they reminded me of the American Marines in the movies.

We got to about quarter of a mile from the point where the resemblance of a path entered the jungle edge, when the leading section took an unexpected uphill turn to the right. The jungle to the right at this point was about one-hundred yards away. We followed the leading section up the steep hill, keeping about five yards between each man, and five minutes later I entered the jungle for the first time.

We kept on climbing uphill for another twenty minutes until we reached the ridge where we turned left. We proceeded along this ridge for another ten minutes before stopping for a break. It had taken us well over an hour to reach this spot, but it had been a lot easier once we reached the ridge with the jungle track climbing only slowly upwards.

I realised that I had made a mistake packing, because with all the weight hanging on my belt, my hips were being rubbed raw. I took the chance to transfer some weight by squeezing some of the kit into my backpack. Everyone had a good drink from their water bottles, which helped to reduce the weight on our belts a little more.

The Platoon Sergeant came around while we were resting. He explained that we had turned right off the track and cut into the jungle lower down the valley, because regiments before us had followed the path into the jungle, only to be ambushed when entering the jungle at that point. Apparently one of the regiments had lost six men there in one engagement.

Somebody said, "Yes that was the Green Howards," but I really don't know.

Another point was, that as we came out of the bright sunshine and into the darkness of the jungle, we were blind for a few seconds in the sudden blackness of it, as it took a few minutes for our eyes to fully adjust.

The signal came to move off. We carried on along the ridge; my belt felt much better, but was still not right, it definitely needed sorting ready for the next time. We continued on along the ridge for about another hour before we moved off the ridge and downhill to the right. After about ten minutes we stopped for another break. Everyone was beginning to feel the strain of the weight that they were carrying.

One of the lads found a leech on his leg and that was it; the next second everyone was searching for leeches. Another three of them were found, but luckily I had managed to keep clear of them for now. We all took another drink from our water bottles; I was surprised to find that I had drunk almost half of the bottle, which was a pint of water.

I looked around and thought, "I am not surprised that we are getting through our water, because everyone's jungle greens had turned black with sweat. We were all completely drenched. This was one time that we could truthfully say that the sweat was running off us."

I looked further out from where we were and into the jungle, beyond the few lads who were sitting near me on the track. Noticeably the trees had become steadily larger the deeper we got into the jungle. The trunks of some of the trees were an unbelievable size. In fact they must have been as wide as two small cars end to end.

Most of the trees didn't grow straight out of the ground as they do in the UK. Instead they had large sweeping roots that started twenty or thirty feet away from the tree. The roots were as solid as a brick wall. They curved inwards and upwards to merge into the tree about fifteen or twenty feet above the ground. The trees were enormous, many times bigger than the largest tree I had ever seen previously. When I looked around, I could see vines everywhere, hanging down from every tree and branch. Some of these vines were as large as my thigh, whilst others appeared as thin as a tiny strand of cotton, and they ranged through every size in between. They were all completely barren, except for the occasional tiny green leaf on their smooth skin-like exteriors. All of them stretched up as far as the eye could see, then appeared to become lost in the dark tangle of greenery that was the jungle canopy, which rose an amazing one hundred and fifty feet or more above our heads.

This dark green ceiling allowed only the odd beam and chink of sunlight to penetrate through, and down into the gloom of the lower greenery that covered the jungle floor around the giant trees. These bright beams of light shining through the jungle canopy were like a thousand theatre spotlights, with some of the beams broken by a buzzing humming multitude of flying insects, that were busily getting on with their lives. They seemed to be completely unaware and uninterested in the human race below.

Where the light coming through the canopy was the brightest, we would find shrubbery growing with branches of long green leaves, each with hundreds of long green fingers, and shrubs with leaves so big that a person could hide in a single one. Everywhere I could see vegetation, with small trees and bushes of every description. Inside them, and over them, smothering everything in their way, were the vines.

I looked at the jungle by the side of the track where I sat, wondering how anyone could make their way through that thick impenetrable tangled mass, where every other bush and branch seemed to grow nothing else but long, hard, sharp spikes, or ragged leaves with sharp saw-like cutting edges.

Underfoot the ground was soft and springy, with over a thousand years of rotting undergrowth, dead insects and fallen leaves; all of which were constantly scrutinised by the army of ants that seemed to be forever on the march. Everywhere around us in the jungle prevailed an overpowering hot damp rotting musty smell, that was forever present, and always around us like a fine clinging mist, until eventually we forgot about it. That was until the smells and the sounds changed, telling us to beware, warning us that something was happening, something was different!

My thoughts and fascinations were interrupted by the signal to move on. We all struggled to our feet and trampled on down the small track. It wasn't too bad for us farther back down the line, because we could tell from the cut branches and vines that the leading section had their machetes out, and were busy making the track a little wider for themselves and the ones behind.

The lad in front of me, the lad behind me and I, decided that we would try our hand with our machetes. There was no unpacking needed because the machete was in a scabbard hung on our belts, so we just drew them like swords.

I took a swing at the nearest vine and was amazed how easy it was to cut through; so for the next five minutes as we made our way along the track, and with the rifles in our left hands, we were all swinging merrily away with our machetes. At least the track would be good and wide for us coming back down and out of the jungle in three days' time. The only trouble was that when we were chopping away and disturbing the vines and branches, we were also disturbing the dirt and all the dead leaves and insects. As we were soaking with sweat, everything stuck to us, so after five minutes we all looked like prize scarecrows. Needless to say, our machetes soon went back into their scabbards.

We kept heading downhill until about half an hour later we came to a stream. This was about twenty feet wide, and when we waded through it, we found that it was only about a foot deep between all the rocks that were sticking up out of the water.

Like the rest of the lads in front I quickly washed my face and arms using my jungle hat to do this. I couldn't believe how cool and refreshing it was doing that, or how peculiar it was to have a quick swill fully dressed, and using your hat as a flannel. It most certainly wasn't the last time that I, or the rest of the lads would be doing that in Malaya.

I waded out onto the far side of the stream and turned left to follow the lads along the stream. I say 'along the stream', but of course in the jungle it's not that easy. So perhaps I should say that we kept the stream to our left. We continued for another half an hour, then everyone stopped and the message came back down the line that this was to be our home for the next three nights.

We all got sorted out in the general area where we had to put up our basha. Like everyone else, I was sharing one with someone. The lad that I was sharing with was called Pete, he was the lad behind me coming through the jungle. We looked around and wondered where to start, where to build, how to build, what to build, how high to build and even what to use to build? Well you can sort of imagine how it goes in this sort of situation. However I will tell you what actually happened. We had a brilliant flash of good old-fashioned British ingenuity.

Before we went any further we would try our hand at making a cup of tea in the jungle. Pete's mess tins were the handiest, and he had packed his tea, sugar and condensed milk inside them, so things were definitely looking up. Unfortunately Pete couldn't remember where he had packed his stove, but I knew exactly where mine was, so in two minutes we were in business.

We used the water out of each water bottle; one cupful of water out of each, then all we had to do was to wait for the water to boil. I fondly remembered that mug of tea many times, as it seemed to be one of the best brews I have ever tasted. It also appeared to be a little bit of England in the middle of nowhere. It's amazing how a cup of tea to the English, has such a great capacity for making everything seem normal and therefore quite acceptable.

We had weighed up exactly what we were going to do while having a brew, and everyone else seemed to be following our example, because around the camp others were doing the same as us; lighting their cooking stoves and brewing up. We had also remembered to check ourselves for leeches, so were all clear to get on with our basha.

We chose the flattest piece of ground, then cleared all the scrub from our small area, as well as between two small trees. Whilst Pete was finishing our small clearing, I went off in search of a long branch to fit between the two trees, then looked for lengths of vine that were about the same thickness as washing line. There were plenty about, but they were vanishing fast to provide cord for the rest of the bashas. The best way to collect it was to swing on it. If you were lucky the whole lot came down from the jungle canopy.

Soon our basha was coming on great and we had tied the roof branch on without trouble. The vine was just like cord to use and was far easier than I expected. Both ponchos had been fastened together with the press-stud fastenings, then hung over the roof branch with the sides tied to convenient trees with vine. We had to make stakes, then drive them into the ground to fasten two corners of the basha roof. To make sure that the roof didn't rain in through the head holes in the poncho, we cut two thicker vines just slightly longer than the holes, then bent the vines which were springy, placing them into the holes so that the neck up-stands were pulled tight. The weight of the vine kept the hole facing down the poncho roof and therefore waterproof.

We managed to get hold of our section's spade and dug the waste pit to one side at the front of the basha. This pit was just for our rubbish, empty food tins and the like. I left Pete doing that whilst I took the water bag down to the water-hole, which being situated only twenty yards to our left, was very handy. We were lucky that we were facing the stream and wouldn't have far to carry the water.

I filled the bag with as much water as I could manage before carrying it back to the basha, tying it to a tree that we had already prepared. It looked for all the world like a green bag of potatoes leaning against the tree. I got the other water bag and went back to the water point, filled it, took it back to our basha and poured the water into the water bag that I had previously tied to the tree, so we now had a completely full bag of water.

The Sergeant came round making sure that everyone was okay and to sort out the perimeter vine. The perimeter vine is an important part of the camp, as it is a positive indicator to the boundaries of the camp. It also serves to stop people wandering off into the jungle in the dark, because obviously they would come up against the vine. It even stopped people wandering off into the jungle during the daytime, which can easily happen in thick jungle, although the longer we were based at a camp-site, the more the small trees and scrub got cut and trodden down. It's amazing how when you first stop at your camp-site there is thick jungle, but within two hours of cutting down the vines and small trees to build your bashas and paths, you can almost see from one side of the camp to the other.

The jungle camp was laid out in sections; let me explain here how a platoon and a jungle camp are made up. Three sections mean that the men in the platoon are divided by three. The outer limits of the camp are divided into three sectors and each is filled with a platoon section and their NCOs; so all around the edge of the jungle camp are the men with their Section Corporals. In the centre of the camp are the Platoon Officer and the Platoon Sergeant, the radio operator who is a member of the Signal's Regiment and is attached to the Loyals, two Iban trackers who belong to the Sarawak Rangers from Borneo and are also attached to the Loyals. On any operation the platoon could also have a Chinese Liaison Officer Interpreter, who would be a civilian or policeman, and we could also have one or more members of the Dog Section, naturally complete with their dogs.

These lads would be members of the Loyals. The dogs were usually Labradors or Alsatians and used for following tracks by scent. I don't know if the British in Malaya were the first to use dogs in a jungle situation? I haven't seen any reference to the use of dogs before then, but I know that the Americans used them later and with great success in South Vietnam, and that was after training in this type of jungle-warfare with us in Malaya.

At the bottom of the camp placed at a convenient spot on the stream, was the drinking water point, which was always slightly up stream from the washing point for obvious reasons. At the other end of the jungle camp at a suitable spot would be a vine tied securely to the perimeter vine, leading out into the jungle for about twenty yards. This vine was called the latrine vine and led to the toilet, which was a hole dug into the ground to a depth that would last the operation. The toilet seat comprised of three wooden stakes driven into the ground, with three suitable branches tied to the stakes to form a triangle about two feet above the ground.

Each day the camp was organised with two sections going out into the jungle on patrol, while the third section remained in camp carrying out all the work that was required to improve the camp, such as making paths around the camp or steps down to the water-hole, all that sort of thing, but mainly doing the guard duties around the camp. The guard duties depended on the camp's location and layout, but they were normally like that first camp with a guard on the water point at the opposite side of the stream to the camp, a guard on the latrine to the inside of the jungle to give privacy and protection to anyone using the toilet, and a guard on the animal tracks that were following the stream downhill and forming a path running through the camp.

Guard duty was usually two hours on and four hours off. It started after first light (stand-to), and finished at dusk (stand-to). Stand-to meant that at dawn and dusk all of the platoon stood at the perimeter vine with weapons ready to repulse an attack by the enemy, as that was known to be the most likely time to be attacked. On the evening stand-to the Platoon Officer and Sergeant would walk around the camp perimeter talking to everyone to make sure there were no bad injuries or sickness, also to give everyone a tot of rum (Navy grog). During the hours of darkness, there would be one guard on duty; he would be based in the centre of the camp. The night guards would each just do one duty of two hours.

So that evening in the camp at my first stand-to I sampled the first taste of Navy grog, which was given to help prevent indigestion and calm the nerves. All I can say about it is that it was a strong rum and very nice. My evening meal was a tin of Swifts steak and onions and half a bag of boiled rice with a cup of tea. The Swifts was an American tinned food and really was first class. Some of the lads made theirs with the curry powder, but it was going to be some weeks before I sampled the delights of curry.

After stand-to we settled down for the night. There wasn't much else to do because stand-to finished on darkness. It did go from light to dark very fast in the Malayan jungle. We weren't allowed to have a torch or anything like that to read with, although the guard in the centre of the camp always carried one for emergencies. We didn't get undressed to go to sleep, but left our jungle greens on, as we didn't know what creepy crawlies were about at night. Quite a few of the lads left their jungle boots on, but as mine were still damp I took them off, but I did leave my socks on.

On every operation after this one I took my light hockey boots into the jungle for pottering about the camp and sleeping in, as most of the other lads did, but you only learn from others with experience. We slept on the ground on top of some large leaves that we put down to make a damp-proof groundsheet. We all carried a thin blanket in our kit, I wrapped mine around me. We didn't need mosquito nets in the jungle because they weren't around to bother us. We were now higher up in the jungle where it was a lot cooler than in Ipoh.

Pete and I chatted about the day's experiences, I could hear the hum of conversations from the bashas near to us. One or two of the lads had a wander around the camp, they stayed for a chat as they passed us. It was already clear to me that most of the lads were not enjoying the jungle experience. Obviously they were not used to going camping, or living in the countryside.

About half an hour after it had gone dark, we were all treated to a display of what really should be called one of the wonders of the world. It was something that I never thought that I would see. I had absolutely no idea that they were here in the Malayan jungle, but there they were - the fireflies. They were everywhere, gently and quietly flying aimlessly around in the dark jungle night, giving out this mystical green light that would brighten up your hand when one flew near to it.

After the display of lights and the day's exertion, both mental and physical, everyone was tired, so about an hour later the camp settled down for the night. I wouldn't say that my bed was comfortable, but it could have been a lot worse. As I was trying to settle myself down for the night I was already making plans in my mind for making my life a lot more homely. At that moment I realised that I had already decided to stay with the jungle. My summing up of the day would be that unlike most of the lads, I found the jungle to be absolutely fascinating; I was looking forward to enjoying exploring and experiencing a lot more of it in the future, but that was providing we didn't meet any of those bad guys who could spoil everything.

Everyone was awake before daybreak; to save time Pete and I lit the cooking stove and put a mess tin of water on it to boil while we were on stand-to. This idea worked great, because just as we were stood down the mess tin boiled. For breakfast I had baked beans and pork sausages and the other half of the rice boiled. Yes rice for breakfast. It was fine as the rice filled the meal out nicely, especially for a non-smoker.

At this point let me say that I went into the jungle a non-smoker, but within the first three days I saw that the cigarette smokers had advantages. One was that they weren't hungry all the time, because the cigarettes curbed their hunger, whereas myself and other non-smokers couldn't carry enough food into the jungle to stop ourselves from being famished all the time. Also the cigarette smoke helped to keep the flies away from you, and when it came to burning leeches off the body, the smokers always had a cigarette ready lit. With the army giving at least fifty cigarettes free issue each week to everyone, it wasn't long before I and the other non-smokers quickly became cigarette smokers. Although I am now again a non-smoker and have been for many years, I must say that there is no doubt that a cigarette then, did make life easier and more relaxing. So please don't moan at any old soldiers because they were hooked by the circumstances of life.

That first full day to which I awoke in the jungle was also my first experience of a jungle patrol. As soon as breakfast was over we were off. The first thing that our Section Commander (Corporal) did, was to check that our rifles were loaded and that the safety catches were on, before checking the ammunition that we were carrying in our belt pouches. He then checked on who was tail-end Charlie, telling him to keep his eyes to the rear, as well as everywhere else. Off we went about four yards apart into the thick jungle, slowly, steadily and silently.

Within one minute we were on our own and lost from the camp, which could have been many miles away. We kept on the move for at least two hours. I was soon ready for a drink, but it was far easier not having to carry around all the kit that we'd carried into the jungle the previous day.

The signal to stop came, so we all sat down where we could and started looking for leeches. I found my first one, which was on my ankle, and although I could not feel it, this was revolting, because I could see the jet-black slimy slug-like creature. Just behind its head that was buried deep into my leg, I could see its neck throbbing as it pumped the blood from my body into its own. To be honest with you, I found this thing so disgusting, that I was beginning to panic inside, while trying my utmost to appear calm on the outside. Nobody had a cigarette to spare, because they were all in use burning leeches off.

I managed to find the matches that I had wrapped up with my razor blade. I was forcing myself to slow down and not shake them out all over the wet ground. I managed to light a match first time, blow it out, then put the hot head of the match onto the leech. It squirmed, but I thought that this is not going to work, then out popped its head. I quickly brushed it off onto the jungle floor, where it was ground into the earth with my heel. The spot where the head had been was bleeding quite readily, but we knew this would happen because of the anticoagulant that the leech had pumped in at the start. I checked everywhere else, but thankfully that was the only one.  It was a bit of a relief really, because thinking about it I felt nothing, but if you had told me then that eighteen month's later I would not be bothered by them, I would most definitely not have believed you. While we were searching for leeches the Corporal came round, advising us not to have a drink of our water until late morning. That way the water would last all day. This was good advice, which I followed until the end of my stay in Malaya.

There was nothing of any note during the rest of that patrol and we got back to base camp at about 15:30. The first thing was a much welcomed cup of tea. Until I went into the jungle I could never understand the love affair between the English nation and a cuppa, but now I truly did understand that it wasn't just the tea we were drinking, it was a little of the traditional English way of life in some isolated and wild corner of the world, where the only intruders were Englishmen.

After the cup of tea I made my dinner, which was again a tin of Swifts and boiled rice. After I had eaten I took my mess tins down to the water-hole, and washed them with sand and water. I then took a walk around the camp.

The path around the perimeter vine was now well-trodden; it was interesting to see how everyone else had performed with the building of their bashas, and take note of how they had built them. I was most interested in the Corporals' basha and bedding. They had built theirs high up, so that they could stand inside them. They weren't sleeping on the ground, but had built hammock-type beds about two feet above the ground.

I asked the Corporal what the bed was made from? It turned out to be parachute silk and he told me all about it. He explained that when you get re-supplied in the jungle by airdrop, you are supposed to carry all of the parachutes out intact, but one or two get damaged, completely by accident of course, usually burnt on the marker fire that wasn't lit. So not wanting to waste anything, the parachute panels get shared out amongst the platoon, and then back in Colombo Camp you get them stitched up so that they can be easily used for a bed in the jungle. Another big advantage with silk was when you were on ambushing duty, the biggest trouble you had then was from the torturous mosquitoes, but they cannot get through silk. The only difficulty was that the parachute had to be a green one, but most of the ones dropped to us in the jungle were white or yellow; obviously we could not have those bright colours wrapped around ourselves in an ambush position.

Well let's face it; the rest of the ambush would think you were a ghost, wouldn't they? Another way was when any old sweats were leaving for Blighty; they would always give their special personal Malayan gear to lads in the platoon who were short of kit, usually newcomers, who by the way, are called 'Joskins'. Don't ask me why, because I have no idea apart from the fact that to josh someone is to tease them, and newcomers certainly got that. It was soon stand-to and rum ration. This time I had a cup of tea brewed ready for after stand-to. We weren't as tired as the night before, so more time was spent talking and watching the fascinating firefly display.

The following day we were out on patrol again. Up to then the day had been very similar to the previous morning, but many times in the jungle you were dealing with the unknown. It was into the afternoon when we came to a part of the jungle that was bright due to a lot of sunlight getting through. When we could see into the clearing, it turned out to be a bamboo grove in the middle of thick jungle. The grove was quite large, at least the size of ten football fields, and as it was directly in line with our compass bearing, the Corporals decided to go right through the middle. It certainly did look like an easy option to all of us, and one that would be pleasant in the bright sunlight that was streaming through. However the Corporal and Lance Corporal hadn't been through a bamboo grove before and had never heard about them, but we were all surely going to find out.

The bamboo in the grove was like the rest of the jungle, absolutely enormous. At times, when we were newcomers to the jungle, it seemed as though we were in Sir Arthur Conan Doyle's 'Lost World' with the only thing missing being the Dinosaurs. Each bamboo plant was as big as four houses, with the bamboo shoots in all different sizes. I don't remember any as thin as the canes you would see in a garden centre today, but I do remember some almost as wide as a dustbin, and probably fifty feet or more in length.

Things were going great at the start and we were getting through nicely, although it did mean climbing over a lot of the big bamboo branches (or should that be shoots) which were bowed right over under their enormous weight. The ends of some of the larger ones were resting on the ground and supporting their own weight. We were almost at the middle of the grove, one of the lads was climbing over a branch that was about three feet above the ground, when, without any warning, there was a loud bang like a hand-grenade and the lad was thrown about two feet up into the air then back down to earth next to us with a thud. We all dropped to the ground and looked around for the 'Commies'.

I was desperately looking for someone or something to shoot at. I heard all the safety catches clicking off, including mine the second we hit the ground. My senses were at an unbelievable height with the split-second fear, which was pumping adrenalin through my body. I was listening so hard for any sound that would give the CTs away, that it became painful. Then I realised that I wasn't breathing. Quietly I let my breath out, then breathed in slowly.

All I could hear was the lad who had been hurt moaning quietly. I have never ever been as frightened as I was at that moment; it seemed to last forever. My eyes were moving rapidly from left to right, looking for any signs of activity. I could see nothing over to my left-hand side, as my head had been turned to the right when I hit the ground. I started to move my head very slowly to the left, terrified that the movement would attract attention.

Someone said, "It's just the branch that's broken."

We all took a quick look before sheepishly getting to our feet, all feeling a bit foolish. One of the Corporals told us all to put our safety catches back on and double-check them. The two Corporals and the lad carrying the first aid bag attended to the injured lad, while the rest of us had a look at the broken branch, which was absolutely shattered.

It was immediately obvious what had happened. The branch was already under enormous pressure with its own weight; when the lad had added his weight, this was the final straw. It cracked, springing everything upwards, including our mate. It could have been a lot worse, if he had been on the break-point when it happened, it would have killed him.

When the bamboo breaks, it then springs up in dozens of long shards of bamboo about two feet long on each side of the break. Each shard is like a sword travelling with the speed of a bullet, so it doesn't take a lot of imagination to know what would happen to anyone near to the break when it occurs. We sat around while the lad recovered. He had been winded, and was badly shaken up by the experience. One of the bamboo shards had just touched his finger, which was cut down to the bone and really needed stitching up.

The Corporal said, "As soon as he was fit to travel we will head back to the base camp."

Somebody came out with some smart remark that made all of us laugh including the injured lad, then all the banter started, which relieved the moment for us all. As soon as the lad was ready we backtracked our way very carefully out of the grove, then headed back to base camp.

Back at base it was decided that as we had only one more day to do, the lad would stay with us and leave the jungle as normal and see the Medical Officer on his return to Colombo Camp in Ipoh.

The following day was *our* day in base camp and the guard duties. There were no improvements that were required for us to do in the camp, so I spent the day relaxing and reading the book that I had carried in. I did hollow out the ground with the spade where I slept, then partly back-filled it to make the ground soft, putting down new leaves to act as a groundsheet. That night I had a comfortable resting place, along with the big as your hand hairy spiders, that found their way under you during the night, obviously attracted by the body heat.

The following morning we were up for the stand-to, then we had two hours to have our breakfast, pack all our kit and destroy our camp, and anything that we were not carrying out of the jungle. We ate all the food that was left and made a second brew. There was a bit of rice left which went into the rubbish pit. When everything had gone into the pit, including the two smashed-up cooking stoves, we then put all the hexamine blocks on top and set fire to them. Once the fire had gone out, we filled in the pit, then emptied the water bag onto it. A few minutes later we were on our way and the going out was easy. We weren't unduly bothered about the CTs, as we had fully covered this area, but don't get me wrong, we were still well alert to any dangers. The track had been well-opened up when we came in; we weren't carrying as much weight now and we were going downhill, so in what seemed to be no time at all, we were out of the jungle and into the clear sunshine. As we followed the track through the plantations there were quite a few Malayan and Chinese workers around; I must say that they did look genuinely pleased to see us. A few could speak good English and greeted us accordingly. Yes it certainly made me feel a lot better knowing that we were welcome there.

We got to the road where we had been dropped off three days earlier and waited for about twenty minutes before our transport came. Within two minutes we were loaded up and on our way. The first thing we did on our return to Colombo Camp was to check our weapons and ammunition in at the Arm's Cote, then to have a shower, a decent shave and a bite to eat. The rest of the day was left up to us to clean our gear or replace any damaged clothing. The following day was pay-day and a debriefing in the morning for us all, then we were free to do what we wanted for the rest of that day and the day after.

I was on Company Orders in the morning to give my decision on the office job, and despite everyone still trying to talk me out of it, I was going back into the jungle. I must have been the only one looking forward to it.

Three days later we received our Company postings, I was going to 6 Platoon 'B' Company. Two day's later that's where I was. With all of the lads in my Training Platoon going into Infantry Companies, this meant that most of us would not see each other again, as we were destined to be in the jungle for most of the time. When we wished each other good luck, we thought we would see each other more or less every week, but it wasn't going to be like that for us out in Malaya. I had no premonition at that time of the fate that awaited.

# CHAPTER FOUR
## *First Ambush, First Tape*

After leaving the training company I reported to the 'B' Company office and was then taken to 6 Platoon's basha and shown to what was to be my bed and my personal little spot for the next eighteen months, or so I thought. The lads from 6 Platoon had just come in from a jungle operation so they were all looking forward to getting cleaned up and going for a pint. They were all talking about getting paid up to date because they had been in the jungle previous to last Thursday, which was pay-day in the army. The routine for that night seemed to be into the NAAFI for a pint of Anchor or Tiger beer, then a trishaw down into Ipoh for a chicken curry. A trishaw is a bicycle-type rickshaw that holds one or two people.

When we went in a trishaw we usually went one person to each trishaw, which meant that it was easier for the Malay or Chinese who was pedalling it. This meant that two people were earning a living instead of just the one. I know that a lot of people in this day and age would say, in a derisory way, that it sounds patronising. Of course it was patronising but why not, they needed the money; we helped in our own small way and felt better for doing this.

The overall banter in the basha was, I suppose, as army banter all over the world, only with Malayan overtones. We wondered who could drink the most pints of the local rubbish, and who could eat the hottest chicken curry? They seemed to be a great bunch of Lancashire lads who appeared to have accepted me as though I had always been there. I was sure that I would mix with them just as easily once they had showered, put on clean clothes to get rid of that rotting jungle and human flesh smell.

I did however find it rather captivating listening to their chatter and jokes; the pleasure and light-hearted banter wasn't just down to them having a couple of days off, but quite obviously to a newcomer like me, it was the relief of once again making it safely back out of the jungle.

The Corporal from the Pay Corps came that afternoon, and I was talking to him while the platoon was gathering to receive their pay. I told him that I had already been paid, so he asked my name? I told him.

"So it's *you* that's given us all the trouble of what to pay," he said.

"I have no idea what you mean," I replied, feeling a little perplexed.

He started to explain, "With the qualifications that you received in Chichester, you are classed as a tradesman, which is the equivalent of an NCOs' rank and therefore paid accordingly. As you have not taken the office job, we did not know what to pay you, so temporarily we are paying you as a Private."

Just then the Platoon Officer and Sergeant came in for pay parade, so I left the basha and went down to the 'B' Company charwallah's for a chip banjo and a cup of coffee.

I had better explain here that the 'B' Company charwallah, was an Indian who had his own little shop that was especially for catering to 'B' Company's needs. Each company throughout the battalion also had their own individual charwallah's with their own little shops, and they were always situated by their own relevant company lines. The charwallah's used to sell tea, coffee and soft drinks, chips, sandwiches made on teacakes, fruit, sweets, stamps, airmail envelopes and cigarettes to mention just a few of the items that they supplied. These were all the kind of things that you would have and need day-to-day, to simply give yourself a break from the army supplies and routine.

Another thing that our charwallah's would do is give credit to anyone in 'B' Co. so if it got to Wednesday and you were broke, you could get what you wanted on your slate, which at times came in very handy. For instance, if you had just come out of the jungle and had no money until pay-day, you could get a chip or fried egg banjo, which was a sandwich served on a teacake without butter. Why they called it a banjo, I have absolutely no idea. Our charwallah was a Muslim, so several times a day he would get his prayer mat out, put it in front of his shop and pray to Mecca, right in the middle of whatever he was doing. I think that he got on fine with everyone in 'B' Co. I know that *I* liked the guy, and I will never forget his dream and driving ambition in life, which was to go to the UK, live in Blackpool and own a fish and chip shop on the Golden Mile.

He knew that I lived just outside of Blackpool, and that I had met my wife in the Winter Gardens. Also my Uncle Bernard was President of the Blackpool Hotel and Boarding House Association, so he was always asking me about the place. When I felt a little bit down it always made me feel better talking to him and telling him about home and Blackpool.

Whether he ever realised his dream or not I have no idea. I do know that for many years after Malaya I would always look into the chip shops when I was on the Golden Mile to see if he was in any of them. I hope he made it, because he was a good and honest human being, and more than fair to us out there in Malaya.

As I was now part of 6 Platoon, this meant that the following day was a day off for me as well. Some of the lads were going swimming at the Kinta Swimming Pool in Ipoh, so I went with them and enjoyed it very much. Transport in the shape of a three-tonner was laid on by the transport section of the Loyals, which of course was free, and if I remember correctly the driver went swimming as well.

The swimming pool was an outdoor newly-built pool. It was a really nice place that was spotlessly clean; I was to visit the place on several occasions during my time in Malaya. One thing that surprised me was that after swimming a couple of lengths of the pool I would climb out and immediately start to sweat with the physical exertion, so most of the time was spent in the water. Another thing that springs to mind when I think about the Kinta Pool is the jukebox there, which seemed to be forever playing all the Pat Boone records, especially *'I'll be home my darling, please wait for me.'* He was always top of the hit parades at that time and was another strong reminder of home. After tea I went down to the NAAFI with my new comrades for a beer as I was now feeling very much a part of 6 Platoon.

The following day we all went to the firing range for practice. It was also my first chance to fire my new FN rifle and sort the sights out. The rifle was nowhere near as accurate as the old Lee-Enfield over the two-hundred yards distance, but why bother? Fifty yards is a long way in the jungle and the FN was just as accurate at that range.

The Loyals had two firing ranges, one was the normal UK type of range that could be used up to three-hundred yards from the targets, whilst the other was a jungle range that was a lot smaller in size, but far more interesting. On the jungle range we could simulate day or night ambushing, or jungle patrol contacts. These all involved pop-up or pop out target figures. When we had night firing on the range, we would use the ground flares and the two-inch mortar parachute flares.

Another reason for using the range on a regular basis, besides keeping sharp with the practice, was that it gave us a chance to use up the ammunition that had been carried into the jungle on the operations. Obviously with the bullets getting wet and being continually unloaded and loaded into the magazines, this meant that they deteriorated, so needed using up before they gave us problems at a time when that sort of a dilemma would be the last thing that we wanted.

There are two things about the jungle range that really stick out in my memory; one was when the New Zealanders were on the range at the same time, so we swapped weapons for half an hour. They were using American carbines that were very light, short, and easy to handle, with very rapid fire on fully automatic, but had poor hitting power. They couldn't believe the hitting power of the FN, but decided that the carbine was better for the jungle as it was light and small. I bet they wished for an FN in their hands when the shooting started!

The second thing that sticks in my memory were the bootlace snakes that were all over the place. They were just like a bootlace, but not as long, probably about nine inches. We were told that they were poisonous and their bite could kill a human, but they only had a small mouth that couldn't open very wide, which made it difficult for them to bite anything, but I can tell you we didn't ever give them the chance!

When we got back to Colombo Camp from the range we were told to get a good night's sleep, because we were starting ambushing the following night. All the lads moaned at this news; it was very obvious that they did not like ambushing. The old sweats said it would be because the monsoon was due. Apparently that would drive some of the 'Commies' out of the jungle and into the homes of sympathisers and relatives. The monsoon was even *overdue* according to one or two of the old sweats. You could always trust them to foretell the future, especially if it was going to be bad. You could say they were harbingers of gloom and doom! I wonder if I was like that when I had become an old sweat? I don't think so, but when I became a Section

Commander one of my jobs was also to try and keep everyone happy.

That evening I saw something else in Malaya that was new, so very different to home and unforgettable to me. It was late afternoon, just after 17:00 I would think, I was sat at the charwallah's having a drink of coffee.

Someone said, "Look at that."

I looked South to where he was pointing. Approximately ten miles away was this gigantic black tidal wave coming up the valley. It was frightening to look at; for a wall of water about a mile high was rolling up the valley towards us. There appeared to be no escape and nothing to stop it; a black mass of swirling clouds lit by bright flashes of sheet lightening made it look like hell on earth roaring toward us. The four horsemen of the apocalypse, with all of them on the loose, loomed large in my mind.

The overall effect was heightened by the monsoon and ourselves being trapped in the same valley. It was a frightening first-time experience that was dismissed by the charwallah.

"It's just the monsoon coming. It will be here in a few minutes," he said rather nonchalantly.

The spell was now broken, and as I looked around everyone was dashing here and there to move everything back under cover. I finished my coffee quickly, went back to my basha to wait with apprehension for what was imminent. Five minutes later the wind started to blow around us. After another five minutes the sun was snuffed out, the rain came with a deafening roar. I think that it was thundering, but the roar of the rain was such that it was difficult to hear anything else above the noise. After about ten minutes of incredible rain, during which we could not see the ground at all, because the rain was bouncing about a foot back up into the air, it started to ease off to very heavy rain, which was just as well because all the drains and ditches where almost filled to the top. I understood then why they were made so deep. The paths were all two or three inches deep in water, and it was running off the roof of the basha like a waterfall.

Amazingly two lads from 'C' Company came walking past chatting away, dressed in the traditional shorts and flip flops, just as if the sun was still shining. I suppose it was time for a shower so they just took a walk around our basha. It rained for about half an hour or just over, then suddenly it brightened, the rain stopped; five minutes later the evening sun was shining again and everything was steaming in the warmth of its rays.

I gave it five minutes then had a walk to the bottom of the camp to look at the monsoon drain. I could see where the water level had been up to and that it was already going down fast. I decided to go to the charwallah's for another coffee, as the last one had been rudely interrupted. As I walked there it was noticeable that all the dust to which I had become accustomed since I arrived at the camp, had been washed away. Everything, including the bashas looked fresh and clean.

As we were ambushing the following night I turned in early along with most of the other lads. The rain had cleared the air and cooled everything down for about an hour, but the heat was back to normal now, I must admit that I was getting more acclimatised to it. It wasn't too bad for getting to sleep early, because the only lights at the bashas were the ones inside. These were electric of course, so if a platoon was having an early night then they themselves switched off the lights leaving the basha in darkness. There were all-night lights that were similar to streetlights but they were up by the cookhouse, toilets, armouries, motor transport parking area, ammunition dump and all along the road that ran though the camp.

We were all up early the following morning. There wasn't an actual reveille call every morning in the camp because everyone was involved in doing something different and at various times. We were after all, a fully operational active service battalion and we all knew what we were about.

We had a comparatively easy day; I went up to our 'B' Co. stores to draw out a tin of insect repellent, two tins of fifty cigarettes that were owed to me, and a new sweat rag. I tried to swap the cigarettes for a piece of parachute silk, bearing in mind what I had been told about ambushing, but nobody had any going spare, so I put the tins into my locker for a later day. One job that I had to do in the afternoon was to draw sixty rounds of ammo and load up three magazines for my rifle, ready for the ambush that night.

I made sure that my water bottle was full, then added some fruit flavouring to it so that it would be tastier to drink. I had some sweets wrapped in a waterproof bag for the top pocket of my jungle greens, plus chewing gum, so I was as ready as I could be. It was apparently worse for the smokers, because they weren't allowed to have a cigarette in the ambush, and from their talk I knew that they were always desperate for a smoke by daybreak.

We boarded the three-tonner in the pouring rain of the monsoon. The canvas sides of the truck were down to keep the rain out, but we were already quite wet. It was not like at home, where when you were wet you felt the cold; there it was more of a refreshing coolness. There were two trucks carrying the whole of 6 Platoon, but we were going to be split into four ambush parties. We had already been told whose party we were with. I was with the Platoon Sergeant's Section.

It was still raining hard when we reached the drop-off point, so when we got off the trucks we were drenched in seconds. The biggest irony was that two minutes after getting off the trucks and getting wet through, it stopped raining, which was typical!

We made our way through a plantation, then around a large tin mine. At the far side of the mine we split into our relevant parties. The smokers had been busy since we left Columbo Camp, smoking just one after another. I was surprised that some of them didn't smoke two at once and do the job properly. I found out that they were allowed to smoke until it went dark, then that was it till morning.

When we got to the ambush position; the Sergeant and one of the old sweats started placing the ground flares and running the wires back to our position. The Sergeant and the Bren gunner were in the middle of the party. I was over to the left next to the end with an old sweat on the end. It was just beginning to go dark, so I wrapped myself up as well as I could with a green towel and sweat rags covered in insect repellent. We lay on the ground on the edge of the tin mine, which was now just a sea of mud about four inches deep. There was a slight rise in front of us, which meant that we could keep our weapons just out of the dirt, though they were already well covered with the mud from our hands. The mosquitoes were beginning to bite and I knew then that I was in for a difficult night, as the insect repellent didn't seem to be having any great effect.

I was trying not to move or make a noise, but I heard the others moving next to me, so I lifted my arm up to get rid of the mosquito that was buzzing in my right ear and driving me crazy. At the same time I plastered some of the mud that I was lying in onto my neck and face, attempting to keep the mosquitoes off. This seemed to work quite well.

There was no moon that night; apart from the light of the stars it was pitch black. The monsoon clouds had gone completely leaving the sky clear. The tin mine water run-off slurry pans were behind us, and at the back of these, but over to the right, were the shadowy shapes of the timber-built mine buildings and washing ramp, starkly silhouetted black against the dark starry night sky. In front of us was the track which ran around the tin mine. Beyond that was scrub land stretching for about two hundred yards up to the smaller trees that were the start of the jungle edge. Behind them was the intimidating black mass of jungle rising up into the mountains. The buzz and humming of the insect world were incessant; the monsoon rains had obviously increased their activity. Mixed into all this hive of noise, coming from every direction, were the loud deep croakings of the bullfrogs, sounding just as if someone was running a wooden stick along wooden oak palings.

We had been warned before the operation that the RAF could bomb the jungle whilst we were ambushing, and I was looking forward to that should it happened. The last bombing that I had been involved in was when our street was bombed during the Second World War. This would certainly be something different, but I did wonder if we would see or hear anything as ambushing was taking place for a good few miles up to the North and along the jungle edge, where platoons other than ours were involved. It was rumoured that the Australians and the Kiwis were up to the North and on the ambushing operation as well.

We had been lying there for over a day, well two hours actually, but it felt like a day. I could see the time on the luminous dial of my watch showing that it was only 21:00. During that time I had managed to quietly get two pieces of chewing gum out of my pocket and into my mouth, complete with mud of course. I lay there wondering how on earth I was going to be able to stand another nine hours of this nightmare? I was wet, and unbelievably actually beginning to feel a little bit cold. I was covered in stinking mud, and the mosquitoes were holding a late Christmas Ball on my back.

I was thinking that nothing could be worse than this, when thoughts of my Granddad Hudson came to mind. I remembered what he'd had to put up with in the trenches in Flanders through all the bad winters, and all the mustard gas, the wounds that he received and seeing his mates being killed around him, including his childhood and life-long friend.

I told myself not to be so soft, that this was nothing. I scolded myself, "Stop feeling sorry for yourself, and get on with it." Somehow it felt as though Granddad was there with me.

The peculiar thing is that my older cousin Raymond felt just the same thing about Granddad while doing his share of national service during the Suez war. I felt that later in the jungle, there were times when Granddad was watching over me and guiding me in my decisions. It may sound daft, but that's truly the way it was to me.

It was approximately 22:00 when the old sweat gave me a slight nudge on my left arm. I looked slowly to the left. In the dark I could just make out his face and his finger pointing to the left and the scrub. I slowly nudged the lad on my right and pointed in the same direction, then I concentrated on the scrub. I hadn't heard the gentle click of the safety catches going off, so I left mine alone.

We had been concentrating on the scrub for what must have been five minutes or more, when the old sweat's safety catch clicked off, followed by mine and all the others. A second or two later I saw movement in the scrub on the edge of the track about one-hundred and fifty yards away. I immediately put it down to some sort of animal, possibly a wild pig, tiger or monkeys, all of which I had been told were around in this part of Malaya.

There had been no more movement from that area for over half an hour so the message came down the line to put our safety catches back on. We continued to scan the area, but there were no further movements that we could see in the scrub. We started to relax a little from the high that we had all been on. I had started to feel a little bit drowsy, and although I wasn't near to going to sleep, I was in more of a day-dreaming situation, rather than concentrating hard. The mosquitoes were still being a pain, but they were not as bad as they had been at the start of the night.

I was brought to full alertness by a peculiar buzzing noise that I couldn't quite place for a moment or two, then I realised that it was a small aircraft coming from behind us and getting louder by the second. Suddenly it was right overhead. I could see from the dark outline that it was a small Auster-type plane, and not very high, possibly between a thousand and fifteen-hundred feet.

I thought to myself, "It wants to start climbing up if it's going to clear the mountains."

Next minute it was over the main jungle edge, then suddenly it dropped a parachute flare. It immediately circled around and dropped another flare. It kept turning until it was overhead again; then it straightened up and flew back over the jungle edge flying on for about a mile and a half before dropping another flare. It was like daylight in our position, you could hear the flares crackling even from that height as they floated slowly down.

One of the lads said, "What are they doing?"

I had a good idea but said nothing, because I could not believe that they were going to do what I thought, so near to us.

Almost immediately we heard them coming, the deep-throated powerful roar of Merlin engines, for it sounded like there were quite a few. I knew then how the Germans must have felt thirteen years earlier with that sound coming nearer and nearer, knowing what was to come falling from them. We had lifted ourselves up and out of the mud to watch the impressive show. I was knelt up. A couple of the lads were standing, watching and listening. I think that we had all forgotten about the ambush because two of the lads had lit cigarettes. The roar from the bombers was enormous. It felt as though the ground trembled with the noise, then we all heard a very slight whistling noise, followed by an enormous explosion that was just into the jungle near to us. The ground rippled under us and I imagine that an earthquake would just sound like that.

We knew that the bombs were not meant for us, but it was frightening enough for all of us to try and bury ourselves into the mud. One minute later it was all over just as suddenly as it had started. All there was left to remind us that we had not dreamt it all were two flares still crackling and floating down to earth, and the fast disappearing sound of engines flying down the valley towards KL.

The Sergeant said, "If anyone needs a cigarette they can light up. They have five minutes for a smoke, but everyone has to keep their eyes open."

I think he was as shocked as everyone else by the experience. I used the time for a drink and some of the boiled sweets that I had in my pocket, and what was left of the chewing gum. All of us, even the old sweats, found it rather nerve-racking. After five minutes we all settled back down into the mud to the silence and our own thoughts.

The rest of the night passed without event, and as soon as the daylight started to appear we broke up the ambush. The ground flares were brought in and the wires folded up, and by the time that was done it was almost full daylight. I looked at everyone, we were just the same colour as the patch of ground we had just left, as everyone was covered in mud from head to toe.

I looked to the jungle where the bombs had been dropped, expecting to see big gaps in the trees, but the jungle didn't look any different. I just could not believe it after the explosions last night. We made our way down the track to the corner of the tin mine, then waited for the other ambush parties to arrive from other directions to join us. Ten minutes later they turned up. The first thing that they asked us was if we had heard the bombing?

We all doubled up laughing.

Someone asked, "Why are you all laughing?"

The Sergeant replied loudly, "Hear it, we were in the middle of it!"

Then someone else said in a female voice, "Well I can believe that ducky, look at the state you are in."

Another round of laughter ensued.

We all made our way back to the road ready to meet the trucks for the return trip to Colombo Camp. After about fifteen minutes they arrived, we quickly boarded and were soon away. Everyone was quiet on the journey back, probably because we were all tired.

I was thinking, "Well that was my first proper operation with my platoon," and spent the rest of the journey putting everything into order in my mind, as well as picking lumps of the fast drying mud from off my uniform.

It wasn't long before we were back at the camp, and we all jumped off the transport. I looked back into the truck to make sure we had everything, but all that was left were piles of mud cakes where we had been sitting.

We got some queer looks from the lads we passed while going to the Arm's Cote to book our weapons and ammo back in. I told Len, who was in charge of the 'B' Co. Arm's Cote that I would be back later to book my rifle back out so that I could clean and oil it.

His replied with a smile, "I blooming well hope you do, so don't forget."

The first job was to get cleaned up. I sorted some clean clothes out from my locker, then went down for a shave, shower and put my clean dry clothes on. This made me feel a lot better, but my back was itching like mad with all the mosquito bites. When I looked in a mirror it was just a mass of bites on top of bites. The rest of me wasn't too bad as the mud had certainly kept the mosquitoes away from the skin where I'd plastered it on.

We weren't ambushing till the following night, so I thought that I must try to find something that would stop the insects from getting my back. Meanwhile I was taking one of the lad's advice and going to the NAAFI shop for some cream and coconut oil to put on my skin, but first it was breakfast time and I was ravenous.

After eating I got on with my chores and also took my mud-covered clothes down to the dhobi man to be washed. The dhobi man used to do all our washing for us. It was all privately run, so we had to pay him of course, but the clothes always came back spotless and perfectly ironed. I can't remember just what he charged us, but it was cheap and well worth the money. The rest of the day was spent pottering around. I had a bite to eat at the charwallah's and a coffee, then I watched the monsoon coming up the valley to unleash yet another drenching on us. When the storm was over, I went to the cinema which was next to the NAAFI, then I turned in for the night and slept soundly until morning.

The following day was spent getting ready for ambushing again, which would be that night, but I had a problem. I had been issued with two full jungle green uniforms, but at the moment with having one in the dhobi for cleaning I only had the one which I had to wear that night. This meant that in the morning when we returned from ambushing covered in mud again, I would not have a clean uniform to put on. Also I wanted to try soaking my jungle greens in insect repellent, ready for that night, which was something I'd been advised to try. I could see that all the other lads had quite a few sets of jungle greens so I asked them if you just went to the Quartermaster's Stores for another set of greens?

One of the lads said, "Well more or less, but you need to have been re-supplied in the jungle, so we will show you how it works when that happens. I have plenty of spare jungle greens so I will give you one for now. You will get your other back from the dhobi when you take tonight's jungle greens for cleaning tomorrow, so you should be okay. If not, don't worry, we will soon sort you out with more gear."

I thanked him and felt a lot better. I could not believe how much easier the army-side of life was here compared to Blighty. I went to my locker, got the two tins of cigarettes out that I had been keeping, and took them to the lads who were sat on the beds at the top end of the basha.

I said, "Here are some fags to share out amongst yourselves in thanks for your help."

They did not want to take them.

I explained, "I don't smoke, and I am very grateful for your help, and I like and approve of your attitude of sharing amongst each other, which is only what I am trying to do myself now."

I left the cigarettes with them and went up to the Quartermaster's stores feeling a lot better, as I now felt far more a part of the platoon and fully accepted as such by the lads. I was going to the QM's to get two tins of insect repellent, that was if I could have two at once, but they gave them to me without any problems, and I got the feeling that you could ask for anything and get it, if it was necessary. Don't get the wrong idea from what I am saying, it had to be needed!

I went back to my basha, got out the jungle greens that I had been given, then took them outside along with the insect repellent left from the night before last, and one of the new tins that I had just got from the QM's. I then soaked the uniform completely in the insect repellent before putting the jungle greens on the basha roof to dry in the hot sun.

It was now getting late morning so I went down to the charwallah's for a coffee and a banana banjo. There were a couple of other lads there, so we all sat talking about this and that, but it did keep coming up that we were all dreading the coming ambush that night. I finished my coffee before returning back to check on my jungle greens, which were now well dry. I then covered the back of the jacket with the thick cream from the NAAFI, to bind in the repellent. I was assured that this would do for one night, but you had to repeat all this before the next ambush However the best thing of all was to wrap yourself in parachute silk.

That afternoon I was lying on my bed relaxing and reading a book, when a voice called out behind me, "So they've got you at last!"

The voice registered with me immediately, and I turned round to see John Hardman standing there. John was an old friend from Kirkham. We had also gone to the Technical College in Preston together for many years. John's job in Malaya was driving the Commanding Officer's Land Rover. This was probably down to the fact that he was a good driver and had driven a Land Rover for a long time back home. I am sure that he was as pleased to see me as I was to see his friendly face. He also told me that another of our friends from home was near and in the band. His name was Ian Bolton. I decided that the following day I would search him out. John stopped for about an hour talking, then he had to get back, whilst I had to get ready for the ambush that night. He couldn't believe that I had turned down a cushy office job and was going out ambushing, but that was my choice, and time alone would tell whether I was right or wrong?

Apart from the bombing, that night's ambushing was just a repetition of the previous nights. We were still in the same ambush spot, which made it more boring than the first night, but at least I knew what to expect and I plastered myself in mud to start with. The insect repellent and cream also seemed to be working well, so the biggest pain was under some sort of control, and the mosquito nightmare turned into just a bad dream.

It was nearly midnight when we heard the aircraft again; we could see the flares, which that night were three or four miles farther up the valley. We could clearly hear the crump

crump of the explosions, and it wasn't surprising that it had been a frightening experience for us a couple of nights earlier, but it was somebody else's turn tonight. The rest of the night passed without anything untoward happening, and once again the morning dawn brought all our lives back to normal, for Malaya that is!

Back in Colombo Camp it was once again clean the mud off everything; my rifle was easier to clean as I had smothered everything well in oil. After breakfast I took my mud-splattered jungle greens down to the dhobi and picked up my other uniform that I had left a couple of days before. Then I went in search of Ian Bolton; firstly to the band basha where I found him, and we had a good chat about home. He didn't know that I had arrived in Malaya, so he was very surprised to see me.

Ian's dad had run the Kirkham Brass Band, so naturally he was a good musician. To get into the Regimental Band you had to be a regular soldier, so Ian signed on for three years, instead of remaining a national serviceman, thereby being able to join the Loyals' Band. A few years after Malaya we often worked together; we became very close friends for a good few years and had many a chat about Malaya. This was until Ian left to live up in the top of Scotland, and I'm sorry to say that I haven't seen him again to this day.

I had to leave Ian because he had a band practice to go to, but I kept in touch with both Ian and John during the rest of my time in Malaya. We did three weeks of continuous ambushing on this operation which was one night on, one night off, so it was a relief when it finally came to an end. Each night was much the same, and the most exciting night was the first night that I told you about, the rest really do need forgetting about.

I never did ambushing for this length of time during the rest of my time in Malaya, most ambushing afterwards was for either one night or three night's duration.

After the last night's ambushing we were given three days off to catch up on our sleep, then get all our equipment back up to standard. In the afternoon I was sitting on my bed writing to Betty when the Sergeant came into the basha.

He said, "You're wanted right away in the Company Office."

When I got there CSM Bull told me that I was going on an NCOs' training course (cadre), the following morning. Once again I was hit with the unexpected. I had been with my platoon for three weeks and I was going to be doing something different yet again. At least this time I kept the same bed.

The following morning I reported to the training section and for more training, but this time there could be something positive at the end like a Lance Corporal's tape. I was determined to pass, because I had already learnt while working for my father, that while responsibility gives you more work to do, it also gives you more freedom at a personal level, and I have never been one for taking orders. The extra money would also be very handy, as I was hoping to buy a new camera so that I could make a record of my time in Malaya and send the photos back home to Betty.

The cadre lasted for three weeks and covered things like compass and map reading, all the weapons that we had covered in jungle training again, plus using weapons that only NCOs used like the Patchet sub-machine-gun, the two-inch mortars and briefings and debriefings for jungle and ambushing operations. They also taught us how to give orders and all that kind of thing. We also received some basic medical training, which told me nothing new apart from the morphine. This was supposed to be given by an NCO to anyone who was badly wounded or injured and in unbearable pain. The injection kit consisted of a thin lead tube similar to a very small tube of toothpaste, which contained the morphine. On the end of the tube was a long cap, which when unscrewed exposed the needle. What you had to do to administer the morphine was to insert the needle into a suitable spot, then roll up the tube like squeezing out toothpaste, and by doing so the morphine was injected into the person requiring it. For some reason I always seemed to be the NCO who had to carry the morphine, and be the one who would have to administer the injection. I always lived with the worry and fear of having to do this to someone.

One thing that I really enjoyed was the work we did with map reading and the compass, and how to relate the two together. It wasn't unknown for a section or platoon to be unsure as to their exact position; I am being polite in not saying lost. A lot of the jungle that we entered was unsurveyed, which was stated clearly in red across the maps that we used. I always got a special kick when I took my section out into those areas. It was also explained to us how to locate a platoon's exact position when you made base camp on the first day into the jungle on a new operation.

What happened was that you got to the location that had been pre-selected in the operational briefing in Colombo Camp. At that area location you then looked for the nearest suitable spot for the base camp. Once you'd found that spot, the radio operator gave the provisional map reference to HQ at Colombo Camp. Later that day, and at a suitable time, two patrols were sent out to verify the location of the base camp by checking on nearby streams or ridges. When they returned to the base camp the confirmation or correction to the base camp location was sent back by radio to HQ Colombo Camp.

A significant event happened to my company while I was away on the NCOs' cadre, and it was in a major way relative to the base camp location patrols that we had been covering, so I will tell you about it in the following chapter.

One of the tests was to go into a local rubber plantation at night. With just the compass and a map you had to find your way from point to point with just a compass bearing to guide you, which in the darkness wasn't easy. I enjoyed doing it and managed to find my way around without problems. The entire course was similar to this, and quite enjoyable. Everyone was treated as if they were already NCOs. At the end of the course we were all sent back to our respective companies.

That night on the notice-board my name was posted for reporting on Company Commander's Orders. The following morning I was there, outside the Company Office, in best uniform and best boots wondering if I had passed the course? I found out before I was marched in to see the CC because the CSM called me to attention by addressing me as 'Corporal Hudson'. I have to say that I was so pleased. It had taken me from being a cadet at thirteen years of age until now, but I had finally managed it.

The CC congratulated me on becoming a Lance Corporal, telling me that I would now be leaving 6 Platoon and joining 4 Platoon. I came out of the CCs' office and the CSM told me to go to the Quartermaster's stores to draw out my new tapes, then go and choose a bed in the Corporals' basha.

The Corporals' basha was a little bit more luxurious, with a small carpet on the floor, a table and two easy chairs and only one door opening, so nobody walked straight through using it as a short cut. The corner bed was free, so I chose that, and except for a month in Hong Kong, that was my own private space for the next sixteen months. My next job was to go and see Len at the 'B' Company Arm's Cote to choose my own personal weapon. I had decided on a Patchet sub-machine-gun. I knew that the hitting power wasn't brilliant, but having heard various tales about platoons and sections getting lost, I had decided that the first thing was to always be where I was supposed to be in the jungle, and to always know exactly where I was at any time.

The major benefit of the Patchet was that it folded up to a small size, with its sling around your neck this left you two free hands for map reading. I took a special pride in always knowing exactly where I was in the Malayan jungle.

# CHAPTER FIVE
## *Under Fire, Pinned Down, and Poisoned*

As mentioned earlier my Company had a major incident just after I had left to start the NCOs' cadre. I must say now that apart from this chapter, I have only put into this book anything in which I was personally involved, but sometimes other events involve you indirectly, and this is one such event. I joined 4 Platoon as a Lance Corporal immediately following the event, and it did have some bearing on my immediate future with 4 Platoon.

A 'B' Company Platoon had gone into the jungle for a five-day operation. They had reached the base camp location, then immediately sent out the short verification patrols to pinpoint the Platoon's base camp location. One patrol went to the West following up the main stream, while the other patrol went to the North following up a tributary. According to the map, this second patrol should come to a very steep hill or cliffs about half a mile away from the base camp location.

After approximately thirty minutes, the patrol reached that location. It did turn out to be a small cliff face. The stream that they had been following, was coming over the top of the cliff forty feet above in a small waterfall. They moved closer to where the water was falling on the rocks, when suddenly shots rang out from a CT sentry positioned on the cliff top.

Most of the members of the patrol were pinned down and unable to move without exposing themselves to the sentry above. It had been a miracle that no one had been hit by the first shots, but now their position was precarious. The jungle was thick undergrowth at this spot, so it was difficult to see up to the top of the cliff without moving and giving away their positions. The cover was limited to big thick leaves and one or two smaller trees.

The Section Commander was to the front of the section when the first shots rang out, therefore he was with the front part of the section that was pinned down. It was difficult for the Corporal, as according to the book, the correct course of action on the first shot, was to immediately charge into the camp and shoot at anything you could see. However on this occasion there was no chance of charging up the forty foot cliff, and now half the patrol soldiers were unable to move without being shot. What could the Section Commander do?

The sentry was above, but a few yards behind him would be the Communist base camp that he was guarding, with probably another fifteen to twenty CTs', some of whom would now have joined the sentry, thus giving them more firepower on top of the cliff. The CT's in the camp would be packing equipment and essentials making ready to flee, while their comrades on the cliff top gave them more time and cover to move more of their equipment which was very difficult to replace in the jungle.

The Section Commander had to make his mind up fast as to what he should do? He knew that he had two advantages. One of them was that not all of his patrol was under fire, and so not pinned down. The CTs' should have realised that, but knowing the way the British Army operate they would not expect the patrol to split up, or at least not for some time. The second, and major advantage, was that the full platoon was only a few minutes away, if they were moving at top speed.

The CTs' would not be aware of that, and would be thinking that it was just a normal platoon section search patrol that they had stumbled upon. So taking advantage of what he had, the Section Commander sent two men and the Lance

Corporal, who fortunately had been to the rear of the patrol, back to the platoon at the double.

The three men made it back to the platoon in less than fifteen minutes, arriving back at the same time as the other verification patrol. Then first things first, the Platoon Officer told the radio operator to contact HQ immediately, whilst simultaneously confirming with both patrols the location of the platoon's base camp, as well as the CTs' base camp location. By the time he had all this information to hand the radio operator was in contact with HQ at Colombo Camp, and the information was immediately passed through to them.

Whilst the platoon awaited orders from HQ they all prepared themselves to move out to help the men who were pinned down. There were two options. The first was to climb the cliff face as near to the CT camp as possible, then sweep around and move into the camp. The second option was to liberate the men who were under fire, then let the RAF bomb the camp. Everyone knew that speed was essential, but each minute seemed like an hour to them as they waited.

The order came through for the first option, which was to take the camp. Within two minutes they were off, leaving just three men including the radio operator, guarding their base camp, with none of them knowing if the men left pinned down were still okay, or what the immediate future held for themselves?

With two extra men, the Lance Corporal and his own two men went back to where his section was pinned down, with orders not to move until they heard gunfire from above. The other two sections, plus the Platoon Officer, Sergeant and Iban trackers went with them for most of the way, then turned to the right heading through the jungle for about three-hundred yards before turning left, then up the cliff face.

Once they were all on top of the rise they made their way slowly towards the CTs' camp with the Ibans and leading scouts to the front. After approximately an hour, the leading

Iban held his hand out pointing down and to the right front. Fifteen yards away it was possible to just make out the edge and roof of a hut. The Officer motioned the Sergeant to move out to the right flank as quietly as possible, with a Corporal between the two, and in the middle of the bulk of the men. The other Corporal and the rest of the men moved quietly to the left. The camp was about fifteen feet below them, and about fifteen yards away. There had not been any sign of movement; in fact the only indication of the camp was the top corner of the hut. Everyone was in position, and it had been managed without a sound being made.

The Officer checked quickly to the left and right then shouted, "Charge!" At the same time he fired his FN towards the camp.

The platoon made their way into the camp the best way they could through the last bit of jungle, firing towards the camp whenever they thought they saw anything. The strangest thing to the lads was to be making all this noise, shouting and firing, when all their time in the jungle had been spent trying to avoid any noise.

The shooting stopped almost immediately, as it was quickly realised that the birds had flown. The most memorable part of that charge, was one of the lads as he came out of the jungle firing shot after shot at a CT, shouting that he couldn't be missing him but he wouldn't go down. Then he realised that it was a uniform hanging on a washing line. It was obvious that they had left a lot of their equipment in the camp, including a clean uniform hanging on the line that was now full of holes.

As there were so many items left in the camp, it would be important for the police and military intelligence to scrutinise them. As this meant the camp could not be left empty, and as it was getting late in the day, and there was a ready-made camp, it was decided to move all the platoon's equipment from their original camp of that morning, to the CTs' hastily departed camp. The Platoon Officer returned to the old camp to report on the outcome to HQ, then the radio could be moved to the CTs' camp and reset. The specialised tracker team was ready to go. It would be on its way into the jungle in the morning at first light to join up with 4 Platoon, so they could then take up the chase.

The following morning after an understandably bad night's sleep by most of the lads, when the tracker team arrived, there was obviously a serious problem with most of the Platoon seemingly very ill. The Medical Officer had to be brought out into the jungle, as nobody could understand the problem. Fortunately for the tracker team they had come in with bottles full of drinking water so they had no problems. Apparently the water hole at the stream had been poisoned due to arsenic being deliberately added to it. This deadly poison was readily available in this part of Malaya, via the tapioca plant which produces the poison as it grows in the plantations that are situated on the jungle edge. Some of the platoon were hospitalised temporarily, but they all fully recovered from the experience, well at least physically.

All of the CTs got away that day, but they were now scattered into the jungle and subject to having their tracks found by the patrols who were constantly probing the jungle for such tell-tale signs.

# CHAPTER SIX
## Section Commander and Observation Point

So here I am, an NCO and a new arrival to 4 Platoon having to get to know everyone again. It would be a little bit different this time. I was a Lance Corporal now, so my priority was the responsibility for my men. It was immediately obvious to me that 4 Platoon had just received a large influx of new blood, including NCOs, and although the platoon had just been traumatised to some extent by 'B' Company's recent experience, I believed that the new blood was more to do with people reaching the end of their service and leaving. It would be better for me as I was new to everything, including the platoon, so we could all have a new start along with getting to know each other.

To my surprise I was immediately given my own section, even though I was only a Lance Corporal and newly-promoted. I was also given the job of giving out the Paludrine anti-malaria tablets to all 4 Platoon members, then marking the tablets off each day against the names in the Paludrine book. Although I didn't know it at the time, I was to keep that job for the rest of my time in Malaya.

The platoon strength was still well down; we were due for further strengthening of men and NCOs in the near future, but until strengthened the platoon wasn't able to go into the jungle, due to being at an unacceptable low level of manpower. This situation did work out quite well though, as it gave everyone the chance to get to know each other, and for me to find my feet as a Section Commander, because we were put onto plantation patrols.

This involved myself and my section being dropped off from a three-tonner at some predetermined spot within a five-hundred square mile area around Ipoh, on a road that was near to a tin mine, rubber plantation, or any type of crop farming area. We would be dropped off at approximately 08:30, then picked up at the same spot at 18:30, after the six o'clock curfew. The times did change quite often depending on where we were patrolling, as well as what we were looking for. Sometimes we would be picked up at 15:00.

We used to carry a packed lunch on these patrols which weren't too bad except for the tin of oxtail soup. Now the tins of soup that we received for lunch were quite interesting. This was due to the method of heating them, as they were intended for use in the sub-zero Arctic. We had to pull a cap off the top of the tin, which automatically lit a heating fuse that warmed the contents of the tin to boiling point, then we could pour it into our mess tin to eat. One important thing that we had to do before lighting the fuse, was to make sure that the tin was open. When it came to the oxtail soup, the can remained sealed. We would light the fuse, then retire fifty feet away to eat our sandwiches, waiting for the tin to blow itself apart. It always managed to do this with a tremendous thump, showering the surrounding area with the hot oxtail soup that was far too obnoxious for us, but no doubt the ants would have cleared the repugnant remains within two minutes.

The plantations consisted of all forms of cultivation, but the largest area was taken up with rubber plantations, most of which were generally up to the North of Ipoh. These rubber plantations would contain thousands of trees, all planted in straight lines, and stretching as far as the eye could see in every direction. There would be tracks running through the trees. Here and there were small wooden huts for storing tools and other items.

In the cultivated areas around Ipoh there was a lot of tapioca being grown; apparently nine-tenths of the world's tapioca was grown in the valley. A tapioca tree grows to about fifteen feet high. It has just one thin, single trunk with a bush of leaves on top, whilst the tapioca crop is in the large potato-like roots in the ground. The problem with tapioca is that the roots are full of arsenic, and the ground and the streams in the tapioca plantations are so full of arsenic that they are deadly poisonous. Naturally we never stopped in a plantation, and knew never ever to take water from downstream of a tapioca plantation.

To the North-East and about ten miles from Ipoh, I found a small grove of lime trees in a secluded and out of bounds area. It was inside the jungle edge near to one of the cultivated areas we used to patrol. They were like small apple trees; the limes were green but looked like small lemons. We used to squeeze half of one into our full water bottle. They were strong-tasting and very bitter, so we didn't squeeze too hard, or we wouldn't be able to drink the water. I have only found out recently that in the North of Perak, Charlie used limes laid out in patterns on the tracks to leave messages. Apparently the military intelligence people gave out the wrong information that the limes were from another Malayan state, as there wasn't a single lime tree in Perak.

Another crop that we came across were pineapples. These grew on the ground in the middle of a bunch of coarse leaves about two feet high. We would help ourselves to one or two, and I must tell you that a fresh pineapple is the most wonderful sweet-tasting fruit that you could imagine. What we buy here in England are just poor imitations of the real thing. If there is one thing that I really miss from Malaya, after my comrades of course, it's fresh pineapple, for that is something that you just cannot buy in this country.

Another tree that was growing everywhere was the coconut. They grew surprisingly high, and we were fascinated by the young men climbing up the trees in their bare feet to knock down the coconuts. The nuts were very big because of the husk. They certainly came down to earth with a fair old thump. The older men waited down below, then they would strip the husks off immediately the coconut had landed. Of course we tried the coconuts finding them very tasty. There was a lot of milk inside the nut, which was very white, and the shell of the nut was quite soft, unlike those we buy in the U.K. where they have obviously hardened due to age.

The banana trees seemed to be growing everywhere, including in the middle of the towns and villages. Rice was also being grown, but not as much as I would have thought, so there must have been areas in Malaya that would be more suited to specialised rice growing. There were also lots of palm trees, which I believe were grown to produce palm oil.

For most of the time, the plantation patrols were very enjoyable, giving us the chance to meet and talk to the local people. Sometimes we would take army bicycles with us and cycle around our patrol area. It obviously depended on the area we were covering, and the type of tracks, but we could cover a lot of ground in the day in that manner. We would also be seen by a lot of the locals who worked in the plantations or the tin mines. I am sure that most of the local people were glad to see us around knowing that the British Army was watching over them at close range, not just riding past in three-tonners.

We would go around the rubber plantations and watch the workers tapping the rubber trees for the latex, or we would go around the tin mines and in and out of the workings and the buildings. The big mines usually had a European manager in charge, and even other Europeans in the management team. They always made a point of showing us around the mine explaining how everything worked. I felt sometimes that it was mainly for the benefit of the local workers, to show them that the army was everywhere, in control and fully trustworthy.

Another thing that they showed us was the gold and silver that they retrieved along with the tin ore during the mining process. The good mines would provide enough gold to pay for the running costs of the mine, so obviously the tin they produced was all clear profit. A few of the managers, including the Malayans, would invite us to visit their homes and to use their swimming pools to relax in on our days off. Occasionally, if we had a free day coming up, we would accept their offers and we always got well looked after when on a visit to their homes.

In one of the plantations, we all had a go at cutting the bark on a rubber tree to tap the tree for the latex. We also all tried panning for tin ore in one of the tin mines. It was interesting, and the locals thoroughly enjoyed showing us how to do things. I am certain that they were pleased that we took an interest in what they were doing.

The tin mines weren't anything like an underground coalmine, or a cave dug into the ground; they were just a massive hole resembling a stone quarry in the UK. The hole wasn't dug out by machinery, but blasted out with high pressure water jets. The slurry that was formed by this process was pumped up to the top of a very large inclined wooden run-off, which was as wide as a main road and about one-hundred and fifty yards long. When the slurry ran down the slope and over the slats of the trays that were placed across the ramp, the tin ore, which was heavy, would be left behind at the slats, thus being ready to be collected by the workers for further refining.

The buildings and ramps were all made out of timber, and reminiscent of the buildings that you see in a Wild West cowboy film. The only solid structures were the concrete bases for the powerful water guns, some of which took two men to operate them, even though they were bolted down onto the solid concrete bases. The run-off areas for the slurry were like a desert landscape, especially in the old mines, and could be as big as two square miles. Over most of the area the slurry would have dried, which left it looking like a white sandy desert that was called a tin slat or tailings.

Sometimes we had to cross them to get to where we wanted to be. While they were great to walk on, just like Southport beach even, the heat was unbelievable. It must have been in the region of 130°F to 140°F plus. This high temperature was caused as the sun was reflected back by the white sand. The first time that we crossed one of these run-offs was a real shock, because of the unexpected heat, but also because we were blinded by the reflected sunlight.

On one of our inspections of a tin mine, we met a Malay manager who was very nice to us. I spent about an hour talking to him about some old prehistoric bones that they had found in the mine. He got his workers to give us tea and biscuits while we were there, and also invited us to visit his home on a free day. He told me how much they had suffered under the Japanese, and how glad they were to see the British back after the Second World War. He really was a charming old Chinese man, who wore a smart grey suit and sported a long grey beard. He spoke perfect English, and was the sort of person that I could never forget. I didn't take him up on his offer to visit his home, but that chance meeting with me saved his, and four of the mineworkers' lives a few months later, although neither he nor his workers were ever going to know anything about it, or that they had been in any danger.

Occasionally we would meet a manager or workers who were obviously anti-British, or even worse, Communist sympathisers. I always treated them as the latter to be safe, the chances are that they probably were. We would search everywhere and make them show us around, then we would closely inspect whatever they were doing. I would keep them guessing as to what we were up to, or looking for, by doing

136

such things as leaving, and returning half an hour later, then doing it all over again.

The following day I would arrange early transport to get us there before the curfew lifted. We would be waiting at their place of work. When they arrived, we'd make out that we were just leaving, but we would check through whatever they had brought with them. We would change over areas with one of our other sections, then they would do the same. As far as we were concerned their place of work would not be used to leave supplies or messages for the CTs to pick up, because it would be too risky.

We didn't worry unduly about being ambushed, because even *we* didn't know where we were going. It was always a case of which track looked appealing or different, and for whatever reason. We all found it very interesting, and to a certain extent relaxing and enjoyable. We never relaxed to the extent that we didn't keep our eyes and ears fully open and alert for any signs of danger.

Another operation that we did within the confines of the plantations, was a three-day observation point duty. I drew the short straw on that one, so my section did the three nights. It was a little bit like ambushing, but you could talk and smoke and suchlike, even make yourself a brew or something to eat, provided that there were no lights shown. One of the lads brought a small radio so we could listen to music or a chat show, but at times we struggled to find a programme in English. The pop music was okay, we would listen to Buddy Holly, Elvis, Pat Boone, Tommy Steele, The Big Bopper, Doris Day, and Ricky Valance to mention just a few of the singers of the day.

There was no danger of being caught out by the CTs because the observation point was on the top of a pinnacle of rock that was about three hundred feet above the surrounding plantations. The top was ideal, it was about the size of a tennis court, with a hollow in the middle, where we could light the cooking stove without showing any glow. There were also one or two small trees around the top. We swapped over with the other section within the curfew times, so that the villagers we were watching about half a mile away, never saw us. Access was gained by climbing up through some thick scrub on a steep dusty slope, then moving around the rocks and on up to the top. It was always worse coming down than going up; we didn't struggle too much, or should I say that we had worse battles with the Malayan Peninsula. I am not sure what we were supposed to see from the observation point! All we had to do was to write down anything that we could see or hear. You must bear in mind that it was pitch black during the night-time. It was surprising how many flashes of light we saw, and dogs we heard barking throughout the night, but everything was duly recorded in the observation book.

After the observation point duty, we had a new intake into the platoon which brought us up to operational strength. However I was to find out that as quickly as we were made up to strength, or approaching full strength, another load of National Servicemen would be off back home, leaving us back to being understaffed again.

Three days later I was going into the jungle with 4 Platoon and my own section on a three-day operation that was taking us about four miles into the jungle. There was nothing special about this operation apart from the leeches that we all kept getting and burning off ourselves. I got my first tick, which made the leeches seem not too bad. I found the tick while I was checking for leeches after getting back into the jungle base camp from the first day's patrol. It was on my left arm just above the wrist. It was a black crab-shaped creature just under the skin, about the size of a large apple pip. They get on you, bury themselves under the skin, then burrow their way along laying their eggs as they go. I could see from the snake-like trail of grey eggs buried under my skin, that the tick had travelled about two inches.

When I saw it, a shudder ran through me. This was far worse than a leech that could easily be burnt off with the end of a cigarette. I would need to cut this creature out with the razor blade that I carried. A couple of bloodthirsty lads offered to do it for me, but I declined their offer. I preferred to personally have control of the depth that the blade was going to go into my skin.

The first thing I did was to try and get things back to normal by lighting my cooking stove to make a cup of tea. While the mess tin of water was warming up, I went and found the medical bag and helped myself to the bottle of iodine. I went back to my basha, made myself a cup of tea, then put the razor blade into the boiling water that was left in the mess tin. I had a sip of tea, got the razor blade out of the mess tin, keeping the boiled water to one side. Then carefully, very carefully, very, very carefully, I cut the skin, following the line of eggs from where the tick had entered, slowly cutting along the grey line. Halfway along I stopped for a break and a drink of the tea. One or two of the lads came to watch me cutting the tick out, but I would have preferred to have been on my own, then I would not have had to pretend that it was just routine, or that I was unconcerned, brave even. I didn't let them know that if I hadn't been so terrified of cutting myself deeper than I had to, my hand would have been shaking like mad. I continued cutting and wondering how I would get the tick out when I came to it?

The thing was still digging away, because it had taken a right turn from the spot where it had been when I first found it, and was still laying the dreaded eggs that would turn into maggots in no time at all. The cut in my arm was already beginning to ooze out the eggs. They were making me cringe. I stopped cutting for a moment, whilst I washed them off with some fresh water. It crossed my mind about salt water, so I got half a dozen salt tablets, dropped them into my mess tin of pre-boiled water, and left them there to dissolve ready for when I had finished cutting out the tick. I continued with the cut before finally reaching the abomination. Its legs were going steadily ten to the dozen; it was still trying to burrow beneath my skin. I put the corner of the razor blade under the back of it and lifted. To my relief out it popped onto my arm.

Without saying a word, somebody passed me a lit cigarette. I put the red-hot end over the tick, which made it curl up and fall off my arm. I was so relieved that although I didn't smoke, I took a long drag on the fag so that the smoke filled my mouth; I then blew it out with a whistle of relief. The next move was to wash my arm with the salt water and to make sure that all the eggs were out. The cut looked like a bad scratch from a thorn, I covered it with iodine and that was it. I got on with cooking my tin of Swifts, hoping that I didn't get any more of those revolting things on me.

Soon the operation was over and we were on our way back to Ipoh and Colombo Camp. I was looking forward to a decent night's sleep. When we arrived back in camp there was a pleasant surprise for us all. On our beds were brand new Dunlopillow mattresses instead of the old straw palliasses, but they were so soft I had difficulty getting to sleep that night. The old sweats reckoned that there must be something nasty coming up for us with them giving us modern mattresses, but the Old Sweats weren't always right.

# CHAPTER SEVEN
*Bamboo Raft, Full Corporal and a Giant Python*

After two day's rest and recovery it was back to the grind. The lads had been having their fun over the last couple of days with the arrival of the new mattresses. The regular send-ups were the traditional apple-pie beds, or to wake someone up in the middle of the night to ask them if they want to buy a battleship, or some other similar and impossible object.

This was the third day back in Colombo Camp when the normal morning routine was that the NCOs had a pre-operational briefing in the 'B' Company Office ready for going back into the jungle the following day. These briefings would be to tell us what we were looking for, and if there was anything special happening or on-going? We would also be informed as to how long we would be in the jungle, as well as how far we were going into the area. Aerial reconnaissance photographs of the patrol region would be examined with special magnifying 3D viewers; these were the sort of things included in a pre-op conference.

The next morning we were back into the Ulu (jungle) and back amongst the giant trees, vines, leeches, ants, snakes and to the same routine patrols. They were just routine with nothing particular happening. My birthday and the months of May and June slipped quietly by without any problems. At the beginning of July we were back on plantation patrols.

I had been in command of my own section for nearly three months by then and we had all got used to each other's ways.

We knew who was the joker (most of the lads) and who was the worrier (me). We had become a good tight-knit unit, all relying on, and fully trusting each other.

The change of routine was welcomed by me because I wasn't feeling 100%. Perhaps the more relaxed plantation patrols might be just the tonic that I needed. I didn't bother going to see the Medical Officer because I couldn't really explain exactly what was wrong with me. I personally put a lot of it down to having the pressure and responsibility of the men in my section. This meant that I was never really able to relax or get a good night's sleep. I suppose that being an NCO was what it was all about, and especially when you cared about your men.

I was not surprised that a lot of the lads drank too much alcohol; it was the obvious release for them, but at times it was difficult to keep the lid on some of the lad's actions and the resulting situations within their rest periods. Some of them tended to forget that they were in the army.

As an NCO you have to accept that it is a 24-hour job with no time out, but the private soldier tended to take rest periods as their own private time, which wasn't quite correct, however most NCOs went along with that, just as long as certain lines weren't crossed over.

I managed somehow to get through my service without ever having to put anyone on a charge. I think that by resolving situations myself, this won me a greater respect from my lads. At the end of the day they were left with no doubt when they had done something wrong. They also knew that there was absolutely no way that I would tolerate any of them stepping out of line on any type of active operation. We really did have a special bond between all of us. It was a relationship that I was very proud of when I used to think about those times after I had returned home. There were times when the lads in my section, unasked and unexpectedly supported me. They even stopped me from giving up my Corporal's tapes on one occasion.

The plantation patrols took up from where we had left off, but about fifteen miles farther to the North, more into the area where the CTs kicked off ten years earlier by killing several rubber plantation owners. I often wondered when we were in that area, just exactly where it all happened, but I never did find out. As we were farther North, most of the patrols were through the rubber plantations, so we were nearly always on bikes. One of the patrols took us to the Western edge of a rubber plantation, where the river Chior formed its boundary.

On our side of the river was the rubber plantation, while the opposite side held nothing but wild jungle. As we made our way along the river on the boundary track, we came across a large raft made from bamboo canes tied together with ropes. The raft was roughly twenty-five feet long by six feet wide, and was secured with ropes at the front. The ropes went up to a wire hawser that spanned the river, which would be approximately sixty feet wide at that point. The raft was propelled across the river by pushing on a long bamboo pole. I couldn't see the purpose of having a raft at this point, especially when there should be no one on the other side, especially so if they didn't want to be shot.

I decided to send the section over to the other bank via the raft to have a quick scout around, also to check if there were any regular tracks of any kind. It's a pity we didn't have our Iban tracker with us, because he would have been able to tell us when the last person had crossed there, where they had gone and how many of them there were? I got the lads to leave their backpacks with the cycles before sending the first men across, while the rest of us covered their crossing from our side of the river. It took them two or three minutes to cross and jump off onto the other bank. As soon as they had got there, we pulled the raft back with the rope that was tied to it for that purpose, then the next three crossed in the same way, followed a few minutes later by the last two lads, leaving only the Bren gunner and me to protect our equipment, and to give covering fire from this side of the river if required.

The lads never questioned why I didn't cross over the river with them; they knew me well enough to know that I would never ask *them* to do something that I wouldn't do myself. I had my camera with me, so I told them I would take their photographs when they were coming back over the river. The real reason that I stayed on the plantation side, was that I was secretly concerned, that should any of them fall into the water, they would not be strong enough swimmers to survive the fast-flowing river. If any of them did fall in, then the two of us on this side could soon get well downstream of them, using the track that followed the river-bank on our side, and pull them out.

This wasn't to happen and the trip went as intended both ways. The lads didn't find anything that seemed to be important, as there didn't appear to be any tracks leading off into the jungle, but I had a strong feeling that the raft should not have been there, so I gave a full report on it at the debriefing meeting, when we got back to Colombo Camp later that afternoon.

The following day we were a couple of miles to the North and in and out of the tin mines that were scattered about that area. Two of the lads were feeling a bit tender after getting tailor ants on them in the middle of the morning break. We had been sitting on some old logs having a cigarette, when one of the lads, quickly followed by the second, jumped up and started swiping away at their arms, one to the left and one to the right. We all rushed to help them get rid of the ants, which fortunately only took a second or two, as they only had the odd one on them. The two lads put their jackets back on and we all made our way to the nearby tin mine; it was only a couple of minutes away and was to be our next stop anyway.

As soon as we got there the two lads stripped off to the waist again, then washed their arms in the water tank that was used for panning the tin ore. The water helped to cool where the ants had been nipping, which helped to ease their pain. The lad with the medical pack offered them a tube of antiseptic cream, which was also supposed to help with stings and bites.

As they were applying this, one of the Chinese girls who panned for the tin ore, and had been watching us since we arrived at the tin mine, came over to us and held out a glass jar containing something that look like a thick marmalade paste. One of the lads took the jar and looked at it, obviously wondering what to do with the mixture? As the girl could not speak English, she made a stroking motion on her arm that meant, rub the ointment on the bites, which they did before handing the jar back and thanking the girl for her kindness, in the best way that they could. This meant much hand-waving and smiles, but I am sure you can imagine how these situations amuse?

We spent about half an hour looking around the tin mine, and as we passed the panning shed on leaving the wooden buildings of the mine, we all stopped, and the lads gave the girls some of the boiled sweets that were included with our rations for the day, to repay their kindness. The ointment certainly worked, because almost immediately all the pain had gone from the bites.

Some months later I was talking to Laurence, who was our Chinese interpreter and he said, "The paste would probably be based on the coconut oil that seemed to be used for everything in Malaya, including sunburn."

We continued on our way around the tracks at a nice and steady pace, which was about all that I was fit for at that time. Lunch time came, and it coincided with us arriving on the top of a small hill that had no undue vegetation growing, so I called a halt for lunch. We didn't have any tins of oxtail soup with us that day, but we did have vegetable soup, which wasn't too bad.

One of the lads rolled a small log over to make a seat. He jumped back and shouted, "Look at this!"

Scurrying away was a green scorpion. We let it go to wherever it was going, but we all double-checked where we were sitting before carrying on eating. When we'd finished our packed lunch, we were getting ready to leave the hilltop, and as the sun had been particularly hot that day, we were ready for finding some shade, and some running water so that we could cool off, at least for a few minutes.

One of the lads got on his bike and started to ride in a circle around the rest of us waiting to leave the hilltop, when we heard a small aircraft approaching from the South.

I spoke to the lads, "It sounds just like the plane that dropped the flares on the night of the ambushing."

The small plane, which I think was an Auster aircraft appeared, and flew right overhead. Then just after it passed us it banked to its left, and flew over the jungle edge. Once again we were treated to a display of aerial fireworks as it dropped its pattern of flares over the jungle. Remembering the night ambush, I told the lads to be ready for being bounced up into the air with the shock waves that were coming. The flares floated down, lower and lower, but there was still no sound of the bombers approach. By then the flares were too low to give the bombers time to get in and drop their bombs, before the bright lights would be swallowed up by the jungle canopy. I looked up at the fine smoke trails slowly drifting towards us in the light wind, and rising two thousand feet up into the clear blue sky, showing the downward path that the flares had taken towards the jungle. It crossed my mind as to just how much that little display must have cost the British taxpayer?

I should really have had my wits about me, then we may not all have finished up together in a heap on the ground along with the bikes, because two Vampire jets whistled over us with no warning sound at all of their presence, until they were overhead. Exactly at that moment they opened fire with their cannons, firing right into the area marked out by the flares. The tracer shells that were interspaced into the gunfire, left their trails as they streaked across the sky and ripped into the jungle canopy. We could hear the noise of the cannon shells going into the canopy, even above the noise of the jet engines and the firing of the cannons. The noise sounded like hitting a cabbage with a spade, but hitting a lot of them, and all at the same time.

One thing that amazed me, was the way that the jets stuttered and actually slowed down, almost it seemed stopping in mid-air, as they fired their cannons. The jets circled around several times, making fresh attacking passes on the jungle. On the last pass over the jungle, they took a long sweeping turn to the left that took them well down the valley, then back up it, and past us at a low altitude. As they flew past us we waved to them; all of us could clearly see the pilot in the jet nearest to us waving back.

To me the fly past confirmed my feelings that the Auster pilot had seen us on the hilltop, and the RAF had decided to give the army a little jolt. I just hope that they didn't see us all hitting the ground on their first pass over us.

We had all enjoyed the breathtaking display of aerial power, and knowing that we could put that firepower down on Charlie without any fear of a response, made us feel a little easier about being in there. Naturally it became another talking point for the next few days, all of which helped to pass the time away.

It was strange out in Malaya because there would be weeks of nothing special happening, then everything seemed to happen simultaneously. It was early afternoon, I was ready to turn the patrol around and start heading back to the pick-up point. I was thinking that it had been an interesting day. Firstly we had the problem with the ants, but I think that we had made some friends at the tin mine. Then we had the green scorpion incident, followed by the two Vampire jets strafing the jungle.

We had just left some old tin mine buildings, and I had just told the lad at the front to head back up the track that we had followed down into the mining area, when we heard the sound of aircraft engines. We looked to the North. Coming down the valley was a twin-engine aeroplane that was flying quite low. It wasn't flying down the middle of the valley; it was obviously following the jungle edge.

One of the lads said, "It looks like it's dumping fuel."

We could all see that there was something falling from the plane. As it got near to us we could see that it was dropping thousands of leaflets that were fluttering slowly down to the ground. I could say that they were like snowflakes, but they were not falling as you would expect snow to fall. Instead they were turning over and over, catching the strong rays of the sun as they fell, making them sparkle like magical fairy lights in the bright sunlight. It was quite a spectacle!

We watched the plane flying down the valley until it was out of sight. By this time we were back on our bikes and were heading back towards the pick-up point. I told the lads to get a move on as we were now running a few minutes late, but we all got to the pick-up point before the three-tonner arrived.

My health had deteriorated during the day, both my arms had large red spots coming up on them. I reported to the Company Office when we got back to Colombo Camp. I told them that I was reporting sick, and going to see the MO in the morning. The following day I found out that I was suffering from septicaemia, the spots that were still coming up turned out to be boils. The MO put me on sick leave for three days on a course of penicillin. On the fourth day I went back to see him and he then put me on light duties for a week. These duties were fine, they consisted mainly of sitting in the passenger seat of a three-tonner and acting as escort for the different platoons coming in from the jungle. I still had my section with me, but it was peculiar trying to do anything with my left arm in a sling that the MO insisted that I wore. The end of my light duty period came and I was feeling much better. I was obviously very run-down, so I made a promise to myself to try and do a little bit less for a while, but it wasn't always easy to do that. My arms were still sore where the boils had been, and as I look down on my arms at this *present* moment in time, I can still see the disfigurement of the scars left behind by those boils.

Just before my light duties ended I went up to the Company Office and put in an application for a week's leave at the army-run Sandycroft leave centre on Penang Island, which is just off the coast to the North of Malaya, near to the border with Thailand. The first free week I would be off to the Island, without a curfew, so without the need to carry a gun whenever I went out for a walk or a bike ride. I returned to the basha and to my light duties, and in what seemed like only two minutes I was throwing my gear up, then climbing onto the back of a three-tonner.

I had that queer taste in my mouth and the back of my throat that I always got on the first day back in the jungle. We were still up to the North of Ipoh and on a five-day operation. We were one Section Commander short, as Billy Fish was away up in Penang on a week's leave. He was coming to join us in the jungle with a couple of the lads out of the platoon who were off for whatever reason, and they were also bringing in three Joshkins to strengthen the platoon. As we were light on men going in on the first day, we had an extra Iban, Laurence the Chinese interpreter, plus two dog handlers, so we were at our minimal lightweight strength.

We alighted on the edge of a rubber plantation just at daybreak, and without any delay we were on our way along a good track which ran through the cultivation. It took us about twenty minutes to get through the rubber plantation, beyond this there was a large open cultivated area along which the track continued. The cultivation was growing all different types of crops. I knew from the briefing that on the other side of the cultivation was an Aboriginal village, which stood on the banks of a river.

Crossing the river by the village was a log bridge which we were going to cross, then follow the track that continued on the other side and up into the jungle. The track leading up into the jungle was an old logging track. It was easy to follow, but we had to be on our guard against being ambushed by Charlie, I never felt easy when we were on these tracks. There were quite a few old logging tracks about at that time; we used them to get deep into the jungle. I would think that the best known one to the Loyals was called the 'Jap-track,' and named as such because apparently the Japanese built it, and had used it regularly twelve years before us, and during the Second World War, to do the same as we were doing now.

I found the native village very interesting; it was a collection of around twenty to twenty-five huts which were all built on stilts, lifting the body of the huts about six feet above the ground. By the side of the track next to the biggest hut, were an old pick-up truck and an old three-ton type lorry. Both looked like wrecks, but I am sure that they were used for the benefit of the villagers in general. I couldn't see many young men about, but there seemed to be dozens of young children and dogs. I was surprised that the Aborigines had been allowed to stay in these villages, whilst everyone else who lived in the countryside and small isolated villages were all resettled into concentrated and police-protected areas that were known as 'new villages'.

The natives that we saw as we passed through their village all seemed happy enough; they didn't seem at all disturbed by us passing through. Once more I got the feeling that they were happy for us to be around. I did find out later from Laurence that the Aborigines had been given a rough time by the Japanese during the war.

We were soon well on our way up the old logging track leaving the village well behind us. Half an hour later we all stopped for a break and a cigarette. I was up on my feet and wandering around for most of the time. My section was leading the platoon in on that operation, and as it's always the lead section that gets hit in a ambush, we tended to be a little bit more careful. We fully concentrated on bringing our training of looking *through* the trees and not *at* them, into full use. I was enjoying reading the map and compass and taking the platoon to the point on the map which was the correct place in the jungle for our base. I had two of the Ibans up front with my section, so I felt better with them being there with us, because they didn't miss very much. They were far better at jungle craft than the 'CTs' who were experts themselves.

I had arranged my section with my leading scout at the front followed by Sanden, my number one Iban, good friend and jungle mentor throughout the whole of my time in Malaya. I placed myself next, followed by the extra Iban, the Bren gunner with the rest of my section following behind us.

With not being happy on a logging track, and after studying the map, I decided to press on up the logging track for another half-mile to where the river split, then just past the river junction, I planned on taking the platoon across the river, moving through the jungle and up the hillside onto the ridge. I decided we'd follow the ridge until I judged that it was time to drop down into the valley and pick up the stream that was going to be our base camp.

With my mind made up, I went back down the track to the Platoon Sergeant and Officer to let them know my intentions and check for approval. I went back up to the front, gave the signal to move off and away we went up the track. Without any problems, we reached the river junction; I signalled the leading scout to head down to the river.

As was customary we all had a quick cooling-off swill while crossing the river. This river was a little bit harder to cross than most, because of the speed of the water as it came down off the mountains. The water was deep enough to come well over our knees, and it really tugged at our legs, feeling like it was trying to pull us down into it, but fortunately there were plenty of rocks sticking out of the water which were very handy for hanging onto in the deeper parts. We picked up some animal tracks that were forming a path coming down through the jungle to a watering point on the river, then started making our way up the track through the jungle towards the ridge.

Rather than going straight up to the ridge from the river, I told my leading scout to go to the left so that we were climbing up the hillside at an angle to the ridge, which made the going easier for us, especially with the weight we were carrying into the operation. For some reason, on a level part of the track I found myself in front of my Ibans and leading scout. It was unusual for me to be there, but occasionally it did happen for whatever reason.

We were in thick jungle, so although it was late morning and bright sunshine outside the jungle, inside and underneath the canopy it was relatively dark. Our eyes did adjust to the darkness so we could see okay. There was a large tree that had fallen across the track with a trunk that was about four feet in diameter. It had fallen in such a way that there was a gap beneath it that gave about five feet of headroom above the track. I bent down to inspect under the tree, but Sanden pulled me gently back; I was quite surprised because the Ibans wouldn't normally touch you at all, but I thought to myself that he was thinking that it shouldn't be me out as the front man.

He gabbled something that I didn't understand, pointing up the track.

I said that we would change over on the other side of the tree. I had a good look around to be safe bending down to go under the tree again.

This time Sanden and the other Iban grabbed me and pulled me sharply back, also pushing back my leading scout, who was up there with us.

This time I knew that it had to be something serious, but I didn't know what? I didn't look at Sanden this time to find out what was wrong; my eyes and mind were fully concentrated under the fallen tree and on the track up ahead, and the jungle to each side of the track. My finger automatically clicked off my safety catch, and I heard my leading scout's safety catch going off. I was straining my eyes to catch any movement in the jungle, but I could neither see or hear anything, that's apart from the chattering of monkeys that must have been quarter of a mile away, plus the never ending buzz of the insect world, together with the pounding of my heart.

I knew something was wrong, but what? Even though it was only a few seconds, the strain of bending down to look under the tree was beginning to tell, due to the tremendous amount of weight in the packs on our backs. I knelt down on my left knee to ease the load.

Sanden touched me gently on my shoulder. I looked slowly round, reluctant to take my eyes off the track up ahead.

The Iban put his finger to his lips signalling me not to make any sound. Then he pointed slowly upwards to above the fallen tree.

I moved my head slowly and looked up. I didn't know what he had seen but I could see nothing. My eyes concentrated on the jungle canopy above and the trees around, but there wasn't a lot to see because we were in thick jungle which restricted us, making our viewing areas limited.

My eyes glanced all around but still I could not see anything to fear.

Then my leading scout whispered from behind, "It's on top of the fallen tree."

I looked up, at first I still not see anything, then a slight movement caught my eye. There on top of the fallen tree was an enormous python, sliding slowly along the tree and heading downhill. Once I had spotted the snake it was obvious to me, but it did show just how clever nature is with its camouflage.

From the Ibans' talk later in the day, plus what I discovered about pythons later, it became obvious to me that this snake really was a giant amongst giants. We watched it slithering by from a safe distance, although what was a safe distance? I thought that we were more than far enough away, probably twenty feet or more, but the Ibans were still very agitated at being that close, and kept pulling us further away back down the track. We couldn't see the head of the snake. All we could see at any time was about six feet of the snake's body, as it slithered out of the leaves from the jungle on the right, before disappearing into the jungle to the left as it followed the trunk of the fallen tree.

The body of the python was at least one foot in diameter, probably more, and I know at this point that anyone who knows about pythons will say that it's impossible for a python to grow that big. Believe me I was there and saw it, and it really was as stated, at least one foot in diameter. We stood there watching it sliding down and along the tree, waiting for it to clear the track before moving on. I would estimate that at its fastest it was moving about one foot every ten seconds. We had been held up for a couple of minutes when the Platoon Officer and Sergeant came up the line to see what had gone wrong and why we weren't moving? We stood waiting, but the snake seemed to be going on forever.

The Sergeant suggested, "Let's go under the tree and the snake."

I replied, "The Ibans are frightened of it, and if they are scared, then perhaps we should be."

The Officer suggested to the Ibans that we proceed under the snake, but Sanden and his mate insisted that we should remain still, they kept squeezing their wrists with their hands and shaking their heads for no. The Ibans weren't easily scared, they were experts in the jungle, so they obviously knew something about pythons that we didn't.

We stood waiting for the snake to pass, but on it moved seeming to be endless, with no reduction in body size to indicate that the tail was coming along. We decided to circle around both the fallen tree and the snake.

There were times when I had to wonder at some of the crazy things we did out there, and this was one of those times. We had to make our way back along the track for about fifty yards before we found a gap into the jungle that was going downhill off the track. There was no chance of going uphill, as it was far too steep, and the jungle was too thick to penetrate without a lot of cutting through the vines and branches. We made our way downhill with everyone back in their correct places up-front. I took the platoon about a quarter of a mile down before directing the leading scout to head to the right.

We had gone about one hundred yards when there in front, sliding downhill along the ground was the python. It had to be the same one, yet once again we didn't see its head. From the Ibans' reaction, and now on reflection after all the years that have passed, we were probably lucky. We did get to see its tail, because this time we waited until it had passed before we continued on our merry way, but we never did get to see the front end.

I have heard stories both then and since, that you will be rewarded with thousands of pounds if you can come up with a python that's over thirty feet in length. Well I don't know to what age snakes live, but if it's a long time, then there may still be one in Malaya that over forty year's ago, was at the very least, thirty-five feet long.

With the snake out of the way we pushed on through the jungle, taking any easy-looking path we found that would take us back up to the ridge. Once there we made our way along until we reached the spot where the ridge took a sharp turn to the right. That point was a very distinctive feature both on the map and the ground. We reached it without further trouble and took a fifteen minute break on top of the ridge. After the rest I took the platoon on a compass bearing down the hillside, and to the point on the stream, which was to be our jungle base camp for the next few days.

Everything was fine with the camp, and there were no undue problems to worry about. The following day I took my section out on a patrol which was just routine, and it was then my turn to have the following day off. When we were sorting the patrols out on the first day in base camp, it worked out that I would be in the base camp for that day, and I was looking forward to the special treat I had carried in for myself on this operation. I had brought a bottle of stout into the jungle instead of my camera, but to be honest after seeing the snake, I was thinking that I could have made a big mistake. It was always the case, I had no camera when it was really needed!

My day in camp went fine. I sorted my section out on the guard duties, then spent most of the day reading as we had very little to do to make the camp more comfortable. Oh yes, and I enjoyed my bottle of stout at lunch time along with the curry that I had made to go with it.

In the middle of the afternoon both patrols came back into camp with no problems to report. When we came back to the camp after being out on patrol we had to make sure that the guard on that section knew that it was our patrol coming in.

156

This was one part of jungle life where it was very important for everyone to know what they were doing. This was the moment in the day when most of us were looking down the wrong end of a loaded weapon, so we had to trust and understand each other.

Most Section Commander's had their own little signal; it could have been a certain whistle sound, or whistling a certain song, or just saying, "Don't do anything rash, it's us."

One of the Commander's used to say, "If you shoot, we're shooting back."

He would always get some smart reply from whoever was on guard at the time; some were much smarter than others.

A regular retort was something like, "You're such a bad shot you wouldn't hit me if you could see me, so you'd better come in with your hands up."

This sort of light-hearted banter went on all the time, and it was a very positive way of not only drawing everyone together, but also served to take the tension out of the stressful moments.

Laurence, the Chinese interpreter was in the base camp that day. I went to have a word with him about the python that we had seen the previous day. "Why were the Ibans so afraid of it?" I asked him.

"I've no idea," he started to explain, "but whilst the pythons may look slow, in truth they can move much quicker than you would ever expect."

It also transpired that Laurence did not speak to the Ibans, nor would the Ibans speak to him. I think that it was to do with that scourge of mankind, differences of religion, but I am not absolutely sure. I must say that personally I found it very sad because I got on really well with all of them, and when I came to the end of my time in Malaya I regarded both as my very good friends.

When the patrol that had been down to the jungle edge came back to the base camp, they had a pleasant and very tasty surprise for us. When they got to the jungle edge they found themselves in a pineapple plantation, so they had cut a few out and brought them back for all the platoon to share. They were delicious!

Stand-to time came around and I had my tot of rum put into my cup of coffee. For a change I had purchased a small jar of coffee from the NAAFI before coming into the jungle. When full darkness came I looked for the fireflies, but this was one area of the jungle where they weren't to be seen. Sadly we only saw them in very few areas. It was possibly down to the type of vegetation that grew in those areas, but I really don't know for sure, but that night I settled down to sleep with the thought in my mind that I now had only a year to do in the army. In twelve months I would be back home again to the green fields, real milk, real butter, real potatoes and a plate of home-made chips, but we still had to sort the bad guys out, as they could spoil everything for some of us.

The following day I was back out on patrol with my section. We headed up and into the thick jungle. The other section went down to the log bridge by the Aboriginal village to escort Bill Fish and the other lads back to the base camp. When we got back into base camp the other section had been back for quite some time, and the newcomers were busy putting up their bashas in the gaps that had been left for them in front of the perimeter vine. There was one important thing that I always had to do immediately after returning from a jungle patrol. When we were back at base camp, and had passed the sentry who was guarding the camp, I had to check all the weapons to make sure that they didn't have a round (bullet) left in the breach, so that there was no danger of anyone getting accidentally shot.

As soon as we were in camp I went to put a mess tin of water on the stove to make a cup of tea, then went to the centre of the camp to tell the Platoon Officer that there was nothing to report from the patrol. That only took a minute, so

I returned to my basha to make a brew and a meal before dark. I decided on a Swifts steak and dumplings with boiled rice for the evening meal. Just as I opened the tin Bill came walking round on the perimeter path. We greeted each other with the customary insults, but we were good friends, and our paths in the army always ran parallel.

"I've some important Company news for you," Bill said. "As from yesterday we are both full Corporals."

The news came as a surprise, but when I was talking to Bill that night we figured out that we should have expected it with the platoon being short of full Corporals, and us both being made Section Commanders' immediately on becoming NCOs. We were both pleased; we decided that in three day's time, and on our first full day back in Colombo Camp we would go out and down into Ipoh to one of the cinemas, then go for a curry to celebrate our promotion, as well as my first wedding anniversary.

The few times that I went out of the camp and down into Ipoh were always with Bill. We were not only good friends, but we were always constant rivals in the platoon for the best results. I always used to tell him that I outranked him, because I had been called-up a few days before him. The only time we didn't spend together was when we went on leave, which was due to only one Section Commander being spared from the platoon at any one time.

Bill also brought into the jungle some more very unexpected news. "With immediate effect, shaving is banned while we are in the jungle."

This news shocked everyone; a soldier in the British Army and ordered *not* to shave, but it did make sense when you considered that a lot of the lads who were in the Infantry Companies were catching a lot of facial skin diseases due to shaving, while on operations in the jungle. It also meant that we didn't have to carry shaving gear into the jungle anymore, which meant just that little bit of extra space in our packs for carrying something else.

The following morning it was a quick breakfast of beans and pork sausages, a small tin of cheese, and two mugs of tea. I didn't have a shave because of the new orders, and I can tell you that by the end of the day it felt most peculiar having a stubbly chin. Once all the section was sorted out and ready, we were off. This time we were back into the thick heavy jungle, but travelling more to the North-West.

I had been warned on the evening briefing that I would be coming up to the edge of 'D' Company area, so to be careful not to stray over into their patch, but more to the point to keep an eye open for them straying into us, and not to shoot them up if they did. The patrol we were on through the thick jungle meant that the going would be slow, with very few animal tracks to follow. We had to cut our way through the vines and small trees for much of the way, making our own path through the jungle. I had one of the new lads in my section, so I had double-checked his rifle before setting off, telling him not to drink too much water before midday. The lad seemed fine, but time would tell, and my lads would keep an eye on him to make sure that he was okay.

We had been underway for a couple of hours; and the going was very slow, with each member of the section having to take their turn at hacking a path through the jungle in front of the leading scout, who would always keep a sharp eye out for the lad up front cutting the track. The new lad measured up fine, but he made the same mistake that we all made at first, by trying to cut his way through the scrub too quickly, which used up too much energy and lost so much salt, but he soon listened to the voice of experience and was fine.

It had got to about 14:00 and we were very close to the 'D' Company boundary, which was about quarter of a mile away. We were all tired after the battle to get through the jungle to that point, which was a small clearing set in a shallow hollow.

I decided to give the section a long rest here, before heading back to the base camp. The clearing that we were in was on top of a low ridge, and the high point of the terrain before dropping down to the boundary stream with 'D' Company.

Beams of sunlight were shining down through the trees; the air was full of bright colours from the multitude of butterflies that were present in that area. There was a pleasant scented smell in the air, which probably explained the butterflies that were being displayed to their best advantage in the shafts of sunlight as they fluttered into them and out again. The lads were sat around the outer edge of the clearing, whilst myself, the leading scout, Laurence the interpreter and the Iban were sat in the middle.

Suddenly there was a loud bang; a shot had been fired very near to us. Everyone dived onto the jungle floor. I looked for a sign of where the shot had come from, and at the lads. They all seemed to be okay, everyone was looking into the jungle trying to surmise where the shot had come from? I looked towards Sanden and the leading scout to see if they had any idea, but they were looking intently into the jungle around us. Sanden looked at me and just shrugged his shoulders.

Then I saw the problem, floating out from the muzzle of the leading scout's shotgun was a feint trickle of blue smoke. I couldn't believe that nobody had realised the shot had been in the middle of all of us.

I looked at my leading scout and said, "What have you done?"

He looked at the smoke coming out of the barrel and said "I've done nothing; my finger was nowhere near the trigger." He lifted the gun and started checking the weapon.

As he did that I was thanking God that the gun had been pointing up into the sky. It was a miracle that he hadn't been sat with the gun across his knees and pointing at one of the lads on the edge of the clearing, but it was very rare for any of the lads to allow their weapon to point at anyone, even by accident.

My scout said, "The gun is faulty because the safety button switches on and off, but if the trigger had been pulled, then the safety button would remain in the off position. I would have been unable to turn it back to the on position until the gun was reloaded." He passed me the shotgun to try the safety button.

I found that he was right about the fault. I said, "I'll have to report the shot when we get back to base camp."

He replied, "Don't report me because it will get me into trouble if I'm found to be responsible."

"Don't you worry about it, your gun is obviously faulty and so it was not your fault. I will have to report it though, because a patrol from 'D' Company may have heard the shot and suspect that it was the CTs. Also as the gun is faulty it must be repaired before it does hurt someone."

We stayed in the clearing, resting as best as we could after the scare, but not surprisingly it had set everyone's nerves on edge, reminding us that our reason for being in Malaya wasn't just for a jungle walk, but also for us to face up to just what could happen at anytime.

When I considered that everyone's heartbeat, including mine, had returned to normal, I gave the order to move out and back down the track that we had spent most of the day hacking out through the jungle. I told the leading scout not to have a round up the barrel, but to be ready to load if necessary. When we got back to camp I reported the accidental shot to the Platoon Officer.

That night after we had all settled down we could hear a wild animal roaring not too far away in the jungle. It sounded as though it was big and nasty, and word came round from the Ibans that it was a male tiger on the prowl. The guards who were on stag (guard duty) throughout that night, unusually made plenty of noise, and also used the torch long and often.

With what happened to the Australians a few weeks later, our guards were probably very wise to be so cautious, but that's for a later chapter.

The following day was base camp duty for my section, and with very little to do apart from guard we all had an easy day, which I spent reading, as well as supervising the change-over of the guards every two hours. This change-over entailed taking the lads who were the new guards to the sentry points being used to cover the camp. At each point the new guard then loaded his weapon, I checked that he had done this, and that the safety catch was on. I also checked the old guard off, making sure that his weapon was unloaded prior to returning into the base camp.

When the Bren gunner was on guard he usually borrowed an FN rifle or a shotgun instead of taking his Bren gun. This was mainly because he was not allowed to cock the Bren gun, due to the likely danger of it going off accidentally. We were taught this in training, and it was then recognised practice by everyone in the Loyals, but at a later date I was unfortunately the one to suffer because of the practice.

The following day we were back in Colombo Camp and without hold ups from any snakes. I also found out that my leading scout and myself were up on Commanding Officer's Orders the next day but one. The Commanding Officer of the Loyal 1st Battalion was Colonel Thompson. He was well known for severely punishing anyone responsible for an accidental discharge, but I told the lad not to worry because the weapon was faulty and so it was not his fault. I had to dash around to get my best uniform ready, all cleaned, ironed and the new full Corporals' tapes sewn on ready for the hearing.

The day of the enquiry came; I was marched into the COs' Office along with the Chief Armourer who had inspected the shotgun. The Armourer was first asked for his findings, and I could not believe what I heard. They had stripped down the gun, cleaned it, then put it back together before trying it for the fault. I and everyone else put the fault down to dirt inside the moving parts, that only the Armouries Department were allowed to strip down and clean.

I told the CO what had happened. Then we were both marched out, and my leading scout marched in to the Cos' Office.

The CO found him guilty of causing the gun to discharge, and fined him two week's pay and four week's confined to barracks.

I could not believe that he had been found guilty, because I knew that he was innocent, and in my opinion the punishment was excessive, because the lad was a regular soldier with a wife at home in the UK. Apparently she would not receive any money for a fortnight either.

As soon as I could, I apologised to my scout for reporting it, then I went to our Company Office to have my say on the matter, and to point out that the problem and reason for the discharge of the shotgun still remained, yet nothing had been done to prevent it from happening again. From then on I always tried to get my leading scout to use a weapon other than that twelve-bore shotgun, and while I agreed fully with the CO that accidental discharges were unacceptable, I had made up my mind that if any of my lads had an accidental discharge, I would cover it up for them. But if any of them did accidentally pull the trigger, or turn off the safety catch, then I would charge them myself, but I had no need to worry because everyone really was always extra careful.

With the COs orders out of the way the next day was special to me because I was going to celebrate my First Wedding Anniversary, and together with Bill Fish our promotion to full Corporal. It was a day off for us, so Bill and I spent the morning going round the other barrack huts looking for Chit-Chats.

Well, Chit-Chats are small lizards which are very similar to the Newt back in the UK. They were very handy things to have in your basha because they would catch all the flies and mosquitoes. When you caught one you would take it back to your basha and let it go onto one of the timber supports to the roof. The Chit-Chat would run up into the thatched roof, then spend its time running up and down catching all the flies. Needless to say that in Colombo Camp they were always in demand and never harmed.

That night Bill and I put on our Civvy Street clothes and went down into Ipoh to the Ruby cinema. We went to get our tickets first, but as we had over half an hour to wait before our show started, we went into a nearby bar for an ice-cold beer. There were already some of the lads from our platoon in the bar so we pulled some tables together, then we all sat having a laugh and a drink together. We didn't forget our leading scout who couldn't be with us that night. The lads decided that on pay-day they would have a whip round for him to help out. Anyway we were all having a good laugh and enjoying each other's company; Privates, Lance Corporals and Corporals with all the army rank forgotten. It was just the men of 4 Platoon together, and of those who had tickets to go to the cinema. None of us made it!

I started by having a Mackeson stout, then I had another. Then I started drinking rum and blackcurrant, because that was Betty's drink, and it was a small way of having her a little bit nearer to me that night, but it was a drink that I hadn't had before, and I have certainly never had since. As I was not used to drinking R and Bs, for the first time in my life, I had too much to drink. But what the hell, it was my first anniversary, and the people I depended on the most at that time were there to share it with me. They made sure that I got back to Colombo Camp safely and tucked me up in bed. The only trouble was that when you had too much to drink and your Comrades tucked you up in bed, they always tucked the mosquito net fully under the mattress so when you wanted to get out of bed in the middle of the night in a hurry, you were trapped by the net. Ah well! I will most certainly never forget my first wedding anniversary, that's for sure!

# CHAPTER EIGHT
### *Royal Navy on Jungle Patrol*

I awoke at 06:45 to another hot Malayan morning. The first thing for me was to go for a shower and shave. I had a thick head from the night before, and I promised myself that I wouldn't drink rum and blackcurrant ever again. My mouth was already feeling a lot better after having cleaned my teeth, so I put my gear away inside my locker and went down to the charwallah's for two aspirins, a coffee and a banana banjo for breakfast. As I sat there eating and feeling down in the dumps because I was not with Betty on our first wedding anniversary, I couldn't help but at the same time reflect on the wonderful country that I was in.

Here I was at 07:15, sitting in the comfortable early morning warmth, wearing just a pair of shorts. The sun was up and shining from over the Cameroon Highland Mountain Range that was behind us to the East. There was a warm friendly earthy smell in the air, something akin to the smell of new-cut grass back home; intermingled with that was the smell of coffee. There was a quiet, but somehow reassuring hum of relaxed laughter mixing with early morning conversation, that could be heard from around the camp. A few lads from the different huts and platoons were walking slowly here and there, simply getting on with whatever they needed to be doing at that time of day. Enveloping all of the placid sounds, smells and warm sunshine, was the music coming from a background multitude of radios that were softly playing throughout the camp.

At that moment I felt at ease and very secure, sitting in the middle of these guys, all just ordinary young men separated, and most not by choice, from their homes and loved ones, who at this moment in time were living their lives on the opposite side of the world.

Why is it that this sort of moment in your life, even though nothing special happened, remains vivid in your memory, like a marker left inside the boring pages of a book that you put down many years ago? Could it be that within those few seconds of my life, I was really beginning to understand my Grandfather's feelings for his gallant comrades, and my feelings and trust in my loyal and gallant comrades?

The moment was broken by the arrival of Bill Fish for his breakfast coffee, which reminded me that we had a pre-operational briefing at 09:00 in the 'B' Company Office, though I hadn't really forgotten about it.

At 09:00 sharp we were at the Company Office for the briefing, which was going to be just a normal scheduled operation lasting five days, and would take place up to the North of Ipoh. The single track Malayan railway line ran through part of our jungle area; our orders were to look out for any signs of activity within the jungle, that might indicate any preparation that the trains were going to be ambushed. One item of news regarding this operation was that four Naval Officers would be coming into the jungle with us, but only spending two nights there. They would be going out on a normal daytime patrol with one of the sections.

The Officers had come up to Malaya from Singapore, so that they could gain the Malayan Medal. A lot of visiting regular servicemen would come into Malaya from Singapore for I believe just one hour, which then entitled them to the Malayan Campaign Medal. I always felt that the medal was demeaned by this, somewhat degrading the memory of the people who truly earned it. Obviously there was nothing that we could do about it.

The four Officers were from an Aircraft Carrier that was visiting Singapore, which I think was called *HMS Bulwark*. We most certainly respected the fact that they were going into the jungle and doing an operation with us. We were reminded of what the Navy thought about the Army, and so we had to try to send them back not only in one piece, but with nothing bad to say about us, so we had to treat them with the respect that an Army Officer would both expect, and receive.

After the briefing, as I didn't expect any involvement with them, I forgot about the Navy Officers and went to sort out my lads and myself ready for the following day start of operations. Before I left the 'B' Company Office, George Tuttall, the Company Clerk, had some good news. My leave had come through, so I would be away to Penang for a week after this operation.

The following morning it was up early and back on a three-tonner with that peculiar taste in my mouth and throat, that no amount of sweets or chewing gum could take away. There were four new faces on the other three-tonner along with our Platoon Officer, and I assumed that these must be the Navy guys. I wondered what they were thinking and what they expected of the jungle? It was strange enough for us at the beginning, but we had a few week's training with people who were experienced in jungle ways before we first went in. I must say that I had to admire them for taking on the challenge of the unknown, especially with their Service rivals - the Army. Added to this was the fact that they weren't as fit and used to walking as we were, but no doubt our Officer would take them out on an easy and short patrol, just to give them the feel of jungle life.

We reached the drop-off point just before dawn, made our way through and past several old tin mines, then followed one of the old water pipelines up into the jungle. We were the back section this time, so we just followed everyone else without any trouble, apart from my lads at the back doing the tail end Charlie, which wasn't easy having to keep looking behind them.

Every time we had a break I would change the lads around, so that everyone had a go. Being at the back meant that I could see the Navy guys who were with the middle section. They were doing okay, better than I had expected actually, although they were only carrying about half the weight of backpack that we were carrying, which would have helped them enormously. Going in and carrying all that weight was always the nightmare part of every jungle operation. I was looking forward to our first night in this base camp, because I had got myself geared up with an old parachute hammock off one of the lads who was now on his way back to Blighty and demob. The lucky devil! At least I would not be sleeping on the ground anymore.

We picked up an old logging track and followed it for about a mile and a half, then the front section turned to the right and we followed, moving down through both the jungle and the river in the bottom of the valley, then onto the far bank before climbing up to the spot which was to be our jungle base camp for the next five days.

My section wasn't asked to put the base camp guards into position, so I was obviously taking my section out on patrol the following day. I finished my basha, made sure that the rest of my section were okay, then went to the centre of the base camp for the next day's briefing, discovering that I had somehow drawn the short straw, for I was taking all the Navy Officers out on patrol.

The Officers weren't present at the briefing, so I questioned the safety of taking them all together, rather than splitting them up so that there were two with each section. I was told that they were all being kept together because that is what they were happiest doing. We discussed the situation, and decided that they were worried that if they were split up, then they would be more vulnerable to be set up for a leg-pull by the army.

I said, "I'm not taking all of my section out with the Officers, as the patrol would be getting too long and drawn out for me to be in full control all of the time."

I was given the okay to organise the patrol to what I was happy with, just as long as the Navy were fine when they were back in the Officers' Mess in Colombo Camp, and having a drink with the CO.

This put me under great pressure. That was the last reassurance that I needed on the night before taking Officers out.

It wasn't all bad though; I was given a choice of where I wanted to go, and how long to stay out? I chose to cover the railway section of the jungle. I didn't expect any trouble there, because it was a couple of years or so since they had ambushed a train. I personally felt that in their now weakened position, they would not be too keen on committing that many 'CTs' to ambushing a train, or giving away their location within an area that was now well-covered by the Loyals, but I could have been wrong.

I was informed that the Officers each had a map and compass to work with, and were under strict orders that I was in charge, and that they had to obey me without question. I decided to take my best two lads, plus my leading scout and Sanden my Iban. One was for tail end Charlie, and one lad to go in between the four Officers, then myself. Sanden my Iban and my leading scout I wanted up front. I had decided to leave my Lance Corporal in charge of the rest of the section as they were being left behind at the base camp. Let's face it; five sets of maps and compasses were more than enough for any single patrol in the jungle!

I didn't sleep well that night, and I don't think that it was the new hammock to blame because that was great, but the following morning I was up and ready for the off. Well not ready, but prepared, if you understand my meaning. I was not looking forward to the day, knowing that I would have to be especially careful not to put a foot wrong or upset the Navy guys.

The day started well enough, with our Platoon Officer bringing them down to the perimeter vine ready for the off. He introduced them to me, stressing that on the other side of the perimeter vine, I was in command no matter what happened. The Navy guys seemed to be fine and at ease with the lads in my section, but they were without doubt perturbed about going into the jungle on patrol. I made sure that the weapons were all loaded correctly. I double-checked that they knew just what the safety catch was all about, and each knew to keep the rifle pointed at the ground at all times, apart from if we ran into Charlie, then for better or worse we were off.

I took the patrol down to and through the river, then up to the logging track where we turned to the right and followed the track South for approximately half a mile. At about the spot where I was planning on heading into the jungle was a massive rhododendron-type bush. I clicked my fingers, and the leading scout looked around at me. I pointed at the bush and he immediately vanished into it followed by Sanden, who also disappeared as if by magic, swallowed up by this monster disguised as a bush.

It was my turn next, but before I went into the bush I turned and smiled at the Navy guys giving them the thumbs up. I knew how they would be feeling, seeing people swallowed up by the greenery, because I remembered how surprised I was the first time that I saw it happening. The bush was about the size of a very large house and big enough to hold all of the patrol. They were always a barb free and convenient way into the jungle, like very handy doorways through the thick jungle undergrowth that always bordered the tracks and clearings in the Malayan jungle.

Once on the other side of the bush and into the jungle proper, I called for a break and got the Officers into the middle of the small clearing, while my lads and Sanden sat around the outer edge looking outward as prearranged.

The Navy Officers asked, "Should we be looking outwards?"

I told them, "It's probably better if you don't, because you don't know *how* to look, where to look and what to look for, but don't you worry you'll be absolutely safe with my lads who are the best." I could tell that they were nervous, but what I'd said seemed to ease their fears a little.

I then asked them, "Do you know where we are?"

They had no idea, even though we had only just got underway, so I showed them on the map where, and how we had come to the clearing, and the direction we were going next. I checked their safety catches, then we were away and heading South. The jungle wasn't too thick in this area, which was helpful, because I don't think that we could have managed a lot of hacking our way through. The Navy guys were beginning to relax because they had begun to make a lot of noise, speaking to each other the odd time, and stepping on and breaking branches that were easy to miss for anyone with their wits about them. The leading scout was becoming miffed with the sounds from behind, and a couple of times he turned and looked at me, screwing his eyes up, and I knew just what he meant.

I called a halt, then went up to the front with the leading scout and Sanden. We discussed the noise.

"I'll have a word with them to try and be silent while going through the jungle. If that doesn't work, then we will have to throw them a frightener, which always works with noisy newcomers."

It was easy for the leading scout to know what was going on, but at first Sanden didn't understand what we were planning. I started to explain to him again what was happening or going to occur, when suddenly he gave me his big golden smile, for the penny had dropped.

I had better explain about his golden smile. The Ibans held their wealth in their mouths. By this I mean that when they had saved enough money, they had their teeth taken out and replaced with solid gold ones. The really wealthy Ibans had diamonds embedded into the teeth when they had run out of teeth to replace with gold. I must say that it did take me some time to get used to seeing a mouth full of gold when I first used to talk to the Ibans, but you really do get used to anything. Everything becomes commonplace given time, even making no sound going through the jungle; I went to have a quiet word with the culprits, but ever so politely.

I asked them, "Do you know where we are on the map?"

Once more they had no idea.

I explained again where we were and how we got there. I asked, "Would one of you like to lead the patrol and decide where we should go?"

They were not keen on this, so they declined.

I then very diplomatically, mentioned about there being too much noise. I then went and had a word with my other two lads about the course of action that we may have to take over the noise level.

When you were in the jungle you made no sound, you even put your foot down on the ground in a special way with first the heel, then the side of the foot, then you rolled the foot over onto the sole, that was so as not to make a sound when walking. The only time that you were supposed to talk was when you were in the base camp. The rest of the time you communicated with hand signals, that were taught to you in training. Of course we didn't follow this ruling to the letter, as out on patrol whenever we had a rest break, we would usually have a quiet chat, discussing anything that we weren't sure about, but a sound that was avoidable just didn't happen.

You could say that we regarded silence as if our lives depended upon it, which of course they did!

Anyway with a plan of action in place just in case it was needed, we set off again, only this time we were heading East and towards the railway line. We came across the railway just about lunch time, so I called a halt for a decent rest. It was not really a meal break, because we didn't have a packed lunch with us in the jungle. Some of the lads sometimes took a tin of beans with them and ate them cold, or snacked on the tin of cheese and biscuits out of the food pack. I used to have some of the barley sugar sweets, and as I now smoked cigarettes like everyone else, I would also have a couple of fags. The chewing gum also came in handy for holding back the pangs of hunger.

In some parts of the jungle the Ibans would show us certain plants and small trees that we could cut up and eat. I remember one that looked very much like a banana tree. We could chop it down very easily with our machete, then we peeled the bark off which revealed a heart that was white, just like the inside of a cabbage and tasted very much the same too. When we found any of these trees we would cut them down and carry as much as we could manage back to the base camp, to share with the platoon. We would then cook it with our evening meal. However in this part of the jungle there was no sign of anything to supplement our diet, so I had to settle on this occasion for the boiled sweets and chewing gum that I carried with me.

There hadn't been any undue noise since the last stop so I didn't bother to mention silence, but I did tell everyone that if a train came along to keep out of sight, because the armed escort in front of the train may not have been warned that we were on patrol or could be next to the line in this area. The last thing I wanted was for us to be shot by our own side, especially with the Navy guys with us, and their safety being my responsibility.

We moved off when I considered that these Officers were ready to start, but they were holding up better than I had expected. Out on patrol in the Malayan jungle was not like a quiet stroll through an English wood. There was also the psychological pressure that really does somehow sap your energy.

We now headed North following the railway, but keeping about fifty yards into the jungle so that we were out of sight of any traffic on the railway line. We had been underway for about a mile when we came to a small clearing that showed obvious signs of CT activity. There was a small attap shelter which had been wrecked. Scattered about were pieces of plastic tablecloth that the CTs regularly used for weatherproofing. The patrol stayed on the edge of the clearing, while Sanden and I checked everything out. It turned out to be at least five-years old, but had probably been used on one of the old railway ambushes. I waved the patrol into the clearing whilst we had a ten-minute break.

There was a panic amongst the Navy guys when one of them found a leech on his leg. I remembered how I felt when I first found one on me, and as I had a cigarette lit I went over and burnt it off him without any fuss, much to his relief.

"Don't worry about it now, just let it bleed until it stops. You'll be fine," I assured him.

Once again we were off and still following the railway line to the North. We travelled for about two miles farther North, before we stopped for a break. I decided that after this I would head the patrol West and back towards our jungle base camp.

The leading scout waved me over and said quietly, "The noise level was beginning to increase again on the last section that we had covered."

"If it gets any worse you know what to do?" I told him.

We stayed there for another few minutes, then we were off, heading West towards the old logging track that would lead us back to the base camp. I could see from the map that we were about one and a quarter miles from the point where we had left the track at the beginning of the patrol to enter the jungle proper. I had worked out the compass bearing that would take us back to that point. As we had to go uphill and down dale, and also around various types of thick jungle undergrowth, large rocks and the like, then I would be more than satisfied to come out and onto the logging track two hundred yards either side of where we entered the jungle.

We had only gone about four hundred yards when the unnecessary noises started again. I should really have warned the Navy guys, because the trouble is when you are new to jungle operations you start to relax when you get near to the end, beginning to think that it's over long before it actually is. You learn with experience, that the time someone gets hit is usually when they least expect it.

The leading scout looked around giving me a wink and a wry smile; then unexpectedly and totally out of character Sanden turned and gave a big grin. To be honest for some reason that really shocked me. I started to worry now about what they were going to do, because I certainly didn't want the Officers being annoyed and upset too much, as that would later be dumped back onto my doorstep. Just as this was going through my mind we heard noises which turned out to be a family of monkeys. They were not too far away, possibly fifty yards.

Sanden, the leading scout and I all dived onto the ground, which would have been the normal reaction anyway to the noise. When I looked around my two lads had hit the deck, but the Navy guys were just crouched down wondering what to do? I rolled over onto my back still watching them, pointing at two of them. Then I indicated a big rock near to where they were, then pointed to a nearby large tree for the other two, gesturing for all four to lie down. This all took about one second.

Doing my best imitation of John Wayne I crawled over to my scout and whispered, "That was lucky."

Sanden smiled at me.

My scout said, "It wasn't luck, Sanden had heard them earlier, and knowing that they were there, he had deliberately took us towards them."

I rolled onto my side so that I could see the lads behind, and hiding the smile, put my finger to my lips to let the Navy guys know to keep quiet. We stopped like that for about five minutes, which was long enough for the monkeys to move sufficiently for us not to be able to hear them. Then the three of us at the front, followed by the rest of the patrol got to our feet. I looked around, and once again put my finger to my lips before giving the thumbs up signal for us to move off towards the logging track.

We just had one more interruption before we reached the track. That was when one of the Navy guys brushed too close to one of the spiky plants that grow everywhere in the jungle. He got a couple of the spikes stuck in his upper arm, but we soon got them out with the tweezers that I always carried in a small tin along with the morphine and razor blade. The lad with the medical pack dabbed a touch of iodine on the two spots, then we were off again.

The Navy guys were exceptionally quiet; I think that the monkey incident had worked, but I also think that seeing the razor blade and morphine tubes that I carried in my medical emergency tin had finished the job off for us. Within half an hour we were back on the old logging track. This moment for me was one of the highlights of my time in Malaya. As I emerged onto the track and looked around, I saw that we had come out onto the track through the very same hole in the bush through which we had entered the jungle that morning, but obviously exiting from a different direction. Knowing that this was too good of an opportunity to miss in impressing the Navy, I waited until all of the Officers were out, and onto the logging track, then pointed to the hole in the bush and told them that this was the exact spot into which we had entered the thick jungle that morning.

At the same time, not wanting to get too carried away I also checked the safety catches on their rifles. Just over thirty minutes later I was checking everyone back into the base camp and feeling well satisfied with my lads and myself. I put a mess tin of water on the stove for a brew, then went to the centre of the camp and told the Platoon Officer all about the operation, especially about the bush, and that the Navy guys seemed to be well satisfied.

The Navy Officers left the following morning with one of the platoon's other sections to escort them out. As it was my duty day in the jungle base camp I saw them off from the perimeter vine.

They all thanked me saying, "That it was an experience that they would never forget."

I found out later that they spent all of that night in the Officers' Mess telling the CO how incredible the army is at using a compass and map, and what a great job we were doing. I believe the CO was very pleased, but of course in true army tradition I heard nothing more about it, but the event may just have saved my Corporal's tapes for me a few weeks later.

On this operation I had again brought a bottle of stout into the jungle instead of my camera. I was celebrating having been in the army for a year, which meant that I now had less than twelve months to do.

"Roll on demob!" I thought.

I know that a bottle of stout is neither here nor there, but to me it was more of a symbolic gesture, just a bookmark in my time, and the stout was a drink that was full of iron which was good to add to our jungle diet.

I looked out for the fireflies that night, but there were none to be seen; it must have been down to the type of vegetation. I really don't know for sure. I settled down in my hammock knowing that elsewhere in the Malayan jungle and back in Ipoh at Colombo Camp, there were other lads from 57/14, the same draft as myself, and my comrades of the Somme Platoon who had shared so much pain and fear with me a year ago back in Ashton-under-Lyne. I had no doubts that they would be thinking the same, one year to go and it's all downhill from here! Unknown and unfortunately though, there were still one or two uphill events to be faced by us all.

The following day I was back out on patrol with my full section, we had a good laugh over the Navy guys, but we admitted to ourselves that they did very well considering that it was the first time out for them, and on balance they had earned their Malayan Medal. We set out over the river and once again back up to the old logging track, taking a right turn and heading Southwards up the old track. We passed the hole in the bush where we had made our entrance and exit with the Navy guys a couple of days earlier. We carried on up the track for a couple of miles before cutting into the jungle to the right of the track.

I was glad to be off the logging track for as you know, I never felt safe on one, but to cover the ground we often had no other option but to use them. The track we had just left had deteriorated over the last mile; it had become hardly recognisable as an old logging track, for it had almost been taken over completely by the jungle. In another six months any trace of it would have vanished forever.

We pushed on through the jungle and up onto the ridge that I was looking for, then we followed the ridge to the South-West for another mile. I was planning to cut down from the ridge to a large stream running in the bottom of the valley. We started going down from the ridge, and had gone about two hundred yards when the jungle started to brighten when it should have remained its normal darkness.

We carried on, wondering what we were coming to? Suddenly we were in bright sunlight; in front of us was a massive clearing that must have been three miles long and at least two miles wide. We could see all of the clearing with ease, because as we had been coming down off the ridge we were above the open space thereby looking down upon it. The clearing had been created by all of the trees falling down. They looked as though they had been that way for some time, because there was no greenery to be seen anywhere. It was really weird, because the trees were just jumbled up together having fallen in every direction.

We first thought that there had been a massive explosion, but it was obvious within a few seconds that if something like that had caused the trees to fall they would all have been laying in the same direction, but these were anything but that. You really can't imagine how strange it all was, because a lot of these trees were real giants. Some of them were so big that they weighed well over one hundred tons. How do you begin to imagine just one of those giants falling down, never mind six or seven square miles of that happening? We wanted to get to the ridge on the other side of the fall, and as it looked as though some of the fallen trees may have been forming a bridge across the valley floor.

I told my patrol, "Let's give it a try!"

We climbed up through the roots and onto the nearest big tree and started to walk along the trunk, which was sloping at a shallow angle downhill. The branches were sticking up from the trunk of the tree, but all the leaves and greenery had gone as had all of the ground greenery, the vines, and everything. We were all a little worried, because when we looked down to where the ground should have been, we could see nothing but a tangle of grey branches, which must have been forty feet or more below us.

I thought to myself, "If any of the lads fell off the tree trunk, then even if the fall didn't kill them, we would never find them down amongst that intertwined mess of timber. Only God knew what malevolent giants of the insect and animal world were lurking waiting for us down there in the tangled blackness?" I gave the order to return to the safety of the hillside.

Once back on *terra firma* I told the lads to take a break while I decided what to do. I took a look at the map and decided that if I tried to go around the fall to the right, then that would take us out of our area, and would also take too much time. I therefore opted to go back along the ridge, then take the section down and around the bottom of the fall, following the stream down to where it joined the other stream that we were going to pick up by coming down from the ridge.

After the rest stop that's what we did, and the rest of the patrol went as planned with nothing unusual occurring. We did have a look at the edge of the dead wood clearing in the bottom of the valley, to try and determine what had killed the trees? It remains a mystery to me still, as to what could have destroyed all of the trees, then scattered them in the way that we found them. I must say that I have thought about it many times.

That evening I was making myself Swift's steak, curry and boiled rice and while I was occupied with that, I was also watching the flying foxes, which were busy that day skipping from tree to tree. The flying fox was like a squirrel, but with membrane wings that stretched across its legs. When it jumped from one tree to another it would sail across the gap, just like a glider, but they most certainly didn't compensate for the absence of the fireflies, which to me personally really were the most fascinating of creatures.

I awoke the following morning to the sounds of the camp coming alive. It was still dark, but we always got out of our pit (bed) in the blackness to be ready for the dawn stand-to on the perimeter vine. I lit a hexomine block, which I had put on the small cooking stove, then I filled the small mess tin with water from my water bag and put that onto the stove to boil ready for the breakfast mug of tea. The next job was to check out the lads in my section; to make sure that they were all awake and ready for the stand-to, and also to make certain that they were all feeling okay. At the same time, I told them that we were off on our patrol at 08:30 and to be ready.

Stand-to passed by okay; we were all busy with making and eating our breakfast. Then it would be time for a quick wash at the water point. All the lads still brushed their teeth at least in the morning, and to do this we all used water which we had boiled on our stoves. We could have done the same for having a shave and then there would not have been any skin problems. I had always used boiled water for a morning shave because I liked using hot water for that purpose, but as I looked around my lads that morning, with all of them doing whatever they were doing and with several days growth of beards on their faces, I thought what a good idea the not to shave order was, because in the gloom of the jungle light, their faces were barely discernible with the hair growth, so obviously more difficult to be seen when out on patrol.

At just after 08:30 we were off again, with all of us wondering what unusual sightings and mysteries we may come across that day? However the day proved to be a nothing unusual day, as the only thing we saw were miles of jungle. That's all we saw, but somewhere along the way we must have got too close to the jungle, because when we got back to the jungle base camp all of us had developed a red rash, mainly to the left arm, but one or two had the rash on their right arms, also one or two had their faces affected. We used to call it jungle rash. As soon as the blisters appeared we would give that area of skin a good wash with soap and water, then rub in some of the special ointment out of the first-aid pack.

Normally by the following morning the rash would have gone, which is what happened in this case. Just the odd time the rash didn't go, and usually developed into something worse. The biggest problem when this happened seemed to be that nobody knew what the infections were, so they just got called jungle fever or jungle sores. These jungle sores were a real nuisance as everybody got them on a regular basis. I can remember having them several times on my arms.

What would happen was that we would awake in the morning with a small blister or blisters somewhere on our body, but usually on an arm or hand. The blister would burst once or twice a day, and the moisture from inside the blister would wet the skin around the blemish. Within an hour or so that area of skin would also come up in a blister, so we finished up with a ring of blisters around the original sore that just kept growing bigger by the day. They were horrible things to have, and the only thing that you could do was to wash the skin often, and keep putting cream on them and loads of powder. The number of tins of body powder that we got through in Malaya, was unbelievable.

We were issued with tins of foot powder and we could have as many tins as we wanted, but most of the lads from the Loyals would go to the NAAFI shop and buy tins of Johnson's baby powder, which seemed to work a lot better on the body. It smelled a lot better as well then, but I cannot even stand the smell now. I never did find out what caused the sores; there were all sorts of suggestions put forward but interestingly we never did get them when we were in the main Colombo Camp in Ipoh.

The following morning, after a good night's rest in my new hammock, we were on our way out of the jungle and back to Colombo Camp. I was feeling good because in three days I was going off on my week's leave to Penang. We got back to camp okay, and the first thing after booking in our weapons and ammunition, was to get shaved and showered and put clean clothes on, which was usually just a pair of shorts. Then most of us would go and get something decent to eat and a cup of coffee or the like.

The next job was usually to redraw your weapon from the Arm's Cote and get it cleaned and well oiled. None of the lads needed telling to do this. They all knew that their life one day could depend on their rifle working correctly. As I remember it was usually about this time when most of the lads were sat on their beds, busy cleaning their different weapons that George would come down from the Company office with everyone's mail from home. Mail was always the highlight of any day, and everyone who got mail would nearly always wander off to have a quiet read and to think of home. I always knew that everyone, including myself, felt a little bit down after being that close to their home life for a few minutes.

This was one of the times when that army comrade spirit was at its best. It would nearly always start with some stupid little remark that would escalate into the full-blown banter which I always felt was the real soul and strength of the British Army. Ten minutes later everyone would have their mind back together, back to the reality of their present life and their comrades. Depending upon the day we got back, but more often than not, there would be the pay parade for the platoon in the afternoon, usually at 14:00, and then after that the lads in the platoon would be free to do what they wanted for the rest of the day and the day after.

These times always reminded me of my first day with 6 Platoon when they had just come in from the jungle, with the relieving tensions, the banter and the jokes and the greatest bunch of men in the world, making the best of being where they didn't want to be. As for me, two days later, I would be at least in one of the places where I wanted to be. My first choice was home, but I had to settle for Penang, and that would do me for a week's rest.

# PHOTOGRAPHS

**No. 1**. The Somme Platoon in basic training at Ladysmith Barracks, Ashton-under-Lyne.

**No. 2.** See page 67. The author having just arrived at the transit camp in Singapore, relaxing on his bed with a good adventure story, prior to his departure the following morning for Ipoh.

**No. 3.** Looking along the barrack room from the author's bed. The photograph clearly shows the timber structure of the army huts.

**No. 4.** See page 72. Ipoh Railway Station - the splendid, and always spotlessly clean building, that was the author's first contact with Ipoh.

**No. 5.** See page 165. The Lido Cinema.

**No. 6.** See Page 165. The Rex Cinema.

**No. 7.** See Page 165. The Ruby Cinema.

**No. 8.** Colombo Camp, Ipoh. The Loyals' base in Malaya, 1957-1959. The Loyal 1$^{st}$ Battalion main area is from left to right, just below the centre of the photograph. The light coloured buildings to the left upper middle, are a part of the Ct's family internment camp. The two prominent hills in the middle distance are where Sui Mah was killed. He was the Communist commander, who was responsible for killing the British High Commissioner, Sir Henry Gurney. This photograph was taken by the author from a Wessex helicopter a few days after Sui Mah's death, in early 1959.

**No. 9.** Kinta Swimming Pool, Ipoh. A regular place for the lads from the Loyals to relax on a rest day.

**No.10.** See page 278. Fire on the Columbo Camp Garrison, and in the 13/18th Hussars area. Photo 10 is taken from the Loyals' camp, and the tents to the right are a part of the jungle training section and home for any new lads from the UK.

**No. 11.** See page 278. Fire.

**No. 12.** See page 278. The fire is very near to the helicopter landing zone.

**No. 13.** The dreaded backpack and armaments just dropped from the author's back on arrival at a jungle edge campsite. Note especially the water bottle fastened to the bottom of the backpack, and not on the belt, the mark of an experienced jungle fighter, with the ability to go without water during the morning. The personal arsenal consists of a Patchet sub-machine gun, four Mills hand grenades, and the tins of detonators for all of the 4 Platoon grenades. To prime them was one of the author's jobs. All up weight, 90 lbs. or more, depending on the length of the operation.

**No. 14.** Jungle edge camp. Panoramic view created by joining several photographs together. To the left is looking towards the jungle edge, and to the right is looking into the jungle proper. This camp had been established for three days prior to this photograph being taken. There are 13 bashas visible in this photograph. (If you can find them)?

**No. 15.** The author removing detonators from the Platoon hand grenades, after returning to the jungle base camp from jungle edge patrol.

**No. 16.** See Page 286. The diabolical water sterilizing kit. After the jungle training section, all the lads preferred to simply boil the water for drinking, but most lads carried a kit just in case.

**No. 17.** Water kit.

**No. 18.** The free issue foot and body powder that we could just collect from the company stores whenever needed.

**No. 19.** The small tin opener that was included in each one day food pack.

**No. 20.** 4 Platoon watching as a casualty from one of 'D' Company Platoons, is carried out on a stretcher, and through our area of jungle.

**No. 21.** One of 4 Platoon's bashas that has been crushed by a falling tree branch. Fortunately no one was 'home' at the time. Falling branches were always a constant threat in the jungle, especially after rain, which increased the weight of the bough.

**No. 22.** A very rare sight - a clump of wild flowers in the middle of the jungle.

**No. 23.** See page 112. Tin mine to the North of Ipoh. This photograph was taken from the top of the slurry washing ramp. 4 Platoon carried out a lot of night ambushes around this tin mine.

**No. 24.** See page 136. Taking an interest in the lives of the local people. Part of the Hearts and Minds strategy that was first applied during the Malaya Campaign. Here the tin ore is being drawn off after its final wash. The black line in the bottom of the jet of water is the fine tin ore, and the bucket is called a pickel.

**No. 25.** See page 136. Lunch time break in a rubber plantation. The author is standing by a rubber tree after a hard morning's patrol, and without his belt, packs, or machine-gun weighing him down.

**No. 26.** See page 137. Observation Point, which was situated on the right hand hilltop, and looking to the South, which is to the right of the photograph. Ipoh is about 12 miles to the right. The path leading up to the OP, and formed by troop movement is clearly evident. The OP is about 350 feet high and was manned continually for several days and nights.

**No. 27.** See Page 138. Private Armitage on the OP. And looking to the South, and overlooking a small village below the OP.

**No. 28.** See page 138. Two of the lads stood in the same spot as above, and also looking to the South, and towards Ipoh, which is about 12 miles away.

**No. 29.** See page 143. Three lads from the author's section crossing the River Chior on a highly suspicious bamboo raft. The film used was a rare early-days colour transparency film.

**No. 30.** See page 143. Another four lads on their way across the river on the bamboo raft. If you look to the right, and above the head of the lad with the pole, you can see the shadow of the wire hawser, that was stretched across the river. This photograph has been used for the front cover of this book.

**No. 31.** See page 149. Corporal Jim Melvin leading 5 Platoon out of the jungle, and over a log bridge after a 5-day operation. Note the damp green uniform and the beard.

**No. 32.** See page 149. The rest of 5 Platoon leaving the jungle at about 16:00hours. The increasing evening jungle mist is quite clear in the background.

**No. 33.** See page 244. The Sandycroft Leave Centre, Penang Island. The old London leave centre bus that was donated 'to our boys in the forces', by the Coventry, Women's Royal Voluntary Service.

**No. 34.** See page 245. The Sandycroft Leave Centre Clubhouse. The Centre of the Centre? Four 'B' Company lads having a drink in the bar.

**No. 35.** See page 245. The Sandycroft Leave Centre beach photographed from the clubhouse bar.

**No. 36.** See page 245. The Sandycroft Leave Centre. The author is at the middle of Sandycroft.

**No. 37.** See page 246. The Sandycroft Leave Centre hire cycles. With two 'B' Company lads holding onto the author's bike.

**No. 38.** See page 245 The Sandycroft Leave Centre beach terrace. A cool and pleasant spot in the evening to enjoy a quiet drink.

**No. 39.** See page 245. The Sandycroft Leave Centre hammock. In a peaceful spot and looking out to sea.

**No. 40.** See page 245. The Sandycroft Leave Centre. The author on the steps leading down to the beach.

**No. 41.** The Sandycroft Leave Centre diving board. This area was protected with a shark net.

**No. 42**. The Sandycroft Leave Centre coast line.

**No. 43.** Hong Kong. See page 293. *The SS Oxfordshire*. The boat that carried the Loyals to Hong Kong, and seen here just unloading the 1st Battalion at the dock in Kowloon.

**No. 44.** Hong Kong. See page 294. The 'B' Company lines at Fanling Camp in the North of the New territories on Mainland China. The clear space to the bottom right quarter of the photo, is the parade ground, known to us as the snake pit. The hut on the top of the hill, with the patched roof, was the 'B' Company Corporals' home (for a while). See Text. The mountains in the background were in Red China. (Communist).

**No. 45.** Hong Kong. See page 294. The well known Bailey Bridge on the main road between the Loyals' camp and Fanling village. At the top of this road stood the border with Red China, mind you, in the New Territories, all roads ended at the Red China borders.

**No. 46.** Hong Kong. See page 293. Lieutenant Colonel Thompson. The Commanding Officer; 1st Battalion of the Loyal North Lancashire Regiment. (The Loyals). Seen here just after disembarking from the *SS Oxfordshire*, and standing on the dockside in Kowloon.

**No. 47.** Hong Kong. See page 299. The small deserted army camp that was used by 4 Platoon when we were in Kowloon, for the riots. The camp was located near to the famous Peninsula Hotel. The hills in the background are on Hong Kong Island.

**No. 48.** Hong Kong. See page 300. Lunch is being served from metal containers.

**No. 49.** Hong Kong. See page 301. The YMCA in Kowloon, where the author and Bill Fish stayed on their weekend leave. The taller building on the other side, is the Peninsula Hotel.

**No. 50.** Hong Kong. See page 301. Looking out of the back of the Peak tram, and on the way up to the top of Victoria Peak. Down the line, and below, is Victoria City, and the water is part of Hong Kong Harbour. Across the water is Kowloon City.

**No. 51.** Hong Kong. See page 302. The author and a Hong Kong policeman on the top of Victoria Peak.

**No. 52.** Hong Kong. See page 302. One of the legendary Hong Kong Star Ferry Boats.

**No. 53.** Hong Kong. See page 301. Looking out from my bedroom window. Across the road is the Kowloon Railway Station, and behind stands the famous Star Ferry Clock Tower. In the distance, and in the early morning mist, is Hong Kong Island and Victoria City. Believe it or not, but at one time, you could catch a train to or from London, at this railway station.

**No. 54.** Back from Hong Kong, and getting ready for an administration inspection.

**No. 55.** Colombo Camp, and looking over the Motor Transport Park at sunset. The evening mist is clearly visible on the far mountainous jungle, which was the Loyals' main combat area in 1957 and early 1958. The top of the ammunition dump is just showing above the edge of the park.

**No. 56.** See page 374. A special memory from the Malay jungle. This photo shows Niambong, who was later tragically killed during an attack on a Communist jungle camp.

**No. 57.** See page 314. A sad day. Lieutenant M. A. Kelly, in the 4 Platoon basha, receiving his farewell tankard from 4 Platoon.

**No. 58.** See page 325. The reformed 4 Platoon. (The Crazy Gang).

**No. 59.** See page 317. The author, in a reflective mood, inside the Corporals' basha.

**No. 60.** See page 313. After returning from Hong Kong, and awaiting the start of jungle operations, the Corporals are all in Columbo Camp, and in a bright and breezy mood. Here are the 'B' Company full Corporals having their photograph taken in the Corporals' basha. The reason for the laughter, is because as soon as the author triggered the timer on the automatic camera, the space that was left for him, was filled with bodies.

**No. 61.** Kuacha Lodge Jungle Camp. See page 344. Looking across the LZ, to the lads who are digging out the waste pit. Lodge camp bashas are situated to the left.

**No. 62.** See page 344. A three-tonner making its way up to the Lodge camp on the three-week old track. Note the growth already overgrowing the track.

**No. 63.** See page 345. Three-tonner going up to Lodge Camp, and stopped on the track to allow the engine to cool.

**No. 64.** See page 347. Part of the trail up to the Lodge. It wasn't always safe to ride on the three-tonner, but it was always an easy walk, with nothing to carry but a rifle. You can tell from the lean, that the lads are going up a steep climb.

**No. 65.** Lodge LZ. in the foreground, and the bashas of Lodge Camp just noticeable in the trees. This photo was taken from the same spot as photo number 344.

**No. 66.** See page 347. This photo was taken from the edge of the LZ and looking into Lodge Camp. Take special note of the two lads just to the right of centre, and reading the notice fixed to the tree, which was a special message sent to 5 Platoon 'B' Company, by her Majesty, Queen Elizabeth II. The message recognized their duty to service on Christmas Day 1958. Also, and of more importance, the fact that they were the **only** men throughout the British Army worldwide, who were actually engaged on active service, that Christmas Day.

**No. 67.** Lodge Camp dog section.

**No. 68.** Lodge Camp NCOs basha, with Sergeant Banks (5 Plt). Note the beard and the stack of cases of soft drinks. Also the tables made from branches, and a large log for a seat.

**No. 69.** Lodge Camp NCOs basha with (5plt) Corporals, Miles Frodsham and Frank Shaw.

**No. 70.** Lodge Camp. The Officers' Mess.

**No. 71.** Lodge Camp waste pit, with Corporal Elson (5plt) stood in the bottom.

**No. 72.** See page 351. The very much alive, but having a quiet moment, wild tortoise.

**No. 73.** Lodge Camp. The steps down to the water point and swimming pool.

**No. 74.** Lodge Camp drinking water point, complete with bamboo stage to keep one's feet dry. Note the bamboo fishing net tucked under the waterfall.

**No. 75.** See page 349. Lodge Camp. The view to the left of the drinking water point, and showing the swimming pool and the dam we built to form the pool. Plus also the ever present guard.

**No. 76.** Lodge Camp. 4 Platoon lads in the late afternoon, and sat in the corner of the main basha.

**No. 77.** Lodge Camp. Listening to the two-way radio at the kitchen basha. The lad on the right with the earphones, is Percy Ashton, who was 4 Platoon's signaller.

**No. 78.** Lodge Camp. 4 Platoon lads collecting their daily food pack in the late afternoon.

**No. 79.** Lodge Camp. The rest of the 4 Platoon lads in the late afternoon.

**No. 80.** Lodge Camp. Stevo, another signaller, seen here outside the main basha, making his evening meal. He was badly injured a few days after this photograph was taken, when he fell off a cliff face.

**No. 81.** See page 350. Lodge Camp 18:30hours 31$^{st}$ December, 1958. The 4 Platoon Officer, 2Lt Rawsthorne and the radio operator, Percy Ashton. 'The last message of 1958'.

**No. 82.** See page 386. First parachute safely down, tonight we can eat.

**No. 83.** Malaya memories. Dark jungle green and bright sunlight shining through on the infamous Jap track. Just time for the leading scout to have a quick smoke, and to get rid of those damned leeches.

**No. 84.** The author, after a night ambush, with a 12 bore shotgun, and a two-inch Mortar over his shoulder.

**No. 85.** The author on light duties with an injured arm. The 4 Platoon basha is in the background.

**No. 86.** See page 445. The Ipoh tree. The man on the surface of the lake, is sitting on a large rubber inner tube. In each hand, which he is using to paddle around the lake, he is holding the chopped roots from an Ipoh tree. The roots contain a toxin that stuns the fish, forcing them to float to the surface, where they are then easily caught by the fishermen. In the background, just to the right of centre of the photograph, is the hilltop, where the observation point was positioned. See page 137.

**No. 87.** See page 445. This is the man seen floating in the rubber inner tube, and holding one of the fish taken from the lake by using the roots of the Ipoh tree.

**No. 88.** See page 429. Match the photos. Photograph taken by the author while on a reconnaissance in a Wessex helicopter, and prior to the jungle edge operation.

**No. 89.** See page 429. Match the photos. Photograph taken by the author, while on a reconnaissance in a Wessex helicopter, and prior to the jungle edge operation.

**No. 90.** See page 429. Match the photos. This photograph was taken from the top of an old, and out of bounds, tin mine washing ramp. The prominent hill is the same one in each photo. This operation was carried out over the Easter period 1959.

**No. 91.** See page 429. The base camp, which is just to the right of the washing ramp in photo 91. This photo was taken on Easter Good Friday morning 1959.

**No. 92.** See page 428. The flooded tin mine slats that we used as a swimming pool. You can see the heads of two lads swimming in the pool, and at the spot where the author lost his wedding ring. Ipoh is through the gap in the hills, and about 12 miles to the left.

**No. 93.** See page 433. The start of the fire that turned the hilltop into a blazing beacon for two days. The hilltop is the one on the right in photograph number 429.

**No. 94**. See page 429. This photograph shows the value of over flying the area, prior to the operation. This area would not have been found otherwise. The hole in the middle is about 400 feet deep, and you can just make out the tops of the tall trees that were growing down there.

**No. 95**. See page 429. The hidden valley from the helicopter.

**No. 96.** See page 429. The same valley from ground level, with the early morning jungle mist hiding the top of the valley, at about 700 feet.

**No. 97.** See page 429. Photograph from the top of the same valley, during an interesting patrol.

**No. 98.** See page 428. Some of the lads sat chatting in the jungle edge base camp. Take note of the old large valve body, that is being used to prop up the left hand side of the basha. Between that and Bill Bailey sat to the left, you can see the large climbing rope, that we used on these jungle edge operations.

**No. 99.** See page 435. Pte O'Rourke, Sanden and the author in the lunch break cave. Quarter of a mile to the left, is where we found the massive cave with the fear-provoking sounds.

**No. 100.** See page 290. The real and proper Loyals' cap badge that was worn for decades by the men of the Loyals, and replaced with the 'Lancastrian Brigade' badge, shortly before going to Hong Kong.

# AUTHOR'S NOTE

The photographs within this book, have been personally taken by the author, or with his camera. They have been selected from over 600 photographs that are held by the Regimental Museum at Fulwood Barracks, Preston. These have been given to the museum by the author, along with other artefacts for safe-keeping. They are open for members of the public to view, at the times that the museum is open to the public.

# THE SOMME PLATOON
## LADYSMITH BARRACKS.
## ASHTON UNDER LYNE

## 25ᵗʰ JULY to OCTOBER 1957

### BACK ROW
BILL HULL  G  SHARKEY   KEN HEY   KEN JONES  N MADDISON

### MIDDLE  ROW
BILL LYNCH  BRIAN MARSH  W RILEY  A RAINER  JOHNNY MORRIS
A CLARKE  FRED HUDSON  BRIAN HOCKEY

### BOTTOM  ROW
B WILLIAMS  B WILLIAMS  J TAYLOR  CSM WALKER  2ᴺᴰ LT MEEKS
SGT BECKINGHAM   B LEWIS  H SEFTON  F  WALSH.

# SINGAPORE

No 2

No 3

No 4

# IPOH CINEMAS

No 5

No 6

No 7

# COLOMBO CAMP    IPOH

No 8

# KINTA SWIMMING POOL. IPOH

No 9

# Fire on Colombo Camp

No 10

No 11

No 12

# Authors  Backpack and weapons

No 13

No 14

No 15

No 16

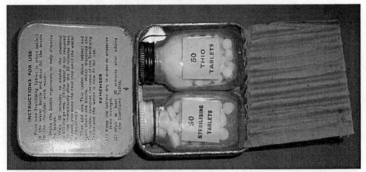

No 17

No 18

No19

No 20

No 21

No 22

No 23

No 24

No 25

# OBSERVATION POINT

No 26

No 27

No28

No 29

No 30

No 31

No 32

# SANDYCROFT LEAVE CENTER ON PENANG ISLAND

No 33

No 34
FROM THE LEFT; *TONY HAIGE,  PRIVATE OPENSHAW,*
*PERCY ASTON  (RADIO OPERATOR),    LEN THISTLETON  (B COMPANY*
*ARMS COTE)*

No 35

No36

No 37                    No 38

No 39

No 40

No 41

No 42

No 43

No 44

.No 45

No 46

No 47

No 48

No 49

No 50

No 51          No 52

No 53

B Company.
L/ Corporal Needham.  Corporal Miles Frodsham.  CSM Bull in the background.
No 54

No 55

# END OF AN ERA

FROM THE LEFT;   ANTARLY,  NIAMBONG,  MR KELLY  AND  SANDEN
## No  56

LIEUTENANT,  M A KELLY.
## No 57

# AND A NEW BEGINNING FOR 4 PLATOON
## (THE CRAZY GANG)

Rear Rank:- Ptes Openshaw, Hough, Smith, Yates, Armitage, Dodd, O'Rourke, Aston.

Centre Rank:- Ptes Nicholson, Jones, Williamson, Moscrop, Bailey, Wilkinson, Murtagh, Campbell, Wallbank.

Front Rank:- L/Cpl Forshaw, Cpl Hudson, Pte Sanden Anak Umai, Sgt McGrattan, 2Lt Rawstorne, Cpl Ryan, Pte Akaw Anak Gawa, L/Cpl Else'i, L/Cpl Quirke.

THE NEW AND REFORMED 4 PLATOON (NICKNAMED THE CRAZY GANG).
PLUS BELOW

CORPORAL BILL FISH WHO WAS AWAY ON LEAVE WHEN THE PLATOON PHOTOGRAPH WAS TAKEN.

## No 58

No 59

From the left; Half of Cpl Hudson, Clp Frank Shaw, Cpl Paddy Donoghue, Cpl Billy Fish, Cpl Pete Hartley , Cpl Frank Tumilty Cpl Miles Frodsham. Leaning over the back wall is Private Rigby.

No 60

# KUACHA LODGE CAMP

No 61

No 62

No 63

No 64

No 65

No 66

No 67

No 68

No 69

No 70

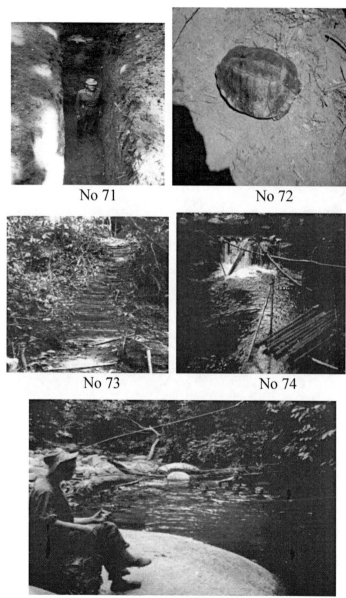

No 71          No 72

No 73          No 74

No 75

No 76

No 77

No 78

No 79          No 80

No 81

START OF MESSAGE. "NOTHING TO REPORT STOP. NEXT COMMUNICATION 08-00 HRS 1ST OF 1ST 1959 STOP. HAPPY NEW YEAR STOP. END OF MESSAGE.

No 82

No 83

No 84

No 85

# THE IPOH TREE

No 86

No 87

MATCHING THE PHOTOGRAPHS

No 88

No 89

No 90

PHOTOGRAPH NUMBERS 82 AND 83 WERE SHOT FROM AN HELICOPTER

237

No 91

No 92

No 93

No 94

No 95

No 96                    No 97

No 98

No 99

241

No 100

# THE  LOYAL  REGIMENT

# CHAPTER NINE

*Penang Island - Large Bomb - Shots in the Jungle.*

Well I was back in the railway station at Ipoh for the first time since I had arrived nearly seven month's earlier, but this time I was on my way to Penang. We had been dropped off at the station by the three-tonner, which had also come to pick up any new arrivals from Singapore bound for Colombo Camp. There were three lads I knew from 'B' Company, who were also going to Penang, which was a good start, because I didn't know whether there was anyone I knew going on leave.

It was the first chance that I had to have a good look at the station. Like the rest of the railway stations in Malaya it was another absolutely splendid building, and spotlessly clean. The train arrived on time; it was preceded a couple of minutes earlier by the armoured escort train. A few newcomers got off and went over to the driver of the dark green Bedford army truck, exactly as I had done all those months before, when I first arrived in Ipoh.

We got on the train, complete with our own weapons this time, and with a full magazine. I knew one section of the line that would be safe from ambush, as I had checked the area out with the Navy guys a few days before. Keeping away from the front of the train, we found seats somewhere in the middle. As soon as we had sorted out our cases and sat down, the train was underway; we were off on our way to the leave centre on Penang Island. The journey would take us about three hours including the stops. It was about eighty miles to the boat ferry railhead at the Kampong (Village) Masjid Timan.

Once we reached the railhead, we had to transfer from the train to the boat ferry, then make the crossing over to George Town and the Island. We were met off the ferry by the Sandycroft leave centre bus, which took us to the centre, which was situated about two miles to the North of George Town. The bus was an old London bus that had been donated by the Coventry WRVS; it also doubled as a tour bus around the Island for anyone staying at the leave centre. I must say that I always regretted never taking the tour on the two occasions that I stayed at Sandycroft.

We handed in our weapons to the small armoury there; we knew that we wouldn't need to bother with them again until we were leaving. The armoury was on the right as we turned off the road and into the centre. There wasn't a basha-type of hut to be seen; all the buildings were more reminiscent of a Butlins Holiday Camp back in Blighty.

To the left were all the leave centre accommodation blocks, and behind those were the dining-room and kitchens. On the right were the staff quarters, and the sports hall for table tennis and suchlike. There was also the hut for hiring equipment, including the bicycles and fishing gear, and the small motor launch that was tied up by the beach.

Access to the beach was down sets of stone steps. It was very clean, sandy and stretched away to the left, but to the right it only went about fifty yards before ending at a rocky outcrop. Built on the leave centre side of the outcrop, was the club bar which was, if I remember correctly, open all day and most of the night also. Inside as I recall were just the bar, a few tables and chairs, and a jukebox.

On the beach were the motor launch and a rowboat, and I remember that on one of the times that I visited Sandycroft, there were also a couple of canoes. About twenty-five yards out to sea was a large wooden tower, which had a good diving board that would be about eight feet high, built onto it. Surrounding the leave centre bay, and about fifty yards out to sea, was a good thick anti-shark net. I was certainly glad to see that!

The beds were comfortable, so I always had a good night's sleep, mainly due I suppose, to the accommodation being so quiet. The food was also good; if we were going off for the day on a bike ride for instance, they would make us up a packed lunch. We had to pay to stay at the leave centre, and although I can't remember how much it cost to stay, I do recollect that it was just a token amount, as was hiring the bikes and other items.

One thing which does stand out in my memory was that we could always go in for breakfast late, then sit in the dining-room eating as much as we wanted, thoroughly enjoying the food, reading the week-old English newspapers, but most importantly, having a good and relaxing laugh with everyone, while deciding what to do that day.

There is not a lot that I can tell you about Penang Island, as most of our time was just spent lazing about and basically doing nothing. I went fishing in the motor launch a few times, even though I have never actually liked fishing. I do not remember catching anything. I enjoyed swimming though, as the water was brilliantly clean and warm. On this Western side of the Malaya peninsula, we were swimming in the Indian Ocean, whilst over on the East Coast, it was the South China Sea. We were warned about swimming and using the diving board if there were thunderclouds about, or during the monsoon. This was because two lads had been struck and killed by lightning while they were standing on the diving board.

The sunsets were always brilliant affairs as the sun didn't seem to go down over the horizon, but it really did give the appearance of sinking into the Indian Ocean. I tried to photograph the sunset on several occasions, but I was very disappointed at the time when not one of the photographs turned out well. However now I am glad that none were successfully developed, because on reflection, one's memory would have been fooled with an image of something, the beauty of which was impossible to capture, even on film. How can one capture the changing colours and tint of the sun, and the rays appearing as steam rising out of the ocean? How can the trickery and images within the eye and the mind, all mingled together with the feelings in your heart, be encapsulated on a photograph? The sunsets were always a poignant moment for me, because I was forever mindful that as the sun sank into the Western Ocean with the reaching tentacles of sunlight hanging onto our day that it was leaving behind, at that very moment the *same* rays of sunlight were reaching out over the Pennines in England to awaken Betty and both our families to another new day apart.

One of the pastimes that I really enjoyed was hiring one of the bikes and taking myself off for the day with a packed lunch. All of the bikes had a saddlebag, which was convenient for carrying the camera, the packed lunch, and of course a most important piece of equipment, a bottle of suntan oil. We had to be extra careful not to get sunburnt, because if the burn put us out of action for a day, then we were up on a charge for a self-inflicted wound while on active service. This was considered a serious offence by the army. Naturally a lot of the lads got sunburnt while they were out there, but they had to treat themselves, because there was no way that they dare report sick. Everyone covered for them in the best way that they could, and that even included the NCOs.

Every evening the bus would leave the centre for George Town; it was free for anyone who wanted to go into the town. It would leave Sandycroft at approximately 18:00 hours, but if we went into town there was no return bus, so we had to get a taxi back, although they weren't too expensive, especially if there were a few of us sharing. There wasn't too much to do in the evening after writing home to Betty or family, apart from spending the night in the bar, drinking and listening to the jukebox or playing cards. Some of the lads enjoyed the boozing and spent every night in the bar. The beer was certainly far cheaper there than anywhere else.

Most of us would have the odd evening in George Town, go to the cinema to watch a film, or enjoy a beer and a chicken curry. The town always seemed to be full of Australians who were connected with the armed forces, but that wasn't surprising considering that Fort Butterworth was just over the water. Many of them were housed on Penang with their families. It made sense, considering that Penang had been freed from the Communists and there was no longer a curfew enforced. There were already international tourists beginning to visit the Island, and to me it had the feel of a sleeping giant that was beginning to awaken. I was right! Now it's considered to be the World's number one International holiday destination. I have to consider myself lucky to have been paid by the army to visit the Island twice, before the tranquillity of the Island was spoilt by hoards of tourists.

Well all good things must come to an end, and the time arrived to leave Sandycroft and return to Ipoh and 4 Platoon. I was thinking to myself that life in the army wasn't too bad now. I was a full Corporal with my own section, which meant that when we were in the jungle I was basically my own boss. So in that frame of mind I caught the ferry back to the mainland, relaxed after my rest, feeling comfortable with the thought of being back with the platoon, and the lads in my section, and a steady eleven month's run-down to being back home. I was on a high, and had a feeling that I would not be coming up against any undue problems, but fortunately we cannot see into the future, and any progression through life seems to me now as, 'the blind leading the blind,' with only hope as the guiding light!

We arrived back at Ipoh Railway Station to be met by a three-tonner that would take us back to Colombo Camp. I couldn't believe that it had been a week since we had last been there, as it felt to me as though we had just been away for a weekend.

It was well into the evening, the driver of the three-tonner said to us, "You can get a meal in the dining-room by telling them that we have just arrived from the station."

However I wasn't hungry, as I had eaten on the train coming down. The meal that I had consumed on the train was a Nasi Goreng, and the Malayan railway was supposedly world famous for providing this delicacy at its best. I must admit that the food was excellent, so much so that I had the same meal every time I travelled on the railway. I have tried Nasi Goreng at different Indonesian restaurants since I left Malaya, but I have never found one that serves anything anywhere near as good as that meal on the Malayan Railway. It really was first class, and if the meal really was world famous, as told by some of the lads in Colombo Camp, then it certainly deserved that accolade.

Once back in camp and with the platoon, I found out that we had a pre-operational briefing the following morning, and we would obviously be back in the jungle the day after. I was in time to catch the last showing at the cinema next to the NAAFI, so I put my gear away, had a quick shower, then rounded my leave off with a quick drink in the NCOs NAAFI, after enjoying the film at the cinema.

After a good night's sleep I was up early in the morning ready for the pre-operational briefing at 09:00hrs. Firstly I went to the 'B' Company stores and drew out my weekly cigarette ration, which was a sealed tin of fifty Senior Service. I also drew out a new tin of Paludrine tablets, which was just for 4 Platoon. Each tin held one thousand tablets, it was still my job to make sure that everyone in my platoon had one each day, and that all allocations were recorded in the

Paludrine book. My mate Corporal Billy Fish had been handing out the tablets whilst I was on leave; I think that he was surprised just how long it took to do it, but it was a job that I had been doing for a few months, and like so many things that are done often, I had got to know the best time of the day to catch everyone together, and thereby make the job quicker and easier.

The briefing went as normal, with the one or two variations that we nearly always had. We were going in for seven days, which meant that we would be carrying in the normal five day's supply of food. We were doing a 'lift and move' jungle base camp on this operation, which meant that we were going well into the jungle, up an old logging track, probably about four miles, and then going to the South for about a mile into thick deep jungle, then building our base camp on a stream there.

On the fourth day we were to destroy the first camp, then move to a new base camp site, coming back down the logging track and building our new camp at the side of the logging track and the river which ran close to the track at the campsite point.

At the new camp we were being re-supplied with two extra day's rations, being carried in by HQ Company who at the same time, were also escorting our Company Commander into the jungle to join us for three days at the new campsite. The Company Commander had been doing jungle check-ups on the 'B' Company Platoons, and now it was our turn.

He warned us to make sure that the sentries all had their weapons loaded and cocked when they were on duty and out on patrol. He had checked on some and found that they were neither loaded or cocked. He sounded rather annoyed about that fact, and I wasn't surprised, because I certainly would not dream of putting a sentry out without his weapon being cocked and ready to fire, nor out on patrol. It's one reason why many times the Bren gunners wouldn't take their Bren gun on sentry duty, because it hadn't to be cocked unless it was going to be fired. Most Bren gunners would borrow a rifle or shotgun from one of their mates for sentry duty, and that was a course of action that was approved of by most NCOs, including myself.

With the briefing over, we wandered back to the platoon basha to give the lads the bad news that they were carrying in five day's supplies, but they were stopping in for another two days, with a re-supply by HQ Company, who were also escorting in the Company Commander.

I knew my lads would be well-suited; I could tell with all the zealous moaning that they were. So to rub salt in I said, "There is more good news and more bad news, which do you want first?"

After more moaning they decided on the bad news first. Their faces really dropped when I told them that we were breaking camp on the fourth day and moving to a new location, then I kept them waiting for the good news. What I was waiting for was the first send-up, the first laugh from the lads to dispel the gloom that had descended upon them.

Someone said, "Is it good, good news or is it poor good news?"

I replied, "I'll tell you the truth. It is poor good news."

At that answer one of my lads, who had come from a really bad home life and was going to sign up as a regular soldier, shouted from the back of the basha, "They are going to send us all back home."

Of course, with that reply, all the lads were doubled up with laughter, so when I finally told them that the good news was that they didn't need to carry in the spare batteries or the rum ration for the extra two days, I had to leave the 4 Platoon basha fast under a hail of pillows, but I knew that the lads were back to normal, on the up, and would do whatever was thrown at them!

I had decided for two reasons not to take my camera in on this operation, one reason being that as it was to be a long operation I wanted to take in a book to read, and the camera would be both extra weight and space, the other reason was that we were catching the back end of the late monsoon, which meant that it would get very wet, which could ruin my camera.

The following morning we were all up early. Again I had that queer dry acidy taste in my mouth and throat. As I heaved my gear up onto the back of the three-tonner, for some reason my Granddad's face appeared in my mind's eye. I remembered how he had to march up to the front line with all his equipment. I thought of the last operation, and wondered how the sailors were feeling back on their ship, and what this op had in store for us?

An hour and a half later, we were in the jungle, and half a mile up the logging track. The river was about fifty yards away through the jungle to our right. Over the other side of the river about one mile from this point, was the cliff face where the platoon had been pinned down by gunfire from the CTs. I knew that some of the lads who were there would be remembering that moment, especially now as we trudged along the track near to that same place. I wasn't certain which of the lads had been involved in that one. One of the peculiarities of our life in Malaya was that when something bad happened, you didn't talk about it. The past was buried immediately.

A regular Lancashire saying at that time was, 'Least said, soonest mended,' that certainly seemed to work well, because the morale was always high, although I personally put that down to all the jokers that we had, not just in my platoon, but also throughout all of the battalion.

We continued our trek up the logging track for about another hour before stopping for a rest break. My section had the easy ride this time, because we were the middle section, so there was no need to worry about the tail-end Charlie or the leading scout.

Poor old Sanden was up front again. It never seemed to be fair the way that we treated the Iban trackers (Sarawak Rangers) as they were always up front and in the firing line, whether we were going in on an operation, or out on patrol in the jungle, yet they only got paid a fraction of the money that we received.

In the main camp back in Ipoh, all they had to live in were tents; it just didn't seem right to me that they were always treated as underlings. I must say thought that they always seemed to be happy, and when spoken to they always had a smile.

After a ten-minute break, just long enough to smoke a cigarette and get the leeches off, we were away again. Before long we were turning to the left off the track and into the heavy jungle. The machetes were out upfront to cut a way through, but progress was slow. There was also a weird smell about; we never did find out what was causing it, even the Ibans didn't know what it was.

I did experience a similar smell just a few years ago, and as soon as I sensed the smell in the air it took me directly back to that operation in the Malayan jungle. The odour that time was where a drilling team were looking for oil, and in the same area, oil and gas were oozing naturally out of the ground, along with the identical Malayan smell.

We reached the stream we had been looking for about an hour later than we had intended, because the jungle had been far more dense than expected in this area. It was one of the features of life in the jungle that we never knew just what we would encounter until we got there. With a bit of good luck we had met the stream at a spot that was handy to cross, and it was also a convenient water-point with an almost level area on the opposite bank for us to build a base camp. We were really lucky to come across such a spot because we were well up a mountainside, which was sloping quite steeply down towards the jungle edge that was some four miles away from us. The first warning as to how that operation was going to be, came on that very first afternoon.

It was late in the day, the base camp was pretty well sorted with all the bashas up and more or less finished. We had made sure that all the bashas had been built quickly, and were able to provide shelter when needed, with the back end of the monsoon around. The sentries were all out on watch around the camp. If it started to rain, they stopped where they were, and got soaked. That didn't matter too much, because it was still warm, and a lot of the lads enjoyed the cooling off effect of the rain. For the sentry on the water-point, the action was different, as that lad was usually on the opposite side of the stream to the base camp. If it started to rain he had to immediately cross back over the water, so that he was on the camp-side of the water-point, then continue his guard there.

In the late afternoon it suddenly, and on top of the usual jungle darkness, turned extremely dark. A sudden wind blew up, which was a sure sign that a downpour was imminent. Sure enough the rain started immediately, and straight away it was torrential, striking the jungle canopy above us with an unbelievable roar that really was deafening.

After a couple of minutes the Lance Corporal from the section who was providing the guards around the camp, went running past my basha heading for the water-point. For a second I thought he was rushing because of the rain, but then I got the feeling that something was wrong because his dash was just *too* urgent. I grabbed my gun, rushed out of my basha into the rain and followed him. As I got to the water-point behind him, I could immediately see the problem. The stream, which was about six inches deep when we crossed it earlier in the day, was now a raging torrent six-feet deep, and quite impossible to cross. Unfortunately the lad who was doing the water-point guard was still on the other side of the water, with no chance of getting back to our side until the water subsided. He was a little worried, being over on that side and on his own. We could see that he was contemplating trying to jump the gap, but there was just no way he would have made it. His L/Cpl told him to stay where he was. I backed up the L/Cpl by shouting across to him that this was an order, and he stayed put.

The next task was to get a couple of the lads to wait on this side of the raging water to give cover to the lad on the other side, just in case anything untoward happened over there. I looked around and found that we were surrounded in the torrential rain, by about ten of the lads who had come down out of interest, and to give their support if needed. I asked for two volunteers to remain there and give covering fire if required.

Knowing the lads, and the way they took care of each other, meant that I really didn't need to ask; they all agreed to stay there until he was back with the platoon on this side of the water. Ten minutes later the rain stopped just as quickly as it had started, and ten minutes after that the water started to go down just as fast as it had risen. Half an hour later the lad was back on our side of the water.

That evening we were informed over the radio that we had to move to the new jungle base campsite one day sooner than planned, which meant we would only have the following day to patrol that area. Having now seen the territory, we were quite happy to be moving a day earlier, for this would have been our patrol area the following day. It was dense jungle with thick undergrowth; the ground sloped in such a way that it would have been convenient to have one leg six inches longer than the other.

The following day I was out on patrol with my section. It was one of those patrols that seemed to be nothing else but hacking away with the machetes, which were really the most trying of the patrols that we did in Malaya, for they really did sap our strength. If we hadn't been carrying salt tablets, we would not have been able to survive the great loss of salt from our bodies.

I remember once suffering from losing too much salt, it was a weird feeling. It was soon after arriving in Malaya, when I was in the jungle-training platoon. We had been making our way through a lot of thick scrub with tall thick grass growing amongst it, which reminded me of sugar cane. I was having a go at being a leading scout, when we came to a scrub area which was growing between two tin mining areas. This was the first proper chance that I had to use this fabulous and massive jungle knife that the army had given to me when I first arrived in Malaya. Like everyone else I had sharpened it to perfection, so it was as good as a razor. I had been busy swinging at the scrub with the machete under the glare of the sun. I was sweating profusely, making up the water loss by drinking from my water bottle at regular intervals. Everything seemed to be going to plan and the path was opening up before me with each swing of the machete. I lifted my right arm to take another swing, when suddenly, before I could bring my arm back down, a feeling of nausea and tiredness, as though I hadn't slept for a week, swept through me. I can remember the two lads behind grabbing hold of me and sitting me down. Then the Corporal came up front and gave me two salt tablets and a drink to wash them down. Within five minutes I was amazingly back to normal, but that was also the last time I ever did leading scout.

We got back to the base camp after the patrol, and the first thing to do, after putting on a mess tin of water for tea and reporting to the camp centre, was a quick and cooling wash at the water-point. After that it was down to making a meal and having a half-hour read of the book that I had brought with me into the jungle. At stand to I took my tot of rum neat, and as soon as we stood down I climbed into my hammock, and because it had been a very tiring two days, I was asleep as soon as my head hit the green towel that I used as a pillow.

I was up early the following morning feeling bright and cheerful after a good and undisturbed night's sleep. We didn't get many of those in the jungle, I looked around at the base camp, which was still shrouded in the blackness of the jungle night, I could see from the small flickering flames of the cooking stoves that were visible from where I was stood, that most of the lads were up and about.

As soon as stand to and breakfast were over, we would be breaking camp, then moving about three miles back down towards the jungle edge to rebuild a fresh base camp, which would last us for the rest of the operation. We had been hopeful of leaving the old base camp by 09:30hrs, but incoming radio traffic (messages) meant that the platoon didn't get underway until after 10:00hrs. This was without doubt one of those operations where when one thing goes wrong, everything goes wrong.

Once underway we followed the path that we had cut through the jungle back to the old logging track, and then downhill towards the jungle edge. After a couple of hours we reached the spot that was to be our base camp for the next four days. The camp was located between the river and the logging track. Two or three of the bashas were built right onto the sloping edge of the track, including mine.

Back up the track in the direction from which we had just come, and about twenty yards out from the camp, was a fallen tree that lay across a slow bend in the track. When we came down the track earlier that day we had to climb over to the left of the tree-trunk, and then back onto the track to continue. Anyone coming down the track would be concentrating on how to cross the tree to keep on going down the track, so we sited the sentry post twenty feet uphill, and five yards past the tree, in a position which gave a good view up the track, whilst also being well-concealed amongst the undergrowth.

A good view in the jungle at that location meant about twenty yards, so the spot was perfect as a guard post. The second guard position was at the jungle edge side of the logging track, which covered both track and toilet, and would be about twenty-five yards out from the camp. The third guard post was in the jungle on the opposite side of the water-point. Everyone who did a guard on that point was warned this time to come to the camp-side of the stream if it looked like rain.

There were a lot of animal noises at that campsite; we could hear monkeys chattering and screaming all the time. Many times you could stand and watch them above you, swinging and jumping from tree to tree; they were obviously not unduly worried by us humans below.

There was also in this area a creature that had a very piercing call. The noise would last three to five seconds and started like the sound of a big four-stroke engine, before rising to a high-pitched crescendo, like a small two-stroke engine screaming its head off. We always thought that it was a large bird in the jungle canopy making the noise, but we were wrong.

I only found out by chance what animal the sound came from, while visiting Chester Zoo some years later. I was walking through the park with my family, when suddenly I heard the same sound. It was coming from the other side of the zoo, about three-hundred yards away. I walked straight over, and there in a large compound was this family of monkeys. One of them was making this piercing call. It did have the name of the type of monkey on the cage, but I can't remember now what they were called. I bet that I am not the first ex-Malayan soldier to hear that sound at the zoo, and be very surprised to find out that it was a monkey producing it.

The following day we had two patrols going out. One was going down the old logging track to the jungle edge, then meeting up with the 'B' Company Commander and the re-supply platoon. My section was given a patrol into the jungle to the South of the base camp. Again it was one of those difficult ones where the land fell away to our left, and rose to the right, thus making walking difficult for us by stretching the muscles in the legs to the most painful limits.

We set off immediately after breakfast, firstly up the track and around the fallen tree, then past the sentry for about two-hundred yards before turning left off the track and into the jungle. The leading scout set a steady pace as the jungle wasn't too thick in this part of our area. We had been underway for about an hour and a half, and I was getting ready to call a halt, when we came upon the remains of an old Communist camp. It looked as though it had been quite a big camp.

Sanden said, "It looks like it held about fifty CTs."

I told the lads that we would have a decent rest there so we could have a good look around. There wasn't much to see apart from the bits of plastic which were scattered around. With the constant damp everything else had rotted away. We reckoned that it was about five or six-year's old. It was a queer feeling standing in the middle of that old Communist camp area with my lads scattered around me, all having a nosy round to see what we could turn up. I thought to myself that not long before then, while I was at Kirkham Grammar School, this spot was a busy camp full of the enemy.

It was time to leave, so I waved the lads to get up on their feet. I took one last look around, then we were off again still heading South. It was late morning and we found it easier going in the shallow valley, which we had entered and we were now heading to the South-West. I was beginning to think about calling a stop for lunch break; well it would have been a lunch break if we had been carrying anything to eat. Most of us settled for a couple of fags and three or four barley sugars to kill the hunger pangs.

Suddenly Sanden stopped and pointed to the left. It wasn't a panic-type stop, more one of those out of interest stops, that Sanden used to do if there was something that was different to him. We were looking at some broken branches, which seemed a little peculiar in the way that they were broken.

I walked past Sanden and the leading scout; just in front of us was a hollow in the ground. It would be about a quarter of the size of a tennis court, and about six feet deep. As I came to the edge of the clearing I decided to take a closer look, jumping for a large rounded rock that was about two feet below the edge of the clearing. Just as I jumped, I looked down, realising that the rock was actually a massive unexploded bomb. Naturally I tried to miss it, but it was too late, the rubber heels of my jungle boots caught the rounded side of the bomb, and my back crashed down onto it.

For a few seconds I was paralysed with both the fear of the bomb exploding, and the unbelievable pain in my back. The next thing, all the lads were around me asking if I was okay?

I worried that my fall on the bomb may have triggered a delayed timing device and I actually asked, "Is it ticking?" Even though I was in agony, I remember chuckling at the reply from one of the lads.

"Why? You're not going to put it on your wrist, are you?"

I stayed down on the ground for a few minutes waiting for the pain in my back to subside. When it started to ease, and with the help of two of the lads, I dragged myself to the side of the hollow which was furthest away from the bomb. The curved side of the hollow was quite comfortable, and was easing my back nicely. I told the lads that we would stay there until my back was feeling better, then we would make our way slowly back to the jungle base camp. I was looking at the bomb from where I was sat. It was unbelievably large, about eight feet long by approximately three feet in diameter. Half the fins had been ripped off the tail end, and the bits left were badly twisted and damaged. Obviously the trees and undergrowth had cushioned the fall of the bomb, preventing the detonator from striking the ground.

I rested there for about an hour before feeling well enough to make a move, but I knew that we had to get moving to be able to make it back to base camp and still have time to make a meal. I certainly felt that I was going to have trouble making it back at all that day. Surprisingly, as we got mobile, the pain in my back started to ease, and after an hour of being underway, and of course taking it steady; my back wasn't feeling quite as bad. Before we reached the base camp the patrol was back to almost normal speed.

I must admit that I was relieved to be feeling not too bad, but I was glad that the following day was our day in camp. We came onto the logging track, then made our way down to the fallen tree where I gave the guard a whistle. After his response, and checking the weapons, we made our way into the base camp. I went to the camp centre and made my report to the Platoon Officer, along with the location map references of the bomb.

The Company Commander had arrived in camp, I could tell that things were different. There was a quiet and more tense atmosphere about the base. After my report I went in search of the lad who was carrying the medical bag to get some cream for my back. When I found him, I asked him to have a quick look to see how bad it looked. He told me that there was a bruise coming up, and I had skinned about two square inches. After having ointment rubbed in I went back to my basha and got on with making a brew and a bite to eat.

That evening at the briefing for the following day, I was told that the RAF bomb disposal squad were coming in to blow up the bomb. That was to be the next day but one, and as I was the only person to actually know where the bomb was, this meant that my section had to escort them. We had to find the bomb again, so that it could be dealt with. I thought to myself that I would show them how my back looked so they would be careful, but decided to keep that one to myself. I was certainly looking forward to seeing the bomb worked on and blown up. Once again I was cursing my luck for not bringing my camera into the jungle on that operation. It always seemed that when I left my camera back in Ipoh, something special *always* happened, but I suppose that's simply sod's law!

That night I didn't have the best night's sleep, as my back bothered me quite a bit. At about 01:30 I rolled out of my hammock and made myself a brew, that's the only time that I ever did that in Malaya, that's to make myself a cup of tea in the night. I remember sitting on the cross bar which supported my hammock, listening to the sounds of the jungle night. I tried to put names to the cries that were all around in the darkness, which made the rest of the camp seem invisible. I think that some of the noise was from monkeys, and I thought I heard the shrill cry of a wild pig, but I wasn't certain. I marvelled how we ever slept at all with all the strange and unknown sounds that came from beyond the edge of our camp, and from out of the frightening and unyielding darkness of the jungle night. After the brew and a cigarette, I managed to settle down and slept soundly for the rest of that night.

I was up in the morning and not feeling too bad, I sorted out who was doing which guard duty, then I relaxed for the rest of the day, sorting the sentries change-over every two hours, and apart from that making brews, a meal, and reading the book I had taken into the jungle. It had got into late afternoon; both patrols were back in the base camp, the C C. had been out with one of the patrols and everything was running fine. It was too good to be true, for nothing runs fine when the boss is around, and the services are no different to Civvy Street in that respect. It got time to change the sentries which once again went without problems. My Bren gunner was on the next guard duty up the track, but instead of

261

borrowing a rifle, he decided to take his Bren gun, which of course, wouldn't be cocked with it being a Bren. With all the guards in place I went back to my hammock, relaxed and read my book.

I was lying back on my hammock with the book in my right hand and up in the air. I was just thinking about getting a cigarette, when what seemed to be a big black fly buzzed past my ear and landed on the top corner of the book. As the black splodge landed on the page, I felt the book tug in my hand.

How fast is the speed of the mind against the speed of sound? I can tell you explicitly that the mind works at a speed that you would not think possible. My mind, in a moment that was far less than a fraction of a heartbeat, calculated everything that the black splodge could possibly be. The answer that my brain gave, had me starting to roll off my hammock even before the sound of the shots reached my ears and awakened all of my senses, pumping the adrenaline throughout my body, and raising the speed of my actions to match the speed of my mind. As I dashed out of the basha I grabbed my machine-gun, which was hanging on the end of the branch holding up the end of my hammock. As I ran around the end of my basha and up onto the logging track, I was cocking my gun ready to fire. I ran up the track past the lads already diving into cover, with quite a few of them choosing the banking that formed the logging track.

As I ran past them someone said, "It's just a wind-up."

I couldn't help a nervous chuckle at that. I was thinking to myself, "I hope my lads don't shoot me by mistake," when I realised that I hadn't got the most important instrument that told everyone that I was with them. This was my jungle hat with the bright yellow marker squares on the front and back. I dare not go on without it, as the risk would have been too great. I turned around and ran back to my basha, grabbed the hat, then ran back up the track.

Much to my amazement I was again running up the track alone with nobody following me or backing me up. I was in a dilemma. The shooting had lasted for two or three seconds, but that was ten seconds earlier. I had my Bren gunner on his own up the track; I was heading that way, but there was no one behind me. I slowed down, then started to creep slowly up the track.

About five seconds later the Company Commander (C.C.) was behind me asking, "What is happening, and was that my man on duty?"

I replied, "Yes Sir it is."

I was told to get up there fast, and find out what was happening. I can tell you that it's very scary walking into the unknown on your own, especially to where bullets had been flying just a few seconds earlier. I was thinking, "Sod the John Wayne stuff; I didn't want to be here and in the army in the first place."

I got to the sentry post, but there was no sign of anyone, and no bodies on the ground. I looked up into the jungle where my lad should have been, shouting his name quietly at first, and then louder. There was some movement from behind a log and small bush. Next thing, the Bren gunner's face popped up with a look of terror written all over it, and I thought no worse of him for that, because I knew exactly how I was feeling at that moment.

So trying to appear laid back with no worries and in the calmest voice I could manage, I said, "Come on down lad, there's only us here!"

You may be thinking that it was all a mistake, there was nobody else around, and he had fired by mistake, all of the shots that we heard. But I, and everyone else in the platoon, knew that the Communists had been there, because we all heard the Bren gun fire. We also heard two other types of weapons firing that definitely weren't ours.

My Bren gunner came down from the guard position and onto the track. "I saw two Communist soldiers coming down the track," he said. "As they got near, I cocked the Bren and opened fire on them both. The CTs heard the Bren being cocked, and as the Bren gun opened up firing, the CTs fired back, and I threw myself down behind the log."

This was exactly where I had found him hiding three minutes later. The C.C. was still coming up the track with about ten of the lads, so I walked up the track to where the CTs would have been when fired on. I had gone about ten yards when I saw five or six items lying in the middle of the track. I can only remember three of these, which were a comb, a pencil and a pocket diary which I picked up first and looked inside. The diary was completely full of Chinese writing from the beginning of the year right up to that very day.

I picked up the rest of the articles and went back to my Bren gunner who was telling the C.C. what had happened. There was no doubting that he was annoyed that the two CTs hadn't been killed. He was really boiling up when my lad told him that the CTs heard him cocking the Bren gun. I knew that I was in trouble when he looked at me.

He said, "I will have words with you later Corporal. I gave implicit orders at the start of this operation, and they have not been obeyed." He became a little happier when I showed him the diary and the other items that had been on the track.

After about ten minutes of everyone wandering about on the track to see if they could find anything else, they all returned to the base camp. I sent the Bren gunner back, telling him to make himself a brew and a meal while I put the next lad onto the sentry post.

He was on a nervous high, as were all of us, and not happy to be out there on his own, so I stayed with him, and to be honest I was happier to be there than under the gaze of the C.C. with whom I knew that I was in trouble. As I sat with the guard I was quietly reflecting on the events of the past hour, and how I had nearly been shot. I hadn't told anyone about that. I couldn't understand how it had happened, because no shots should have come anywhere near to me.

I stayed with the guard until it was time to go for the following day's briefing. I wasn't looking forward to that! I sent another of my lads out to join the guard who was now on his own and I then went to the briefing.

I was first to arrive; as I did I could see that the C.C. was busy looking at the diary. I did wonder from the way he was engrossed in studying the book whether he could understand Chinese, but I dare not ask him, so I never did get the answer to that question.

He asked me, "Why wasn't the Bren gun loaded?"

I explained, "We had been told in training that you never cocked the Bren until you were ready to fire it, so that was the accepted practice throughout the battalion."

Just as I was saying that to the C.C. Billy Fish arrived for the briefing, and bravely, much to my admiration, he confirmed to the C.C. that what I was saying, was correct, and everyone had been trained NOT to cock the Bren until ready to fire.

It took the heat out of the situation at that time, but the C.C. said to me, "You will be on Commanding Officer's Orders when we got back to Colombo Camp, and charged with disobeying a direct order while on active service in the jungle."

Then we got on with the briefing, which was that the RAF Bomb Disposal team had been cancelled, and Captain Bruce Merrie was coming in with the tracker team to try and backtrack where the CTs had come from, and where they had gone?

We all had to remain in the base camp in case we were needed to back up the tracker team when they arrived. With the briefing finished, we all returned to our bashas ready for the evening stand to. I wasn't too happy; a week ago I was on leave and quite happy, and now in such a short time, I was on CO's Orders when we got out of the jungle, and on a serious charge. Both me and one of my lads had nearly been shot, and my back was still crippling me with pain. I got into my hammock that night, but with everything that was going on in my head, I didn't get a good night's sleep.

One of the other sections went to the jungle edge early to bring in the tracker team. I knew then that I was in real bad books with the C.C. because I was sure that under normal conditions, it would have been my section who would have been asked to do that.

The tracker team arrived with us at about 09:00hrs, which was early, but they wanted to be on the trail. I didn't hold out much hope for the tracker team following the CT's scent, because we did have a heavy shower in the late afternoon after the incident.

I had better explain the tracker team. The Officer in charge of the team was Captain Bruce Merrie, and it seemed to most of us, that he had a personal vendetta against the 'CTs' in the way he led his team. The purpose of the tracker team was to pursue the CTs after the Loyals had some form of contact with them. The team contained several top Iban trackers, dog handlers and leading scout types. They always travelled fast and light, by only carrying enough food to sustain them for the day, and they were both known and feared by the CTs. The dogs were there for following the scent trails which had been left behind, and the Ibans were the best trackers that we had. They could almost tell you if a spider had walked across the jungle floor the day before, but the CTs were so skilled in jungle craft that they would leave only the trail of a butterfly. Sometimes, if the tracker team were in luck, it was a big and clumsy butterfly.

Unfortunately there were no clumsy butterflies this time. The tracker team followed the trail after the shooting and found that the CTs had run back up the track for about one hundred yards then cut off into the jungle. They then swept around and came back down onto the track, which they crossed about a mile away from the base camp. Then they made their way through the jungle and down to the river, which they then followed upstream by actually wading in the river, so the tracker team lost contact with them there.

The following morning we broke camp and headed back to Ipoh and Colombo Camp. Once there I spent the day sorting the gear out from the operation, and also finding a spotlessly clean uniform ready for the CO's Orders, which was to be at 11:00hrs the following morning.

I was dreading it! I should really have been going to see the Medical Officer, because even though it was improving, my back was still giving me a lot of grief. At the first opportunity that arrived that day I went to the NAAFI shop and bought a bottle of aspirin painkillers. This time the lads didn't help at all over the CO's Orders, and although they all came to give me their sympathy, they all also commented on what punishment they thought the CO would hand down to me. The *best* prediction suggested was that I would lose one of my tapes, and be busted down to L/Cpl. Another train of thought was that I would be taken right up to a court martial, but most of the other NCOs thought that I would be busted back down to a private soldier.

The following morning I was on parade in front of the CO's office, under the command and watchful eye of the Regimental Sergeant Major. I was marched into the CO's office where I was asked to explain my actions, which I did.

I had my say telling the truth, "That we had all been trained NOT to cock the Bren gun until ready to fire, and that was the practice throughout the battalion, and why most Bren gunners borrowed a rifle to do sentry post."

The CO then questioned me, "What is the name of the NCO who told you that?"

I replied, "I can't remember," I didn't want to get him into trouble with me. However I can still clearly remember his name even to this day, but I am not giving it here.

The CO sat there writing at his desk for a few seconds whilst I was stood stiffly to attention in front of his desk, dreading what was coming. I was proud of my tapes; I had worked hard at being a good NCO and Section Commander, and now ironically, I was probably going to lose them because I followed the instructions that I had been given in training.

The CO put his pen down, looked up at me and said, "Corporal Hudson, you did disobey a direct order, so I am punishing you with a severe reprimand, which will go onto your records. Dismissed!"

The RSM marched me out of the office, and once outside dismissed me to report back to my Company office with the result of the Orders.

I made my way back up the road to the Company office. I was quite happy with the result, because getting a severe rap could restrict my future promotions, but as a national serviceman I was already as high as I could get in an Infantry Battalion. I went into the Company office and relayed the result. Everyone seemed to be genuinely pleased that it was nothing worse, which made me feel a lot better. I was going to book in with my back for the MO's orders the following day, but I was informed that I had to go with my Bren gunner to Sungi Seput Police Station the following morning, to make out a Police Report on the shooting incident.

I left the company office and made my way back to my basha. I was ready to get changed into my shorts, put my flip-flops on and relax a little. It had been a tense few days for me, and of course the rest of the lads. I was thinking of winding them up when I got to the basha, but decided that over the last few days we had all had enough.

I walked through the doorway into the Corporal's hut. Most of the NCOs, and one or two of the lads were waiting for me to return. I told them immediately that I had got a severe dig but that was all. After explaining what happened, and also that I now had to go to the Police Station up in Sungi Seput the following morning, I went to the charwallah's for a coffee and a cigarette to try and get my head back together.

That afternoon, when the Battalion Orders of the day were posted on the notice-board, one of the orders was that, the practices of **'Not cocking'** a Bren gun on sentry post, will stop with immediate effect.

The following morning we were away up to Sungi Seput to make our report to the Malayan Police. We went in one of the Land Rovers. It was very pleasant driving through the Malayan countryside in an open top vehicle, on a clear hot sunny day. I was thinking that it was just over a week ago that I had finished my leave, but so much had happened in that time that it seemed more like a month had gone by. All that rest and relaxation that had made me feel so much better, had been blown into oblivion by just one bad week.

We arrived at the Police Station to make our report, which was necessary as Malaya was now an independent country. We spent approximately one and a half hours at the Police Station, before we set out to return to Colombo Camp. I have to say that it was white European Police Officers who questioned us, but I must tell you that I was shocked at their attitude. They made us feel and treated us as though **we** were the terrorists.

When we got back to 'B' Company lines, I found out that we had a briefing the following morning ready for the next jungle operation, which meant all my rest days between operations had been blown, so I had no chance of getting to see the MO without ducking out of the next jungle operation. I couldn't even think about doing that after what we had just been through.

Some of the lads may have thought that I was running away scared, which to be honest, I might have been, but for many reasons I had to go back in, if only to be with the crazy gang who thought I was mad for running up the track towards the shooting, on my own, and without my jungle hat with the identifying flashes.

That should have been the end of Chapter Nine and the end of that Operation, but I must bring it to a close for you with the consequences.

## FOOTNOTE TO CHAPTER NINE

Some months later, we did hear that the diary was invaluable to Army Intelligence, as the CT to whom it had once belonged, had filled every day with information on movements, camps, pickup points and all the sort of good information that our operations were based upon.

Three weeks later, and about twenty miles to the North of that operation, the CT to whom the diary belonged was shot and killed in an Australian ambush. In his shoulder was a three-week-old bullet wound, that was probably caused by a .303 round from our guard's Bren gun. That would mean that when he was hit with the bullet, he would have been knocked onto his back, which explained how the items on the track fell from his backpack. It also explained how the bullet buzzed past my ear. When he fell and hit the ground, he must have unavoidably pulled the trigger, so firing a round that passed under the fallen tree and through the book that I was reading.

For many years after leaving the army having completing my national service, I was continually troubled with unexplainable stomach and back pains. After an especially bad period of pain my doctor sent me to the hospital for various tests that continued for some weeks. After failing to find the problem, I was finally sent for a series of x-rays just in case they would pick out something.

The specialist who studied the x-rays was Mr Garden who was the father of Graeme Garden, who is one of the famous Goodies in the TV series of the same name. The specialist told me that my problems were there because I had three completely crushed vertebrae in the lower part of my spine. He dated the injury back to the time when I was in Malaya. He also told me to make the best of life, because as I got older, the back and the pain would get worse. Unfortunately he was right!

Do you remember at the beginning of the book I told you about strange coincidences? Well what about this one? About five years after finding out about the damage that was caused to my spine by the bomb in Malaya, I was talking to a BAC test pilot who lived in Wrea Green. It turned out that he was an Ex RAF Wing Commander who served in Malaya at the same time as myself. I told him about the injury that I had received on an unexploded bomb. He asked me to describe the area and the bomb. It turned out that he was the pilot who had dropped the bomb. Now isn't that an amazing twist of fate?

Whilst this operation was the one to give me the most physical grief even still to this day, the one that was to give me the lasting nightmares for many years, is still yet to come.

# CHAPTER TEN
### *Chinese Voices in the Night. 4 Platoon Missing*

So once again it was the early hours of the morning, we were pulling away from Colombo Camp in the back of a three-tonner and I had the usual bad taste in my mouth. The lads were full of themselves before we set off, but they went unusually quiet once we got underway towards the drop-off point. I kept trying to think of something that would get them going, but nothing came to mind, so we reached the end of the journey and the drop-off point with everyone still in the same apprehensive mood.

We jumped off the three-tonners; and loaded ourselves up with all our gear. The weight wasn't too bad this trip, as we were only going in for three days, and we were only going into the jungle for about a mile. We were also going straight in with no old logging tracks for us to use, or for me to worry about.

We were the lead section this time. I had said at the pre-operational briefing that my section was going to do the lead-in, because we needed to do that; in order that all of us could get our acts back together after the last operation.

We set off through the plantations in an eerie sombre silence, that just wasn't normal for 4 Platoon. I really was beginning to worry about the lads. The jokers weren't joking, the send-up merchants weren't sending-up; everyone seemed to have withdrawn into the depths of their own thoughts and concerns. We reached the jungle edge and entered into the jungle darkness with which we had all become familiar over the past months. The jungle was kind to us on this operation; we made our way through the tropical forest with very little trouble, arriving at the base camp location sooner than expected.

We had set up the camp by mid-afternoon and everyone was busy making their own particular space more homely, by doing such things as building a table, or a bench to sit on, finding somewhere to hang their clothes undercover of the basha, all those resourceful kind of things.

A few of the lads helped the radio operator sort out the aerial for his receiving and transmitting unit. He was having trouble getting a radio signal to Colombo Camp from this location. My understanding of the situation from him was that it was all down to the mountains that surrounded us, and the wavelength of the aerial wire. It was actually all double Dutch to me, but the lads enjoyed listening to the radio at night, so they didn't mind helping the radio operator who was attached to the Loyals from the Signals Regiment.

In the evening after it had gone dark, any of the lads who wanted to listen to some pop music would go to the centre of the camp to where the radio operator was based, they would then share the headphones, one ear-piece to a lad. If a few of the lads wanted to listen together as a group to some particular programme, then they would hang up a couple of mess tins, hang the headphones into the tins and turn the volume up full. They were then able to just hear the radio from about three yards away. This allowed a little bit of home comfort in the middle of the black, and at times intensely menacing, jungle night.

Stand to time came around, and the lads were still very quiet, but I did hear the odd little bit of laughter which was a good sign. It was certainly better than the arguments that I had been expecting to erupt amongst them. I had my tot of rum put into my coffee that I had made prior to stand to. I had nearly finished drinking it when Bill Fish came to my basha.

"Are you coming to the camp centre for a chin-wag?" he asked.

I finished my coffee, then we both made our way there, stumbling and feeling our way through the darkness. The first indication that we were near to the centre was the soft glow of light from the control panel of the radio. There were about six of us sat on the ground next to the Officers' basha, talking quietly about this and that. The camp had somehow slipped into the darkness, and the low soft hum of conversation from around the camp had subdued slowly, then quietly vanished without notice. It had got to about 22:00hrs, and the next lad who would be on guard from ten to midnight was due. I was beginning to feel tired, so I was ready for heading back to my basha when somebody crawled up to us on his hands and knees.

I thought at first that it was the new guard. However it wasn't the replacement sentry, but one of the lads from the bottom end of the base camp.

He motioned to us to keep quiet whispering, "We've heard the Chinese just outside the camp."

My first thought was that it was a send-up, but he really looked too frightened for it to be that.

The Officer instructed the guard, "Go and see what is going on?"

I volunteered to go with him, asking him to give me the torch to use if needed. I wasn't really worrying about going down there, because the CTs were just the same as us, and didn't often move about in the jungle at night. It was too dangerous, and far too easy to get lost. I picked up my Patchet machine-gun, put the sling around my neck, then we set off to the bottom end of the camp. I could just make out in the blackness, that the lad who had come to tell us that something was amiss, was still crawling along on his hands and knees.

We got down to the bottom section of the camp, but as I made my way along the perimeter of that section of the camp I began to get worried. Even the hard men of the platoon were hiding behind the fallen logs and trees. Their weapons were in the ready to fire position.

I asked as many of the lads as I could where they thought the noises had come from? Then I went to the place on the perimeter vine nearest to that area. I passed the word along that I was going to shine the torch into the jungle, but no one had to open fire unless I did. By this time the fear of the lads had gripped hold of me; I was now terrified of what might happen when I turned on the light, because I would obviously be the number one target. Don't start thinking that I was being brave, because I wasn't! My legs started to shake with the fear that was building up inside me, which was getting worse by the second. I thought that if I don't do it now I will lose my nerve altogether.

I had found a friendly tree to stand behind, so I cocked my Patchet and held it in my right hand with the safety catch off, and my finger on the trigger. In my left hand was the torch, with my thumb poised ready on the switch. I poked my gun around the right hand side of the tree, along with half of my right eye, before extending my left hand to the left of the tree, and as far to the left as my arm would allow. I think that I managed to get my hand about ten feet away from my body; well I know that's not possible; but I certainly **tried** for ten feet.

I gritted my teeth, shut my eyes tightly for a second, then opened them and switched on the torch. There was nothing, absolutely zilch, except for the trees and undergrowth. I shouted softly to everyone to hold their fire, and to make sure their safety catches were on. I then told everyone to stand up and come to the perimeter to see if they could see anything moving?

One or two had managed to get hold of a spare torch, and a few of the lads would take small torches into the jungle, and these were all now shining into the jungle darkness. The lads were now talking quite loudly; all the fear that was so apparent a few moments ago, had vanished into the night.

I picked up a lump of wood and threw it at a nearby bush, just in case there were any wild animals that had made the sounds and were still lurking around. All the lads followed my lead and started throwing lumps of wood and stones into the darkness to frighten off anything that could still be hanging around. I sent the night guard back up to the camp centre to report that there was nothing to worry about, and that it was probably a wild pig that the lads were now chasing off.

Next I went along the line checking each lad, just to make sure that their weapons were unloaded and safe. I certainly didn't want to be on COs orders again because I had failed to do something. As I made my way along the line, two things were very noticeable, one was a new respect for me, after the ordeal of the last op for still having the courage to shine the light into the jungle. I didn't enlighten them to the fact that if anything at all had moved out there, I would probably have fainted. The second, and more important factor, was that they were all laughing and pulling each other's leg. The nerve-tingling moments, followed by the lights from the torches, and the shouting, had not only rolled back the darkness and the fear, but had also rolled away the pessimistic cloud that had descended on 4 Platoon.

I went back to the camp centre to let them know what was happening at the bottom end of the camp, then went to my basha to make another mug of tea to help settle my nerves, which were still on a high jangle after the last fifteen minutes. I filled the mess tin with water, put it onto the cooking stove that I had already lit, then got a cigarette out of my tin and bent down to light it from the cooking stove.

As I stood back up I saw something that made me grab my machine gun, cocking it and flicking off the safety catch as I brought the gun to my shoulder in one swift and well-practised movement. Bobbing up and down and coming towards me through the jungle was the pale light of a torch. I can still remember distinctly the thoughts that flashed through my head. As far as I knew, no one else in the camp had seen the torchlight, so I was on my own.

I thought do I open fire now and so warn the camp, or wait until they were nearer to me and in a position where I could not miss? As I was trying to make up my mind the torchlight went down to ground level and then around my legs. I could not believe it, but I had mistaken a firefly for the light from a torch. Obviously such was the state of my nerves at that time. If there had been lots of fireflies around then I would probably have realised right away that it was a firefly, but that was the only one I saw in that base camp.

The rest of that operation went as planned without problems, and the third day saw us heading back out to the rendezvous point for the transport to take us back to Colombo Camp in Ipoh. When it arrived, the drivers had a shock for us, greeting us with the news that in a week or two we were going to Hong Kong. We confirmed with the drivers that it wasn't just 4 Platoon going, which is what we thought the drivers first meant, but it was all of the battalion, and we were going for a month.

Like the rest of the lads I was thinking this was wonderful. It was a place that I had always fancied visiting but never thought that I would ever get the chance. Now we were all going to be paid to go there. The journey back to Ipoh was full of talk about our forthcoming trip, with all the little titbits of what anyone knew about Hong Kong thrown in for good measure, but in reality none of us really knew a great deal about the place.

I got more information about Hong Kong at the operational de-briefing in the 'B' Company Office. We were going mainly for a rest and retraining in European Warfare, but we were also going to be trained in the riot drills, as we would be going out on riot patrols in Hong Kong. Apparently the year before there were a few small-scale riots from both the Nationalists and the Communists on their relevant special days, which were only a few days apart, and we would be there on these particular days to give support to the local garrison.

I was to be the 2.5 Anti Tank Rocket Launcher Instructor for 'B' Company, and that was to be my only job in Hong Kong. I had to pick up the manuals for the 2.5 launcher (BAZOOKA) and study them. After the next operation I was to attend a training course on the 2.5 Bazooka.

We had, or should I say that I had, my normal in-between operations rest this time. Everyone was talking about going to Hong Kong for a month, and we were all looking forward to the break away from Malaya, which was going to be most welcome. We were having a four-day break this time between operations, which was more relaxing, and on the second day I was lying on my bed after returning from the Kinta Swimming Baths after an afternoon swimming. I was reading a book when I heard someone shouting.

"Fire, Fire!"

I jumped up and dashed out of the basha to see what was happening, and sure enough over the other side of the football field rose black smoke from a fire. I dashed back into my basha, got my camera from out of my locker, checked that there was some film left in it, then dashed back out making my way towards the trouble.

The fire wasn't in the Loyals' part of the camp, but in a supply section belonging to one of the support Regiments.

Four of the huts and their contents had been destroyed by the time the fire had been brought under control. It was one of the things that always worried me in our camp (THE LOYALS COLOMBO CAMP) because all of the living quarters were made out of dried attap leaves, which would make it very difficult to put out a fire if one started. As the huts were so close together it would have meant that a fire would quickly spread from hut to hut. Fortunately that was one problem we never had to face, for it would have been an impossibility to replace our personal effects if we had suffered that fate.

With the trip to Hong Kong looming there was a very relaxed atmosphere about the camp. That night Bill Fish, one or two of the other lads and myself went into Ipoh to one of the air-conditioned cinemas, then afterwards for a Chinese chicken curry in one of the restaurants that tended to be frequented by lads from the Loyals. I remember wearing my blazer, because the last time that I had visited the cinema I had felt the chill. The only trouble with the air-conditioning, was that when you came out of the cinema the heat hit you, and it took a good few minutes to re-acclimatise to the temperature.

The following day was spent getting back into our normal Malayan routines. We totally forgot about the dream of Hong Kong, as we were thrown back into the realities of fighting a war of stealth, and back into the middle of the unbounded Malayan jungle. That operation was totally different to anything that we had done before, and I never did find out why? No doubt it would be based on some titbit of information that seemed to indicate that maybe there would be a result from doing it.

We went about two miles into the jungle and built our jungle base camp next to a suitable stream. The operation was to consist of four days of ambushing in the jungle. All the platoon's available personnel were on ambushing, and we all went out from the base camp together as one unit, then got dropped off in small groups of four, about one or two-hundred yards apart, and as far as we could stretch along a ridge, which was located into the jungle, and about a mile away from our base camp.

We would set out from the base camp immediately after breakfast and make our way to the ridge. We would then walk through the first ambush position, dropping off four of the lads at that point. The procedure would be repeated every one or two-hundred yards, until the last four men reached the furthest point that could be managed with the men available. Obviously there was no problem in dropping everyone off, but we had to be more than cautious when the procedure was reversed at the end of the afternoon, because that entailed walking back into each ambush setting. The ambushes were kept in place until very late in the day. The last ambush in position was the first one to move, but they did not lift until 17:00hrs. Then they had to pick the other positions up on the way back which meant by the time we got back to the jungle base camp, we had very little time before stand to and darkness to do everything that required doing.

I had the next to last ambush position; I must say that it was a bit peculiar ambushing in the jungle and not on a track or pathway. Instead of concentrating your eyes and mind on one particular spot, you had to keep looking all around the whole time. The jungle in this area was comparatively thin, and I suppose it could be compared to a dense British forest, which meant there were several spots around us where the Communists could appear at any time.

The first day went okay, although it was a long and boring day's ambushing. We had to be careful with our water, because we had no chance of refilling our bottles until we got back to the base camp. It was a case of a small sip from the water bottle when the need arose. Most of us would carry the daily sweet ration and the chewing gum, which helped to stave off the pangs of hunger, and we would usually have a small tin of cheese or a tin of cold beans about midday, along with a cigarette that also helped to keep hunger at bay.

It was getting late afternoon, and the jungle was beginning to darken as the sun, which we could not see, dropped down towards the horizon that lay behind the mountain tops over to our left. The 17:00hrs deadline arrived, and with relief we stood up and put our packs on ready to leave as soon as the last ambush party made contact with us. About five minutes later we heard them whistle to us from outside our ambush position. They appeared within a few seconds of hearing my respond whistle, which informed them that we knew they were there, and that it was safe to approach us.

There was never at any time in the jungle or Colombo Camp any of the traditionally perceived bull of, 'Halt who goes there, friend or foe, advance and be recognised'. Well I say *never,* but there was of course the occasional send-up.

As soon as they appeared at the edge of our ambush clearing we moved out on the opposite side heading for the next ambush position. As we got near to them, we slowed down from the top speed that we had been travelling through the jungle, to a more normal and safe pace.

It was a very daunting experience to be heading into an ambush position; even though they knew that we were due to be there. I gave a warning whistle, which they immediately answered, so we entered the small clearing, only to walk through it and follow those lads into the jungle on the other side, and so on to the next ambush. This procedure was followed through the rest of the positions until the platoon was fully reunited. We then made our way down into the valley that was behind us in the ambush positions, crossing over the river that was running down in the bottom, then scrambling up the other side of the valley to the animal track that followed the river all the way down to our jungle base camp.

When we arrived at the base we had just enough time to cook our evening meal and make a brew before the stand to and darkness arrived. I remember that there were still a few cooking stoves on the go in the darkness that followed. We certainly didn't have much time to do what had to be done. On top of making a meal, we had to clean and oil our weapons, carry water up to our bashas from the water-point, wash our clothes and ourselves, our mess-tins, and all of that sort of thing. And don't forget that there was always the relentless removal of leeches, ticks and other creepy crawlies that seemed to just become part of one's way of life in the middle of the Malayan jungle.

The following morning I had quite a shock. I normally lit my cooking stove and put a mess tin of water on to boil for a brew immediately after stand to. That morning, fortunately for me, I was running a little late, so I hadn't had the time to do that. When I lifted my drinking mug out of the water bag in the daylight after stand to, there in the mug of water was a large, and very much alive brown scorpion. The lads who had the nearby bashas came to have a look at it, then I tossed it, along with the water, into the jungle undergrowth. For a long time after that I always had a good look into the water bag before sticking my hand in. I had enquired about the scorpions in Malaya after we had the incident with the green one, and my understanding was that it was very unlikely that a scorpion sting would lead to one's death, unless there was some illness or other weakness present in the person stung. I also knew that the lighter the colour of the scorpion the less venomous, with a black one being the most dangerous, but nevertheless any sting would cause you to become very ill.

That day's ambushing was just a repetition of the previous day, with the platoon strung out in the same positions, and with the same people manning them. The day was another of the arduous ambushing state of affairs that everyone in the Loyals had to endure. We were all relieved when 17:00hrs arrived, and we could stand-up and stretch our legs within the confines of the jungle clearing. At 17:05hrs we were ready for the whistle from the last ambush lads, and we waited quietly listening intently. 17:05hrs turned to 17:30hrs with still no sign or sound from the lads from out of the next ambush position. 17:30 became 17:45 hours, yet there was still no sign of the lads. I was now very concerned, because I could think of no reason as to why they had not arrived at our position. If there had been any shooting we would have heard it with us not being too far away from them. I was now wondering what to do? Should I take my lads to the ambush position and find out what had gone wrong, or should I keep waiting? I considered the options that were open to me, stop where I was until it was too late to do anything because of the darkness which was now approaching fast, go to their position to find out what was wrong, or abandon them and carry out the fixed plan of heading back to base camp and picking up the other ambush positions. The NCOs in command of those positions must now themselves be considering what move to make.

I had just made the decision to go and find out what had gone wrong, when we heard their whistle from outside the clearing. I think that we all whistled back in reply, and as they dashed into our open space we dashed out at the other side, heading for the next ambush position, with them hot on our heels. We didn't bother too much about not making any noise as it was late in the day, and I got the message back that the Platoon Sergeant's wristwatch had started running slow, and they only realised what had happened when it started to go dark. When we got to the other ambush positions they were all still in place as we had been, and worrying about what to do and what had happened? Nobody stopped to discuss what had gone wrong. We were running far too late in time to stop for anything, but the message was passed back and forth from man to man along the line of the platoon as to what had gone wrong.

As we crossed the river in the bottom of the valley, and started the climb up the other side to get to the track that would take us back to the base camp, we knew that we were in trouble. That side of the valley was in the shadow of what was left of the daylight that was still coming over the horizon. When we reached the path we could hardly see the man who was immediately in front, nor the man behind us.

We had progressed along the track for about five minutes when the order was given by the Sergeant to stop. He had decided that it was too dangerous to proceed any further in the closing down darkness that was now approaching the pitch black of the jungle night. There was a small clearing where we were which was about the size of a medium bedroom, and forming part of the track. It was decided that we would all spend the night there sitting in a tight group, resting as best as we could. We didn't bother having a sentry on duty; no one was going to get much sleep, and a lot of the lads talked the night away.

We had two main problems, one was that all sorts of wild animals could come walking into us; after all we were on a track that was created by large wild animals who followed the river up and down looking for prey. But the lads talking and smoking would have taken care of that problem. The other was that we were all short of water.

We did an assessment as soon as we stopped to check the amount of water that we had per lad. We did this by simply shaking each water bottle. It worked out at less than an eighth of a water bottle to each person, which was just less than half a cupful per lad. This meant that we could just keep our mouths moist until we made the base camp in the morning. Perhaps half a cup of water doesn't sound too bad to see the night out, but remember that our Malayan jungle night was a hot twelve hours long, and we had been conserving our water all day, with the expectancy of replenishing our bodies with water at the base camp in the late afternoon. I suppose that we had learnt to live somewhat like camels, drinking a lot when it was readily available, but only taking sips when it wasn't, so as to conserve the water we were carrying.

The night passed with relative peace; there was a gentle hum of conversation throughout the night, which I heard on waking from the catnaps that I managed to get. Also in the darkness there was always the glow of a cigarette, which was somehow very reassuring within the black and unknown surroundings full of fear-provoking sounds, and that try as we may, we could never put a name to. During the night I wondered what sort of panic there would be back at Colombo Camp? It must have been an unusual radio message to receive, that 4 Platoon had failed to return to the jungle base camp from a simple ambushing operation. No doubt it brought up the habitual fear that something always happens when least expected, but I was going to have to wait to find out what was thought about our failure to arrive back at the base camp.

Day dawned, and when we were able to see clearly in the early morning light we immediately set off for the base camp lower down the valley. I took the lead with my section, and travelling at top speed we arrived near to the base camp location within twenty minutes. I brought my section down to a slow pace, as I didn't know what sort of response to expect from the sentry. Well that's not quite accurate. I knew what I expected from the guard on duty, even though we were some fourteen hours late. The unknown to me was, with us having gone missing; how much on edge were their nerves, and how light or otherwise, were the fingers on the triggers.

It was a great relief when my whistle was answered immediately, and when we got to the sentry position to find that the Platoon Officer, who had remained in camp, had sensibly put two lads on guard together, so as to relieve the pressure on the lookout. The relief of the few lads we had left in the base camp was clear; they had obviously been very concerned when we didn't return the previous night. It turned out that they expected us well into the night, and had placed guards out on the track with torches until a 20:00hrs deadline.

A message was immediately transmitted to Colombo Camp that all personnel had returned safely, so the operation was to progress as normal, and the lads back in Ipoh who were as I understood on standby to come and search for us, were stood down.

The first thing that we did, as you would guess, was to put a mess tin of water on the cooking stove for a brew. We were all gasping for a drink, but we had to wait for the water to boil before we could manage to have one. We couldn't just drink the water that was available to us, because it was polluted with whatever type of life or disease was present in the region. Once the water reached boiling point, we had to let it remain boiling for at least ten seconds to ensure that all the nasty bugs had been destroyed, and only then could we use it to make a mug of tea, or pour it into our aluminium water bottles to cool ready for drinking.

*Please note here that after our time, it was discovered that more than twenty minutes of boiling were actually needed to kill all the bugs.*

However then, we nearly always filled our water bottles with boiled water, which to me was always the easiest and cleanest way, although we did carry a small tin with purifying tablets. The tin held two glass bottles of tablets, one with blue tablets and the other with white tablets. What we had to do was to fill our water bottle to the top, then drop one purifying tablet inside, put the top on then give it a good shake. We had to let it stand for half an hour, then put the other tablet in and give the bottle another good shake, letting it stand for another five minutes before it was fit to drink.

The second tablet was to take away the taste of the first tablet, but that didn't seem to work as the water always tasted horrible. My wife used to send me a parcel of strawberry fruit crystals to add to a bottle of drinking water, in order to make the boiled water palatable.

When the mug of tea was made and ready for drinking, we then made the meal that we should have had the night before. We were of course hungry as well as thirsty, but in Malaya we did find out the reality, that you can go without food for a long time, but you cannot go without water. In the short time that we had in the base camp, meals were made and eaten, drinks were made and drunk, water was boiled and water bottles filled, clothes were changed and washed, weapons were stripped, cleaned and oiled, and the ammunition was checked and reloaded, plus all the other little bits and bats that we needed to do.

We had arrived in the base camp at about 07:00hrs, and at 08:30hrs we were heading back out from the base camp and to the ambush positions. Even though we had lost a night's sleep, the ambush operation continued as normal. It turned out to be just another boring day's ambushing, and we all had difficulty keeping awake. By the time 16:45hrs arrived, we all stood up and got ready to leave. We had decided on the way to the ambush positions that morning, that we would lift the ambush at 16:45hrs, instead of the pre-arranged 17:00hrs. It would just give us those few minutes extra to do everything that we needed to do, and everyone was happy with that arrangement. Everything worked as planned this time, so we made it back to base camp in nice time to do all we needed to do. At stand to that night, everyone who had been out of the camp the night before got a much welcomed double ration of rum. That on top of missing the previous night's sleep, meant that we all slept like logs. The following day's ambushing was just normal with nothing unusual happening.

The day after we were heading out of the jungle, and Hong Kong was back on the discussion agenda. Back in Colombo Camp the preparations were well in hand for our departure to Hong Kong, which was to be the following week. After our two days of rest and recuperation following the jungle operation, I was on the training course for the Bazooka rocket launcher. It was quite interesting, with it being a weapon that was totally different to any that I had previously experienced. But to be honest I got the feeling that the instructor's course was to be of no importance when we got to Hong Kong. We had no rockets for the single weapon that we had, so none of us would ever get the chance to fire a rocket.

When we got to Hong Kong my initial feelings proved to be correct for the rocket launcher wasn't even mentioned, but I didn't complain, because it gave me more time to myself, and after all we did go to Hong Kong for rest as well as retraining! The course on the rocket launcher only lasted for the day. I imagined that all we had to do now was to get ourselves ready for the trip to Hong Kong in a week's time, but that was not to be as the next day I found myself on plantation patrols, but unusually this time with the full platoon including Mr Kelly (Lieutenant), our Platoon Officer.

The operation seemed a bit meaningless, and I think that it was a case of making our presence known to the villagers before we left for a month, and getting us away from Colombo Camp.

What is the saying? *'Idle hands make work for the devil.'*

On one of the days that we were out on patrol, we were due to cross over a river and check out one of the Aboriginal Villages on the other side, but the only way to get there was going to be by crossing the river in a dugout canoe. We managed to attract the attention of some of the natives on the other bank, and two of them paddled over to see what we wanted?

We explained the best way we could, that we wanted them to transfer us to the other side in their canoes. Several of us had been weighing up the canoes, while the discussions were taking place on transferring all of us over to the other side, and we had our doubts about the dugouts being able to carry the weight. The dugouts were well down in the water with two natives sat in them, and the Aborigines are a very small race, and I must say that they were always very nice and friendly towards us, and always seemed to smile whenever we saw them.

After much discussion it was decided to try the heaviest load first, which turned out to be 'Bill' Bailey, one of the Bren gunners. The Bren gunners were always the big lads of the platoon, and they nearly always got the short straw when something like this was in the offing. The canoe was about four feet below us down a steep bank, and holding just the one native to paddle, so we lowered Bill down and into the dugout. He sat down very carefully, but the canoe was very close to sinking, for there really was only about an inch of canoe showing above the water at one point.

Some of the lads of 4 Platoon had seen that, and realised the likely outcome, but before any of us NCOs could say, 'You had better get out very carefully Bailey', the lads had quickly passed down his Bren gun and ammunition. I will never forget the look on his round and always cheerful face, as the canoe sank under him to the strains of *'Rule Britannia, Britannia rules the waves'* whistled and sung by most of the lads.

Bill Bailey then had the problem of hauling himself out from the river. It wasn't too deep next to the riverbank, probably about four feet, but the bank was about four feet high and at a very steep angle. The lads had taken his Bren gun and ammunition back as soon as the boat began to sink, but pulling Bill Bailey out was a different proposition. The lads were after extracting all sorts of promises from the big friendly guy before they would pull him up the bank.

I suppose that moment summed up the mood of 4 Platoon just prior to leaving Ipoh and the Malayan jungle for a month, and heading for the safety and bright lights of Hong Kong. There was one bad moment for 'B' Company before we left; all of the battalion were in camp waiting for the move to Hong Kong. It was the first time that I had known Colombo Camp to be full, and of course this meant that the dining-room and NAAFI were also filled to capacity.

A lot of the lads would go down into Ipoh for their night out and a quiet drink, and one of our Corporals, belonging to 5 Platoon was no exception. It was three nights before we were due to leave for Hong Kong. Cpl Jim Melvin had gone into Ipoh to visit the cinema and to have a quiet drink. The following morning we were informed that he had been shot in the back by a Chinese man. I never did find out just what had happened to Jim, apart from that fact that he returned to the 'B' Company 5 Platoon basha just before we left for Hong Kong. He was wearing a large plaster over a wad of lint dressing to the wound on his back right shoulder, that had been caused by a shot from a revolver, but apart from that he looked fine. His trip to Hong Kong was cancelled due to his medical condition, but I got the impression that he wasn't unduly worried about that, and was looking forward to the peace and quiet of Colombo Camp without the battalion.

Jim probably holds the distinction of being the last Loyal Regiment soldier to be shot wearing the Loyals' cap badge, because in Hong Kong, the Loyal Regiment became a part of the 'Lancastrian Brigade'. But I and the rest of the lads were still 'LOYALS' despite the new cap badge.

# CHAPTER ELEVEN
## *Hong Kong and Riot Patrols*

Our train bringing the battalion down from Ipoh, arrived at the dockside in Singapore We walked slowly over from the train to the ship, joining the queue to climb up the gangway and go on board. Everyone was loaded up with the army issue of small packs and backpacks, and of course the familiar and very full kit bag. The ship that we were about to board was the troopship *SS Oxfordshire*. She was completely white, except for a wide blue line high up on the boat, and she weighed in at approximately 28.000 tons, which was quite large then, but may be classed as a mini now.

Soon we were on board with our bunks sorted and our gear stowed away. Everyone was wandering around the boat to find out where everything was, discovering the general layout of the boat. The popular spots were the ice-cold fresh water drinking fountains, where we had to queue to get a drink. It tasted wonderful after the warm polluted water that we had been used to drinking in the jungle. The lads who had travelled from the UK and out to Malaya on board one of these troopships, were looking forward to sampling the British beer that was sold on board.

Two hours later everyone was leaning on the rails to watch as we left the quayside, sailing away from Singapore and bound for Hong Kong, which was three day's sail away. On board ship there were film shows every night on the open deck, and the food was very good, but apart from that the boat trip was very boring, so most of the time was spent reading or playing cards.

Another of my amazing coincidences occurred on the last night before arriving in Hong Kong. We were issued with a meal card on boarding, as the dining area only held so many troops at one time. I was leaning on the deck rail waiting for my meal, just standing and looking down at the water, watching the flying fish jumping in and out of the South China Sea. I had been leaning there for about five minutes, when I looked at the lad next to me leaning on the rail and got a real shock.

Standing there with his hands on the rail, also watching the fish jumping, was Stanley Worthington, a lad who I knew well from my old hometown of Kirkham. Stan was an electrician, and we had worked together many times during the previous five years while we were serving as apprentices. Stan worked for an electrician called Freddie Ireland, whose wife was the manageress of a confectioner's shop that stood on the corner of Kirkgate and Poulton Street in Kirkham.

About eighteen months before I started going out with my wife Betty, Stan and I were working near to the confectioner's shop, and Stan got his afternoon brew from his boss's wife, Mrs Ireland. Stan forgot to take the tray and teapot back to the shop, and so Mrs Ireland sent the young sixteen-year-old girl assistant to retrieve the teapot and tray. I will never forget that lovely sixteen-year old girl, who was blushing like a pink English rose at having to come into a room full of workmen to ask for the tray. That was the very first time that Betty and I saw each other, I would never have guessed then that three years later we would be married.

Stan was as pleased and surprised to see me as I was him. We had a good chat; it turned out that he was doing his national service with the Engineers and he was based in Singapore, and was going to Hong Kong on a fortnight's leave. I explained that I was with the Loyals and that we were going to Hong Kong for a month's rest and retraining.

He replied, "That explains to me why there are so many Loyals on board ship."

When it was our turn to enter the dining area. I said, "I'll see you later," expecting us to have another chat about old times before we docked in Hong Kong, but sadly I have never seen nor heard of Stan Worthington from that day to this.

One of the problems with national service was, that in those days, many good and close friendships were torn apart for at least two years, and with the years of enforced void, and all the various other reasons that do occur in life, contacts were never regained.

Hong Kong itself is an island just off the Chinese mainland, and a part of the mainland was also a part of the Colony. The harbour was between the island and the mainland, and also between the two Cities that formed the major part of the Colony of Hong Kong. On the island stood Victoria City, while on the mainland was Kowloon City, which is where our ship docked.

It didn't take us long to disembark. We had to form up on the quayside in our respective Companies. All our packs and kitbags were loaded onto the familiar three-ton Bedford army trucks. The full battalion was then marched through the Kowloon streets to the railway station, where we boarded the train that was waiting to take us to Fanling village in the North, which was to be our new home for the next month.

Fanling was a small Chinese village near to the border with Red Communist China. The mainland that formed that part of the Colony was called 'The New Territory'. Here is another of those amazing twists of fate: Quite often I would go for a curried chicken take-away from a shop in Bamber Bridge that was owned and run by a Chinese family. One evening while the shop was devoid of other customers, I was chatting to Janet, the daughter of the owners. and it turned out that she was born in Fanling Village at the very same time that I was stationed there.

The train took us up to Fanling and along a part of the coast of the mainland of the New Territories. It was about fifteen miles from Kowloon City; I remember that Hong Kong Island and the New Territories seemed to be very mountainous. We arrived at Fanling Railway Station and were met by the familiar camouflaged green-painted three-ton Bedfords. Once aboard the trucks we were driven from the railway station, through the village to our camp, which would be about one and a half miles from the station. I can remember that we passed over a small Bailey bridge, which was within the confines of the village.

The camp was to the right-hand side of the road on the outskirts of Fanling, and as we drove through the main gates, the guardhouse was in front and slightly to the left, and about fifty yards in from the main entrance. To the left of the camp was a steep hillside and the 'B' Company Lines (Barrack rooms and offices), were to the extreme left of the camp built on the hillside.

The Company Office and Quartermasters Stores were situated at the bottom of the hillside, and to the right of the road that led to the hillside and the 'B' Company barrack rooms. To the left of the road and opposite the Company Office, was a small parade ground known as the snake pit. This was a little piece of China that we were going to get to know quite well.

Perched on the hilltop and standing on its own, was the barrack room that was to be home for a month for all the 'B' Company Corporals, but unfortunately for the NCOs, that situation wasn't going to last. I have absolutely no idea where or how the other Companies of the battalion were billeted within the camp. 'B' Company was over to the left and out on its own. In the time that we were there I never entered into the rest of the camp.

The first night in camp was okay, it was like being on leave as there was no undue threat. We had been worried about being cold with the temperature being well down after Malaya, but we had been issued with an extra blanket, so I think we all slept fine for the whole of the time that we were in Hong Kong. The first day was going to be general training for everyone, but there was no sign of a two-point-five anti-tank rocket launcher, nor the course for me, so I went down to the Company Office to see what there was for me to do, and was given my first job in Hong Kong. I was given an amount of the local Hong Kong dollars from the Company petty cash, and then I headed down into Fanling Village to buy various sized paintbrushes, a tin of Royal blue and a tin of Canary yellow paint, which were the 'B' Company colours.

Two points of interest from this trip were how much wealthier we were in Hong Kong compared to Malaya. We received nearly ten dollars to the pound there, as against nearly four dollars to the pound in Malaya, and on top of that, everything in Hong Kong was far cheaper. The other point of interest was the mode of travel from the camp to the village, which consisted of a pillion seat on the back of a standard bicycle. I went through the main gates of the camp that morning planning on walking down into the village, and was met by about a dozen of these contraptions all touting, or should I say *pedalling* for business at the main gate.

"Well it beats walking," I thought, so I singled out the Chinese guy who looked the strongest, and off we went, down the road over the Bailey bridge, and about four minutes later we arrived at the shops in Fanling. I walked along the row of shops, and went into the one that looked the most promising. Within fifteen minutes I was on the back of a bicycle, and on my way back to the camp loaded up with tins of paint and brushes to create all the 'B' Company signs that where required around the Company lines.

Once I had dropped the purchases off at the Company office I was free to do what I wanted, so I spent the rest of the day writing to Betty and the rest of my family, and reading. It quickly became clear why we were in Hong Kong, rest and retraining were part of it without doubt, but the main motivating factor was that we would be there for the big celebration days of both the Nationalist Party and the Chinese Communist Party, as they fell within a few days of each other.

Apparently before we arrived in Hong Kong, the newspapers there were full of the Loyals' achievements in Malaya. We were described in the local media as a force that had to be paid the utmost respect, or suffer the penalty, something like the media attention that the SAS receive today. It also explained the reason for the Loyals being marched through Kowloon from the quayside to the railway station, to let the local inhabitants know that we had arrived.

In the previous year there had been a few small scale riots between the two main protagonists, and the intelligence services in Hong Kong believed that they were just the rehearsal for the following year when the lid was going to blow off. The answer was to bring in some backup that was used to action, so the Loyals were the perfect answer, along with the glorifying media blitz that had preceded us.

After two or three days of arriving in Fanling we started anti-riot training drills on our small parade ground, the snake pit. There were two main I A. (Immediate action) drills that we practised, one was for when we marched down a street where there may be possible rioters, whilst the other was for when we were facing a mob of people who were rioting.

The drills basically consisted of carrying out a lot of armed military movements as a platoon, but with only just one word of command being given by the Platoon Officer to start the ball rolling. The idea was that such a professional and imposing military machine, with everyone knowing exactly what to do without being told, would frighten the rioters into behaving, but we were told that the last option would nearly always work; a white chalk line drawn across the street, and anyone crossing the line was told that they would be shot.

I found that I really enjoyed the I.A. drills, and it always gave me a lot of pleasure to see 4 Platoon performing just like a well-oiled clockwork motor, twenty-six movements, and all without any further words of command after the first order had been given. Of course it wasn't all like a well-oiled machine at the beginning of training, and we did have a good few laughs along the way, but 4 Platoon's I.A. drill was eventually good and polished, and it was ready for use if the first call ever came.

We had been in Fanling for about a week and a half when we had our first proper encounter with Kowloon. We had been informed that we would be spending two nights in the City, so we were packed accordingly when we climbed aboard the two three-tonners that were to carry 4 Platoon down into Kowloon. It was quite a large convoy of lorries that carried all of the Loyal Battalion Platoons who were going to be involved in keeping the peace operations in Kowloon, and we got underway from the camp at about 09:30hrs that morning.

It was only about fifteen miles to Kowloon, and we were in the outskirts of the City after about half an hour. We had arrived through a small pass, and then, for some reason, just through the pass, the convoy of lorries stopped on the roadside for a good half-hour or more. We had stopped at a place where we could look along the road and down the hillside, looking into Kowloon and over the harbour and the various bays that were below us.

It was a hot sunny morning, at that moment it felt to me like one of those warm lazy English summer days that you sometimes have, when everything seems to be just part of a dream that is drifting around you. The atmosphere was as clear as a bell, which was very characteristic of the weather that we had for all of our stay in the New Territories. I don't remember it raining at all during our time there, although it probably did.

I could see Hong Kong Island and Victoria City clearly, and the harbour between the mainland and the island was full of Naval and Merchant vessels. Just below, and to the left of Kowloon City, was the airport, with the long runway stretching out into Hong Kong Bay and the South China Sea. The world famous Star Ferry boats were clearly visible, scurrying across the harbour between Kowloon and Victoria City, and I decided then that at the first opportunity I would sail across to Hong Kong on one of the Star Ferry boats.

Many of the ships in the harbour were American Navy vessels, which was due to Korea still rumbling, and the war in Vietnam just kicking off for the Yanks, and Hong Kong was an obvious, and very handy staging post for them. There were several large white boats in the port, and it was clear that they were passenger ships which would be bringing the international tourists who were just beginning to visit destinations throughout the world such as Hong Kong. Air travel had not yet made its mark on the tourist trade, and fast flying passenger jet planes were still a dream to be delivered at a later date, although the Comet jet airliner had started flying a passenger service on middle distance flights.

The message was passed along that we were now ready to roll, and a few seconds later we were heading down the road and into Kowloon City. The one thing that remains vivid in my mind about the outskirts of Kowloon on that first morning, were all the high-rise apartment buildings built into each, and every available space. All of the flats appeared to have their own little balconies, and each balcony seemed to have its own quota of children's faces peering through the railings from beneath the multitude of washing that fluttered from every dwelling in the gentle morning breeze. It somehow made me feel at ease with these people, who were trying to live and bring up their children in what appeared to me to be, a clean, normal and respectful way of living. I was praying that we would not have to wield the big stick against any of them in the days to come.

The battalion was scattered all around Kowloon. I suppose it was a case of wherever there was room for the Loyals. 'B' Company was billeted in a small collection of Nissen huts that were built by the side of the bay on the South East corner of Kowloon, and a few yards away from the famous Hong Kong Peninsula Hotel. It didn't take us long to each sort out a bunk in one of the huts, and then it was back onto the three-tonners. While we were sorting out our beds the drivers had removed the canvas covers from the three-tonners so the backs were now open.

We were now in full view of the general population as we sat in the backs of the lorries on the bench seats, which were down each side. We were dressed in full best uniform, complete with the two belt ammunition pouches, steel helmets, and rifles with fixed bayonets. Then all the platoons went their own way, driving around the streets of Kowloon and showing everyone, that we meant business. I remember driving around the airport, and the supply roads around the runway a few times.

There was one especially magnificent moment that I will never forget, I can see it all now in my mind's eye, just as if it had happened this morning. We had left our small camp in Kowloon for the first time, and of course we were on the first tour of Kowloon. We had been out on the road for about a half-hour, and we were in a narrow street in a busy section of the City that was packed with shops and people. We were slowly passing a jeweller's shop, and as the street was so narrow there was not a lot of room left on the pavement. The first three-tonner had just passed the shop, when a middle-aged, and obviously American couple came out of the door, both carrying some parcels. The guy was the defining model of the all-American wealthy middle-aged male, sporting a white Panama hat, and rimless glasses. He was overweight and red-faced; his flowered short-sleeved open neck shirt was loud against his check pants, black and white shoes and a massive cigar stuck between his teeth. I could see his face whiten as he saw the first lorry carrying part of 4 Platoon, and then as we drew level with him I saw his eyes drawn to the bayonets fixed to our rifles. He just managed to grab the cigar with his free hand, before it fell out of his mouth.

I was surprised at his reaction, as he looked at my white Corporals tapes and then at me, I could not resist giving him a wink and a big smile. If his reaction was anything to go by then, what we were doing was having some effect, and if it worked as well on the locals to prevent any trouble, then that was going to be really good.

We spent the full day just riding around and flying the flag, then it was back to our mini camp for the night. Our meals were brought to us in containers, just like meals on wheels. They were not over brilliant, but it could have been a lot worse. What we didn't like was that we were not allowed out of the small camp, which meant we had very little to do there.

The following day was a repetition of the first, except that we stayed out longer and into the evening, as it was the most likely problem day, but I didn't see any more shocked Americans. The third day was just a case of riding around Kowloon in the morning, then back to Fanling for a break and sorting out our gear.

As soon as we got back to the camp in Fanling I decided to put in for a weekend pass to visit Kowloon. I checked with Bill Fish to see if he fancied a weekend down in the City, and we both got a leave pass without any problems. Late on Friday afternoon we were back on the train, and on our way from Fanling Station to Kowloon. The journey didn't take long, and we were soon booked in to the YMCA, the forces centre in Kowloon, which was next door to the Peninsular Hotel, and also near to the small camp where we had been based a few days earlier. We had an early tea before visiting a large NAAFI forces centre that was near to the waterfront. It did have its own special name, which was something like *'The Cheerio Club'*.

It was a busy place, and there were more than a fair share of the Loyals in there. Apparently the beer was a lot cheaper than in the City, so we stayed for a couple of hours, then about ten of us, who were all 'B' Company lads, went out into the City to find a good Chinese restaurant, and in Kowloon that was not difficult. I can remember that we had a good laugh about nothing, just stupid little things, which indicated to me just how relaxed we had all become after unwinding from Malaya.

I slept well that night, and we were all up bright and early the following morning. After a good traditional English breakfast, Bill, a few of the other lads and myself set off to the Star Ferry Terminal. We didn't have far to walk as the ferry head was near to where we were staying. It probably took us about ten minutes of what was an interesting walk along the Chinese waterfront. It was amazing how many junks there were in the harbour, either sailing or moored to the quayside by the dozen, and all of them appeared to have large families living on board. Some of the boats that were tied to the quayside were dropping to bits and just not fit to be on the water. It was at that moment that I realised from where the saying *'a pile of junk'* might derive, but even they had large families living on board.

When we got to the ferry terminal there was already a boat loading, so we bought our tickets and went on board and were underway almost immediately. The waters of Hong Kong harbour were relaxing, as they soaked up the warm early morning sun which poured down from a clear blue sky, but the tranquil waters seemed to be out of step with all the activity that was taking place on the surface. There were dozens of ships anchored out in the harbour, or tied up at the various quays, and even more small vessels scurrying around the harbour. That was apart from the Star Ferry boat we were on, and the other Star Ferry boats that have for years scurried back and forwards across the harbour. It was very pleasant to be sitting on the ferry watching the Island draw near. Towering over the Island was Victoria Peak, which is nearly 2000 feet high.

Just before we got married and I joined the army, Betty and I saw a movie, which was called *'Love is a many splendored thing.'* It was about an American news reporter who married a Hong Kong Chinese girl and then got killed in the Korean war. I found myself whistling the theme tune to the movie many times during my stay in Hong Kong, and I was looking forward to taking the mountain railway to the top of Victoria Peak just as they had done in the movie. William Holden, a famous actor, was the star of the movie, and he was actually present in Kowloon making another movie while we were there. Some of the lads from the Loyals met him when they called into one of the Kowloon bars for a beer. He talked with them for an hour or more, and bought them all their beers, which was a kind thing for him to do, and that happened in the evening of this very day that I am now writing about.

We landed at the ferry terminal in Victoria City and decided to firstly visit a park, which I think was called Tiger Balm Gardens. Anyway it was a park that was full of sculptures of brightly coloured dragons, tigers and Buddhas and several lakes and waterfalls, all of which I would imagine to be typically Chinese. We left there about midday and made our way through Victoria City to the Peak tramway. The public transport that we used to get to Tiger Balm, and then to the Peak Railway Terminal were old red UK double-decker buses, which provided the public transport all around the City. This was quite a surprise to me, but I must say a pleasant one.

We all booked onto the Victoria Peak Railway, and away we went on what was a very steep, but enjoyable ride to the top of the peak. The views from there were splendid, and I took a few photos from the top. There were one or two policemen up there, and I had a chat and my photograph taken with one of them. There were also quite a few American sailors around, who were obviously from the Naval ships that we could see down in the harbour. We stayed on the top for about an hour before making our way back down into Victoria City where we found a place to eat. After that we made our way back to the ferry and over the waters of Hong Kong harbour to Kowloon. We went back to the Forces Centre, had a wash and brush-up, and then went out on the town for the night starting at the Cheerio Centre or whatever it was really called.

The following day Billy Fish and I had some business to attend to for 4 Platoon. We had found out that Mr M. A. Kelly (Lieutenant Kelly), our Platoon Officer was leaving the battalion when we got back to Malaya and returning to the UK and the home of the Loyals, Fulwood Barracks in Preston. He was a respected officer and well liked by every single member of 4 Platoon. Everyone had expressed their concerns on hearing that he was leaving us. We had held a collection amongst the platoon members, and every soldier put something into the pot. We had decided as a group that we would buy a gift in Hong Kong, where we would be able to get a better deal for our money. Billy and I were chosen to sort that out on behalf of the platoon, so that is what we were going to do that day.

We spent about an hour looking around Kowloon, in and out of different shops, then we entered one that seemed to be okay, and had a good selection of various gifts and also various types of drinking tankards, which is what we were thinking of getting for Mr Kelly.

A Chinese gentleman who was the proprietor, came over to us. From that moment, and for the next four hours we were engrossed in the Chinese art of bartering. It really was a most fascinating experience, and at the end of the day and several ice-cooled beers later, as provided by the proprietor, we all finished up good friends and with the gift that we wanted. Later that day we were on the train and heading back to the Camp at Fanling along with Mr Kelly's farewell gift from 4 Platoon.

Monday morning dawned and we were back to practising the I.A. drills, and that was probably because we were going back to Kowloon again in a few days. I think that the next event was for the Communists, because everyone was expecting trouble to break out during those celebrations. The following day was down to more practice. We all got finished early, and rather then everyone getting totally bored, we called it a day, well after all, we had been sent to Hong Kong for a rest as well as retraining.

One of the Lance Corporals, two or three of the lads and myself decided that night to go to the Garrison cinema, which was to the far side of Fanling. After tea we all got a bike ride each to the cinema. I don't remember the film that was showing, but I do remember that we were sat near to the back of the cinema. Sitting on the row in front were three or four Sergeants out of the Loyals, whose faces I knew vaguely. During the interval between films I was lighting a cigarette, when I accidentally dropped my cigarette lighter. Naturally I bent down and picked it up, and obviously thought nothing about doing that.

After the show we all headed back to the camp and went to the guardroom to book back into the camp, when incredibly all of us were immediately arrested and put into a cell. When I asked why, I was told that we would soon find out. I questioned the other lads in there with me, but everyone was completely in the dark as to what was going on, so we could only wait to find out the reason for our imprisonment.

About ten minutes later the Sergeants who had been sat in front of us, booked in, and then cleared off apart from one Sergeant who I knew to be from HQ Company. We were let out of the cell and all asked to empty our pockets. To cut a long story short, the Sergeant who was questioning us had been the one sat in front of me in the cinema. He had lost his wallet from out of his back pocket, and was accusing me of picking it up from the floor in the cinema and pinching it.

I had never in my life been so insulted, and became so angry with our treatment and his accusation, but I managed to keep control of my feelings at that moment. Of course like everyone else, I was relieved that we were being questioned about something that we, or I, had not done. I didn't sleep well that night, as I was still very angry about what had happened, and first thing the following morning I went to the Company Office and told the 'B' Company Sergeant Major (C S M Bull) what had happened the night before. He immediately took me in to see Major Stone who was our Company Commanding Officer, and I reported the matter to him. Typical of the army, I never heard anything about the matter again, nor did I ever see that particular Sergeant again. So what happened about the affair I really don't know. There was one thing about the affair that everyone, including myself, had thought about and agreed upon, and that was what sort of an idiot would carry a wallet in their back pants pocket with the strong chance of it falling out, not to mention all the pickpockets that were supposed to be around the Hong Kong area, and about whom we had all been warned.

Two or three days later all of the 'B' Company Corporals were in trouble. We had enjoyed the atmosphere of Hong Kong, and also living in the peaceful surroundings on top of the hill, and we were well away from any of the agro or noise that any army camp can at times generate. To be honest, we had relaxed **too** much. Most mornings, and when there was nothing much to do that day, we would still be in bed well after 07:30 hrs. We were supposed to be up and alive at 06:30hrs. but we had got that we didn't worry too much about that. That is until this particular morning when the CSM decided to pay us a visit to find out where all the 'B' Company Corporals had gone? We hadn't gone anywhere, we were still in bed!

Needless to say we were in trouble, and within an hour we were all back in the barrack rooms with our respective platoons, but that's all that happened to us and there was nothing ever mentioned again regarding the Corporal's inattentiveness. On reflection afterwards, I thought that Sergeant Major Bull was very lenient with us, but I think that he appreciated more than anyone, that back in Malaya we had been working hard and under difficult and hazardous conditions for the past few months. I spent one and a half years under the watchful eye of CSM Bull, and I must say that at the end of my army service, he was one of the people for whom I had the utmost respect. As a CSM he made sure that the army and the Battalion Orders were adhered to within 'B' Company. He managed this by being heavy-handed with plain commonsense, and I think that most of the lads in 'B' Company held for him the same high esteem that I felt for the man. We would never have dared to tell him that though.

A day or two later we were back in Kowloon for another three days, with two nights sleeping in the half-rounded corrugated steel Nissen huts. The routine was going to be the same, with the platoon riding around Kowloon with fixed bayonets wearing steel helmets. This time we were going to have the addition of members from the Hong Kong Police Force with us. Each platoon was allocated two or three policemen, who travelled around Kowloon with us on the patrols. I could never understand the purpose of placing the policemen with us, because none of them could speak English. The lack of the ability to communicate was to make life difficult for me, when for some reason unknown to me, I was given the job of looking after the welfare of all the policemen who were attached to the Loyal Battalion.

We had arrived at the harbour side mini camp early on the first morning of our second visit to Kowloon, then we went out on our flying the flag and bayonet routine. There was a change at lunch-time; instead of returning to the mini camp for a bite to eat, we went to a major barracks in Kowloon. The reason for visiting these barracks was to pick up the policemen who were going to be attached to the platoons. Also we were using the barracks for a freshly cooked meal for lunch.

I still haven't fathomed out why I was chosen to take care of the policemen's needs. One would have thought that it would have been a situation for at least someone of a Sergeant's rank, if not higher. Maybe someone knew that none of the Chinese policemen spoke a single word of English, or maybe someone had explained that Kirkham Grammar School taught Chinese, which of course they did, but only the diplomats sons! Not the language.

There would be about thirty of them altogether, and I was completely on my own. I had to try and explain where the toilets and washing facilities were to be found, then sort out the dining-room for them, plus cutlery and suchlike. Everything went quite well really, and we all had a good few laughs along the way. The dining-room was a self-service cafeteria layout, and I was scratching my head to a certain extent when it came to making sure that they all received the necessary cutlery. It soon became very clear to me that they were obviously not used to using knives and forks. How do you explain that one when you don't speak the same language? Fortunately a few of them actually carried their own chopsticks, which was the first time that I knew of the

Chinese custom to carry their own private eating utensils, which I suppose is very hygienic. But we all overcame that problem which again created a few laughs.

I was thinking, "Well it wasn't too bad, and we overcame the problems with very little trouble, so what can go wrong now?"

All *they* had to do was walk along the food counter and choose what food they liked. Lets face it; everyone knows what they like to eat. I could see from the back of the queue, and from where I was organising the eating utensils and trays for them, that they were choosing meals that looked fine, and were basically what I would choose myself. I went along the food counter last, feeling happy that everything had worked out okay.

My first misgivings came when I reached the end of the food counter and arrived at the sweets section. The lad who was serving the sweets, asked me if I would like rice pudding? He then looked up to heaven, then asked if I would like it on top of my chips just like everyone else?

"Oh no," I thought, looking around slowly, to check that they had done this.

Well that was it, there was nothing I could do except have my rice pudding on my chips, sit in the middle of them, and pretend that this was wonderful English food. To be honest it wasn't too bad, and I certainly had eaten a lot worse in the jungle back in Malaya, but I must admit that I have never tried it since. The things we used to do for Queen and Country in those days. Still it was an experience that has given me many a laugh since, and fortunately everything else went according to plan. But I was relieved when I handed the Hong Kong policemen over to their respective platoons.

The rest of the operation went according to plan, and the continuing high profile that we presented to the people of Kowloon must have done the trick, because there was no trouble at all whilst we were in Hong Kong. We headed back to Fanling after the second night in Kowloon; I think that we were all feeling a certain amount of satisfaction at a job well done.

Once back at the camp we sorted out our gear, before a few of us decided to visit the cinema again! Someone said that if there were any Sergeants sat in front, behind or to the side, we'd all move seats, so with that agreed, off we went to the NAAFI for a drink and then to the movies.

A couple of days later, the platoon spent the full day on the rifle range. We took a packed lunch for our midday meal. Normally there is nothing special to write about being on the firing range, but in the New Territories it really got a little bit frightening. We had been target shooting for about half an hour when the first local Chinese started to appear on the range after apparently hearing the firing. The frightening thing was, that they would appear on the butts behind the targets every time we stopped firing. They were digging the spent bullets out of the sand to sell on as scrap metal, and there were quite a few young children amongst them.

They had obviously done it all before, because when the next group lay down and prepared to fire, all the Chinese moved away to the sides. When the shooting was over they all poured back into the area behind the targets like a swarm of locusts. If they had done that in the UK there would have been a public outcry against people being allowed to be that daft.

The following evening I was back in the guardhouse, but this time I would be the one doing the locking up, because I was the Guard Commander. It was a post that normally would be filled by a Sergeant rather than a full Corporal, but my memories of the Loyals are that we always seemed to be short of men to fill the variety of positions. But I must say that I always felt somehow that it was an honour to be trusted with such a responsibility, and especially so with me only being a national serviceman. I had done Guard Commander once before back in Malaya at Colombo Camp, and I remember that I was terrified of making a mistake. I was given strict instructions by the Provo staff (Regimental Police) that if the Military Police (Red Caps) brought in a prisoner to be locked up for the night in our cells, then under no circumstances was I to allow the Red Caps to step inside the guardhouse. I didn't worry about the order, because it was very rare for prisoners to be brought into the guardhouse from outside of the battalion.

In Colombo there were six cells and just one prisoner locked up when I took over the guard. That night I had two visits from the Red Caps, once with a New Zealand lad and the second visit with two Australians. I locked them up without trouble, but the strange thing was that I had to keep ordering the Red Caps out of my Guardroom. I know at the time it felt most peculiar to be ordering two Military Policemen around, but I was the Guard Commander and that made me the boss. I never did find out why I must not allow them into the Guardroom but when the Red Caps left, we made sure that the prisoners had whatever they needed, that's apart from their freedom.

In Fanling there were only two cells, and I never saw any Red Caps in that area so there were no problems. I finished the guard, and was told that I was required in the Company Office. My heart tended to sink when I got that sort of message, as my mind raced, pondering everything that I had done over the last few days that might be leading to trouble, but I had no need to panic When I got to the Company Office I was informed that I was taking an advanced guard to the docks in Kowloon, and sorting out the accommodation on board the ship, that was to take the Loyals back to Singapore. That was the end of my time in Hong Kong.

As we sailed out of the harbour I felt rather sad to be leaving, and within the hour Victoria Peak was a distant spot on the horizon, and the flying fish were still trying to escape from the South China Sea.

Two footnotes to Hong Kong are that some of the lads from the Loyals sailed back to Malaya in a TLC, that's a tank landing craft, you know the boats that have a flat front, but I have no idea why they did that or how long it took to get back?

The second footnote, and to us the most important happening in China, was that somehow, and sadly we thought at the time, and with the loss of our cap badge, that the Loyals had *died* in Hong Kong, and that we had become a part of the Lancastrian Brigade. None of us accepted that fact, we really were Loyal to the end.

# CHAPTER TWELVE
*Needless Trouble. New Sergeant and Officer*

After an uneventful trip from Hong Kong to Singapore, we were back on the train heading North up the Malayan Peninsular to Ipoh and Colombo Camp. I got the feeling that most of the lads felt as I did, which was looking forward to getting back to Colombo Camp and the normal routine that we had all become comfortable with, prior to Hong Kong. But we were all also feeling the apprehension of a return into the jungle, after the relaxed atmosphere and bright lights of Hong Kong and the New Territories. I suppose that 4 Platoon and I were feeling a little more anxious than everyone else. We were travelling back to Ipoh, and to a certain extent into the unknown. We were without a Platoon Sergeant, about to lose Mr Kelly our Platoon Officer, and we had no idea who was going to replace either of them?

There was also the steady draining of lads who were all good mates, but they had nearly completed their service and were going to head back to the UK and home. Lucky devils!

The fanciful and wonderfully engineered structure, known as Ipoh Railway Station, appeared outside the carriage windows. In no time at all we were back in Colombo Camp and climbing out of the three-tonners with all our gear. I made my way back to the Corporals' basha, and apart from the absence of my photograph of Betty on top of the locker, everything looked the same. It did feel quite good to be back in familiar surroundings.

The first job was to unlock my cupboard just to check that everything was okay. I started to unpack all the gear that I had brought back from Hong Kong. As soon as I got to Bett's photo I put it on top of the locker, then went down to the charwallah's for a coffee and a pack of cigarettes. The charwallah was pleased to see me and the rest of the Company. It turned out that he had gone back home for a holiday to India while we were away.

After a brew and a cigarette I went back and finished unpacking, and making my bed up; then Bill and I went to the cookhouse for a bite to eat. In the queue before us there were three very white faces waiting to get served with a meal. They were very obviously new lads from the UK. As Bill and I joined the queue to wait behind them, they nervously moved out of the way to let us Corporals through to the front.

"There's no need to do that now you're with the battalion lads, as you'll find that everyone waits their turn," I informed them.

I watched the Joskins go to a vacant table feeling some sympathy for them. We had all been there, and in that nervous state ourselves.

I turned to Billy, "Shall we go and sit with them as soon as we've got our meals to have a chat. I think they badly need to hear a friendly voice." I suddenly felt that we were 'old sweats'.

So we did just that, which we felt help them to relax a little.

The battalion was going to go through a couple of weeks of jungle retraining before we entered into jungle operations again. I personally didn't think that it was necessary, but it would help to shake the bright lights of Hong Kong out of our systems. It would also help us to re-acclimatise to the body-sapping heat.

One of the more considered aspects of the Loyals was to always have the battalion, both mentally and physically, as near to 100% fitness as possible. I believe that is the sole reason why the battalion had the best record of any battalion that served in Malaya. That's apart from the unbelievable luck that we all had at times, and I include myself in that sentence.

There are two old sayings, *'It's the attitude of mind that creates the luck'*, and *'It's funny how people who practice the most, always seem to have the most luck'.* I would say that both were appropriate to the Loyals in Malaya.

The following week brought some regrets when 4 Platoon said its goodbyes to the Platoon Officer Mr. M. A. Kelly. To mark the occasion he was presented with the memento that we had bought in Hong Kong. The presentation was made by one of the lads of the platoon. Mr Kelly was well-liked and respected by the lads, and we all knew that we were going to miss him, especially now that we were without a Platoon Officer or Sergeant. He left through the open doorway of 4 Platoon's basha, and that was the last time we saw him. I didn't know it then, but for the next two weeks without our Officer, 4 Platoon's life was going to be a nightmare.

A day or two after Mr Kelly left, I was informed that our new Officer-to-be, was a national serviceman, and our new Sergeant-to-be, was a Sergeant McGrattan. The frightening news was that he was the Ex-Provo Sergeant of the SAS. The platoon was well deflated at that news; there was a lot of speculation as to what we were getting, and how bad he was going to be?

Just about the time we received that news, the platoon started to get a lot of nasty little niggles from outside of the platoon. My lads were being ordered to do jobs that should really have been done by others. There was nothing that neither I nor the other NCOs of the platoon could do, as we were junior NCOs. We could have gone to see the Company Commander and complained, but we weren't going to do that because of the trouble it would have caused. Also we thought that they were just having a laugh and sending us up, so we just had to tolerate what was happening in the best spirit we could muster.

I was really annoyed one day when I came back from the Company Office to find my platoon doing work that once again should have been done by others. I was now looking forward to the new Officer and this Ex SAS. Sergeant McGrattan, joining us, for no matter how bad he turned out to be, it would at least put an end to the nonsense that was going on, and steadily getting worse. The lads in the platoon were beginning to get sick of what was happening, for the joke had most definitely worn thin. They were beginning to complain, and demand that the NCOs do something about it, because it had now gone way beyond a joke.

I suppose that if things ever came to a head over the affair, then it happened the following day, when I was ordered to carry out a mundane Private's task in front of my section. I had no option but to obey the order, and was prevented from passing the task down to my lads. By the time I had finished the chore, my lads had left and vanished into the middle of the platoon.

I went and sat on my own to think out what I should now do? As far as I could see, my authority with 4 Platoon had been completely undermined, so I reasoned with myself that there was no point in retaining my rank. I also had a feeling of hopelessness at being unable to do anything about what had been happening to 4 Platoon since Mr Kelly had left. I made up my mind to see the Company Commander, Major Stones, in the morning, to give up my Corporal's tapes, and to fully explain why. I sat there on my own with my back to a tree and smoked a cigarette. I had been there for about fifteen minutes and was halfway through my second cigarette when Billy Fish appeared.

"What's going on here?" he asked.

I told him what had happened, and that I was going to give up my tapes the following morning. Bill tried to talk me out of doing that, but I was adamant that I was going to do it. I also told him that I was going to give the exact reasons as to why I was relinquishing my tapes; I didn't give a damn as to what trouble it caused, because at that moment in time I had just had enough.

Word must have got around all of the Company, because for the rest of the day everyone kept out of my way. In fact nobody was talking at all; everyone in the platoon was in a silent and sombre mood. I went for a coffee followed by a shower.

When I returned to my basha, the Corporals' room was filled with the lads from my section. Basically they had come to give me their backing as to witnessing the reason for my decision; they would prefer me not to go down that road, but for me to hang on to my tapes and remain as their Section Commander. I felt very honoured, and thanked them for their support. I told them that I would think about what they had said, and make my final decision first thing in the morning.

Word had certainly made its way around 'B' Company. Just after teatime I had a visit from two 'B' Company Sergeants. It was immediately obvious to me that they were concerned about what they had heard. I told them what had occurred, as well as the action I was contemplating taking the following morning. They agreed that I had every right to be angry, and that what had taken place was totally out of order, but if I took the course of action I was thinking about, it would create a load of trouble for the Company. They went on to assure me that they would personally see to it that the situation would not happen again, and that in a few days time 4 Platoon would have its own Sergeant and Platoon Officer. As they left I told them the same as I had told my own lads, that I would sleep on it and make my final decision in the morning. The spontaneous and unsolicited support that I received from everyone certainly made me feel a lot better.

When the two Sergeants turned up bright and early, I'd had a good night's sleep, and was up early. I had already made up my mind not to pursue the matter. It wasn't really their problem, but they were obviously very relieved when I said that I was going to let the matter drop. True to their word, until 4 Platoon's new guys arrived, the Sergeants always seemed to be around to help out with any problems.

That day we got a little bit more information about our new Officer. Apparently he was a Lancashire lad, Second Lieutenant Rawstorne. I wondered about which part of Lancashire he came from, but we would all know in a day or two. The other two platoons in 'B' Company were now operational, and they were due to go into the jungle at any time. We were non-operational until we had a Platoon Officer and Sergeant, which would be in a day or two.

The Loyals area of operations had now moved farther to the North, as the Communists had been driven further up the Malayan Peninsular towards the Thailand border, where they could escape for a while to lick their wounds. To me our trip to Hong Kong appeared on reflection, to act as a dividing line in the battle against the Communists in Malaya. When we returned to Ipoh and Colombo Camp, we heard that many of the zones to the South of the country had been declared White Areas, which meant they had been effectively freed from the Communist insurgents.

Once again it was Thursday pay parade, and when Lance Corporal Tootal, the 'B' Company clerk arrived in the 4 Platoon basha, he told me that I was wanted at the Company Office after pay parade. Again my heart sank, but when I got to the office I was asked if I would like to volunteer to command the armed guard at Ipoh racecourse that coming Saturday afternoon?

I knew the saying, *'never volunteer for anything,'* but I was very grateful to be asked to do it, so accepted immediately. The advantages in doing the guard were that we got paid privately, I should add, **well paid**, and we were also provided with vouchers for meals and drinks. I had to get a Lance Corporal and six lads from the platoon to volunteer for the duty, and although it wasn't quite as easy as I had expected it to be, it wasn't an undue problem. I think the extra money, food and free drinks made all the difference to the volunteering.

When Saturday arrived we were taken to the racecourse in a three-tonner from the Loyals Motor Transport Section. The driver dropped us off at the racecourse just before 12:00hrs, and I told him to be back at 16:30hrs to pick us up. Surprisingly the place wasn't the hive of activity that I had been expecting, and the horse-racing was due to start at 13:30hrs. I had been told to report to the clerk of the course when we arrived, so I left the Lance Corporal with the lads and went in search of his office.

I found him almost right away; he turned out to be a very pleasant and very well mannered Chinese gentleman. He told me the areas that he would like us to cover, before giving me the meal and drink vouchers for the lads and myself.

It became obvious to me that we were there with our weapons, just to give a greater sense of security to the wealthy who were attending the horse-racing. I put two of the lads to wander around the start and finish area, two to wander around the stands, and two to hang around the cashiers' offices, where the money would be deposited throughout the afternoon.

I told them all not to go for a drink or a meal without letting me know first, so that I could make sure that there were only two off duty at any one time. Then the Lance Corporal and I wandered around the stables, office areas, and bar and restaurant. We could help ourselves to whatever we wanted in the bar and food areas, and the people in charge just wouldn't take the vouchers that we had been given. It was a top class race meeting, and needless to say, so was the food. I felt sure that by the end of the Saturday afternoon I had put on a couple of pounds in weight.

In the middle of the afternoon, we bumped into Corporal Jim Melvin, the lad who was shot in the back just before we went to Hong Kong. It turned out that he loved horse-racing, and having a bet on the gee-gees.

I asked him, "Are you winning?"

In return all I got from Jim was his very wide and cheeky smile, which probably meant he was doing okay.

The afternoon soon passed; I found it quite enjoyable. We talked to a few lads from the Loyals who were there enjoying the racing. I must be honest here and say that I find horse-racing absolutely boring, and just cannot understand anyone enjoying the pastime, but of course it's everyone to their own. I have only ever been to two horse-race meetings, this one, and then back there again in Ipoh a few months later, when I was asked to volunteer again for the job.

Well anyway, I didn't have time to watch the horse-racing, I was too busy eating and drinking. Just before 16:30hrs I went to the Race Course Office to sign us off and pick up our money for the day. Then it was onto the three-tonner and back to Colombo Camp for Saturday tea, although none of us were hungry.

That weekend saw the other 'B' Company Platoons back in the jungle on operations, but we were still stuck without a Sergeant or Officer; although both were due to arrive in the coming week. I was up early Monday morning taking an early shower, then off to the charwallah's, for a hopefully, uninterrupted coffee.

The camp had returned to its normal tick-over routine, and with most of the Infantry Platoons back into the jungle on operations, there was a blissful peace, after the crowded and noisy place it had been with everyone in camp. As I walked back up to my basha in the bright warm morning sunshine, I was wondering how we would handle the surprises that army life held in store for us this week? I was about to find out one of the answers.

In the shade of 4 Platoon's basha, a darkness that was enforced by the bright sunshine from outside, I could see a stranger walking slowly down the middle of the basha.

"Better go and see," I thought to myself. So with the trepidation that seemed to have become a part of everyday army life, I walked into the 4 Platoon basha.

The stranger was approaching the end of the basha into which I had entered, and in the second that it took for my eyes to adjust to the gloom, I could see that he was a big man, very smart and very military. There were three very white Sergeant tapes on his sleeve, plus a wings badge indicating that this Sergeant had made at least seven parachute jumps.

I swallowed the lump in my throat and said in my best and strongest, couldn't care less voice, "Sergeant McGrattan?"

He replied with, "Yes," and a radiant smile.

His voice had that little touch of pleasant musical Irish lilt, and as I introduced myself, I knew instinctively that this was a person who I was going to get along with.

Again I addressed him, "Just give me a minute to put my things away, then I'll show you around 'B' Company and 4 Platoon."

By the end of the day everyone had met our new Sergeant, and thankfully we all got on fine together, which was a good start for the new 4 Platoon team. We were told that Mr Rawstorne would be joining us the following day; I just hoped that the new Officer would be as well received as our new Sergeant had been.

The next morning we were sat in 4 Platoon's basha with the Sergeant, swapping tales about various jungle operations, when this young Officer, with a freshly sunburnt face, walked into the basha.

"4 Platoon?" he questioned.

We all stood and introduced ourselves to Mr Rawstorne. Once again, as on the previous morning, I had the feeling that this was another person who I was going to get along with.

I was told that he came from Croston, which is a village just to the South of Leyland. Apparently his father was the local vicar, and two of the lads in the platoon who were from that neck of the woods, knew of him. All they could say was that as far as they could remember he was fine, well liked and would be okay with us.

With time, and now in retrospect, my first instincts proved to be correct, and I like to think now that, although the differences in rank were always respected, in the jungle we all served together as comrades, friends and members of a great team. I am sure that Sergeant (Paddy) McGrattan and Mr Rawstorne will not mind me telling you these stories. As I have written previously, I was very proud of my jungle skills, especially when it came to map reading. I always had a very special regard for knowing exactly where we were at any given time. I am sure that Paddy would be the first to admit that his map reading in the jungle wasn't his best attribute.

When I think back to those days, and the men I still hold in the very highest esteem, I chuckle to myself when I think of the op when I was leading the platoon into the jungle, and up one of the countless jungle tracks. We had stopped for a few minutes rest; the track ran straight up the hillside in front of us for about half a mile. The track was also pointing straight at a mountaintop about three miles away.

We had been stopped for a few minutes when Sergeant McGrattan came up with the map in his hand, waved at the hilltop to where the track was pointing and said, "We are going right over that hilltop."

"No," I replied, "We are turning 90° to the left and off this track."

"Are you sure?" he asked.

"Yes," I replied.

"You'll be in trouble if I'm right," he said.

"Yes, I understand that, but I know where we are going," I answered.

"All right," he said, and off he went back down the track to the middle of the platoon, along with his well-known and well-loved cheeky smile.

Now from the beginning, the new Platoon Officer wasn't too bad at map reading, but at first, map reading in the jungle was a skill that had to be developed. Part of that skill was deciding if a stream or ridge that you had come to, was on the map, or had been missed by the cartographers, or if they had put a feature into the map that wasn't really there? These things happened everyday when you were in the jungle, and when you were going through some of the more difficult terrain, where there were no obvious points to double-check with and confirm your location, then it was very easy to get lost, or should I say confused. It was due mainly to the jungle not being surveyed on the ground, and the thick jungle canopy, one-hundred and fifty feet or more above us, hiding all of the ground features from the air.

The self-confidence that I had with my map reading, led to me really enjoying the challenge of going into the operational areas when the map was stamped across with the words UNEXPLORED AREA. Mr Rawstorne and myself had a lasting and friendly competition as to who was correct in pinpointing the map reference for the jungle base camp position.

After discussion at the end of the first day of each operation, I am proud to say that it was always my map reference that was radioed back to the operational headquarters at Colombo Camp, that is except for the last jungle operation I was involved in. On that operation Mr Rawstorne was greatly pleased in radioing back to HQ, his map reference, for the jungle camp.

All I can do now, and after all this time, is to say that, "Mr Rawstorne Sir, if you are reading this, you were definitely wrong with your given position. We were unquestionably two-hundred yards farther to the West!" Such was the rivalry and camaraderie that existed between us all, which was to remain so for the rest of my service in Malaya. If it hadn't have been for all the interruptions by the bad guys, life would have been great, but everyone in the Loyals did their bit to improve everyone else's life, and to make up for being so far away from home and our loved ones.

The next day, the first full day of the platoon being a unit complete with Officer and Sergeant, we all went to the jungle firing range, where we had an enjoyable day. We had some good laughs and got to know each other better. The following day we were a fully operational platoon again, ready for action, and the morale of the lads was back at the top.

# CHAPTER THIRTEEN
## *Man-eating Tiger. Guarding Ipoh RAF Base*

After a break of nearly two months, 4 Platoon were climbing onto the backs of the three-tonners, and once again I had that peculiar taste in my mouth and throat. No matter what sweets I sucked, or what change of breakfast I had, or didn't have, I never did rid myself of that weird taste. We now had to begin our journey a few minutes earlier in order to reach the jungle operations area before sunrise. The active area was now in a part of the jungle that was further to the North, so obviously the journey took that little bit longer. This operation was just a general sweep, search and destroy mission, but I had the feeling that it was more getting accustomed to that area, and a shakedown operation for 4 Platoon, with it being the first time we had all been out together in the jungle.

We had been warned at the pre-op briefing that there was a man-eating tiger in the area, although it was thought to be much further to the North. Apparently it had killed two natives from one of the kampongs, and two weeks earlier, it had dragged one of the Australian soldiers out of his bed. This had happened at their jungle base camp in the middle of the night. Fortunately his mates chased it off, but the lad's legs were badly mauled. The Australian lads were with the 3rd Battalion Royal Australian Regiment, and their main camp was up to the North near Sungai Siput.

We arrived at the drop-off point just on daybreak, making our way through a rubber plantation, reaching the jungle edge just as full daylight emerged. It felt warm and very pleasant, which meant that we must have readjusted back to the Malayan climate without problems. I was looking forward to cooking my own meals again, and at a personal level I was feeling okay. I was glad that when I first arrived at the battalion I had chosen to go into the jungle, rather than being stuck in Colombo Camp. In the jungle, although I had the fears and a lot of responsibility, I was more or less my own boss.

We weren't going too far into the jungle on this trip, just over a mile, and it was to be for five days. As we entered the darkness, for some reason, it felt good to be back under that dark green canopy. I suppose most of the feeling of euphoria was down to being in there and with my close friends. Well no! Not friends, Comrades, for they were more than close friends could ever be. I suppose that moment, and the other times out there in Malaya when similar feelings came to me, is a part of the reason why I am sat here writing this book. I presume as much as anything for me, it's a way of addressing the guilty feeling, and the remorse of brushing the Comrades from your mind as soon as you are away from the dangers and safely back home.

Later on you reach an age where your memories drift back to the friends and the days that will never return, to the bygone times when you knew men who really were something special. Along with the memories, are the unhappiness and the sorrows of not knowing where they are, or how they are now, and I regret not keeping in touch at the commencement of a normal home life.

I remember that a lot of the lads from around the Preston area agreed to meet up each year in the only pub that we all knew, the Blue Bell Public House on Church Street, Preston. On a certain day, and at a certain time, Betty and I went to the first year reunion, but unfortunately nobody else turned up. We had a couple of drinks in there, then left never to return.

However back in the jungle, it didn't take too long for us to reach the base camp position, probably two or three hours, as the jungle was easy and not heavily overgrown with thick undergrowth. It was one of the areas that occasionally we came across, where the misty clinging atmosphere that we were breathing in, had a sweet and very pleasant smell and taste, for at times you could really taste the atmosphere in the jungle.

It was the first time for the Officer and Sergeant to be with 4 Platoon in the jungle. It was the start of, 'we must be absolutely certain of the location,' which certainly gave us some friendly rivalry over the coming months.

Sergeant 'Paddy' McGrattan was then, as he always remained during the rest of my service, a very much laid-back tower of strength. That night we were treated to a marvellous display of fireflies which had to be seen to be believed. It is impossible to put pen to paper and describe the wonder of seeing all the pale green lights moving around in the dark jungle night. Also you must realise that they weren't just flying around us, and that's all around us, they were also flying behind the trees, and in and out of the foliage of the massive undergrowth, vanishing and reappearing at will. The very finest displays of fairy lights at Christmas, come nowhere near to challenging the displays of the fireflies, and we had five nights to watch them. I know that I keep mentioning them, but they really were something special, and to me without doubt, one of the wonders of the world. If you want to see them, you will have to go to Malaya, and then into the jungle at night, you cannot capture the magic on film, so you will never see them on your TV.

The following morning saw me back out on jungle patrol with my section, and Sanden as my tracker. We were going up the mountainside following the stream by our camp. We were always extra careful on the tracks that were running alongside a water course, because obviously they have been made by some animal or other. The Iban trackers would usually know what animal had made the tracks. Sanden would warn me if the tracks were a bit dodgy, or could lead to trouble, but most wild animals would head the other way if they knew humans were about. But some wouldn't retreat, and would quite readily attack. Of course, other animals would use the tracks for convenience of travelling through the jungle, just like us, so it was impossible to know for certain what we might encounter, and every patrol was a journey into the unknown.

I was certainly well relaxed on that operation, enjoying being there on that patrol. The day was perfect; there was a lot of sunshine penetrating through the jungle canopy, which made our surroundings at jungle floor level easy to observe. There was a multitude of airborne life that was clear to see, especially with the shafts of bright sunlight illuminating them as they passed through the beams. The butterflies in that area were especially brilliant, and I realised that we always seemed to find them in the areas where the jungle had a pleasant or slightly different smell.

We continued up the track following the stream to the West, climbing uphill all the time until the stream ran dry. We then headed North until we reached the top of the ridge, before following the ridge back down towards our base camp.

We were about halfway back to the base camp when Sanden stopped and pointed up the tree he was standing next to. He was very excited about something, so we all gathered around the tree, all of us looking up to where he was pointing.

About twelve to fifteen feet up the trunk of the tree, the bark had been ripped off, and the bare trunk of the tree had deep gouge marks, which would be three or four feet long. I could not think of an answer to the question from one of the lads.

"What the hell has done that?"

I looked at Sanden and said slowly, "What has done that?"

"Tiger," Corporal Hudson. Tiger, big Tiger, very big, sharpen claws."

"Good God!" I exclaimed, "It can't be possible for a tiger to grow that big."

The scratch marks were up the tree, three times higher than our tallest lad. I looked around the lads and they all had one eye on the claw marks, but the other eye on the jungle around us, and so did I. It then crossed my mind that the tiger may have only just done that, because the strips of timber on the ground, below the scratch marks, looked very fresh.

"Sanden," I asked, "How old are these markings?"

He picked up some of the strips, smelled them, then said to me, with one finger in the air, "One day."

I thought back to the day I first entered the jungle, when the size of the trees and the scrub that formed the undergrowth beneath the trees, made me think of the Lost World. That caused me then to think that it only needed the big dinosaurs, to make it complete. I looked up at the claw marks that were way up the tree and wondered.

Although we had been warned about a tiger in the pre-operational briefing, I decided that with something so big and dangerous on the loose in our area, it would be advisable to get back to the base camp to warn the rest of the lads as quickly as possible. We continued down along the ridge as quickly as the terrain and safety would allow.

We had been underway for about ten minutes when we heard a family of monkeys kicking-up a terrible racket down in the valley to our left. We all stopped and looked to the direction from where the din was coming. The noise seemed to be coming nearer and towards us. I wondered for a moment as to whether we were invading their territory, and now they were going to attack us. That isn't as unusual as it may sound to you, for several times platoons have had to move their jungle base camp, because they found that they were sharing the same water-hole with a family of monkeys.

If I remember correctly, baboons are the primate with the worst temper, and therefore the most feared. You shared nothing with them, but to keep everything in perspective, just remember, that the animal species that was most feared by all the jungle animals was ourselves, man. That fear of man could have been working for us then, because the noise started to move away from us, back down into the valley towards the stream that would obviously be there. I turned and looked at Sanden.

He replied to my look with, "Monkey, monkey, maybe tiger." Then he did a clawing-like action with his hand, plus a big golden toothed snarl, "ahaarr."

Me and the other lads who had seen Sanden do that, couldn't help but laugh, although Sanden wasn't trying to make us laugh, though he was happy that he had, and of course, laughed with us.

I am still more than happy with the fact that I regarded Sanden as a good friend, and I am still proud of Sanden regarding me as his very good friend.

As the sound of the monkeys receded down the valley over to our left, we headed along the ridge and back towards the base camp that was down in the valley to our right. We were making good time, as no doubt my section was spurred on by the thoughts of the tiger that we believed to be behind us. This belief was underlined by a sound that we all thought to be the roar of a tiger in the distance, and from the area we had just left.

Sanden just shrugged his shoulders at that one, so it probably wasn't, but we were hearing a lot of noise from the various waterfalls in the stream just below us. Sometimes falling water has the peculiar knack of making sounds that are identical to the ones you are listening for, or is it your imagination that does that? It's also surprising how your fears and nerves can turn sounds and shapes into something that you are expecting them to be, but hoping that they are not.

We made it back to base camp with no further scares, but the tail-end Charlie was a nervous wreck by the time we had made it back, and he had a real crick in his neck from looking behind him all of the way back. I didn't say anything to anyone, but I was annoyed with myself for not thinking about the tail-end Charlie, and getting each of the lads to take it in turn, but I had been too intent on getting back to the base camp as quickly as possible to warn the others.

To reduce the risk factor to a minimum, that evening after we had all eaten our evening meal, everyone in the platoon buried any food that was left into the waste pits, ensuring that the remains were well covered over. The idea was to eliminate any smell of food that might attract the tiger. It was something that we had not bothered about prior to that operation, but it was an act that we performed on a regular basis after that. If there is one thing that the Loyals did well in Malaya, it was to learn quickly from mistakes, and with experience you didn't ask if you could do that, you just immediately did! Burying the uneaten food was an example of doing that, and we also had small wood fires burning on top of the cooking stoves up to darkness, because wild animals don't like fire, and the smell of wood smoke would linger all night. But as I have just written, we all learned from our mistakes, and two days after that I did the most stupid of acts that very nearly cost me my life. You have all heard the saying, *'within an inch of my life,'* well I can honestly say that this mistake was within one thousandth of an inch.

That night after stand-to, and when full darkness arrived, we all sat watching the wonderful display given by the fireflies, with the faint smell of wood smoke in our nostrils. A lot of the lads had rescued the old and empty tin cans, then tied them together on the perimeter vine so that they would jingle together if the vine was touched. Of course, as no doubt you have already guessed, some of the lads took pleasure out of rattling the vine and jangling everybody's nerves. It wasn't too easy getting to sleep that night, although eventually everyone did, but it was late on into the night, and with the thought of that Australian lad getting dragged out of his bed by the tiger.

The following day was our turn to remain in base camp, so I spent the day putting more protection up around my basha. This consisted of cutting stakes about four feet long, then driving them into the ground around the basha, to form a type of simple fence. Then I tied vines around them all to form a perimeter, then hung empty tins onto the vines, just so that I would sleep a little easier that night.

The following morning, after a decent night's sleep, I was back out again on jungle patrol with my section. We were once again heading up the stream that we had followed two days earlier. Once we reached the top at the spot where we had previously turned to the right, this time we turned to the left. The jungle wasn't too bad, so we reached the ridge up to the left without much bother. This ridge was one of those that we sometimes came across where the top was very uneven. It had a lot of very large rocks sticking up along the ridge-line, turning it into a dragon's back that was impossible to walk along.

There had been no sign of an animal track as we came up to the ridge, but after so many months in the jungle you get an instinct of what to expect, and if there wasn't one on that side of the ridge, then I would have been surprised if there hadn't have been one over the top and on the other side. All through the jungle there are tracks that are made by the different animals, both large and small. Like us humans they choose the easiest route. One of the ways being along a ridge, or in this case just below the ridge. Sure enough when I took my patrol down off the ridge, there was an animal track. It was about thirty to forty yards below the ridge, and followed the line of the ridge. The track wove in and out of the large boulders that lay below the hilltop, and wasn't too bad for making our way along.

We reached a particularly large boulder, where the path curved around the rock and out of sight. The leading scout made his way around the boulder with Sanden close on his heels, and I followed close behind Sanden, with the rest of the lads close behind me. If you suffered from claustrophobia then this was certainly not the place to be.

The track we were following was only about a foot wide. It was bounded by the large house-sized rocks on both sides. From between the boulders grew the normal jungle trees that had all the time in the world to push their roots down into decent nourishment, which showed in the dense dark jungle canopy that was over our heads, turning the track into a dark green tunnel that was only penetrated by the odd vivid beam of sunlight. With the shafts of bright lights bouncing off the rocks to our left, the effect was something that you would expect to see in a magical wonderland tunnel on Blackpool Pleasure Beach.

We were all keeping an eye open for any wild animals, including Mr Tiger, and we were all on our guard for any snakes that there might have been around, for this really was ideal snake territory. It was also perfect for scorpions, as well as the spiders that were frequently seen in the jungle, although more often than not, they were seen first thing in a morning.

As I rounded the boulder, the leading scout and Sanden were crouched down, and looking into a cave that had been formed by a large boulder rolling down and onto the tops of the two large rocks that formed the sides of the cave. It was really more of a tunnel, because there was an opening at the other end, about twenty-feet away from the side we were on.

I looked up to the left to where the hillside, over a few hundred years, had worked its way down onto the top boulder. I thought to myself that it looked easier to go up to the left and over the top. I looked at Sanden and the leading scout. They were both looking through the tunnel, busy trying to work out if there was anything alive in there that could be a bit dodgy.

I decided to climb up the left hand side to see if it was an easy route for us to follow, which indeed it turned out to be. As there were plenty of hand and foot holes, in ten seconds I was on top. There appeared to be an even better path going down the other side, and back onto the track that we were following. I decided to have a quick look to make sure that the path held no surprises for us, then I would go back and tell the lads to come this way. I moved a couple of yards down the path to have a look, when at that very moment to my right, the leading scout came out of the tunnel and onto the track.

Out of the corner of his eye, he saw my movement, and in a split second he swung his shotgun around and pointed it right at my head. I know it was pointed right at my head, because I was looking right down the barrel of the gun. Once again I was into one of those heart-stopping adrenalin pumped moments when time stands still, well almost stands still. I could see his eyes clearly over the top of his shotgun, so clearly that I could see the shock in them. This was a look that I had never seen before, and thankfully have never seen again to this day. I saw his thumb push the safety catch off, and his finger end moving further out of the trigger guard, as he started to squeeze the trigger. Then the gun swung away to my left, and pointed down towards the ground. The safety catch clicked back on, then my leading scout gave me a tongue-lashing, the like of which I had never heard before, nor do I want to hear again.

I stood there and accepted that from a Private, because he was absolutely right, and I was totally wrong in what I had done. His quick eye and reactions had, in a fraction of a split second, saved my life, and the bright yellow square operational patch stitched onto the front of my jungle hat also helped. That hat, complete with the patch, is now in the Regimental Museum at Fulwood Barracks. Should you ever go there and see my jungle hat on display, remember that the simple yellow square on the front helped to save a life.

I was angry with myself for making such a childish and stupid blunder, and apologised to my leading scout and my lads for the upset. We had a good long break, then headed back to the base camp without any further problems to worry about. The amazing thing to me about that incident is, that I can still remember it clearly, and I remember it didn't perturb me at the time or since. I must admit that I do find it quite amazing that it didn't give me nightmares at the time. I can only think that I had so much trust and faith in my lads to get it right, that I didn't ever have that psychological hang-up then, but the dilemma of my nightmares was still to come.

The following day we were out again, and this time it was to be an interesting map reading exercise as I had to take my patrol to the North, which meant up hill and down dale, and into tiger country. After my stupid foul-up the day before, I was still concerned as to the reaction of my section towards me. I needn't have worried though, because I got the friendly ribbing of not getting too far in front this time, or if I did, would I keep shouting to let them know where I was? It lasted for a few seconds, but I didn't mind and joined in the laughter. I was relieved to know that I had been fully forgiven for my mistake.

It had got to about midday and I was getting ready to call halt for a lunch-time break. We were heading up a steep hillside and I had decided to stop when we reached the ridge. We could hear an aircraft in the distance, and it crossed my mind that they could be dropping leaflets. The patrol had nearly reached the top when suddenly we heard Chinese voices on the ridge. Everyone in the patrol immediately froze, not wanting to drop to the ground and so make any extra undue noise. We were all trying to spot the Chinese, and were intently using our jungle training of looking through the trees. It was difficult for us to locate just where exactly the talking was coming from, as the voices were somehow fragmented, and had a hollow ringing sound to them.

It suddenly occurred to me that the Chinese might be in a cave near to us, and not on the ridge above. I looked slowly to my left and then to the right, and as I moved my head to look to the right, my eyes were drawn to Sanden. He was giving me a big golden smile and had his finger pointing upwards. I looked up realising what he meant, indicating where the voices, or rather voice was coming from.

Up above and coming nearer to us, was a voice broadcasting Dakota aircraft. I had heard about the type of aircraft that had just given us a fright, but this was my first experience of one. The idea of the broadcast was to call upon the CTs to surrender, telling them that they would be well treated and receive money. I suppose basically, the same messages put to Charlie, by the leaflets dropped from the sky.

With the scare over we continued up and onto the ridge, which took us all of one minute, but once we had found a suitable spot, we settled down for a lunch-break. The day up to then had been bright and sunny; we could tell what the weather was like above the jungle canopy, by the amount of light that penetrated down to us at ground level.

I was just about to start the platoon back on the patrol, when it suddenly went dark; obviously a cloud had crossed in front of the sun. I told the lads we were waiting for a while until either it got darker, or a wind sprung up. It was unusual for us to get rain in the middle of the day, but not entirely unknown. Ten minutes later it was still dark, so I made the decision to abandon that patrol and head back to the base camp.

We had covered nearly three-quarters of the mission and found nothing, not even a trace of the tiger. I wasn't abandoning the patrol because we were bothered about getting wet, we would have been okay with that. This patrol was across country, over the streams and ridges, and I was concerned that if we got a heavy and prolonged rainstorm, we would not be able to make it over the streams, due obviously to their increase in size.

As I wrote in an earlier chapter, a small stream can become a powerful river in just a matter of seconds. It wasn't unknown in Malaya for a platoon to be crossing a stream, and to become split in half by the waters suddenly becoming a raging torrent. We were back in the base camp a couple of hours early, and my judgement wasn't questioned when I explained why. Needless to say, the sun broke through the jungle canopy when we were about ten minutes out from our base camp, but that's sod's law isn't it?

We got into Colombo Camp the following day, and I was glad to be back there. It had been quite an action-packed five days. Once again if one thing happens, you can almost guarantee that something else will also happen. I was beginning to wise-up to the fact that this was always going to happen in Malaya.

It was now well into December, so a few of us were beginning to look forward to our last Christmas and New Year's Eve in the army. We heard that most of the platoons would be in Colombo Camp for Christmas, but we didn't know then who they would be. The big news, or should that have been rumour, was that the Australians were building a big deep jungle base camp for 'B' Company. I did ask one lad who would probably know, and although I didn't get a yes, I did get a big maybe.

We had our rest days, and our pay-day and I had a night out in Ipoh with my lads, a hot chicken curry, a beer and a good laugh. Our first duty, after the recuperation days, was the dreaded guard duty on Colombo Camp. It was rare for us to do a guard on the camp, as we spent so much of our time in the jungle. The Training Company or HQ, usually carried out the guard duties on Colombo Camp. Surprisingly, I was looking forward to this guard tour of duty, because I had been given the job of doing Guard Commander on the RAF Airbase at Ipoh Airport. I am not one hundred percent certain, but I think that I was the first one to do that duty for the Loyals, and I believe the first to be provided by the army. The reason that I was given as to why we were doing the night guard duty on the airfield, was that according to Military Intelligence, via surrendered CTs, Charlie had been using the airfield as a short cut. It was said that some of them spoke to the RAF personnel on a first name basis. It all sounded very unlikely to me, but as I have said before, out in Malaya, the unlikely and not possible, all to often became the reality.

I arrived at Ipoh Airport in a three-tonner just before 18:00hrs, along with my section who were in the back of the dark green army lorry. We drove through the main entrance to the RAF base continuing on past the guardhouse, and up to where several three-tonners were parked. They were identical three-ton Bedford lorries to the one I was in, apart from the fact that ours was dark green with the Commonwealth Brigade, and the Loyal badges on the front, and they were the dark RAF blue with the RAF red, white and blue roundels on the front.

We turned around, then drove back and stopped in front of the guardroom. We all climbed out, and were then met by a couple of RAF Police Corporals who had come out of the guardroom to greet us. They quickly showed my second-in-command and myself around the guardroom. I believe that my two IC then, was a regular soldier called L/cp Critchley.

The RAF guys showed us where the kettle was, where to get water and the keys to the cells, and I think that was about it. The patrol areas around the airfield and the buildings had to be defined by us. To be fair to the Boys in Blue, it was probably better that we defined the patrols as we saw fit, which was the area to cover with the men we had available. I also got the feeling that they were embarrassed to be handing over the base guard to the army.

I decided that we would cover three areas with one man to each, the accommodation buildings and NAAFI, the aircraft hangers and the parked aircraft. With three men for each area, that would have meant two hours on and four hours off for each man in the section. I abandoned any idea of patrolling the airfield itself, as it was far too big of an area for us to cover with the men available. I had a walk around the accommodation and NAAFI area. The NAAFI was in full swing; it sounded as though some of them in there were getting well tanked-up.

If I had been in Colombo Camp, I would have been quite entitled to go inside to make sure that there were no drunken problems arising, but here I didn't want to push my luck. It did cross my mind that some of the boys in blue might make my army lads the prime target for trouble when they came out of the bar, having had too much to drink. I made up my mind that at the first sign of trouble, when the NAAFI closed, we would take the offender into custody and lock him up for the night. In the event, the RAF lads were more than pleasant with my lads, much to my relief and my self-embarrassment, for thinking the worst without reason, of those dedicated young men who were simply noisily enjoying themselves in a distant land.

The Officer of the Guard came from Colombo Camp to check on us at the airport, just to inspect us, and make sure everything was okay. It would have been just after midnight when he came over from Colombo, but he only stayed for a few minutes. After he had left, I took a walk around the parked aircraft. I was surprised to find the doors to many of the aeroplanes unlocked. Needless to say, I tried several different pilot's seats that night, and found it a very different and enjoyable guard duty experience.

At 07:00hrs the following morning I handed the guard duty back to the RAF, and climbed aboard the three-tonner that had arrived to transport us back to Colombo Camp. It had been a pleasant change to the normal guard duty, and I was hoping that if I had any more to do, then I would be sent there.

A couple of days later we found out that the gossip about a deep jungle camp was true, and 5 Platoon were about to go in there for seven days. That meant they would be in the jungle for Christmas. 4 Platoon was going to replace them, which meant that I would be spending Christmas Day in Colombo Camp and New Year's Eve in the jungle.

# CHAPTER FOURTEEN
## *Kuacha Lodge Jungle Camp*
### *Christmas and New Year*

So it was true, 'B' Company were getting a permanent deep jungle base camp, and 5 Platoon were going to be the first to use it. Unfortunately for them, it was going to be over the Christmas period. The camp was being built by the 17th Troop of the Royal Australian Engineers, and it was situated further to the North of our old jungle area. There was to be a pre-built landing zone (LZ) for helicopters, but general access was to be in three-tonners, using a track that had been dynamited and bulldozed through the jungle, to the site of the camp. The permanent base camp was several miles into the jungle, and was called Kuacha Lodge. The name 'Kuacha' means to stop, or to quit now, but who named it that I have absolutely no idea, but we always called it Lodge Camp.

5 Platoon were loaded up and underway a couple of days before Christmas. There were three, three-tonners going up to Lodge Camp, instead of the normal two that would generally be needed to carry the platoon. The lorries were also carrying supplies up to the camp, and an armed escort for coming back down the jungle track, just in case they were ambushed on the trail, which remember, was cut through virgin jungle that was also enemy territory. Guess who was doing the escort duty?

Well I didn't mind nor did my section. We were all interested in what this new base camp was going to be like, especially as we were going there to stay the following week.

Also Colombo Camp was getting busy, with all the Infantry Platoons coming back for Christmas in peaceful surroundings, plus a ride into the jungle and back to Colombo would be a nice change, and it would also save us from being assigned to do something else.

We entered the jungle on a newly bulldozed track, that was immediately climbing upwards into the trees. This was the first time that any of us had been carried into the jungle on transport, that's other than our own two legs, so needless to say it was a new and interesting experience. There had obviously been other three-ton Bedford lorries up the track before us; the wheel tracks of these vehicles were plain to see in the reddish-brown surface of the new track. There were no real straight bits to this trail, as it turned and twisted its way up the mountainside, in, around and out of the big trees.

The smaller trees had been dynamited and bulldozed out of the way, and any spoil from the track had been bulldozed downhill away from the roadway. Where we had entered the jungle at the beginning of the track, the spoil, which had been pushed to the side nearly three weeks earlier, was already greening over. It is absolutely amazing to us Europeans, to see just how fast nature grows out there, and the greenery takes over everything in no time at all, that is when there is nothing to stop it.

The three-tonners had dropped into four-wheel drive as soon as we entered the jungle, but even so they struggled to get up some of the slopes. Some of the tight and hairpin bends on the track had to be seen to be believed. They were so tight a bend, that it was actually impossible for a lorry to steer around, because they didn't have a tight enough radius turning circle.

So the Australian engineers cut deep grooves around the bends to match the width of the wheels on a lorry, so as to act as tramlines, and it worked. It was an amazing sight to see the three-tonners pivot around under their own power. The only person on board when these manoeuvres were carried out was the driver. The reason for that was, that with the engine revving, and all the wheels spinning, the lorry could easily flip itself over the side and roll down the hillside, or at least down to the first big tree. With the chance of being ambushed, the armoured pigs would have been the safe vehicles to use going up through the jungle to Lodge Camp, but there was absolutely no possibility of them making it up that track with the weight of those vehicles, and the lower ground clearance. When we first used the track to go up to Lodge Camp, most of the lads would hang onto the metal framework that supported the heavy green canvas cover over the back of the lorry. Obviously with the track being so rough, if you weren't holding onto something, you would get bounced about like a ping-pong ball. The problem was that the track was just wide enough to take a three-tonner, so for much of the way the lorries would be pushing past overhanging branches and shrubbery. The first week in getting to the camp resulted in several badly bruised and grazed hands, and one broken finger.

The 'B' Company lads were not that daft, the main problem was that for the first day or two, the canvas covers were fit in place over the back of the lorries. Obviously no one in the back of the Bedfords could see when an obstruction was about to be brushed past, so there was no warning, so therefore no time to remove one's fingers that were already hanging on for dear life. There were logical reasons for having the covers in place, one was that if Charlie was spying on a convoy going up to, or leaving Lodge Camp, then they would not know who or what was on board. Also if the convoys were ambushed on route, then Charlie would not be able to throw hand grenades into the backs of the vehicles. We soon made sure that the CTs had been cleared from the area, and then wisely, removed the covers, thus eliminating the damaged hands problem. Quite a few of the lads acquired pieces of rope to tie onto the metal framework, then they could hang onto those quite easily, which made life more bearable when travelling up to Lodge Camp.

The track progressed further and deeper into the jungle climbing all the time. We passed through thick and heavy jungle, though at times the jungle thinned out into areas that had been previously logged, or more than likely burnt down, because there were no signs of any old logging tracks within that area. But for most of the time, we had the thick green jungle canopy over our heads and no sun. The first sign of the approaching Lodge Camp was the bright ring of light at the end of a dark green tunnel. It was a satisfying feeling when we finally edged out into the bright sunlight, which was shining down through a large hole in the jungle canopy. This had been created out of the virgin jungle, by blasting and cutting the trees to make a helicopter LZ the size of a football ground.

We had finally arrived at Lodge Camp, when we moved out from the dark jungle into the newly opened ground of the LZ; it took a second or two for our eyes to adjust to the bright sunlight. Once we could see clearly, then what we saw before us was a large open space. That was the LZ that had been cleared by the 17th Troop of Australian engineers. On the opposite side of the LZ from where we had entered, the ground seemed to be rising slowly up into a valley leading into the mountains. To our right the ground appeared to be rising up to a mountainside. Perhaps this sounds a little vague, but even in a clearing the size of the LZ, it was difficult to see the surrounding terrain with the jungle still overwhelming everything in sight. Around the edge of the LZ was an absolute confusion of toppled and broken trees with smashed branches, all of which obviously, after being blasted, had then been bulldozed to the edges of the LZ by the Australian engineers. The space left by the clearance would be large enough to comfortably take a couple of helicopters, which was a big LZ in the Malay Jungle. It did mean that a platoon could quickly be flown in or out by helicopter, if and when that was required.

To the left of the clearing, the ground dropped away and down into the valley, where the river and water-point were situated. Immediately to the left was a smaller clearing, where the base camp was still in the process of being built. I only had a few minutes to look around, because as soon as the lorries were unloaded, we would be ready for leaving, but only after making a brew and taking a tea break.

It was certainly different in the Lodge jungle base camp. Amongst the equipment for the camp were packs of food supplies, which we would have normally carried in on our backs, but were now going to be issued daily to the lads. Also there were crates of beer, pop, and soft drinks, as well as cartons of cigarettes. All these kinds of luxury items would be booked to any of the lads who wanted something, then the cost would be paid back on the first pay-day back in Colombo Camp.

The camp consisted of several huts that were made from timber and inter-woven attap leaves. Of course all the material required was readily available in the jungle around the camp. There was no sign of the Australians, who had obviously finished what they had to do, then had packed up and left. The Aborigines were really interesting, they had been drafted in to help with the building of the long house that was going to house the platoon; they were sat on their haunches, busy plaiting attap leaves that were to be used to roof the huts, and also fill in the walls. I cursed myself for not taking my camera in there with me, but I certainly would take it in the next time, along with a few rolls of film, because there was no problem with carrying extra weight up to Lodge Camp.

As I stood watching the Aborigines, the drivers came up to me saying, that it was time for them to be leaving. I wondered for a moment why they had come to me, then realised that I would be the senior NCO going back out of the jungle, and then back to Colombo Camp. The return journey went without event and was just a reversal of the passage into Lodge Camp.

I remember one special moment that happened later, when going up to Lodge Camp in a three-tonner, and there was just myself and the driver. I was bringing someone out who had broken a tooth in a fall, so had to visit the army dentist in Colombo Camp. It had rained the night before, making the track exceptionally slippery, forcing the three-tonner to slip and slide more than usual, which in turn led to the engine running hot and overheating. The driver stopped on a level part of the track to let the engine cool down. It was another 'stored in the memory' moment for me.

We had heard nothing for the previous half-hour but the roar of the engine, accompanied by the noise of the bouncing, screeching wheels and tyres, with the more than too-often stones, that were picked up by the tyres, then thrown with some force to crack against the underside of the truck, or to rattle like a machine-gun on the inside of the mudguards. There was all this plus the rattles and bangs from the drop-down sides, the back and all the other bits and bats that can move and make a noise. Altogether it was a kaleidoscope of ear-bashing noise, the volume of which wasn't realised until the driver stopped and turned off the engine. Just for a moment, the silence gave me the impression that I had suddenly gone deaf. But it was only just for a moment, then the sounds of the jungle were upon me.

It was like a heavy mist of sound, descending down onto me from the jungle canopy above, like a fog rolling along the ground, around the trees and through the undergrowth, to wrap itself around me, then to soothe my eardrums with the gentle and continuous jungle sounds, which by that time, and after a year's experience, I had become so accustomed to, and was even comfortable with.

Christmas Eve 1958 was, well I don't know what to write about it actually, because the day was basically just a normal day. There was a game of football in the afternoon, in the hot sunshine. Would you believe it? Talk about *'Mad dogs and English men go out in the midday sun.'* That evening there was a very solemn mood about the place, a feeling that I had never known before that time. There was a midnight Christmas Mass in the dining hall, which was conducted by the Loyals' Battalion Chaplain. I was surprised just how many of the lads attended the service; I would think about half of the lads who were in camp at the time. The carols that were sung in the service, didn't lift the solemn mood, and if anything, they seemed to make it worse. It was very obvious that at that time, these lads were badly missing home and their loved ones. I know that I was, and I had been very lucky to have spent the previous Christmas at home.

The lads of Somme Platoon, with whom I had trained in the Ladysmith Barracks a year and a half ago, were spending their second Christmas away from their homes and their loved ones.

Christmas day was a little more upbeat, and I think that once it had arrived, then we all just had to make the best of it; at least it was another day off from any duties. But of course, we couldn't stay in bed and have a lie in. We were in the army, so still had certain things to do. I normally didn't bother going to the dining-room at lunch-time, preferring to just nip down to the charwallah's for a coffee, banana banjo and what had become the customary cigarette. However that day I decided to go to the dining-room for Christmas dinner, and to sample a traditional army institution.

It was always the custom in the army at Christmas, for the dinner to be served to the other ranks by the Commissioned Officers. I think that I received mine from Captain Williams, who was the son of the Brigadier, Mr Williams also became 'B' Company's Second in Command; I must say that I always found him to be a real gentleman. He was one of those Officers who would, if you knew what you were doing, let you get on with it without interference. He once went out on a jungle patrol with my section and myself, and despite the preceding apprehension, we all enjoyed that rummage around in the jungle.

As Christmas Day was more of a downer than an upper, I think that I will leave it there, except that I must tell you about what was to me, an important event for 'B' Company, and the Loyals. As you know 5 Platoon were in the jungle at Lodge Camp. Apparently they were the only British troops anywhere in the world, who were actually engaged on active service that Christmas day. To recognise that 'Duty to Service,' they received a special Christmas message directly from Her Majesty The Queen. The radio message was proudly fixed to a tree in the middle of Lodge Camp, and in the middle of the Loyals jungle, for all to read.

Christmas Day fell on a Thursday, this meant that it was more or less turned into a long weekend for us. Monday and Tuesday were the days for getting ready to go back into the jungle, and some the lads were looking forward to seeing Lodge Camp for the first time. It was easy to pack for this one, as there were no food packs to worry about, and everything was being transported in for us on the lorries. There were also a few extra luxuries being taken in. One or two of the lads took in pillows, someone took in a portable radio that was purchased in Hong Kong, some smooth-talked the cookhouse lads, purloining fresh fruit and vegetables, of which we the NCOs, knew nothing at all about until we were in Lodge Camp, but more about that shortly.

On the Wednesday, we bounced and bumped our way up to Lodge Camp to replace 5 Platoon, who then did the reverse trip back to Colombo Camp.

We arrived at the jungle camp quite early in the morning, so everyone spent the day assessing what could be done to further improve the amenities of the camp, so continuing what 5 Platoon had started. The camp was intended to house one platoon for as long as required. There were several huts that had been built of different sizes, which were all made from wooden logs and attap leaves. There was a small hut for the Officer, with the radio operator to the side, and one slightly larger hut for the NCOs. All the equipment delivered to Lodge Camp was stored in either the Officers' hut, or the NCOs hut for safekeeping. There was a small hut for the dog and dog handler, and a small hut for the kitchen, and one long house and a smaller long house, which would hold a platoon and the Iban trackers, plus any supporting personnel, such as the Chinese Liaison Officer, who in our case was Lawrence, who was of Chinese extraction.

I had many a jungle evening chat with Lawrence and we became good friends. He was born on the Island of Penang, my leave Island, and he would relate how the Japanese treated them during the war. How human beings could act to others, as the Japanese did then, is totally beyond my comprehension, but as I was to find out later, even we had our pitiless characters, who tried to play their evil games with the young children.

Some of the lads of the platoon were set to work on enlarging the camp waste pit that had been started in the top corner of the LZ; this hole, when finished, was about eight feet deep, five feet wide, and about twenty feet in length, so it looked really big. Other jobs were down on the river. There were steps to be finished off that were leading down to the water-hole, and a bamboo platform for the fresh water-point.

The 4 Platoon Ibans made a fishing net out of bamboo, which was fastened under the waterfall that fed into the fresh water-point. The net was constructed by splitting a large bamboo pole many times, down and around one end, then opening it up like a large funnel, with the bamboo being held open with slivers of bamboo. It was checked every evening, and always had fish caught inside, so there was fresh fish everyday, for those who liked it.

Remember the lads I told you about, who had purloined fresh fruit and vegetables from the Colombo Camp kitchens? Well we had been in Lodge Camp for three days when we received a visit from the Loyals' Commanding Officer, Colonel Thompson. As he would be with us at lunch-time, some of the lads said that they would make a special meal for him, and they wouldn't take 'no' for an answer. Second lieutenant Rawstorne was worrying what they were going to produce?

Sgt Paddy McGrattan said, "Just leave them to it."

I'm sure that Paddy had a good idea of what was going to appear before the CO. He was one of those NCOs, who didn't say much, but also didn't miss much.

When lunch-time arrived, the CO was treated to freshly-made fish and chips, complete with salt and vinegar, followed by fresh fruit for sweet. Afterwards, the Colonel commented on his surprise and pleasure with the meal. I think that the most pleasure acquired from the meal by the CO, was the resourcefulness of his boys.

Another project that was underway at the water-hole, was that the large pool below the water-point was being enlarged and deepened by building a dam across the water outlet. This was so that the pool could be used as a safe swimming pool, which would also be under the watchful eye of the sentry, who would be on guard over the water-point.

He would sit on a large rock, which was ideal for the job, and on the camp-side of the water-point. The rest of the work at the Lodge was generally tidying up the area, removing all the smaller lumps of wood and what have you, that had escaped the Australian's bulldozer blade.

The second day in Lodge Camp was New Year's Eve. I took my section out on patrol and we headed South-west and up the valley. The night before we had all been discussing the reason for building Lodge Camp in this place. We decided that from a defensive point of view, if we came under attack, the camp was perfect, on the jungle side to the North and East, we had the open ground of the LZ. To the South was a small patch of jungle that held the toilet, and was bounded by the new track and the river. To the West was a very steep bank that dropped twenty-five feet down to the river.

We were all a little bit on edge on this patrol, because the conclusion of the debate the previous evening, was that there must be a lot of Communist activity in this area, to want to build a camp of that size and permanence. So we were all of the opinion that there was a good chance of running into Charlie within the coming days. It certainly made us all silent on the patrols, you couldn't even hear anyone breathing, never mind a footfall. Isn't it always the same? You always worry about something that didn't matter in the first place! But I did worry enough on that first patrol to forget all about New Year's Eve until we had got back into Lodge Camp.

That evening at about 18:30hrs, just as the last light from the sun was being swallowed up by the jungle, I saw the Platoon Officer, Mr Rawstorne and Private Ashton, the Radio Operator sitting on a log outside of the radio shack. They were transmitting the last message of the day, and of course, the last message of 1958. I dashed back to my basha, grabbed my camera and returned to take a shot of that poignant moment.

The most exciting occurrence was on New Year's Day. I was in camp with my section, and when the other sections arrived back in camp, one of them had found and brought back a large tortoise. I had no idea that they were to be found in the middle of the Malayan jungle, but there it was, and I took a photo of it, so that no one could argue that they didn't live in Malaya. There was some dispute as to what was going to happen to the tortoise. The Ibans wanted to eat it, as they were regarded as a tasty delicacy. Our lads wanted to take it back the following day and leave it back where they had found it. They argued that in Lodge Camp there was no shortage of food, which was very true, so you will be pleased to read that this early day's attempt at conservation won the day, and the tortoise was returned to its place of abode the following day. The Ibans were kept happy with an extra day's food pack as part of the haggle, so no one suffered loss of face, which was always important.

That was about it for Lodge Camp, all a big huff and puff over nothing. We left at the end of our week and were replaced by 6 Platoon, and we never went back to Lodge Camp, so what that was all about, I have absolutely no idea, and we never did find out. Maybe some of the other Company Platoons went in there, I really don't know, but we never heard a word from any of the lads in Colombo Camp that they had been in there. The big news for me at Lodge Camp was that I was then into my year of demob and only had six months left to do in Malaya.

# CHAPTER FIFTEEN
## The Artillery Big Guns - The Last Plateau

We were once again back on plantation and jungle edge patrols. This time we were bashed-up in the worst possible place, just inside the jungle on the edge of the plantations, and just out of sight of the plantation workers. It was the worst place for a base camp, because once the sun had gone down over the horizon, we were absolutely plagued by the dreaded mosquitoes. Whatever happened to Lodge Camp, swimming-pool and all? We knew just what to expect from that area, due to the ambushing experiences we had been involved with, in and around the tin mines that were operating there, so we went to that base camp as best prepared as we could be. Best prepared meant that we took in extra insect repellent, and also a new anti-mosquito weapon for us, as recommended by one of the platoons from 'D' Company, a large bundle of joss sticks.

When we reached the base camp-site, the bashas were built as airtight as possible, but with what little we were able to carry in, an airtight approach was not over brilliant. We managed as best we could with the help of the large leaves from the jungle around us; then as the sun went down at the end of the day, we covered everything with insect repellent, and lit the joss-sticks inside the bashas. A joss stick is made from a scented paste, and in Ipoh you could buy different smelling sticks, they were very cheap, as the Chinese used to burn them in their homes as a part of their religion. We would light them with a match, and they would then smoulder for one or two hours, filling our bashas with a sweet-smelling fine smoke. The smell of the insect repellent, mixed with the aroma of the joss sticks certainly gave a most peculiar smell, but it did work to a certain extent, reducing the mosquito annoyance by about 75%.

The first day in camp was our turn to remain on guard duty. We only needed two guard positions in this camp, and as there was very little camp improvement to carry out, the lads spent most of the day reading, smoking, talking and cooking, and most of those events were carried out in the bright sunshine that bathed most of the camp, as we were right on the jungle edge.

The following day, I was patrolling up to the North and along the jungle edge. We didn't stay inside the jungle all the time, but occasionally ventured out onto some of the vast unfolding areas of sparkling white sand forming the tin mine slats. They ran all along the jungle edge in that area, which was obviously rich in tin ore. The sun was beating down that day, so it was unbelievably hot, especially when you were walking on the tin slats with the sun being reflected back up from the surface.

I took my section up into the jungle for a lunch-break; we followed a small tumbling stream up to a friendly looking spot by the side of the cooling stream, where we stopped for our break. We had been there for about half an hour, and it was one of those areas where there was a profusion of brightly coloured bugs and butterflies of all sizes. We had been sitting in silence for a few minutes with all of us I think, fascinated by the multitude of life fluttering around us in the jungle, when we heard a loud crashing sound from behind us. It was about one-hundred yards away, up the hillside into the jungle.

We all swung around with our weapons at the ready, looking in the direction from where the noises were still coming. All the lads in the section had served in the jungle long enough to realise that Charlie wasn't making the sounds, and we all had a good idea what animal was causing the noise, but we all looked at Sanden for his confirmation.

"Pig, wild pig, many pig," he cried.

Within two seconds, and with no order from me, we were heading back down to the jungle edge and to the open tin slats. We weren't going to hang about in an area where there were wild pigs, because they were dangerous animals. They were like the wild boar that used to inhabit ancient Britain, and they really were wild. The chances were that they would attack and savage a human on sight. That's why I didn't hang about in that place, nor did the lads need any telling.

We made our way further, following the jungle edge for about half a mile. It was early afternoon; the temperature was high in the hot sun, so we moved back into the jungle and under the protection of the cooling shade of the jungle canopy. We were on a hillside, so had a commanding view of the tin slats as I followed the jungle edge from about twenty-five yards inside the jungle. The patrol had travelled about a quarter of a mile along the jungle edge, when the lad behind tapped me on the shoulder. I looked around. He pointed behind and down onto the tin slats below us.

I stopped the patrol, and we stood contemplating the group of figures walking along on the tin slats. They were heading towards the jungle, and were coming from behind and from the left of us. The group would be about quarter of a mile away when we first spotted them, and from the large round hats they were wearing, we assumed that they must be Chinese. They were all carrying something, but they were too far away for us to be able to identify what? Then they vanished from our sight down into one of the valleys that had been formed in the surface of the tin mine slat.

Over to our right as I looked out over the tin slat, was one of the large steel pipelines that ran down from a river water source higher up in the jungle. They supplied the tin mines with the vast quantity of high-pressure water that they needed for their mining operations. The hillside we were on, was already beginning to curve round into a valley that stretched up into the jungle, and up into which the pipeline would obviously have been laid. There was always a path that followed a pipeline into the jungle, which allowed for maintenance to the pipe, and the dam from where the water would be sucked into the pipe. There was absolutely no maintenance allowed within the jungle without notification to, and permission from, the authorities, and an armed escort for protection, while the maintenance works were carried out. If anyone entered the jungle to carry out maintenance without permission, and they were seen, they would be shot as CTs. I knew that no one had applied for permission, that is unless we should have been notified at the briefing and somebody had fouled up, and that wasn't unknown.

At top speed I took my section to a point in the jungle where we could observe the group coming out of the valley, and onto the path that followed the pipeline up into the jungle. We came to the perfect spot and there we waited.

The lads asked, "Are we going to shoot them as soon as they appear?"

I really had my doubts about this group, as my brain kept telling me that the chances were that someone had fouled up, so I ordered the lads to keep their safety catches on, and only to fire if I told them to do so.

We waited and waited for what seemed like an eternity. I was beginning to think that I had got it all wrong, and that they had gone in a different direction, or turned back to where they had come from. Suddenly, about one-hundred yards away, a figure appeared from behind the lip of the valley, quickly followed by four more.

The first person was a male Chinese who was carrying a spade. He was followed by three Chinese females, who were also carrying tools. The last person was carrying nothing more than a walking stick. He turned out to be the charming old Chinese man with the long grey beard, with whom I had chatted quite a few months before.

I heard one of the safety catches go off, and I told them quietly, "Keep your safety catches on. I know them."

Unbelievably two of the lads wanted to open fire on them, and when I said, "No!" they even started to argue that we should.

Again I said, "No, and that's an Order."

I had a quick look at the map to see where the dam was situated; the barrier would be holding the water back, and so forming the lake that would be supplying the pipeline. From the map I could see that the valley curved behind us, so I took a compass bearing on the lake, then took my section up to the lake on that reading, as quickly and silently as possible.

As the jungle was not too dense at that point, we made good time, arriving at the lake in less than ten minutes, and well before the Chinese party's arrival. The lakes that formed the pipeline heads were never large areas; they were more just a widening of the river, and redirecting some of the flow of water down into the large steel pipe. I knew we should be getting near to the lake, when sure enough we could see the glittering water through the trees.

We kept ourselves hidden, watching as the Chinese party arrived, and then cleaned out the filters that guarded the entrance to the pipe. They spent about twenty minutes carrying out that chore, and then they left, retreating back down the path that they had followed up to the lake.

As soon as they were out of sight, we went and checked the area around the pipe entrance, just to make sure that they hadn't left anything, then we followed their tracks back down the path. Just as we reached the bottom, at the point where it broke out from the jungle, we caught sight of the back of the group just disappearing down the valley that ran through the tin mine slats. We turned left, heading back along the tin slats leading to our mosquito-ridden base camp.

As I took my patrol back to the base camp, our feet were sinking slightly into the silvery sand of the tin slats, and the world, well my world was somehow contradictory. I suddenly felt, well it really is difficult to say how I felt at that moment. I knew that I felt different, but I didn't know why. There was something different, like I had lost something.

My brain started to tick over, check-listing everything mentally. Had I seen the Chinese do something that was important, but hadn't registered as such? I realised one thing that should have struck me sooner, if they had reported to the authorities that they had repairs to do, and we had not been told about that at the briefing, then the Chinese should still have had their armed escort with them. If I had realised that sooner, would I have opened fire on them? I thought about that, but only to myself, and at the start of the journey back to the base camp. Those thoughts you do keep to yourself, they were the lonely thoughts when in command and on active service, the absolute responsibility for any individual; the moment when you realised that what you have seen, and what you have heard, affect the decisions that you take, or don't take, and might mean life or death for someone. And of course, those thoughts obviously always affect what you do. But that's what was missing for me at that moment, the responsibility for the lives of five human beings. Five people with ordinary lives, and no doubt normal families, and for a short time their lives, and their loved ones futures, were held entirely in my hands.

I was perfectly happy with what was then, and without a doubt to me now, the correct outcome. What I am really trying to say is what really affected me the most, was that at that moment I realised that my decisions were taken without any personal emotions. Had I become dehumanised?

The rest of that operation held nothing more exciting than the nightly battle with the mosquitoes, and we returned to Colombo Camp glad to be away from them, and of course the smell of insect repellent and joss sticks. The affair with the Chinese working party was reported at the debriefing. A few weeks later I was told that they hadn't notified the authorities, but apparently they were told that they had been watched all the way, and they were lucky that it was the Loyals watching over them, and for any of them to still be alive.

We were now hoping that the next operation would take us back to Lodge Camp, and all the home comforts that it held for us. We still weren't to know that, despite all the work we put into the place, we would never see Lodge Camp again.

The next operation was well up to the North of the Perak State, and on the Western side of the valley, on the opposite side to where we had just been. It was only going to be a three-day operation, and we were going to enter into the jungle by following an old logging track that firstly wound its way through an old and unused cultivation area.

As we arrived at the drop-off point in the three-tonners, it was just turning daylight. We could see the rays of the sun reaching up from behind the Cameroon Highland Mountain Range that was some thirty miles to the East of us. It was on one of the roads in the mountains up there, where Sir Henry Gurney, the British High Commissioner to Malay, was ambushed and killed by Charlie. British soldiers, mostly national servicemen who were escorting Sir Henry, also died in that ambush.

We spent a few minutes sorting ourselves out, and five minutes after the lorries had left, we were underway. My section were doing the lead in, and so I was up to the front of the platoon. The leading scout was out in front, followed by Sanden and then myself. In front was a wide valley, and the floor of the valley was just perceptibly climbing upwards towards the jungle-covered hills. In the distance the valley narrowed, then started to rise up into the heights of the mountain range. With the sun behind us, we could see clearly to the front, and the direction in which we were heading. We could feel the sun already beginning to burn the backs of our necks, and it had the beginnings of another very hot Malayan day.

The old cultivation area that we were in was enormous, and I would think that it had an area of something around five or six square miles. There were no trees at all, not even surprisingly any palm or coconut trees, but there was a multitude of different types of bush and shrubbery that were taking over the area, and these were scattered about in groups. The river that ran down and through the valley, was well over to our left, and we were planning on using the river as our water source, but three miles or more further up the valley.

With the valley and the cover being the way it was, this meant that it would have been an ideal place for Charlie to ambush us, if he had a mind to do that, so I turned around and opened my arms to the rest of the platoon, which told them to spread out, leaving more space between each man.

We had been underway for about one hour. The ground under our feet was still more or less on the level, and the old logging track was a bit on the dusty side. There were thick scattered bushes to each side of the track, and the sun was definitely building up for a scorcher of a day.

Suddenly there was a most peculiar sound, that seemed to be all around us like a swarm of hornets, and then more of the sounds were added to the first. We all had time to look quickly around, and the adrenalin pumped-up brain, that had stopped time in its tracks, was unable to assimilate what was happening, or what the sounds around us were?

Then came the sounds of gunshots banging and thumping our eardrums, and echoing in the valley. Everyone dived for cover, which meant for all of us, under the nearest bush.

There were more bangs and thumps, only this time further away.

"My God," I thought, "we are surrounded by dozens of them and without cover."

Then I heard Sgt Paddy McGrattan shouting, "It's okay, it's okay, it's the artillery firing *over* us."

We all stood up, and I will not say that we felt a bit foolish because we didn't; it was a frightening moment for us all. The shells were still going overhead, with a distinctive whoosh-crack and exploding at the top of the valley, just beyond where we were going to build our jungle base camp. We stopped in that spot until the radio operator had set up his equipment, and Mr Rawstorne had sent a message back to base to find out what was happening?

While we were waiting for all this to happen, the lads were spending their time pulling out all the long, black, wood spikes that where sticking from our bodies. They were acquired with thanks to the bushes that we had dived under for cover. Believe it or not, but my wife Betty was still pulling black spikes out of my back over a year after I got back home.

We got a message back to proceed with the operation as planned. Apparently we should have been told at the pre-operational briefing that we were going up the valley under the covering fire of the howitzers of the Royal Australian Artillery. It was a bit late to tell us now that the Artillery would be giving covering fire at 08:00hrs; and it was certainly a scary moment for 4 Platoon. If we had been warned beforehand, it would have been a very interesting experience. But as I have said before and to be safe, you could not take it for granted that nothing had been missed in the pre-operational briefing. When information was missed out, you could almost guarantee that it was further up the line and beyond the powers of the Loyals.

At about 11:00hrs, we were crossing over the river that was to our left; we were fortunate to immediately find a spot that was ideal for our base camp. It was about fifty yards over the river, on the top of a low ridge that was running downhill following the line of the river. The water-point was at the place where we had crossed the river, and there was an ideal spot for the sentry to guard the water-point, and also keep the track we had travelled on, under observation. Doing that provided a permanent daily one-man ambush on the track, which was still running through the cultivation, though now it was very narrow old open cultivated land, running high up into the valley.

There were only two sentries needed in this base camp as there were no tracks anywhere, and the area was overgrown with large ferns and a type of briar tangled amongst the trees. The toilet point was downhill but still on the ridge, so the second sentry was guarding that spot; but lower down the ridge.

The following day I was out on patrol with my section. We were heading further up and along the track on which we had travelled coming up the valley. We left the base camp, by first travelling uphill and walking in the river, so as to leave less evidence of fresh tracks entering into our base camp from the old logging track. We crossed out onto the track and then made our way uphill. We followed the track climbing upwards for a couple of hours, had a quick break, then made our way into the thicker jungle on our right.

We had gone past the area that had been shelled by the Australian Artillery, but there was no sign at all of any damage. The going was now naturally much slower than travelling on the track, but we were still making good time, and the jungle was at the sort of density that I preferred, which was thick enough to give you good cover, but thin enough to get through without too much bother.

We had been underway on this compass bearing for about an hour, and the ground was a peculiar series of rolling vales, which were most unusual, and the only time that I found that type of ground feature in Malaya. One thing that was really noticeable in this area, was the amount of wildlife that abounded with virtually every step we had taken; I had seen more snakes and centipedes on this patrol, than probably in all of my time in Malaya up to that date. It was the same with the monkeys who were also prolific in that patrol area.

I addressed Sanden, "With there being so much wildlife around, will there be more chance, or less chance of there being CTs around here?"

All I got from him was, "Maybe, maybe."

To be honest, I don't think that he fully understood what I was trying to say, or mean. Suddenly appearing through the jungle twenty-yards in front of us, was a vertical white cliff-face, rising as high as we could see from where we were placed. It took us just a few seconds to get to the rock-face. Ten yards from the cliff, there was very little growing on the ground, due to the rocks both large and small that had fallen, or been washed down to ground level, where we were standing. We looked up to where we could see a little bit of bright sunshine shining on what must have been the top of the cliff-face. We reckoned that it must have been about two-hundred feet high.

I was amazed that the cliff was there at all, because there was nothing shown on the map, and for this area the maps were pretty good and accurate. I studied the map for a feature that showed a cliff-face, just in case I had missed something, and my map reading wasn't as good as I believed. Perish the thought of that, but just for a second I did wonder. But on the map there was nothing, not even a prominence that the cliff had been mistaken for.

We had a ten minute break, then I took my section along to the left following along the rock-face, we were all on our guard, as we knew that Charlie had a liking for having their camp high up, with the sentry on the edge of a cliff.

We had been following the rock-face for just over half an hour, and it was slowly curving around on itself. I had just about made up my mind that this was a small Gunong, that wasn't shown on the map, when we came to a ramp that was leading up the side of the cliff-face. It looked quite natural, and wasn't man-made as far as we could tell, but it was a perfectly sloped angle for someone to go up and down in a wheelchair. We could see that it was climbing up and following the curve of the rock-face.

I wondered where it went to, and if it did make it to the top? All the lads were also wondering about those possibilities, so were also intrigued. I was not about to try and find out, without first checking all the way around at ground level, that was assuming that it did go all the way around. Half an hour later we found out that it did, because we arrived back at the spot where we had first seen it. We immediately turned around and started back to where the ramp was climbing the rock-face. We were running out of time, but there was no way that we were going to leave that place without finding out where the sloping ramp finished?

For some reason, we were all convinced that it would reach the top, and we were all filled with a certain amount of excitement as to what we might find if and when we got there. It only took us twenty minutes to get back to where the inclined path started. We were able to move through the jungle at a good speed, because we had just covered the ground, so we knew that everything was clear and relatively safe. We were also no longer worried about Charlie being up there. He wouldn't trap himself without an escape route. There would be no fresh water up there, and there were no tracks showing any recent movement on the inclined path.

I checked with the lads that they were all okay with going up the incline? Everyone was more that keen, and ready for the off. The path was about six-feet wide at the start, and remained that width until we were about eighty-feet above the ground. It was quite hard going, so we were being extra careful where we put our feet, with being so high up and not wanting to stumble on some rock or other. We came to a dog-leg in the path, where it swung around a crevice in the rock face. On the other side of the dog-leg, the path reduced to between three and four-feet in width, but was still climbing steadily.

I didn't like heights then, and I still don't, but I was used to working at heights on tall buildings, and I think that my estimation of us being about eighty-feet above the ground would not be far wrong. But when we looked over the edge of the path, it looked far higher, with the trees growing by the side of the path and still towering above us. When we looked down it gave us a tunnel effect, for the ground appeared to be much further away. I was not very happy I can tell you, and I was definitely thinking to myself that this was a bad idea. I looked up and could see that we still had a long way to go. I don't mind admitting now, that a little shiver ran up my spine when I thought of climbing further up on that slope.

I had called for a rest at the dog-leg, whilst I took the chance to weigh up the options. I could tell that one or two of the lads were enjoying the experience, but I could also tell by the way they were hanging onto the rock-face, that two of the lads were frightened of the height, and getting worse as the height increased. I didn't tell them, but I really did sympathise with them, because I appreciated how they were feeling, but as the leader of the patrol, I just dare not show my fear, and I knew that I just had to go on.

I knew that it may seem pointless for me to do something that I didn't want to do, especially when I could just order my lads to get on with it. The greatest respect that I got from my lads, including the hard knocks, was that I would never ask or expect them to do something that I would not do myself.

However, being the section commander, did give me a certain advantage, and I could make life easier for myself with nobody realising that I had done that.

What I did, was to leave the two lads, who were obviously not keen on heights, at the dog-leg, to guard the path that we had just come up, but to also guard the equipment that the rest of us, who were going all the way up, were leaving behind. We left everything behind on the path, including the water bottles and spare ammunition. As I carried more gear than anyone else, a large pack of maps and a compass for example, I then left more gear behind than the others. I also had the advantage of a lighter weapon, that folded up into a small easy to handle unit.

So against my better judgement, onwards and upwards we went. As we got higher, it actually became easier mentally, because we had entered the jungle canopy, and in places the branches overlapped the path. It was weird when we broke through the canopy and into the sunshine, because that also brought us to the top of the cliff-face and onto the top of the gunong. It explained why the aerial mapping had not picked out the prominence. The top of the gunong was level with the top of the jungle canopy, so the green shrubbery growing on top would have made it look just like the tops of the trees.

We had a wonderful view from up there as we could see out over the treetops, and right down the valley that we had travelled up the day before. But for the hills to our right, we would have been able to see all the way to Ipoh. We spent about fifteen minutes searching the top for any sign of past life up there, but disappointingly and surprisingly, we found absolutely nothing, and it had got past the time to head back.

When we arrived back to our jungle base camp, we found that the other patrol, or at least the Iban, had caught and killed an iguana lizard and a python snake. They too had found an abundance of wild life in the area. That night we all tried, well at least those who wanted to try, a taste of python and iguana meat. The python steak wasn't too bad, and to me was like a cross between chicken and crab-meat. The iguana lizard was a different proposition, and was absolutely diabolical. It was just a lump of fishy-tasting gristle, that had to be sucked to get the meat off.

Sanden enjoyed it, as to the Ibans it was regarded as quite a delicacy. Well each to their own, I suppose. The following day, we were back out on patrol, but there was nothing of any significance to be seen, and certainly not as interesting as the previous day. But that evening had one moment that was a little bit different and sticks out clearly in my memory. I wonder how many of the lads out of 4 Platoon remember this one, and from all of the hundreds of memories that we have all carried with us down the years?

It was late afternoon and still very bright and warm with the sun still well up above the hills behind us. One of the Lance Corporals had been down the ridge and to the toilet. When he returned back to his basha, he realised that his army issue watch was missing. He knew that he was wearing it before he went down the ridge to the toilet. It was a serious offence for an NCO to lose his army issued watch or compass. I only wore mine when I was on an operation, otherwise I wore my own personal wrist-watch.

All the lads that were available joined in the search, up and down the path from the base camp to the toilet, but all to no avail. I wandered down to where they were searching, and made a suggestion that had them all looking at me as though I was daft.

All I said was, "Why not divine for it?" I know that most people think that divining is not really possible, or that it is just a magician's trick. I was taught how to divine for metal objects by my father, who used the technique to locate buried cast-iron stop tap boxes, and I might add, with a great deal of success.

To divine for metal, you need two lengths of thick metal wire, each about two-feet long, which are then bent in a certain way. But where do you find two lengths of metal wire in the middle of the Malayan jungle?

I had already thought about that before I made the suggestion. The radio set had a canvas hood to darken the dials, which enabled them to be read easily in daylight. The hood was held rigid by removable metal rods, which were just about the right length. The Corporal who had lost his watch was desperate to try anything, so off I went and acquired the wire rods from the radio operator. As soon as I got back to the track, I bent the rods as the tradition required, before starting to walk slowly down the path towards the toilet area, watched by the lads who had now stopped their search. One or two of them were quite amused by the event, and of course provided the expected caustic and amusing comments.

I had gone about one third of the way down the path when the divining rods swung across to the right. I turned to the right, straightened the rods, and then moved forward. Within a couple of feet, the rods crossed over each other, and there, immediately below the tails of the divining rods, lay the missing watch. The lads could not believe that it had worked that easily, for within two minutes from starting divining, the watch was found. Needless to say then that all of the lads wanted to have a go after that.

There is just one thing of note about our waterproof army watch. When I was issued with mine it was the first time that I had seen a nylon wrist-strap. Up to that time the straps on watches were mainly leather, or expanding metal types. The straps, just like everything else in the jungle, got dirty and smelly, but with being nylon they were easy to wash and dry, and didn't rot. The familiar nylon watch-straps that most young people wear nowadays, were originally made for army personnel to use in the Malayan jungle.

That event was just about it for that operation, and the following day we were back in Colombo Camp, getting paid up to date, and drawing our free issue of cigarettes from the Company stores. I suppose that the final curtain to that operation came down later that morning when Mr Rawstorne came down to the Corporals' basha.

"Corporal Hudson!"

"Yes Sir."

"That divining trick that you did in the jungle."

"Yes Sir."

"Well I don't want you to show me any more tricks again in the jungle."

"Right Sir. May I ask why?"

"Yes Corporal." Then, with a broad smile, he told me that he didn't want to be laughed out of the Officers' Mess again, as he had been the night before, after explaining how to divine with metal rods for a lost object.

I did say in the jungle that, *'When you do it, you have to relax your mind and let the force do it for you.'* I wonder if 2Lt Rawstorne wrote about the stars and wars, and under a pseudonym in later years?

# CHAPTER SIXTEEN
## *The Scared Camp - The Death of a Friend*

It now seemed to be non-stop, with one jungle operation after another. On reflection, I would put it down to the fact that Charlie was on the run, and they were heading steadily for the Thailand border and sanctuary. We were going to do our bit to make sure that Charlie kept on running. Our next operation was going to be shared with 5 Platoon. This was due to so many national servicemen, out of both platoons, going back home to Blighty at the same time.

We were only in the jungle for five days, and on the third day, nearly half the men were leaving the jungle base camp to return to Colombo Camp, and then a couple of days later were off down to Singapore to catch the boat for home. For some reason, I wasn't worrying about this particular operation, and the jungle when I got in there had a little bit of a friendly feel to it.

We were not too far into the jungle, and one of the large tin mine water supply pipes was running up the valley, and did pass quite close to our base camp. As there were so many of us at the beginning of the operation, when we built the jungle base camp, the perimeter was of a far greater circumference than normal. Nobody worried about it at the time, but to save space, two of the lads and myself built a triple basha. There were, for some reason, quite a few tracks criss-crossing in that area, and one of them passed the front of our basha. It was about ten-yards away into the jungle and slightly downhill from us.

I have no idea what animal or animals had made the path, but it was obvious that it was used regularly. Please don't have the idea in your mind that these paths were as you would see in your local park or wood, that is like a path you could just walk along. A path or track in the jungle, would normally be a hole that was obvious, because it penetrated through the thick jungle undergrowth, and the ground would be compressed hard, and generally devoid of major plant life. The tracks could be, and were used by any form of life, and if they were large enough, this included humans.

The second day I was out on patrol with my section; we headed up into the mountains, and at the start we followed the pipeline path. We found nothing of particular interest in the area we were patrolling, and made it back to camp with plenty of time to prepare a meal. Shortly after we had got back into base, whilst I was making my evening meal, for some reason I noticed a certain air of depression about the camp. It was nothing undue, and I put it down to a good few of the lads leaving the following day to return home.

I was surprised that the lads who were going to be leaving the jungle, and were spending their last night in there, weren't going around sending everyone up, because they were going home, and we were staying in there. I put it down to last minute nerves, and not wanting to stick their necks out, with still being in the jungle. The two lads who I was bashed up with, were also showing nerves, and kept on for me to move the basha away from the track that ran near to us, more into the camp.

The following day was our day in the base camp. The morning was a little peculiar, as it was so busy with the number of lads that were in there, packing up and getting ready to leave. They were soon on their way, lucky devils; and in the space of thirty seconds, the camp had moved from a hive of activity, to a quiet, lonely and almost empty place. There was a definite air of sadness, because some good mates had just left, and we knew that we were probably never going to see them again, or ever share a cigarette and a laugh at a bad moment. But the most depressing thought was the regret that you knew they were starting a journey that would take them to their loved ones, whilst we were still stuck in the middle of the Malayan jungle.

The two lads kept on for the rest of the morning about moving our basha away from the track, and more into the centre of the camp. This worry of theirs kept nagging at me, because it was so out of character for them to be troubled to that extent. When it got to lunch-time, I really did become concerned, because they offered to do all the work involved in moving the basha, which was really out of character. But I had an ever-growing pessimistic feeling that something was very wrong. It was just small things that were happening, and it wasn't just those two lads who were causing me to worry. **Everyone** was very quiet and tending to circulate in the middle of the camp. Everyone carried weapons all the time. The lads on sentry duty, so they weren't on their own, would have a mate sharing the guard with them, and that was most unusual, and the moment when I realised that there really was something wrong.

I had already agreed with the two lads that we would move our basha back and nearer to the camp centre. It was a logical move anyway, because the bashas that had been around us at the beginning, had now gone. The lads who were bashed up in them, were amongst those who had left for Colombo Camp, so that was leaving us out on a limb.

We rebuilt our bashas nearer to the camp, and this time I built my basha for myself, and the other two lads built together next to me. But they were still very uneasy, but when I finally started asking what was wrong, all I got back was that everything was fine. The next two days didn't change much in the platoon's anxious attitudes, and when we moved out of the base camp to return to Colombo, I was still no wiser.

The amazing thing was, that as we reached the jungle edge, the mood immediately lifted in the most amazing manner, which left me with no doubt at all, that something was very wrong with that area, or in that base camp. On the three-tonner back to Colombo, I tried to pump the lads as to what had been troubling them, but all I got were negative answers.

I toyed over what could possibly have been worrying them all, but I could think of nothing, apart from that someone had seen some type of apparition. Once we reached Ipoh I forgot about the problem. I thought that I would never penetrate the wall of silence, so there was no point in trying, and whatever it was that bothered the lads, would have to remain a mystery to me forever. It was quite some time later when I found out about the problem. What I was told seemed to me to be absolutely unbelievable, but I will tell you about that later.

Three weeks later, and in a valley just a mile or two to the South of that frightened jungle base camp, Captain Bruce Merrie, of the MMG Company and leader of the Renowned Loyals Tracker Team, was out with his tracker team on a training exercise. Captain Bruce Merrie's idea of an exercise was to do the training in the area where you were most likely to run into Charlie. It was said that when he went into the jungle, he travelled light and fast. All he took with him were his weapon, spare ammunition, water bottle and a pocketful of rice. I think that was a bit of an exaggeration, because whenever I saw the tracker team, they all carried packs on their backs, but the idea wasn't that far from the mark.

The tracker team hadn't been long off their transport, and were making their way up an old logging track near to the jungle edge. As they came to negotiate a fallen tree that was across the track, the leading scout saw two CT's coming down the track. At the same time, they saw the tracker team.

The CT's immediately vanished into the undergrowth, but from what I was told about the incident, there was no exchange of fire. The tracker team had a full complement of Iban trackers and dog handlers, but try as they might, they could not find any tracks at all in the undergrowth into which the CT's had vanished.

You have to realise that Charlie was an absolute master at hiding his tracks in the jungle. You could say as if his life depended upon it, which of course it did!

Captain Bruce-Merrie then took the decision that if Charlie hadn't left any tracks to where he was going, and because he had been spotted, then maybe he had left tracks back to where he had come from. What the tracker team didn't know, was that the two CTs headed back to the base camp they had just left, so as to warn their comrades that they might be backtracked.

The tracker team decided to give the dogs a try in picking up the scent of the CT's, and sure enough, one of the dogs picked up the scent and was away with the dog handler in tow, closely followed by the top Iban tracker, Niambong, the other Ibans and the rest of the tracker team. I knew Niambong well, and regarded him as one of my friends out there. He was a chief's son from Sarawak, and was the first Iban I went into the jungle with back in the jungle training Company. He was the first person who tried to teach me the art of jungle craft, and I remember him showing me how a leaf on a bush, or on the ground would turn, if someone brushed past them. The tracker team was travelling at top speed, so there was no time for a break, as speed was essential if there was to be any result from their endeavours.

They had been following the scent for about an hour and were well up the valley and into thick jungle. The dog handler's bootlace had come undone, so he stopped and knelt down to refasten it. The laces on a jungle boot were very long, which allowed you to wrap the lace around the top of the canvas boot several times, preventing anything getting down and inside of the boot. We would normally undo our boots each time we stopped, to check for leeches and suchlike, and also to let the blood circulate to our feet. We would then obviously retie the laces, trying to make sure that they would not come undone, because with being so long, we could easily trip over them. Of course, the tracker team hadn't stopped, so the dog handler hadn't had the chance to check his bootlaces, but now that one had come undone, he had no option but to stop and tie it.

As the dog handler knelt down, Niambong passed him checking for any sign of tracks left by the CT's. A shot was heard coming from the jungle up to the right of the track they had been following, and Niambong fell where he had been standing, having been killed instantly, as he was shot through the head.

The rest of the Ibans, having seen what had happened to Niambong, instantly ran past his body, and into the Communist camp with the rest of the tracker team hot on their heels. The response was so quick and savage from the Ibans and the tracker team, that Charlie had hardly time to stand and fight. There was an instant mêlée of hand-to-hand fighting, with so I was told, the Ibans throwing down their rifles and resorting to using their machetes on Charlie.

At the end of the battle there were, if I remember correctly, four CT's killed, and the rest scattered and escaping into the jungle, our loss was sadly Niambong. I have to tell you that although his grandparents had been head-hunters. I always, and without fail, found him to be what I would call, a real gentleman, and I am writing this now, because I personally want people to know that fact.

Why have I told you about that incident? Well for one thing, it's my chance to finally pay my respects to Niambong, but mainly it's down to our old base camp and why the lads were so ill at ease. The reason was told to me during one of the evening chin-wags that we sometimes held, in the night-time darkness, inside one of the jungle base camps and a long time after both events.

The reason for the anxiety of the lads in that base camp was that the day before the lads were due to leave for Colombo Camp, one of them, who shall remain nameless, was on guard duty in the afternoon on the West side of the base camp. The guard post overlooked a small hollowed clearing. In the middle of the guard duty, a CT walked through the clearing, heading South.

Knowing that if he shot him, the lad would have been held back in Malaya for quite sometime, he let him go on his way, with Charlie unaware how close he had come to being killed.

That's what I was told by my lads out in Malaya, and I believed that to be so for many years, but an old Comrade from the Malayan days, Major Maher (Slim), has recently at Fulwood Barracks, told me that the true story wasn't as I thought, or had been told. Major Maher and I were Corporals together in 'B' Company, but not only were we together in that jungle base camp, but Slim was the Section Commander of the lad who was on guard duty that day, so obviously knew far more about what actually happened on that afternoon than I do. According to Slim there were two CT's who walked into the clearing that afternoon, and the lad concerned actually spoke to them and told them to clear off, or words to that effect.

No wonder everyone was concerned. They all knew that Charlie was about that area, but also that Charlie knew where we were. When I first heard about Charlie walking past the guard, my immediate thought was that he must have been heading for the CT base camp that the tracker team attacked, which was situated over the hill to the South. What would the future have been for everyone, and especially Niambong, if he, or now they, had been shot?

Our next operation was back on the dreaded ambushing; this time we were going to be doing that for three nights on the run. We were going to ambush the track, or possible tracks, leading from the village, that we had under observation when we were on the night-time Observation Post. The 4 Platoon Officer and all the NCOs did a daytime patrol in the area. It looked just like a normal plantation patrol, but we were actually surveying the ambush points. Nobody knew that we were all NCOs and an Officer, because in the plantations, or in the jungle, we all dressed the same, and never ever wore our rank. Anyone who didn't know us would think that we could all be just Private soldiers.

The track that we were all ambushing ran along the bank of a wide river that went around two sides of the village. I must have drawn the short straw, because my section was ambushing the most likely point, which was where the track crossed the river to the village. At this point, the track followed the river, then took a sharp turn to the right, went up the river-bank which was about five-feet high, and then over the top of the river-bank dropping about seven-feet to the water level. The water in the river at that point would be about six inches deep, but the river would be about fifty-feet wide. The river-bank on the village side of the river, was a repeat of the bank on the ambush side.

That evening after curfew, we moved into the ambush position, which I set up on the outside of the bend that was leading up to the bank of the river crossing. I set the ground flares in place, then ran the wires back through the undergrowth to our ambush position. I then settled down in the middle of the section, coupled up the wires to the battery and switch. The two-inch mortar was next to me, along with four parachute flare shells. There were still a few minutes of daylight left, so we all had a last cigarette before settling down for another unpleasant night, which in Malaya meant twelve hours. It wasn't quite as bad as we had been expecting with the mosquitoes being very few in number at that spot, which served to make it a little more bearable for us.

We were still fully alert to any movement in the undergrowth around us, where we were was an ideal place for the snakes, scorpions, spiders and everything else that could bite or sting. We had been lying there for about an hour, when the moon started to rise above the mountains of the Cameroon Highlands over thirty miles away to our right. It was a full moon that night, and when it occupied the sky above us, it really was the most wonderful sight that you could ever wish to see. It seemed to be ten times greater than how you perceive the moon in the UK, for it really looked enormous, just as you would expect it to look through a pair of binoculars back home in Blighty.

When you first see a tropical moon, it's difficult to understand just how the atmosphere can make so much difference to what you can see. But that night it certainly made everything around us stand out clearly, with it being almost a silvery daylight.

We could hear the sounds of the village from the moment we arrived at the ambush position, the music playing on the radios, and the occasional laughter all coming to us through the shrubbery of the cultivation, and faintly from the distance. There was the odd sound now and again of metal being hammered, like someone banging on a corrugated metal sheet, and a couple of times we heard what sounded like a motorbike engine being revved. There was also the odd dog barking, occasional shouting at whatever, and in the early evening the sound of young children playing, probably as back home, some ball game. Overlaying all the sounds of the village, was as always the sounds of the Malayan night, the constant buzzing and hum of the insects, and the infrequent wildlife sounds that we could never put a name to, and with being so near to the river in that particular spot, the sporadic deep-throated croaking of bullfrogs.

By nine that evening, the sounds were decreasing, and by eleven the village had become as silent as the grave, with not even a dog bark echoing to us through the plantations, or across the river. The hum of the insect world had a tendency to lull you to sleep, and you had to guard against that while ambushing, which usually meant giving the lads on each side of you the occasional nudge, and them you, especially if you thought someone was beginning to fall asleep. I had just looked at the glowing dial on my wrist-watch; it was showing nearly 00:30hrs.

I thought to myself, "If Charlie was going to use this crossing tonight, it's going to be anytime now, or he won't have time to make the cover of the jungle before daylight."

Just at that moment I heard a sound that sent a shiver down my spine, from the far side of the river had come the sound of a footstep in the water, just a quiet splash in the river, but a sound we had been listening for. I was just about to nudge the lads on each side, but they both beat me to it. As it turned out later, all the lads had heard that first footstep in the water.

With each step, the sounds of the water splashing became louder and nearer. At the second splash, I heard the safety catches clicking off.

I whispered very quietly, "Wait for me to fire."

Splash, splash, splash, the sounds came nearer and nearer, and then crunch, they had reached the slope of the bank seven-feet down on the other side, and the first footstep had left the water and crunched into the gravel that formed the track on the river-side of the bank.

Crunch, the second step now boomed out to us, sounding like church bells ringing out with the noise, and seemingly as loud. Crunch, we all drew in a lung filled with air, and then stopped breathing, holding our breath in anticipation. Crunch, crunch, crunch. Where were they? Where had they got to?

Their heads should be showing now above the bank but there was still nothing.

Another step crunched from over the bank. Had they followed the bank up-stream? Suddenly, there was movement coming over the bank, a head just beginning to show, up and over, our fingers tightened on the triggers.

"Come on, come on," I thought to myself, "come on show yourself."

Then with a heart-stopping leap the figure was there, standing on the top of the bank and looking down at us. We all beheld a blooming great scraggy dog, which that night had to be the luckiest dog alive, or should I say *still* alive. It was an absolute miracle that nobody opened fire, because we reckoned afterwards that we all had the triggers down at least halfway and onto first pressure, when the dog made us all jump as it leapt onto the top of the bank. We all kept absolutely still while the dog looked at us.

I had heard from somewhere that sometimes Charlie used dogs to check if the coast was clear, so I kept the lads where they were until the dog had a sniff around and then paddled back over the river. I waited for another ten minutes, before telling the lads to make sure that their safety catches were back on, then I went very quietly to the top of the bank and looked very slowly over.

Everything stood out clearly in the bright moonlight, so bright in fact that it was throwing distinctive shadows from every object. But there was no sign of the dog, and nothing was moving wherever my eyes looked.

I was just behind a bush that was growing on the bank top, so I stood up very slowly. I could then see part of the track that was leading to the village. In the moonlight it stood out like a large shiny silver snake, making its way through the cultivation towards the settlement. But there was no movement at all to be seen. I stood there perfectly still for about ten minutes, with just my eyes moving; all the time studying the sides of the track leading to the village, but there was nothing.

I went back down to the lads, looking at my watch. I was surprised to see that it had got to 01:45hrs. It was getting too late for Charlie to be coming through the crossing, but you never could tell. The lads were still very much on a high, but the rest of that night passed by with no further incidents, as did the next two nights on that bend, but I did wonder for a long time after that, as to whether the dog was on its own, or was there someone with it?

Back in Colombo Camp things were looking as if we were in for improvements. Work had just started on two large new buildings. One was going to be a new NAAFI shop, whilst the other was to be a new cinema, but with a stage built in, so that it could be used for other events. Both were to be air-conditioned. We had also had another little luxury installed, which was hot water to the wash-basins and showers; just as when I first got to 'B' Company, the old sweats reckoned that something bad must be coming up.

I was an old sweat myself by then, and I agreed. Well you do learn that you don't get too many good things, so the chances were that you would be right, and if you weren't, it was simply a bonus. Another notice appeared on the notice-board saying that they were going to start an aeroplane-modelling club if there was enough interest within the battalion. I had always been keen on building model planes, so I thought that I would have a go at that if it takes off.

Somebody said, "They're making things so good for us, that we won't want to go home when the time comes, well what do you think?"

The next operation that 4 Platoon was to embark upon was going to be the longest time spent in the jungle by any platoon from the Loyal Battalion. We were going in for at least three weeks, and we were to be re-supplied by parachute drop. It all sounded very interesting at the briefing, but it did mean carrying a fair amount of extra gear into the jungle. For the air-drops we had to carry large marker panels; one was bright red and the other bright yellow. When opened up they would be about twelve-feet long and two-feet wide, and were made from rayon, which is a material similar to nylon. Then there were the smoke grenades, the flare gun plus the flare cartridges of different colours. It was all extra gear, that had to be carried into the jungle, along with everything else that we needed, and by shanks's pony.

We were going deep into the jungle, and the first night's stop was going to be just a case of making a meal and putting our head down for some sleep. The following morning it was off again, deeper into the jungle, to our first permanent base camp location.

With regards to seeing Charlie, the operation was a bit of a damp squib, and you could say a month wasted, that is with the exception of leaving our tracks all over the place, so that if Charlie did come back into the area he would get the message, that even that far into the jungle, he still wasn't safe. He would get the message that we had been there, we were there, and we would be back there. We did find one old and major Communist base camp that was even complete with a small parade ground, and what I believe was a firing range. As I stood in the middle of the parade ground I was once again filled with the self-satisfying thought that I was the master of all I surveyed. Yet just a short time before, and while I was attending Kirkham Grammar School, that area was the domain of the Malayan Communist Army.

Although Charlie was in short supply, this operation was not without its interesting moments. After five days we moved the base camp a few miles to a new location that was on the edge of a small natural clearing, which had been spotted on the aerial photographs of that area. The clearing was to be the location for our parachute re-supply late the following afternoon, and as we would have run out of food by then, we were all keeping our fingers crossed that the clearing would be okay, but until we got there, we just didn't know.

The journey through the jungle to the new location wasn't too bad, and our backpacks were very light as we had no food to carry, but we were filled with a certain amount of trepidation as to what we were going to find with regards to the clearing. If it was unable to take the air-drop then we were in trouble. We would be out of food, and there was no other area that was near to where we could redirect the drop.

We got to the clearing mid-afternoon, and the first quick look into the clearing lifted our spirits. There seemed to be no problem for a parachute drop to take place. The thing that had worried me the most, was that the area was only showing clear on the aerial photos due to it being a swamp. It was a little smaller than I had expected, but it would do, that's with a bit of clearing out of the undergrowth the following day before the air-drop.

We all got on with building the second base camp, as this was going to last us for over a week. With the air-drop due the next day everything was fine and nothing now could go wrong, could it?

The rest of that day was spent building a decent camp. We were all already smelling to high heaven. The lads planned on damming the stream that we were based on, so as to form a small swimming pool. They had all decided, after Lodge Camp, that a pool was a necessity to clean living in the jungle. It certainly helped, for you did feel a lot better and healthier when you were clean. But it was very rare to find a location that would facilitate building a dam, and was also safe from attack by Charlie.

It was planned to clear the drop zone area the following morning. Meanwhile everyone had to make a list of all the gear that they needed to be dropped in the following afternoon. At a personal level, that consisted of things like new jungle uniforms, green towels, jungle and hockey boots, socks, soap, cigarettes, matches, mail and the like. The general platoon requirements consisted of firstly the amount of food packages for how long we were to remain at that camp. Also there were fresh radio and torch batteries, new maps, new cooking stoves and hexomine solid fuel tablets, naturally enough insect repellent, and all that type of thing, and not forgetting the rum ration.

The entire list of requirements were radioed to Colombo Camp that evening, along with the normal daily contact to base. You may be surprised that new jungle uniforms and boots were on the list, but after a week in the jungle, with the constant dampness, and battling our way through the undergrowth, parts of our equipment were rotting away, and more than likely, also torn and ripped. When we replaced damaged or worn out items in the jungle then, whatever we had to replace was supposed to be totally destroyed, and then buried.

Of course what we used to do was to carry the damaged items out of the jungle at the end of the operation, then exchange them for new goods at the Company Stores. That's why at the end of our service in Malaya, we had a locker-full of new equipment that was then on leaving, given to other lads in the platoon, or to the 'B' Company Quarter Master for his stores.

The following day was just a matter of clearing the undergrowth in the morning, then waiting for the radio messages on the air-drop. After lunch we put the red and the yellow panels out in the middle of the clearing in the form of a cross. We put the yellow one on top, as that was the brightest, and would show up better in the bottom of the clearing, to anyone flying over. We got a radio message that the gear was still being collected and packed, so the parachute drop would be late afternoon at approximately 16:00hrs.

I was in charge of the smoke grenades and flares, and the air-drop had to follow set army air-drop procedure, which was smoke grenade at the first sound of the aeroplane engines, and then on first sight, to fire a green flare if it was okay to drop, or a red flare to clear off and don't drop. We got a radio message at about 15:15hrs to say that they had just taken off from Ipoh airfield, so should be with us at about 16:00hrs.

We were certainly in need of the air-drop, as we had run out of main meals and needed the re-supply for our dinner that night. Everyone was also desperate for the supply of cigarettes, and we had all been sharing the few we had since the day before. By sharing I mean one cigarette lit, and four or five people smoking that one. It seems a nonsense now, especially with having been a non-smoker again for so many years, but I can still remember being desperate for a smoke. To be honest, cigarettes were a tremendous comfort in the middle of the jungle-enhanced anxiety, and when I finally gave up many years ago, it was also in many ways to me, like giving up the last direct link with my old comrades from within the Malayan jungle.

At 15:45hrs I was on my own, and at the jungle edge on the left hand side of the LZ. I had my Patchet sub-machine gun, my camera, and the Very-flare pistol slung around my neck. In my right hand I held the phosphorous grenade for the smoke. As I was alone and away from the base camp, I had fortunately found a big handy tree to give me cover, just in case, Charlie was around. One always had to be on one's guard when in the jungle.

I stood quietly waiting for the sound of aircraft engines. I knew that there was more than one plane, because the radio message had said that the planes had taken off. It was getting very close to the drop time, so I was listening intently, until I heard the engine sounds that I had been waiting for. I moved slightly away from the tree, pulled the safety pin from the grenade, then threw it to the edge of the clearing. I had put a five second fuse into the grenade, so five seconds later it duly exploded. The small phosphorous globules flew in every direction, actually a lot further than I had expected. I had just time to dive behind the tree that I had been using for cover, before the hissing globules flew past.

I thought, "My God that was close!"

I hadn't time to dwell on how close I had just been to being badly burnt, as I now had to be ready with the flare gun. I moved well away from the tree. The smoke from the grenade was drifting away from the clearing and into the jungle. It was rising slowly up through the trees, but I could see that it still had yet to reach the open sky above the canopy. I took hold of the flare gun, which I had already loaded with a green flare; pushed off the safety catch, then I watched the patch of bright blue sky showing through the hole in the jungle canopy.

Suddenly the roar of the engines was right above me, and the instant the front end of a plane appeared over the clearing, I fired the flare gun. Bang, the hissing green flare arced upwards towards the bright blue opening in the canopy. It climbed upwards leaving a white smoke trail in its wake. Above, and silhouetted against the clear blue sky above the dropping zone, were now three single-engine Auster-type aircraft.

Once again the adrenalin pumped through my body, slowing time for me down to a snail's pace. As soon as I had pulled the trigger, and the green flare had left the pistol, I knew there was going to be a problem. As the three aircraft rapidly approached the centre of the airspace above the clearing, so did the loudly hissing green flare. I was transfixed and helpless as I watched the flare pass the height of the jungle canopy, before converging with the line of flight of the three aircraft.

Suddenly the three aircraft and the flare were together in the blue sky, and I do mean **together.** I have absolutely no idea how they missed being hit by the flare as they took rapid evasive action to first miss the flare, and then each other. It really was a mêlée of flare and planes that took place in that clear blue patch of sky above my head. How they all missed each other I will never know. I have relived that moment many times in my mind, and in my mind's eye there is never enough space for them NOT to miss each other, but thank God that somehow they did.

As the sound of the aircraft died away, we received a radio message from the Flight Commander, which simply said. "Please, no more flares. Thanks."

He needn't have worried. There was no way that I would have sent another flare up after what I had just experienced, regulations or otherwise. It didn't make sense to me from the beginning as to why we didn't just use the two-way radio, but that incident did lead to the army regulations being changed immediately, with regards to flares being used from inside the jungle on air-drops.

The sounds of the aircraft grew louder as they returned to make their drops to us. I was filled with a certain amount of apprehension as they drew nearer, and the trepidation wasn't just down to the two incidents that had happened with the phosphorous and then the flare. It was that my mind was fixed on one inescapable thought that, *'In the jungle everything always happens in threes.'*

The first aircraft flew over the edge of the clearing, and as it reached the edge, the engine cut for a second, and from the aircraft dropped a large bundle, which within a couple of seconds, was floating down to the centre of the clearing, and landed almost on the marker panels. I managed to get a good photograph of the first parachute drop, and was ready for the second, but unfortunately that one came down behind some shrubbery, so I wasn't able to take a photograph, as I was not able to see it. I could hear the third aircraft coming towards us, and as it passed over the top of the clearing, a large bundle detached itself from the aircraft, and like a rocket, shot across the top of the opening in the jungle canopy, and about halfway down into the dropping zone, before the bundle disappeared into the jungle, on the far side of the clearing and away from us.

As it hit the ground unseen from us, we all felt the impact as the ground shook slightly under our feet. It was obvious that the parachute had failed to open. I just knew that something else was going to go wrong, for in the jungle you did develop a sense to trust in your feelings and instincts. Like everyone else, I was upset that we had lost a part of the air-drop, but we still had to find it to see what had been destroyed? The thought did cross my mind as to what could have happened if the package had landed in the base camp amongst the lads, instead of out of the way, somewhere in the jungle. Despite losing part of the drop, I think we had been very fortunate on that re-supply, as the whole operation could quite easily have ended in a terrible tragedy.

While most of the platoon set to retrieving and unpacking the bundles that had been dropped safely, I set off into the jungle with one or two lads from my section, and my mate Billy Fish. It took us about twenty minutes to locate the container, and when we did, it was to find that the load of food packages from the drop had been crushed to a third of the height that they should have been, and the whole lot was almost fully buried into the soft ground. That was over two day's food supply lost, which meant we must rescue as much as we could from the wreckage buried in the ground. I sent a message back to the platoon not to open any food cans for the evening meals, but instead to send more help to retrieve the damaged food packages, and transport them back into the base camp. A lot of the food was irretrievable, and we had to bury it in the hole it had made on coming down to earth. To give you some idea of the damage, out of a total of three-hundred tins, there were only two that hadn't split open, and those two were badly crushed.

We carried what we could back to the base camp, then it was a case of everyone taking out of it what they wanted to make for their evening meal, and whatever anyone thought they could use from the rest. It wasn't too bad in the end because we all seemed to finish up with a big meal that night. I remember that I had scraped out of the tin Swifts steak, with scraped out beans and pork sausage. You could say that we did scrape through, so it turned out to be not as great a problem as we first thought it would be.

There were a few extra food boxes dropped with the re-supply to replace any that may have got damaged on landing, and the Ibans also found us trees that we could cut down and use as a food supplement. We also got plenty of cigarettes with the addition of our free issue on top of our order, so that night the lads stomachs were full, they were all smoking, and relatively happy.

As one or two of the lads said, "It could have been a lot worse, it could have been the rum ration."

We stayed in that base camp for quite a long time, and when we moved on to our next jungle base camp, which was towards the jungle edge, we had been in the jungle for well over a fortnight. Once again, as we moved to a new location for a base camp, we were low on food having only one day's supply left.

We were moving closer to the jungle edge, and to a location where we could be re-supplied the following day by HQ Company. At least getting supplied by HQ on the ground, and not by air-drop, would prevent one of the lads getting two day's food supply all at once, and on his head. We found a suitable spot for the base camp, then radioed into Colombo Camp, our requirements for the re-supply. Everything went as planned, both for the re-supply and the rest of that operation, but there was just one thing of note that I must mention.

When the re-supply column arrived at the base camp, the Officer in charge, and I have no idea now who that was, had brought with him into the base camp, a supply of cards to be made out and then sent back home. The cards were issued by the Red Cross, and were just tick a box replies in response to such questions as; I am well; I am not well; I am a prisoner; I am not a prisoner; I am being well looked after; I am not being well looked after; all that type of pre-printed question and answer material.

We all duly filled them out and returned them to him. Apparently a few parents had been telephoning Fulwood Barracks in Preston, the home of the Loyals, to say that they hadn't heard from their sons for over a week, so they were worrying that something was wrong. I must say that I was quite surprised at that, because there were very few of the lads who would write home every week. However the end result was that nobody at home ever received the Red Cross letter cards, so what happened to them I have no idea. A few days later we finally got out of the jungle and enjoyed a few well-deserved days off.

# CHAPTER SEVENTEEN
## CT's Ambush. Kuala Kuang New Village

We were going to be on our way back into the jungle, but this time we were doing what I had become accustomed to when I first got to Malaya, going into the jungle for what used to be just a normal three-day operation. I say normal, but of course, what was ever normal in those jungle operation days?

We were again short of men on this operation, due to some of the national servicemen leaving for Blighty, and one or two of the lads being away on a well-deserved leave, including my good mate Corporal Billy Fish. The night before he went on leave, we went down to the Corporals' Mess for a drink. On the way back he said something to me that we never ever said to each other.

"Be careful in there," meaning the jungle.

For some reason, after Bill had gone off on his leave, that remark seemed to play on my mind. It still sticks in my mind, and is just another of the memory bookmarks that I have told you about. It played on my mind enough for me to joke to the lads about it. I remember joking about them all taking an extra ammo magazine, because Corporal Fish had said that we had all to be extra careful, due to us being without him on that operation.

I remember dreaming the night before the operation about Granddad. I dreamt we were on the Somme, and in the front line; a whistle blew, and I started to climb up out of the trench.

Granddad pulled me back whispering in my ear, "Not yet."

That's all I remembered about the dream, but these memories that I have just told you about, all came flooding back three weeks later, and have stayed with me vividly until this day. As you get older, you realise more and more that life is nothing greater than a small cloud, floating this way and that, and all on the wind of fate. The only question we must ask is, who does the blowing?

We were on the three-tonners heading to the drop-off point, I thought to myself, "On the last few operations I was happy and relaxed, then everything went wrong, so this time I'm worrying again over nothing, so everything will be okay."

Well that was logical thinking wasn't it? I always envied the lads who had a fatalistic approach to life, and so never seemed to be concerned about anything. As we got to the drop-off point, I couldn't help but worry about the small size of the platoon.

My section was down to five men, which meant very little firepower, if it was needed. Most of the Loyals Infantry Platoons were involved in that area of the jungle we were going into. We were informed at the pre-operational briefing, that apparently, military intelligence had good information that there was a Communist base camp in that area, supposedly holding fifteen CTs.

We weren't too far into the jungle on that operation, and so we were at our jungle base camp location in just over a couple of hours. The spot we found was ideal for the camp, and located in the fork of two fair-sized streams, which provided us with two good defensive boundaries to the camp.

The first full day in the jungle was also the turn of my section to remain in camp as a rest day, and to guard our base. Of course, we were fortunate to have found such a good spot for a base camp, as we only needed one sentry point, and he was able to cover the water-point as well as the toilet area. With being short of men on this op, it would have made covering two sentry posts difficult, but it worked out better than normal, which was one worry less for us.

The Platoon Officer took Bill's section out on the first patrol. He was going to do a difficult one, that was relying very heavily on judging distance and using the compass. At the evening briefing, I thought to myself, that even though his map reading was first class, with his still limited jungle experience, he would do well to manage it. I also remember a certain amount of leg-pulling about getting lost.

His search and destroy patrol consisted of leaving the base camp at 08:30hrs, crossing over the stream that formed the northern boundary of our base camp, and crossing over the animal track that was over on the other bank of the stream. Then it was required to head North-West on a compass bearing up to the ridge, that lay about two and a half miles to the North-West of the camp. He was then going to head to the West along the top of the ridge for about two miles; then when he considered the patrol to be at the correct spot, turn left to head South and downhill to pick up the headwaters of the stream, which was to be the main object of the patrol.

They were then going to follow the stream down until it joined our base camp stream, a couple of miles higher up from where we were based, before following the animal track down to where they had crossed it at the start of the patrol, and back into the base camp. In effect they were going around in a large square, one corner of which was our jungle base camp. That way of patrolling a suspect stream, was by far the safest way for us. It meant that if there was a CT's base camp on the stream, we would come down onto it from up-stream. As it was very unlikely for British soldiers to come down from the ridge, as if they were coming in through the back door that was locked with thick jungle.

Charlie wouldn't have a guard above the camp, and would normally have just the one sentry placed on the stream down from their base camp. That was to prevent us finding their camp undefended, and by the normal, easy and obvious way of following a stream back up the mountainside to its source.

The Officers' patrol returned safely later that afternoon. At the evening briefing, it turned out that they had come down off the ridge too soon, and so followed down the wrong stream. In fact he came down the stream before the one he had intended to follow. No doubt you'll already have realised, as did the Naval Officers' a few months before, that pinpoint accuracy in the dense jungle and over many miles distance, really was the most difficult of tasks. It can be compared to finding your way around a strange city with only a compass, in thick fog and in the blackness of the night.

It did mean that the patrol that I was to have done the following day had been covered. So I was then going to patrol the stream that should have been done that day by the Officer's section. By the very nature of the tasks, that sort of a reshuffle happened every week in the jungle.

I had a good night's sleep waking up early with plenty of time before stand to. We had breakfast. At 08:30hrs we left the base camp, by first crossing over the stream to the North and then turning left at the track. This time we were going to patrol the stream of uncertainty, by the normally accepted method of following the stream up to its source.

It had the makings of another hot day. In Malaya, at this time of the year, the sun was almost directly overhead for much of the day, and the rays were already shining brightly through the gaps in the canopy. As we walked through the bright beams of sunlight shining down and onto the track, the intense heat of the sun penetrated instantly through our jungle greens and onto our bodies, only to be replaced, a second later, by the cooling shade of the jungle canopy. Where the fingers of sunlight touched the jungle floor, and the areas of dampness along the banks of the stream, small fine wisps of warm mist rose up into the atmosphere, adding to the dampness of the jungle morning air. Having then become a seasoned veteran of living in the jungle, and also enjoying the experience, led me that morning to feel at peace with the world and my surroundings.

The day was warm, and the jungle had a pleasant and soft damp kind of smell that wrapped itself around me. The insect world was busy creating the mantle of sound that was forever present in the jungle, whilst the stream close at hand, was generating the soothing sounds that only a babbling brook can produce. Every shade of green was displayed, from the almost black, where it was suffocated by the depths of the jungle darkness, to the bright and dazzling silver greens caressed by the morning sunlight shining down onto the edges of the stream. The waters of which reflected back all the greens you could see, in a sparkling reverberation of green light, and all to comfort one's eyes, as only green can do.

Away in the distance, the chattering of two different families of monkeys could be heard, while near to us came the call of some kind of bird.

I remember thinking to myself then, as I did many times in the jungle, "How can anyone not fall in love with this wonderful insight into what nature can do, to create a truly peaceful place, and all without the help and interference of mankind?" But with a job to do, my thoughts were put to one side, and I pushed on with the patrol.

After about an hour, we came to a place where the stream curved away to the left. From the map, it was apparent that the stream curved around and then back on itself, so forming a gigantic horseshoe bend. I decided to cut half a mile off the patrol by going straight over the ridge, and down to the water on the other side. It only took us ten minutes to get to the top of the dividing ridge, and once on top we found a small clearing where I called a halt for a drink, a boiled sweet or cigarette break, plus a chance to get rid of the leeches that had locked onto us.

One of the lads who had been in my section for only a few weeks, was about to sit down on a patch of ground that had an area of about six square feet, which was clear of leaves.

"Don't sit there," I quickly stopped him, "that spot will be full of ticks." I explained to him, "When the birds come through the jungle canopy and down onto the ground, they cannot just fly in and land as in the UK, because of all the trees that are in the way. What they have to do is flutter straight down to the ground, like a helicopter coming in to land. Of course, when they finally came to rest on the ground, the beating of their wings had blown away all the loose fresh leaves. When the bird comes to fly up and away, it leaves a lot of the ticks, those that it was carrying on its body, behind on the ground."

We stopped there for ten or fifteen minutes, before continuing on our way off the ridge, and down to pick up the track and stream at the bottom of the hill. We carried on following the stream up the valley, during which we passed the two streams over on the other bank that were due for checking out the following day.

At about 11:30hrs, we reached the confluence of the stream we were following, and the one we were going to patrol. It was close enough to midday for our lunch-time break, so we all enjoyed relaxing in the shade. The hum of the insect world was still evident around us, but all the other animal noises had gone relatively quiet in the heat of midday, as they obviously preferred to nap with the sun turned up onto full heat. *'Only mad dogs and Englishmen'* once again sprang to my mind.

We were beginning to relax a little too much, which was always easy to do in the energy-sapping heat. We were suddenly brought to full alertness by the crack-crack of what sounded very much like rifle shots just upstream from us. Sanden looked at me and smiled, and I did the same back. Apart from the newest member to the section, we all realised within a split second, that a large boulder rolling down the waterfall, which was just upstream from us, had caused the sound. It wasn't too unusual to hear that happen in the jungle streams, and especially during the monsoons, but it never failed in jangling the nerves, reminding us why we were there and what could happen.

I stood and clipped up my belt, "Come on lads, it's time to get on."

It was a good time to get moving, while everyone was wide-awake. The path was very distinctive, which made it easy to follow, and it was rising gently up towards the ridge. We were thankful to have a decent track because the jungle to the right was very thick, and it would have taken us over an hour just to travel a few yards. To our left was the stream that we were following, and the jungle between the path and the stream wasn't too bad or thick. We nearly always found that when we were on gentle moisture-holding slopes that faced to the South; then the jungle always had a tendency to be that little bit thicker. Under those conditions, a good track was always welcomed.

We were taking it steady and carefully, checking everything along the way. This was ideal Charlie territory, and we had been told that they were in the area, somewhere! The wait-a-while trailing vines, where a particular pain on that section of track. The spikes constantly tangled in our jungle greens, slowing us down, and interfering with our concentration.

My leading scout was up in front, followed by Sanden, myself and two lads behind me. It was only a small section, too small really, but at least that did give us the advantage that there was far less noise produced by us; not that we normally made a lot of noise. We just didn't!

We had been underway for about an hour after the midday break, when a flurry of sound coming from the right caused us all to drop down to the ground. A few seconds later we heard the chattering of monkeys that were scurrying through the treetops and away from us. I stopped the patrol there for a break, and we sat silently checking our bodies for leeches, and having a quiet cigarette, whilst keeping our eyes and thoughts on the jungle around us. We couldn't see the stream we were following, but we could hear it a few yards away to our left, gurgling away through the trees, but it was now getting much smaller in volume.

We had a ten minute break there, just enough time for the nerves to settle back down again, before I got the lads up and underway. We were all fully alert on that patrol, or should I say on edge, especially now that we were getting near to the headwaters of the stream. We all knew that there was a strong possibility of CTs in the area, which had certainly concentrated everyone's mind to the job in hand.

We pushed on up the track with the stream we were following getting smaller and smaller. The jungle had also very noticeably thinned, which would be due to the ground becoming much drier as it was higher up the mountain, and also that little bit cooler. Suddenly the stream that had become just a faint trickle, vanished into the ground.

This wasn't unusual, but many times the headwaters of a stream would reappear further on, only to disappear again, which could happen several times. The jungle seemed to have a certain air of expectancy about it, or was it just that our nerves were on edge now with being on the headwaters of the stream?

The jungle noises were still the same; yet somehow seemed different. On reflection I can only describe it, that all the normal near to sounds were still to be heard, and all the far away sounds were still there, but there was somehow nothing in between. I couldn't have told you then, and I still can't tell you now, exactly what it was that was missing?

We pushed on for another twenty or thirty yards, but there was no sign of the stream reappearing. Up ahead it looked from the brightness, as if we were just coming to the edge of a clearing. Sanden had just moved ahead of the leading scout, when he held up his hand, then went slowly down onto one knee. Slowly we all followed his action, remaining motionless for what must have been half a minute, silent but listening intently.

I had never known Sanden to remain motionless for so long, but after half a minute, my heart was just beginning to beat a little slower. I was about to move up closer to Sanden to find out what the problem was, when Sanden clenched all the fingers on his still held-up hand, except the index finger. That meant absolute quiet, no movement whatsoever.

My heart started to pump extremely fast, as did everyone else's, because I heard the gentle click of all the safety catches coming off the safety. I held one finger up to enforce Sanden's silence. We all remained like that, absolutely motionless for at least five minutes, although it could have been half an hour, I just couldn't tell. It was a very frightening moment for all of us, and it gave the impression then of lasting forever.

It was a great relief when Sanden suddenly rose to his feet and said, "Monkey, monkey only monkey."

My first words were, "Put your safety catches back on lads."

I looked at my watch and saw that it was well after 14:00hrs. I told the lads that we would take a break there, and then head back down to our base camp. We all sat at the end of the track just before it entered the clearing, and the open space would be about half the size of a tennis court. There were no large trees in that area of the jungle, which allowed the sun to shine right down into the clearing.

While the lads were having a rest, I got up and walked casually out from the track, and into the middle of the clearing. There was still no sign of the stream reappearing, and nothing else of interest that I could see, so I went back to join the lads. I too had a five minute rest and a cigarette, before we backtracked our way down to the base camp.

The following day we patrolled one of the streams on the other side of the water, which turned out to be just a normal nothing to remember, and nothing exciting type of a day. It was just the sort of day, that if all our time out there had been like that, we would have had no tales at all to tell when we got back home. That evening we got a radio message that our transport would be at the pick-up point one hour earlier than planned.

On returning to Colombo Camp, all NCOs had to report to the Company Office for an urgent operational briefing, and the platoon had to remain present within the Company lines. We didn't even bother trying to guess what that was all about.

I did say that, "It sounds like we are going straight back out," which proved to be correct.

### *Footnote to the Above Operation*

Three weeks after the above operation, 4 Platoon were based approximately one mile over the ridge that was above the stream described in detail in the above patrol. We were re-supplied by HQ Company, backpacking our food and requirements into our base camp. They followed the route that I had taken with my section, up to where I had turned the patrol around just before the clearing, and where Sanden thought he had heard something.

From the headwaters of the stream, the re-supply party were to proceed on a compass bearing, which would take them over the ridge and down to our new base camp. They had several Iban trackers with them, who were able to read the tracks we had left from our patrol. When they passed through the clearing where we had stopped, they found that just through the clearing, twelve CT's had lain in ambush waiting for us to enter the open space. Just beyond their

399

ambush was the base camp that they had vacated three weeks prior to that re-supply. When I had walked into the centre of the small clearing, I had only been a yard or two away from them, and in the middle of the ambush. There is no doubt that if I had passed through that clearing with my small section, we would have been annihilated.

We made it to the pick-up point without undue trouble, and the drivers got us back to Colombo Camp in double-quick time, well not that fast really, but they certainly didn't hang about. We reported immediately to Company HQ, and found out that we were going to surround one of the new villages called Kuala Kuang, which was a few miles to the North of Ipoh.

It was all hands to the pump on that one, and was going to involve all available Loyals, the New Zealanders and the Gurkhas. We had just less than an hour to get ready, before boarding the three-tonners, which would take us to the village. That meant a quick dash around for a bite to eat, a quick shave and shower, then collect the free cigarettes issue, all those sort of things that usually took us at least half a day when we got back into Colombo Camp from a jungle operation.

But in less than one hour, we were climbing on board the three-tonners and ready for the off, all scrubbed-up clean and tidy, full of food, smart and soldier-like, and with the lads complaining bitterly about not having their free days off after an operation. If it had been any different I would have been worried about morale, but everything was okay, and with the grumbling, things were as normal.

The three-tonners started up their engines, and we were immediately pulling away from the Motor Transport Park. It looked as if all of the Loyals' vehicles were engaged in this one. We turned to the right as we came off the MT Park, and the long line of vehicles drove along Canning Road, which ran through the top end of the camp, and continued on until we reached the main road that ran up to the North. Once we were on the main road, the convoy stopped and waited for the correct timing before we moved again.

4 Platoon were in the first two lorries of the convoy, which was being led by three land-rovers. I was in the second lorry, and behind us stretched the long line of army lorries that were carrying all available personnel from the Loyals, including a batch of new lads who were with the Jungle Training Company, and just out from the UK. This was going to be just a quick half-day operation, as we were due back at Colombo Camp that night, but as always that did not take into account, *'the best laid plans of mice and men'*.

This operation turned out to be full of incidents, and the first one happened right in front of me as I was sitting on the back of the three-tonner. The canvas covers had been taken off all the lorries, so that we could all jump off as soon as we stopped at Kuala Kuang. I was sitting looking out over the road, when a body went flying past about eight-feet up above the ground and upside-down. A Chinese man who had been riding his push-bike, had come straight out onto the road from between the two lorries carrying 4 Platoon. An army land-rover that was patrolling the convoy, could not avoid him, and cart-wheeled him down the road. We had an army ambulance in the convoy, so their personnel attended to him, taking him to the local hospital. He looked in a bad way, but we never did hear if he recovered or otherwise. The medics were still attending to him when the order to roll came, so the convoy moved off and headed for Kuala Kuang (K.K.)Village.

To get to K. K. Village we had to first go into the small town of Chemor. In the middle of the town, we took a left turn, which took us down to K. K. about a mile and a half away. When we were a couple of miles away from Chemor, we all lay down in the backs of the lorries so that no one could see us while going through the town, and give the game away. It would only have taken a few seconds for a sympathiser to telephone a warning through to Charlie in K. K. that something was afoot.

Once we were well clear of Chemor, we all sat back up, and made sure that we were ready to jump off the backs of the lorries. The arrangement to surround the village was a little bit complicated, but it did work perfectly. The plan basically consisted of the Loyals' convoy driving down the access road to K. K. As the lorries got to the entrance gates, which were set in the high barbed wire security fence that was around the village, they would stop briefly, before driving into the village; this would allow everyone to jump off, and start running around the boundary fence to their allocated spots on the village perimeter.

The Loyals were covering the boundaries along the front of the village to the left and right of the main gates, and the right-hand side village boundary. The Gurkhas had been hiding in a rubber plantation at the back of the village, so took up their positions along the rear boundary fence when a bugle call sounded the charge. The New Zealanders were covering the left-hand boundary, and I think that they were also hiding in a rubber plantation over to the left. The most important point, was that the two miles of village perimeter was covered by the troops in under two minutes.

As mentioned previously, 4 Platoon was in the first two lorries, so we were the first platoon off the transport and running. There was a special reason for this, which was that we had been given the most important place on the perimeter, and that spot had to be covered within seconds of the start of the operation to surround the village. The reason this location was so important, was that it was the place that Charlie used, and was out of sight from the guard posts. It was at the right-hand corner of the surrounding eight-feet high barbed wire fence, and had a ditch running underneath the barbed wire. That was the bolt-hole, which apparently Charlie used to get in and out of Kuala Kuang.

4 Platoon were given strict orders at the briefing to guard the ditch at all times, as the CT's just might try to break out using the bolt-hole. There was no chance of them coming through there with us guarding it. Anyway we should have known that the CTs were far too smart to risk that. I believe that I worked out how Charlie escaped from Kuala Kuang Village a day or two after the event, and I think that I personally may have, without knowing, helped them to succeed in doing that.

We had been in our position for about ten minutes, when some of the lads out of the band came along, and with them in charge, was the Staff Sergeant who was known around the Loyals as 'Drumo' as he was the Drum Major. I really should have realised that 'Drumo' was just a nickname, but I never had a reason for thinking about it, or him, prior to that moment.

The first thing that I knew about a problem was when 'Drumo' started to order my lads to move around the corner of the perimeter fence, as his lads were going to guard that section. I went over, and because I was fuming with him and without thinking, blasted him verbally for ordering my lads about. Then I shouted at him for being in the wrong place, and told him off for trying to take over a strategic point on the perimeter that we were specially guarding on the direct orders of the Commanding Officer.

I actually said to him what he had said to my lads, "So get your arse out of here Drumo, and round the corner to where you should be."

He looked me up and down, and I still hadn't realised what I had done, until he immediately replied, "Right Sir," and toddled off around the corner with his band of men.

Fortunately I didn't see them again. When I looked around, my lads were doubled up laughing.

One of them said, "You really should have told Drumo not to call you 'Sir', Corporal."

Covering my embarrassment over what I had just done, my reply to that was, "If he comes back, you had better **all** call me Sir."

You must remember that when we were out on operations no one had any indication on their uniform as to their rank, as we all dressed alike.

It had got to mid-afternoon, and they had obviously not caught the two CT's who we were after. We received orders that food was going to be organised for everyone around the village perimeter, and meanwhile my section was going to search a small patch of undergrowth and trees, and where the stream ran through the area we were guarding.

We started off in a straight line, slowly making our way into the shrubbery. It wasn't particularly thick, and we would have been about twenty-yards apart as we made our way through it. I was in the middle of the section, and we were nearly out of the undergrowth.

Suddenly Bill Bailey, who was on my immediate right, let out a terrible scream, and started running out of the undergrowth shouting, "Hornets."

A second later we were all on the outside. We didn't see any hornets, but Bill had been badly stung on his head by a few of them. The army ambulance came and took him up North to the military hospital, but before he went off in the ambulance, and very much to our shame, he had to do something.

As he ran out of the shrubbery, he dropped his rifle and hat, but quite naturally he had kept on running. They had to be retrieved, but nobody would go back and pick them up for him; so despite the pain he was in, he had to do that himself. He was in hospital for a couple of days, and we were all glad and relieved to see him return to Colombo Camp. It was believed in Malaya that seven hornet stings were just about enough to kill a man.

About one hour after Bill had been taken to hospital, we had food delivered to the main gate; so I sent one or two of the lads down to gather up our allocation. We had something else delivered shortly after the food, and the delivery gave us the clear message that we were here until morning. We had a supply of flares complete with flare-gun, and a two inch mortar, complete with an enormous load of parachute flares, and a couple of torches. We were definitely in for a miserable night, although there was a bit of dangerous fun going on up till about 02:30hrs that kept us and the villagers awake.

Just before darkness, a water-bowser arrived by the main gates to the village, which was a relief to everyone as the water bottles were almost empty. We were beginning to consider options for refilling them. Four of the lads took all the 4 Platoon water bottles down to the main gate to refill them, and came back with the bottles all filled, plus a load of fresh fruit that had also been delivered for everyone, and some bread rolls.

The deliveries of water and food eliminated our immediate concerns, and word came round that we were definitely spending the night surrounding the village. The Military Intelligence boys, and the police were absolutely certain that Charlie was inside the village somewhere, and they were busy searching the homes of all the known sympathisers.

Night arrived quickly as it does near to the equator; you have daylight one moment, then ten minutes later, it's dark. The darkness replaced the senses of what we could see with our eyes, to what we could hear and smell. All the sounds that hadn't been apparent to us during the daylight hours, now seemed to have unexpectedly turned themselves on.

Suddenly the village had humans living in there. The savoury smells of Chinese cooking drifted over to us, as the villagers prepared their evening meals. The village dogs seemed to suddenly detect our presence at the barbed wire fence, because those living near to the boundary started what seemed to be a choreographed chorus of barking. From all over the village, or at least on the side we were guarding, there were the sounds of babies and young children, crying and shouting. One or two adult male voices could be heard shouting in Chinese. I thought that this was addressed to their dogs to try to shut them up.

There was no street lighting in the village, but the flickering lights of lanterns could be seen through the open doors and windows of the scattered shacks, that made up the homes of the villagers. All that normal Malayan evening village life was about to change, at least for that evening.

From the Kiwi's side on the left-hand village boundary, there was a bang, followed by the white flare from the gunshot, arching its way up into the dark night sky, and then back down to earth, burning itself out just before reaching the ground, and then throwing everything into utter blackness after the bright silvery glare that almost hurt the eyes. Bang, another flare from the Kiwi's; this time with a lower trajectory, that took the still hissing and crackling flare into the Gurkha positions on the rear boundary.

The Gurkhas responded with a flare back at the Kiwi's, and also one into the Loyals on our right boundary. Then somebody sent up a two-inch parachute flare and that was it. The village was bathed for the next few hours under the lights of the flares and parachute flares, and the surrounding troops battled it out with each other. It was nothing to really worry about, and just one of those friendly conflicts that sometimes just 'flare' up!

The highlights of this friendly battle, were when the empty steel casings from the parachute flares fell back to earth, and occasionally landed on top of one of the corrugated iron roofs that covered the huts. When that happened, there was a tremendous crashing and ringing noise, followed by a loud cheer from all the soldiers surrounding the village, which always accompanied the occurrence.

The morning arrived with the sun climbing into a clear blue sky; it was obviously going to be another hot day. Food containers arrived once again at the main gates to the village; this time bringing breakfast for everyone. I think this consisted of mainly loads of toast, baked beans naturally, and rashers of bacon. We still had some fruit left over from the previous night's delivery, so we weren't starving, and water was no problem as there was a water-bowser now parked all the time by the main gate.

I suppose that it was quite a massive operation for the transport section of the Loyals, because there were lorries coming and going all night. No doubt the kitchens back in Colombo Camp would be busy preparing food to be sent out to us, and the cookhouse staff would be about the only ones left in Colombo Camp.

The searching of suspect homes within the village, by military intelligence and the police, continued all that morning and well into the afternoon. Our presence there had stretched from being just for a few hours, to a day and a half. I wondered how it was all going to end, because I got the feeling that everyone knew that Charlie was in there, and we were not leaving until he was caught.

I was getting fed up with being there, it was really getting to be boring staring at barbed wire all the time, and everyone else was feeling likewise. We then got the unexpected orders to get all our kit together and load it all onto our three-tonner, but keep our normal jungle patrol equipment on, which meant ammunition and water bottles and suchlike. We were going to do something that we all thought was not allowed, and that was to go into the village and search everything inside and out.

"Great!" I thought, "I was finally going to see inside one of the new villages. I'd often wondered what they had inside, how they did their shopping and that sort of thing?"

We entered the village through the main gates and followed the road that swept to the left and up a slow-rising incline. My section's job, was to sweep around the left-hand side of the village, and along the inside of the boundary fence that the New Zealanders had been guarding. When we reached the middle of the fence, we had to spread out in a long line, then slowly make our way forward, searching everything and anywhere. The area where we started to search was more like the garden area, and there were all types of vegetables planted and growing, along with various types of fruit trees. I kept to the middle of the lads, and just kept my eye on what was happening, ensuring that all the huts, both big and small, were being checked out; in fact anything at all was thoroughly checked that could possibly hold a person.

The inhabited huts were well away from us on both sides and were being searched by others. We were making our way slowly uphill, and on top was the shopping centre. Well, that's what we would call it nowadays. Then it was just a collection of shops that were all built with corrugated iron sheets. It was like a short road on top of the hill, and the shops were built on each side of the road. There would be about a dozen shops altogether, with just the normal mix of goods that you would expect here in the UK. in food shops, clothes, fruit, fancy goods, a shoe shop and so on. All the shops were closed and locked, and there was nobody in sight. In fact the whole village gave the appearance of being deserted. I have no idea whether the villagers had been ordered to stay indoors and under a daytime curfew or not? I don't think that had happened, and for some reason, I had the feeling that it was more of a Holy day.

The main reason, when I thought about it afterwards, was probably down to the fact that they were too frightened to come out, possibly the older villagers remembering the cruelty of the Japanese a few years earlier.

When we arrived at the rows of shops, the lads tried to see inside the shops by looking under the metal sheeting, or through any holes that there were in the sheets, but that proved to be impossible, so they asked me what to do? The shops had no windows at all in the walls or doors, and were built completely from corrugated iron sheets. The only space that there was where the lads could possibly gain access, was a large gap at the top of all the doors.

I told them to try and climb over the doors, and failing that to break the locks off. In the end, we had one lad who proved himself very apt at climbing over, along with the help of the rest of the lads. It took us nearly an hour to check out the shops and the area surrounding them. On leaving the shopping area, we had to swing around to the right and downhill towards a row of huts that were obviously living quarters. Outside some of them, washing hung lifelessly from washing lines that were strung from the huts to poles by the side of the hard-baked, well-trodden paths that led to, what turned out to be, the outside toilets, and other relative buildings. We were about seventy yards away from the living quarter buildings.

My lads were all strung out in a line, and very obviously searching everything, when a young lady came out from one of the huts. She walked towards us, then turned and entered into one of the outside buildings about fifty yards away from us.

She was a very striking young woman in her early twenties, with the jet-black hair that was typical of the Chinese. She particularly caught everyone's attention, because all she was wearing was a large bath towel, which was wrapped tightly around her. In her left hand she carried what appeared, from that distance, to be a large soap bag. When we got near to the building that she had entered, it became obvious to us that she had gone into a shower cubicle. There were six cubicles in a row, and she had gone into the second one along. We could see into the other cubicles and they were all empty. We could clearly see her head above the door, over which the bath towel was draped, and as the door had a gap at the bottom of at least one and a quarter feet, we could clearly see her legs and the water and soap bubbles running down onto the floor.

"What an idiot she is!" I thought to myself. "Surely she must have seen us searching everywhere before she entered the shower. What would she have to say if I sent my lads to search the shower with her inside?"

As we could see into all the other empty showers; I waved my lads away from the shower, telling them to go around each side of the shower area, and then down to the huts and back onto the road.

There was a young girl, and what looked like her younger brother standing by the last doorway entrance to the living quarters. It was a surprise to see somebody else besides the lady who had gone into the shower. The locals had been especially conspicuous by their absence. I had a couple of barley sugars left in my ammunition pouch, and as we passed the children, I gave the sweets to them, remembering as I did, the lasting memory of the kindness of the American Servicemen to us 'kids' back home during the war years.

We arrived back at the main gate where some of the other platoons were already assembled having finished their search of the village. Within fifteen minutes we were at last, on our way back to Colombo Camp for our well-deserved break. The good news the day after we returned to Colombo was that Bill Bailey had returned from the hospital, and appeared to be none the worse for his experience, and much to his credit and his character, he held no grudges for having to retrieve his own rifle and hat.

## Footnote to the Above Operation

In Colombo Camp a few days later, I was taking a shower, when the difference between our showers and the ones in the village suddenly came to me. They had a seat fitted across the back of the shower cubicle. That thought was also accompanied with the realisation that the seats in the village showers could easily have held two men, sat with their knees under their chins and out of sight. Ever since then, I have believed that is how the two CTs escaped from Kuala Kuang. What other explanation could there be for the young lady to act in the way she did?

I was told in 2003 that the Malayan Government instructed our Commanding Officer, Col Thompson to burn the complete village down as a punishment for hiding and protecting the CT's. The Colonel refused to carry out the request, pointing out that the village complex had cost the British taxpayer a lot of money to build, most of the inhabitants were innocent civilians, and the British Army would receive the blame for that course of action. He was a real and genuine, officer and gentleman.

# CHAPTER EIGHTEEEN
*Perak River Dam. Pangkur Island. Water Agony*

Our next operation was of interest from the beginning, and involved us in leaving later than normal that morning, making our way up to the North of the Perak state, and to the large Perak River Hydro-electric Works and Dam. We drove into the middle of the complex, then unloaded our equipment from the three-tonners, which had parked on the large car park next to the dam. It was just after 09:00hrs, and it did seem peculiar to be donning all our equipment with quite a few of the Malayans and Chinese workforce watching us.

We had to start late so that the workmen would be ready for us and able to take us through the dam. One of the other platoons in 'B' Company had been through this dam a few weeks earlier, and I thought that they were joking when they told me about the dam being a hollow structure.

The enormous white concrete structure curved away from us with a gentle sweep that took it across to the opposite side of the valley, a quarter of a mile away. Two-hundred feet or more below us, we could see the bottom of the valley, and against the base of the dam lay a group of large square concrete buildings.

Cascading out from the bottom of the dam were concentrated streams of water that had been channelled to follow the old watercourse. The dam looked as if it was a solid lump of white concrete, but the brown thick steel double doors, that were set into the end of the dam, and thirty feet below the top of the dam, were the first clue that you could access the structure.

The doors were thrown open, allowing us to enter onto a concrete walkway that was suspended nearly two-hundred feet up inside the dam. Large concrete columns arched gracefully backwards and forwards across the inside of the structure, while below us water flowed from ducts in the lake-side wall of the dam, following smoothly sculptured canals that flowed downwards to vanish through the outer wall at the base of the dam.

Everything inside the dam glistened under the dazzling white light that issued from a multitude of arc lights, turning the inside of the dam into a sparkling Cathedral-like structure from fairyland. We made our way along the suspended walkway towards what appeared in the distance, to be a tiny doorway at the far end of the four-feet wide sky-walk. It was very interesting inside there, but by the time we got to the other end I was ready for getting out and into the sunshine, as I was really feeling the cold from the icy interior.

As we organised ourselves in the warm sunshine on the outside of the dam, the thick steel door slammed behind us, and we could hear the locks sliding into place, giving one the feeling of sudden isolation from civilisation, and being pitched into a battle with whatever came out of the jungle. We didn't wait for something to attack us though. We didn't have the time to wait, and the platoon disappeared into the leafy dark green jungle, back into the life to which we had become so accustomed, which was seek and destroy the enemy.

We were heading slowly through the jungle towards the location for the base camp. There were many animal tracks in the area, and we followed the ones that were heading in the general direction in which we wanted to travel. We had been making our way through the jungle for about one hour when we took our first break. While we were sat there having a cigarette, looking for leeches or any other scraggy living thing that had chosen to stick its head under the skin, my leading scout walked down to the stream that was a few yards to the front, and through which the path that we were following, crossed.

He attracted everyone's attention by waving his hand, and then putting his finger to his lips, motioning us to keep quiet, and then pointed down into the stream. Sanden looked at me, and I nodded towards the leading scout. Just the two of us made our way down to where the scout was standing motionless in the stream, with his shotgun ready, and looking around into the jungle. As we got a couple of yards away from him, he held up his hand for us to stop, and then pointed down into the water, and just a foot up-stream from where he was standing.

In the sandy-bed of the stream was a perfect human footprint. Sanden bent down to study the footprint, while I waved three lads from my section to come down to us, two to give extra cover, and one to instruct to fetch the other Iban and to tell the Officer and Sergeant what we had found. We all stood around keeping a close watch on the jungle, while Sanden and his mate studied the impression in the stream.

After a minute they decided that it was from the day before. The only problem appeared to be though, that it was a bare foot imprint. We discussed the situation for a few minutes before deciding that it had been left by an Aboriginal native from the village that had been built on the banks of the lake about two miles to the North of that location. We continued on our way to find the place for the base camp, but the footprint had increased everyone's alertness, so it was a very quiet 4 Platoon that one hour later reached the base camp location.

We built the base camp on a convenient stream, and in an area where the jungle was, for some reason relatively thin but with a friendly feel about it, or was that just me? We found nothing of particular interest over the next three days patrolling, so we were ready for making our way out of the jungle. There had been an increasing air of tension about the platoon the nearer it came to packing up at the base camp, and leaving. Normally the lads couldn't wait to pack up and head for Colombo Camp, but this time it was going to be a little bit different, and this was the only time in Malaya that I can remember, when the platoon was not looking forward to the journey back to Ipoh.

The reason for the foreboding was that we were going into the Aboriginal village, and getting them to take us over the lake in their dugout canoes, and of course everyone remembered Bill Bailey, the Bren gunner, sinking in the dugout on the river. This time the water was half a mile across, and two-hundred feet deep. I wasn't over happy myself with the situation, because most of the lads were not strong swimmers. I also had obviously realised that if a problem developed, then with all my swimming experience, including several years as a lifeguard on Blackpool Beach, I would be the one who would have to do the rescuing.

We got to the Aboriginal village by mid-morning, and then the Platoon Officer and Sergeant negotiated with the Chief Tribesman over the price, and what type of payment he required for us to be rowed across the lake in their dugouts. The haggling took about half an hour, and was settled as payment in Malayan Dollars. We always called them Dollars, but the correct name is Ringgits. The payment was to be left at the post office stores in the little Kampong, where we had arranged for the three-tonners to pick us up later that day. The dugouts were all different sizes; some would hold three of the lads, some two, plus of course the native to paddle, but most would only hold one plus the Aborigine.

I warned the lads to unclip their equipment and place it in the bottom of the canoes, as that would give them more of a chance if the canoe tipped over, and sod the rifles and the rest of the gear. Once we got organised, it didn't seem too bad, and I could tell that the lads were feeling happier, for there was the odd joke flying around, which was always a good indication as to the level of confidence.

I was in a two-man dugout, which meant that I was on my own with one of the natives who naturally couldn't speak English. The first thing I did after getting into the canoe was to take off my jungle boots and my jungle greens, then I stored them carefully in the front of the dugout with the rest of my equipment. So I crossed the lake sitting in the dugout, wearing nothing more than my underpants and jungle hat. I thought that I had better be ready for diving into the lake, just in case one of the dugouts flipped over, but everything went according to plan so we all reached the far shore safely.

We climbed out of the canoes and got ourselves organised, then set off along the track that ran through the plantations. The cultivated area that we were travelling through stretched down to the lake from the Kampong, where our transport was due to pick us up later that day. We arrived with about an hour to spare, so we found a place in the shade by the roadside and on the edge of the village.

We had been there about ten minutes when the young village children started to gather around us; just the way children do, wherever soldiers are in the world. We looked through our packs and gave them the chewing gum and barley sugar sweets that were left. I got the feeling that the children had not had sweets or chewing gum before, but they soon learnt what to do with them. Some of the lads were throwing the sweets into the air for the children to catch, and that to me was fine as the children were enjoying the game.

Then two of my lads started a game with the children that I just could not believe. When a car was coming along the road, they were throwing sweets into the road for the children to chase, and just into the path of the oncoming cars. I was enraged with them, and that was the only time that I came really close to the point of charging any of my lads. I managed to restrain myself, only just though, but I made sure that those two lads suffered for the next couple of weeks.

The transport arrived on time, and inside two minutes we were on board and underway for Ipoh, Colombo Camp and a very pleasant surprise. Over the past month or two, there had been some feeling of bad blood, which had been growing between the New Zealand lads, the Australians and the lads from the Loyals. This tension between the groups seemed to be at its worst when the lads had just got back out of the jungle and were having their first night out in Ipoh. The release of the pent-up tension, plus a fair share of the local brew, was leading to arguments, and small fights taking place in Ipoh itself. The problem was resolved in a most generous and unexpected way.

We arrived back in Colombo Camp and the 'B' Company lines, to be welcomed with the news that we were being taken immediately to Pangkur Island for a two-night unwinding break. This entailed the platoon being taken in three-tonners on a one-hour journey to a small coastal village called Lumut, where a large motor launch was waiting to take us across to the Island of Pangkur.

When we arrived at the Island, the motor launch ran up onto a sandy beach where we unloaded all the supplies that had been sent with us, and were intended to last us over the next two days. Along with all the food supplies and fresh water containers, were dozens of smuggled tins of cigarettes, courtesy of the British Customs and Excise men. But most importantly to the lads, included with the supplies were also bottles of Tiger and Anchor beer by the crate load. In fact the stack of crates on the beach looked like a delivery from a brewery.

After we had finished unloading, I looked at the stack of beer crates, and thought to myself, "We'll never drink that lot in two days, but we, or should I say they, most certainly did."

We bashed up on the beach where we had landed in the launch, and the first night, with having just got out of the jungle, everyone slept well; although as you would expect one or two of the lads were already well drunk.

The following day was spent reading, swimming or going for a walk along the beach and suchlike. There were quite a few huts on the edge of the beach, which obviously belonged to the fishermen and boat builders. A lot of the lads just spent the time drinking the free booze, and later in the day one or two of them were becoming a little difficult to keep under reasonable control. As I didn't like the beer, I was absolutely sober, and was already of the frame of mind that this break, with all that booze was not the good idea that I had first thought it might be.

The local young native boys were hanging around our camp and beginning to be a nuisance. In the middle of the afternoon, they all vanished, and five minutes later we found that a brand new camera belonging to one of the Corporals, had vanished with them.

That evening, and just after sunset, a few of us were swimming in the ocean. The sea was warm and relaxing, and I was enjoying the experience when without warning, one of the lads shouted that he had been stung or bitten by something. We all rapidly made our way to the shore, and away from the unknown danger that had been swimming below us in the water. When we examined the lad's foot, it appeared to be a bad sting, but with regards to what sort of creature had caused it, we had no idea. We gave the lad some painkillers, and after that incident we kept out of the water.

We were due to be picked up by the launch early the following morning, so while I had the chance, I decided to get my head down early for a decent night's sleep. Most of the lads were still up and about, intent on finishing the beer no matter what. They had lit a fire on the beach next to our camp to burn all the rubbish that we had created with the food boxes and wooden beer crates. They were all in good spirits, and having a sing-song with all the bawdy army songs at the top of their list. Foraging parties were out and about looking for anything else that would burn, and so be destined for the fire and their all-night beach party. I was still trying to get to sleep nearly an hour later, but it was proving to be very difficult with all the noise, especially the singing, that can only be graciously described as absolutely appalling.

I was brought to full awareness by the odd word being shouted from the fireside, and in the distance farther up the beach. I lay there for a minute or two trying to hear what it was that they were saying, and to determine what it was that they were trying to do? I decided, after hearing the words boat, fire and Viking burial, that I had better get up and go to see for myself just what it was that they were planning?

I crawled out of my basha making my way up the beach towards the noise. Coming towards me along the sandy beach was a large white rowing boat. To the front and the back were a few lads from 4 Platoon pushing, pulling and grunting with the effort that was being made into getting that boat to the fire.

I ordered them, "Why don't you pull, push and grunt the boat the other way, straight back to where it came from?"

One or two of the lads, with being well intoxicated, were quite prepared to argue with me, and to disobey the direct order that I then gave, "Return the boat to where it belongs."

A long time before then, I had learnt the lesson of handling my lads when they were in that sort of mood. I gave my order directly to the lads, who for the sake of a quiet and untroubled life, would always do what was asked of them, even though at times they would grumble. I found that it was always easy to exploit the chinks in the armour, and without too much trouble, provided you went about it in the right way.

I found out a few days later that they had already burnt the oars and the rudder, prior to me stopping them from really pushing the boat out.

The motor launch arrived as planned the following morning, and as it appeared around the rocks to the left of the bay, with perfect timing, the last of the beer was being downed by the lads. We loaded the boat with our equipment, and checked the beach where we had bashed-up, to make sure that nothing had been left, including any rubbish. We hadn't invented litter in those days, that's apart from what the cat had!

I made sure to be sat right up on the bows of the launch for the trip back to the mainland. After all the drink that had been consumed the night before, and that morning for breakfast, it was obvious to me that before we reached port, most of the lads would have to relieve themselves over the side of the boat. The speed of the launch made being in the bows of the boat well up-wind, and there are worst things than spitting into the wind!

We arrived back at Colombo Camp in the early afternoon, and back to the normal routine that had been interrupted with the relaxing trip to Pangkur Island, very well relaxing for some I suppose. I was quite happy to go back to the normal routine and not have to worry about what the lads were up to. In the event 4 Platoon never received a return trip to the Island, much to the lads disappointment but to my relief. There was now plenty to do in Colombo Camp with the aeroplane model-flying club having got into full swing, and flying every Sunday morning on the football field. New floodlit badminton hard courts had been built next to the living quarter bashas, and there was talk of playing some of the locals, especially with badminton being the National Game in Malaya.

The new and large air-conditioned NAAFI shop had just opened, along with even better news, a very large and air-conditioned cinema, that showed up-to-date films. We felt that we were living in luxury with the new cinema. The old one was tiny by comparison, and just had four of the tropical fans hanging from the ceiling, and as they did, permanently spinning with a steady hum, which was just another noise that you had to get used to in Malaya.

A day or two after arriving back at Colombo, we were sitting in the 'B' Company Office and being briefed for the next operation. This one sounded really interesting, that's apart from the Charlie aspect, because we were going about twenty-five miles to the North-East of Ipoh, and deep into unsurveyed jungle, which lay over a mountain range that we had to cross. We were going to carry in five day's supplies, which would be hard work with going over the mountains, and we had to find a suitable clearing in the jungle over on the other side, so that we could be re-supplied by parachute drop. We also had to, while we were looking for any signs of Charlie, look for traces of a herd of wild elephants, of which nothing had been seen since the late 1930s. Apparently the elephants made their way from East to West and then back again, and always remained within the valley we were going to patrol behind the mountain range. We were told that it took the herd twenty-five years to travel the length of the valley and back.

One of the problems that we could see from looking at the map was going to be a supply of drinking water while we were making our way over the tops of the mountain range. We worked out a route through the range that would, if we were unlucky, leave us without water for a couple of hours on the second morning, while we were making our way down to the headwaters of the nearest stream. But as always, and once again, *'the best laid plans of mice and men'*.

The road was following the jungle edge at the spot where we unloaded our equipment from the three-tonners. According to the map, we should have been at the beginning of an old logging track, and the traces of the old track entering the jungle could just be distinguished in the brightening early morning light. As we donned our equipment by the roadside, the three-tonners that had brought us vanished down the dusty and narrow Malayan road, and with the familiar growling Bedford gear changes vanishing with them as they picked up speed.

We all helped each other to lift the backpacks into position on our backs; we were carrying five day's supplies, so the packs were on the limit as to the weight that we were able to carry. Like everyone else, once the backpack was in position, I then tightened the straps to pull the pack in close to my body so as to make it easier to carry.

We entered the jungle via the old logging track, carefully at the beginning, so as not to leave any noticeable signs to anyone passing on the road that we had entered onto the old track. My section were doing the tail-end Charlie at the beginning of that operation, and we were going to take over the lead in the afternoon, when we got up and into the mountain range. I was trying a different flavoured chewing gum this time, to see if that would remove the queer taste in my mouth and throat, but it was all to no avail.

As I made my way along following the faint remains of the old track, and not having the responsibility of leading the platoon, my thoughts turned to home and what little time I had left before I would be on my way back there. It was just a matter of weeks now. Like everyone else, the nearer I got to leaving Malaya, the more I worried about not making it back to Blighty.

Nobody ever spoke about their fears in Malaya, at least not until we were all on the boat and sailing for the UK and home. Everyone then opened their hearts and discussed their fears about Malaya, and how we all thought when we went out there, that we would not see home again. The fears were not just down to the fact that we could be killed out there in the jungle, the world was deep into the cold war with the USSR and Red China, and we had all grown up with the strong possibility of a World-wide Nuclear War.

When we had left home for Malaya, the Suez Canal was still blocked after the Egyptian war, and the Chinese were still threatening the rest of the world via Korea where the war had not long been over. So our fears were not just for ourselves, but also for the safety of our loved ones back home.

It had got to mid-afternoon, and we were battling against the jungle and the steep terrain in making it up to the top of the mountain pass where we intended to camp for the night, before making our way down into the valley and the nearest water the following morning. We were already in trouble, due to the stream that we followed up the mountainside running dry. That happened well down into the valley, and far earlier than expected. With the difficult terrain and thick jungle making us sweat profusely, and sapping our strength; this meant that by mid-afternoon, we were almost without water. We had to push on, and reach the proposed campsite at the top of the valley, so that at least by the following morning, we would only be two hours away from a water supply at the headwaters of the stream we were going to follow, and leading down into the valley over the other side of the mountain range.

We reached the top of the pass at about 17:00hrs, and by then we were all desperate for a drink of tea, but there were no cooking stoves lit that night to make a brew, because we had no water to make one with. But at least one of our objects of the operation was achieved, because there, right on top of the pass, were a multitude of elephant tracks that Sanden said were just a few months old and heading to the East.

We spent a restless night sleeping in the tracks, and I distinctly remember hoping that the elephants would not make an unexpected return. But the inability to sleep wasn't down to the elephants, it was due to the lack of water, and with each passing hour the agony increased. For my evening meal I had warmed two tins of beans and sausage, due to the large fluid content in the cans. I regretted swapping the tins of frankfurter sausages, as they were in a tin full of brine water and the lads were drinking that. The Platoon Officer contacted Colombo Camp with the evening messages, and the news could not have been worse for us. We had to abandon the operation, and leave the area immediately at first light, as the RAF were now going to bomb the region.

So now instead of being two hours away from water, we were five hours away, and heading back the way we had come. As soon as it was light enough to move, we were underway and heading back downhill. Anything that had moisture amongst the food we were carrying had been opened and sucked, including the Nestlé's condensed sweetened milk tubes. The lads who had the brine water from the frankfurters were now suffering, because the salt content had by morning, made them even thirstier.

I cannot explain just how bad it was to go without water; it really is something that you have to experience to know. I will say that it was, without any doubt, my worst physical experience in Malaya. We tried all the tricks, including sucking on small stones. Sanden showed me how to select and cut from the vines that were hanging down from the jungle canopy, and then suck on the vine. They had to be cut to the correct length, and the ends splayed at just the right angle to easily extract the fluid from them. The liquid that dripped from the end, was a thick fluid and tasted like a mixture of bitter treacle and vinegar.

I don't remember a great deal about the return journey back down the mountain and to the nearest water, but I do remember that it was very difficult to concentrate on what I was doing, and ensure that we kept on the track that we made on the way up the mountain.

Trying to concentrate on what you were doing was comparable to being very drunk and in pain, yet trying to appear sober and normal to anyone watching. Thank goodness that we had Sanden and our other Iban with us, helping to make sure that we kept to the track made the day before, and to keep us heading towards the nearest water.

There was something that happened towards the end of that journey, and a phenomenon that has remained with me to this day, a recurrent reminder of that nightmare journey. When we were about half a mile from the stream, I could smell, or should I say taste the water, because the sensation was a mixture of both. I can only describe it as a sweet smell that seems to just touch the back and the roof of your mouth. As always, and with still shaking out my footwear, the smell of fresh water is also for me, an ever-present link back to those times in Malaya.

Probably the worst time was when we reached the stream, we had to fill our mess tins with water, get the cooking stoves out and lit, then wait for the water to boil, so that we could make a brew of tea. We kept water on the boil until our water bottles were filled with boiled water, and the small stream was full of the platoon's water bottles and mugs of tea, all put there to quickly cool and so be drinkable. What a wonderful photograph that would have made, but with no space to spare on that trip into the jungle, my camera was in my locker back in Colombo Camp.

While we were stopped and replenishing our water, most of us made the meal that we could not eat the night before. When we finally got moving from that refreshing place in the jungle, we all felt one hundred percent better, but I shudder to think what might have happened if we had stumbled across Charlie while we were in that condition.

We arrived back in Colombo Camp and into the preparations for a big administration inspection, which also included a drill parade for each of the Companies. As we were now more used to blacking our faces for night ambush, or crawling on hands and knees in the jungle, we naturally were not very good at marching on the parade ground, well the motor transport park actually. The admin. and drill parade passed by without, as far as I know, any problems, but I do remember some of the lads still being upset over an accident that had happened in the USA a short time before.

A Beachcraft Bonanza aeroplane had crashed to the North-West of Mason City in Iowa; all on board the aircraft were killed. The passengers included Buddy Holly, Ritchie Valens and 'The Big Bopper' J B Richardson. The news of their deaths flashed like wildfire around the camp, and it reminded me of the day when the news about Manchester United's air-crash spread around the camp. I mention the accidents, and the effect on the lads, because I think that at the time it was important and relative to the way we all thought, and the way we handled the problems together as close comrades. The only thing that most of the national servicemen wanted in Malaya, was to get back home and return to the life that we had enjoyed before being called up to do our two years. But every major and minor change, no matter how small and insignificant, meant that the way of life we had left behind and wanted more than anything to return to, was, with the passing of time, fading away from us. There was nothing at all that we could do; as in those days Malaya really was the other side of the world, and a lifetime away.

The greatest wretchedness to me then, and on reflection still, were the goodbye letters that a lot of the lads got from their girlfriends and fiancées back home. The army has a name for those letters, 'Dear Johns.' I will never forget the look of bountiful joy on some of the lads' faces on receiving a long awaited and long overdue letter from a girlfriend back home, to be replaced immediately with a look of absolute devastation. It was an essential time for the comrades to be near, and unfortunately the comrades did get a lot of practice.

I became of the opinion that the kindest females, if you could say kind, were the ones who just never wrote again, and the affairs just died a protracted death, which was always tinged with the hope of a letter. I know that I spent more than my fair share of time and along with the rest of the lads, in trying to cheer up a lad who had just received a 'Dear John'.

Without fail, once you got them to laugh, then you knew they were going to be okay. The British Army may march on its stomach, but without doubt it survives through its comradeship, and advances on its wit.

# CHAPTER NINETEEN
### Hill Top Fire, Hand Grenades,
### The Cave and the Noises.

We were back on the jungle edge, and about ten miles to the North-East of Ipoh. This time we had a great camp, which was on the site of an old tin mine, and next to a large lake that had formed in the old mine workings, and came complete with a wonderful white sandy beach that sloped gently down into the water. Needless to say, most of the lads spent their spare time swimming, or just sitting in the cooling waters of the lake. The real downer for me at this spot, was that I lost my wedding ring in the lake while swimming. It simply slipped off my finger, and although the water was only about three-feet deep at that spot, and search as I might during the rest of the days spent at that base camp, it was lost forever.

This area was very different to what we had become used to, and the jungle edge was basically determined by the high cliff faces and rocky outcrops that stretched for about fifteen or twenty miles. The extra equipment we carried for this area was a selection of climbing rope, extra ammunition and hand grenades. The reason for the ropes was so that we could climb down the cliff faces that formed some of the gullies, and then to access any likely looking caves that were present, and needed checking out. The extra hand grenades were so that any potential caves that were really difficult to access, would get a grenade thrown inside, and the extra ammo was so we could send a burst of gunfire into any of the caves that were high up on a cliff face. We only fired into the ones that were less than one-hundred feet up the cliff face, but there were a lot of cave entrances that we could see.

Some of them were three or four-hundred feet above the ground. We all thought that we were little John Wayne's on that operation, lobbing hand grenades into caves, and then a burst of gunfire. I must tell you that we found it impossible to pull the pins out of the grenades with our teeth, as they do in the war films, but we did try. The only thing that was missing on those patrols were the rousing background military music, and a bugler sounding the charge.

I took my section out on patrol the first full day in that area, and we headed up to the North. I had flown over this area a day or two earlier in a Wessex helicopter, and I spotted what looked to be an interesting valley a couple of miles to the North of our base camp, and I wanted to take a closer look. I had taken a photo of the valley from the helicopter, so I took my camera on the patrol hoping to take a photo from inside the valley.

It seemed a little peculiar to be going out on a jungle patrol loaded up with all the extra equipment that we were carrying, as normally we travelled light. With it being one-hundred feet in length, the rope was the heaviest single item, so the lads took it in turn to carry it, with each stint lasting for about half an hour. When we got to where the valley started, I thought at first that we would not be able to gain access due to the start, or should that be the end of the valley being about thirty-feet up the cliff face. The entrance seemed to be through a very narrow cleft in the rock face. I was thinking of abandoning that patrol, and making our way to a valley further North.

The leading scout said, "I'll be able to climb up there with no trouble."

So I told him, "Well then, you give it a try."

In the event it proved to be a far easier climb than it looked from ground level, and we all managed it without any need to use the rope. The narrow cleft that we had climbed up and into, stretched away from us, and slowly climbed towards the true valley. The sides of the cleft towered over us, and probably rose two-hundred feet or more above our heads. It was as if a giant had smashed an enormous axe down on top of the cliff, splitting it all the way down to the narrow path where we stood.

I was filled with a very positive feeling that we would find something in this secret valley. It was ideally located for easy access to contact the local Communist supporters, and for getting into Ipoh, yet still perfectly hidden. We would normally have walked right past the entrance, not even realising that there was a valley there, but on this occasion, I had seen the valley from the helicopter.

We made our way slowly and carefully along the track. It would have been about fifty yards in length, and led into the narrow valley above us. The cleft in the rock was so narrow, that if we had held our arms out to each side at shoulder height, and all the way along the path, then our fingers would have touched the rocks to each side. The cleft suddenly opened wide to display to us light jungle growth, and the start of the hidden valley. The sun was shining down from the top right-hand side of the gorge, and directly onto us, almost as if we were being especially picked out by a powerful spotlight.

I warned all of the lads, the leading scout and Sanden especially, to be on their guard for any booby traps that may have been put in place by Charlie. I still had a strong sense of foreboding, and the more I saw of the valley, the more convinced I became that we would find something, or that something might find us!

We had all been warned in jungle training of the dangers that could lie in wait for us. Most of Charlie's booby traps involved sharpened bamboo stakes, either on the surface or more than likely, buried in a pit, and also more than likely with the stake's tip covered in some sort of poison or human excrement. These booby traps had several names, Choler, Panji or Punji beds, and a few other apt army slang terms, but no matter what the name, they all meant real trouble if you put your foot into one. There was also the possibility of land-mines having been planted. We had been casually warned of the slight danger of land-mines in training, but with the jungle being what it is, no one worried about them again. I considered then that if I were holed-up in that valley, I would have definitely put land-mines in place, that's if they were available.

I decided to change Sanden and the leading scout around, and told Sanden to carefully check the ground for any disturbance, and for the leading scout to watch up-front and over Sanden. So in that order, we very slowly made our way along the path and up into the valley. It probably took us over half an hour to cover the first hundred yards, but everyone in the patrol had caught the atmosphere of the place, and we were all concentrating intently on every little corner that we were able see within the valley.

Even though it was only mid-morning, it was unbelievably hot, and the lower end of the valley formed a natural sun-trap that was with the absence of any shade, cooking us alive. We had already taken to drinking our water early, and also with an added salt tablet, we had to replenish our body moisture losses that had already turned our jungle greens black. It was to our great relief when we reached the shelter and relative safety under the shade of the canopy provided by the bit of jungle that was growing there within the valley walls.

After a long break to cool off and regroup our thoughts, I took the patrol over to the right-hand side of the valley, where it was cooler still, with the added shade of the cliff wall that formed the side of the valley. As we made our way up the valley following the rock face, we found several caves that contained nothing of interest, apart from one that had an old skeleton, along with several large jars that were packed with old bones. It was obvious to us that the cave had been used for burials many years before then. So out of respect, we left their remains in peace.

At the top of the valley were a scattering of potholes, and we could tell that some were very deep by the length of time it took for the rocks we threw, to reach the bottom. Two of the potholes were accessible, and probably about thirty-feet deep and about fifteen-feet wide. The bottoms of both were sandy, and had two or three caves running off at the base. Rather than risk life and limb, and at least an hour's time by climbing down to investigate, we lobbed down a couple of hand grenades, and sorted them out in one minute flat. We then made our way back down the other side of the valley, checking out the caves in the rock face as we headed down to the narrow gully outlet at the bottom of the valley.

We found nothing of interest, and we didn't linger on the way back to our base camp in the old tin mine by the lake. We were very nearly out of water, and none of us wanted to go through even having a small sample of that agony again.

The following day was my section's rest day, which was spent in swimming, reading, cooking and making brews of tea. I also took a few photos for the scrapbook. It was just like being on a luxury holiday, well almost! The lads had to do their guard duties, but even they were easy to do, and with no chance of Charlie getting within a quarter of a mile without being seen by us.

The Platoon Officer, Mr Rawstorne had taken a patrol out into the jungle, which was to the South of the base camp. They were going to make their way to the top of a large hill which was clearly visible from our base camp, and would be about two-thousand-feet high.

It had got to mid-afternoon when one of the lads said, "The hilltop is on fire."

I looked up from the book that I was reading, and sure enough there was a wisp of smoke rising above the area that the Officer's patrol was checking out.

I watched for a few minutes, and it seemed to be getting worse, so I got my camera and took a photograph of the smoke rising above the hilltop. There was nothing that I could do about the problem, apart from worry, so I went for a swim in the lake.

As the day wore on the fire got worse, and I must say that I was relieved when Mr Rawstorne and his patrol returned safely to the base camp. The fire was putting out quite a pall of smoke by then, and I can remember wondering if anyone would bother about it?

The Officer said that they had their dinner break right on top of the hill, and obviously someone had left a cigarette end or something burning up there. When it had gone dark, and after the stand-to the flames had become clearly visible, and we could see that the whole of the hilltop was ablaze. It was a gigantic red beacon, and there was no chance of us hiding the fact that we were around. About an hour after sunset, the radio operator received an urgent message from the Commanding Officer saying that he was coming into our base camp later that evening at about 22:30hrs.

I really could not believe that the C.O. of the Battalion would be coming into a jungle base camp in the middle of the night. To me, and everyone else, it was unheard of, and I would not have thought the fire was that important. It was arranged for myself, along with my section, to meet the CO's. transport on the main road at the top of the old mining track, which would be about one and a half miles from the base camp. We were then to guide the CO. and his party to the base camp, and also to act as guard to the party.

We left the base camp early, then waited out of sight by the roadside for the CO's land-rover. We had been waiting there for about half an hour, when we heard the unmistakable sounds of the land-rover coming up the road, which was my cue to step out onto the side of the road. I pointed to the track at the side of the road, and waved for them to drive down. I had been worrying all evening as to whether or not I should salute the CO when he arrived, obviously not wanting to make him a target with us being on the jungle edge. When I got a proper look at him in the darkness, I could see that he was in jungle greens.

I just said, "Good evening Sir," and left it at that.

We led the way back along the track to a space nearest to our base camp for the land-rover to park. I left my section with the vehicle and driver, and guided the CO. to the base camp a quarter of a mile away, and around the edge of the old tin mine. The CO. stayed for about half an hour, then I escorted him back to the transport, and then back up the track to the road. I have no idea what was discussed at the meeting between the CO and the Platoon Officer, and I kept well out of the way, but much to 4 Platoon's embarrassment, the fire burnt merrily away for over two days, and was clearly visible from Colombo Camp back in Ipoh.

The following day I took my section further to the North, and up into a narrow valley that curved first slowly to the left and then to the right. Once again we had high cliffs to each side of the valley, which would have been about two-hundred yards wide. I would normally have expected a river to be flowing down the valley, but there wasn't even a small stream. You could say that the whole area was bone dry.

I put this down to the region being nothing else but mountains of limestone rocks that were not only porous, but also full of caves and potholes that swallowed up the water as soon as it rained. It was an area where the landscape was in utter confusion. I was told by a local tin mine manager that the region had been formed by Ice Age action, many millions of years before.

If you can see in your mind's eye, the bewilderment of limestone mountains, gorges, valleys, potholes that were up to half a mile wide, and five-hundred feet deep, caves that were of every size and depth imaginable, cover it all with jungle, then that's the area that we were in at that time.

We slowly climbed upwards and had followed the valley's contours for about three hours. Suddenly the valley opened up into a gigantic bowl, with the walls towering two or three-hundred feet above us. In front of us the ground angled down to a depth of about one-hundred feet, and at a slant that was quite easy for us to walk down.

When we reached the bottom, we stood silently for a moment in awe at this other world that Malaya was displaying before us. The light we received in the bottom of the pit was indirect sunlight, that was bounced off the white limestone cliffs, to give a pleasant reddish tint at ground level. All the normal jungle sounds were different, the bird songs, the monkeys' shrill calls, and the constant overriding hum of the insects all echoed around us, contained by the limestone walls of the gigantic hole, and with a difference in sound that was quite pleasing to one's ear. I decided to circle anticlockwise around the base of the sump, checking out anything we found that may be of interest, along the way.

We made our way slowly along the base of the cliff, and as it came up to the time for a lunch break, we found a nice little cave that was set into the base of the rock face. When we looked inside there was evidence of past occupancy, which we thought was from British forces during the Second World War, but the tins were almost rusted away. I spent the break thinking about the last ones to sit in that cave, and wondering what happened to them?

The break over we moved on, and fifteen minutes later we came across a massive opening in the rock face, which led us into the largest cave I have ever seen. It was enormous, you really could have put St Paul's Cathedral in there, along with the Houses of Parliament and Westminster Abbey for good measure. One of the lads had some hexamine cooking blocks, so we made some torches with the blocks, using branches that we cut from one of the bushes outside the cave.

We went inside the cave, best prepared as we could be, and made our way carefully as the limestone floor of the cave was criss-crossed with large cracks, that obviously went down to various depths. The floor of the cave sloped at about 10°, and down into the bowels of the earth, and that's the direction we followed. I was annoyed that we didn't have a torch, as that would have made life safer, and we would have been able to see much more of the cave and down into the large cracks in the floor. Who knows what mysteries they contained?

We made our way carefully down into the cave, and we did find that it got easier to see as our eyes adjusted to the flickering light of a hexamine block. It took us well over half an hour to get to the bottom of the cave, and there to our surprise at the end of the cave, we found a sump hole. We could see the floor of the sump was about ten feet below us, and had a sandy floor. There were no footprints, or other marks obvious in the sand, and the side of the sump had ledges that were forming an easy ladder down onto the sandy bottom. At the base of the sump was a cave running through from left to right, and the height of the cave would be about five feet.

I made the decision that we would climb down into the sump and investigate the cave that was leading further into the hillside. We lit another hexamine block, so that there were two torches burning. The leading scout got hold of the new torch and climbed down into the sump. It only took a second or two, and with the ledges it was just the same as going downstairs back home. Sanden was the next one down, and then I followed him. Just as I reached the sandy floor, the leading scout held up his hand.

He whispered, "What's that noise?"

I told the next lad who was just starting his descent to "Hold it," and then I said to all of the Section, "Quiet!"

We listened intently for a few seconds, and from down inside the cave that we had been planning on investigating, came a most peculiar sound, that was unquestionably getting louder and coming towards us. It was a noise that I find very difficult to explain, and the nearest that I can describe it for you is, that it was a combination of a rolling wave of water rushing along the cave towards us, and the beating of bird's wings against the walls of the cave. We couldn't see into the blackness of the cave, and so could not tell what it was that was heading rapidly our way, and from the proximity of the noise was now only a matter of a few yards away.

I just said one word, "Out!"

Three seconds later, we were all twenty-feet away from the entrance to the sump-hole, and looking back to see what was going to come out of the black hole and into the faint light of the main cave. My first thought was that we had disturbed a large colony of bats, but why had none flown out and into the main cave?

I asked the lads, "Did you think it was bats down there?"

The consensus of opinion was that's what caused the noise.

I said to Sanden, "Bats?"

He shook his head saying, "Me don't know."

I could tell in the pale flickering light that even he had been frightened by the sound we heard.

One or two of the lads suggested, "Why don't we throw a grenade down the sump?"

I was worried that if I missed the hole in the darkness, we would have the shrapnel flying around our ears. I was also concerned that the concussion of the explosion, may well bring a part of the cave roof down on our heads. We didn't go back and have a look down into the sump-hole, and I decided that this time, discretion really was the better part of valour, but my decision to leave the cave left a mystery that has remained with me to this day.

"Was it bats? I don't think that it was, because there was no guano at all in the cave, or down in the sump, and the bats would surely have roosted in the main cave, which was ideal for that purpose."

Sanden also didn't think that it was bats, but he was reluctant to discuss what he thought we heard down there.

What do I think now? "Well I have heard that the Australians found giant scorpions near to that area of Malaya. I think that we were nearly found by giant cockroaches, who knows, but whatever was living down there, it didn't leave any tracks in the sand, and no droppings."

When we left the cave, it had somehow got to mid-afternoon and time to be heading back to the base camp, so I left the rest of the big hole for another time, and pointed my leading scout down the valley, towards the old tin mine and the still burning hilltop.

The following day was a Friday, and we all had the day off apart from guard duty. One of the other sections went up to the main road to meet and bring the Battalion Chaplain into our jungle camp to hold a Service, and give Communion to anyone in the platoon who wanted to join in.

I can't remember now whose idea it was to ask about having a service in the base camp, but I remember being asked by some of the lads to put the request in to Mr Rawstorne, who with being a vicar's son, was more than pleased to pass on the request to Colombo Camp via the radio. Before you get too confused with 4 Platoon's sudden, and 100% conversion to religion, I should tell you that it was Easter and Good Friday. I thought that it was a splendid idea to ask for the Chaplain to come into the base camp, and I wished that I had thought of it myself. But it was typical of those lads, that they always had the ability to rise to any occasion, no matter what.

I still feel a great deal of pride in having been a small part of such a great team. I could tell from chatting with the Padre that he had been delighted to receive a request to hold a service for a platoon inside a jungle camp. He stayed with us for at least an hour after the service, sitting and chatting to the lads, having a drink of tea and sharing out cigarettes.

The following day we were back out on patrol, and further to the North. I think that everyone in the platoon felt better for having had the Padre in the day before. I know that it made me feel a lot better, and was a positive link with our past Christian way of life back home. This patrol was once again a case of a small climb to access the valley, that we wanted to have a closer look at. I had already discounted finding Charlie, even though it was perfect terrain to hide away from anyone searching. I had realised from what we and the other sections had found, that although the area was perfect for Charlie, the main ingredient, water, was missing. I said at the previous evening briefing that rather than look for Charlie, my section was going to look for any signs of water. That meant looking for greener greens, and darker earth if you know what I mean?

If we found traces of water we just might find traces of Charlie. So with that in mind, we slowly made our way up the narrow valley into which we had climbed. The narrow track leading upwards was reminiscent of the other valleys that we had patrolled over the last few days, with very little width to the ravine at the start of the climb.

We had travelled about a mile along the track without it widening to any significance, when it suddenly seemed to end about fifty yards in front. When we got to where the track had seemed to end; it did in fact to a quick dogleg, and then immediately opened out onto a broad ledge that would be about one-hundred feet long and forty-feet wide. Amazingly the ledge gave the appearance of being perched on the side of a cliff face inside another large pothole, but unlike the last pothole, the only way down to the floor of this one was by climbing down about eighty-feet.

While I made up my mind as to what to do, we sat down at the edge overlooking the ground level, and took our lunch break. It was another quite amazing place that could have been created by Hollywood. When I looked down I had an overview of the green undergrowth that filled the bottom of the deep hole, and I could just see through the growth of trees to the rock face on the other side. Two-hundred feet above us, through the round hole formed by the cliff walls of the pothole, I could see the blue sky.

I made up my mind, deciding that it was too dangerous for us to climb down to explore the base of the pothole, so we headed back early towards our base camp. With us being so early, I took the section back through the plantation area, as we were walking along one of the dusty tracks that criss-crossed the plantation areas, we saw a dust cloud approaching us along the track that we were walking on. The cause of the cloud was obvious to us, as the dust was being stirred up by two of the new six-wheeled Saracen armoured personnel carriers, belonging to the 13th/18th Hussars, who were also based at the Colombo Camp Garrison. The leading vehicle pulled up next to us. We had a few minutes chat about what was happening, or mainly **not** happening, and then we both went our own ways. It was a pleasant little interlude, to have a chat with lads from another British Army Regiment, who like us, were a part of the Commonwealth Brigade.

We got back to the base camp earlier than normal, so I had a swim in the lake and another fruitless search for my wedding ring. It was our turn for a rest day that was spent generally cleaning the camp and getting ready to leave the following day. Once again we arrived back in Colombo Camp, and once again to the chore of sorting out, renewing and cleaning our equipment. We already knew that our next operation was going to be back into the area we had just left, but yet further North again to the last position, but everything was subject to change in Malaya.

After fifteen months in Malaya I had got used to that, so a change of plan came as no surprise, but where I was asked to go was a surprise. I was to take some documentation up to the 3rd Battalion, The Royal Australian Regiment at Camp Lasha, and then bring the documentation back when it was ready.

The following morning, while the lads of 4 Platoon were enjoying their rest day, I was getting a packed lunch from the cookhouse. I went to the MT Park and picked up one of the small scout cars that had been ordered for me the day before. The small armoured vehicle just had room for the driver and a passenger, and above the passenger seat was a gun turret with a mount for two bren guns.

I told the driver, "Pull up at the end of the MT Park by the 'B' Company Arm's Cote, while I book out a couple of bren guns and ammunition."

As soon as I had fixed the bren guns onto their mounts, we were off, and on our way to the 3rd RAR. at Camp Lasha. I was standing inside the scout car with my head and shoulders protruding out of the gun turret, and the barrels of the two bren guns were side by side and pointing up into the sky.

"This is great," I thought to myself with the cooling wind blowing in my face I felt like one of the Desert Rats. But it didn't last, because as we picked up speed, the flies and anything else that was floating on the wind, smacked you hard in the face. Enjoyable as being carried that way was, I gave up and slid back down into the seat.

The reason behind me going to Camp Lasha, was that for some reason the Diggers were pulling out of an important ambushing operation, and we were taking over from them. If I remember correctly, 6 Platoon was also involved in that ambushing operation, but I am not 100% certain. We never did find out as to why the Australians left the ambushing to us. It may have been down to an act of conscience on their part, but I really don't know. I sometimes wonder as to the ethical rights and wrongs of that ambushing operation, and even as to whether I would now on moral grounds, have refused to go on the operation.

Military intelligence had found out that one of the female CTs was pregnant, and the baby was due at about that time. They also knew that her family lived in the small Kampong near to the Australian's Lasha Camp, and they were expecting her to be escorted out of the jungle to have the baby there, or to bring the baby out of the jungle to leave with her relatives, if she had already given birth.

We started the ambushing operation the following night. This consisted of the platoon being taken in the late afternoon to Lasha camp where we waited until after the curfew had come into force. Then we walked up the road back towards Ipoh for about half a mile, before the ambush sections started to vanish into the jungle on our right. My ambush section was holding the last position, so we finished up walking up the road on our own, and a good mile away from the Australian camp.

To the left of the road as we walked along, were scattered plantations, no doubt belonging to the suspect Kampong. To the right of the road was the jungle in which we were ambushing the tracks that could be used to get to the Kampong.

We were obviously the last ones into position, but still had plenty of daylight left to set up the ambush, and to put the flares out and run the wires back to our position. We had our last cigarette and then settled down for the night, but not a full night. On this operation we were lifting our ambushes at midnight, 00:01hrs to be precise. Intelligence obviously didn't expect the female to be making her way through the jungle later than that. After battling with nothing worse than the mosquitoes, midnight duly arrived, and we broke the ambush position. Just as we were leaving the ambush location, we heard on the road that was about one-hundred yards away, an army vehicle going towards Lasha camp. I thought nothing about it, as any military movement on that road should have been warned that there could be troop movement in that area.

We made the road, and headed towards the Australian camp. A couple of hundred yards down the road I could see, stopped in the road, the lights of the vehicle that had just passed us. From about a hundred yards away, I could see that it was a scout car, and the lad in the gun turret was talking to what was obviously a group of our lads standing on the side of the road. We were about twenty-five yards away, when the lad in the gun turret swung around with his gun pointed ready to fire at us.

I heard Corporal Frank Shaw shouting, "Hold it, hold it, don't shoot, they are our lads."

I was furious with the lad in the gun turret, who turned out to be one of the Australians from Lasha camp. The Digger who was driving the scout car apologised for his mate's behaviour, explaining that they had been to Ipoh for a night out, and that they were on the way back to Lasha. The Digger in the gun turret had been involved in a gunfight with Charlie two or three days before, and his nerve had gone to pieces.

But to me that was no excuse for him being quite prepared to have a shot at us. There was no way that he should have been allowed anywhere near alcohol, with a gun in his hand when his nerves were in that state. It turned out later that the driver had stopped him shooting up our other ambush sections, who were walking along the road and back to the Australian camp. The Australians said that they thought that they saw, in the headlights of the scout car, figures running across the road and into the plantations.

I was so mad at the guy in the gun turret, that I got out the torch that I was carrying in my ammunition pouch, and then while everyone else stayed where they were, went to the edge of the plantation and shone the torch into the shrubbery. There was nothing to be seen, and no movement, but it didn't worry me at all shining the torch. I had already been down that road of fear in the jungle, plus this time I was really angry. It was only by the grace of God that 'B' Company didn't lose some of its lads that night.

By the way, Corporal Frank Shaw was out of 6 Platoon, and I am almost sure that it was Frank who called out the order, "not to shoot," on the road.

We got back to Lasha camp shortly after the disturbance on the road, and our transport then took us back to Colombo Camp and a late night's sleep. We did another two nights ambushing at Camp Lasha and then called a halt to that operation.

We were still down for completing our sweep of the rocky and disturbed area to the East of Ipoh, but again we were sent out on a different operation to the North of Ipoh. This one was what I have always called my being insulted operation, and I know that the rest of the lads felt the same as I did.

We arrived at the jungle edge well to the North of Ipoh, on a five-day operation. There, without prior notice to us, we met up with others, and were then made to sign the Secrecy Act, and told never to disclose to anyone what we were about to do on that operation, and of more importance who we were with? If we had simply been told that it was a secret operation, and not to talk about it, then that would have been fine, but we all found it very insulting as British soldiers, to be pressed into signing the Secrets Act.

We had been told that what we were doing must not be disclosed to anyone, ever. How long is ever? That's why I am not going to tell what it was that we were asked to do, and I am sorry for leaving you wondering, but I considered that as this book is a full and true record of my time during national service, then it is appropriate that the occurrence should be recorded here. I must add also that the ramifications of that operation have remained vividly with me to this day.

Back in Colombo Camp the various new activities had taken off, and were being enjoyed by many of the lads. I was enjoying the aero-modelling side of life, along with our 'B' Company Sergeant Major, CSM Bull, who was also an expert modeller. I was busy building a control line model of a twin-engine Mosquito. It was quite amazing how you could leave your model aircraft, or indeed anything else that was too big to be packed away, on top of your locker or under the bed, and when you returned from a jungle operation weeks later, everything would still be there untouched. If you couldn't trust your belongings to your comrades, how would you be able to trust your life to them? Which you did, unwaveringly.

After our post operational days of rest, we finally made it back to the last section of jungle edge to be checked out by us. I had been hoping that one of the other platoons might have been given the task, as it wasn't the best area to be in. I didn't think that we would be lucky enough to have a swimming lake by the side of the camp, and I was right. But it wasn't too bad, and we had a handy water supply that was pouring steadily from the bottom of the cliff face, which is obviously where we built our base camp.

On the plantation side of the base camp were a series of large fishing lakes. We were lucky enough to be able to watch the Malayans catching fish. The way they did that was quite unbelievable. I had my camera on that operation, so took photos of them fishing. What they do is sit on an old rubber inner tube, then paddle around the pool with their hands. In their hands they are holding the chopped-up roots from an Ipoh tree, which produces a poison that knocks out the fish, which they then gather from off the surface where they are floating. At night, and after the curfew we went fishing ourselves. We didn't have any Ipoh tree roots, so being resourceful and army trained, we used what we had, which just happened to be the Mills hand grenades. This kept us in fresh fish while we were in that base camp, and we didn't need to purchase a rod licence.

There were only two things that happened on that operation that were of any note, that's apart from fishing with the grenades. The first was discovered on my first patrol along the edge of the cliff face, which also formed the jungle edge boundary. There was an area of scrub-land, about two-hundred yards distance from the rock face, and up to the start of the plantation area. This area was out of bounds at all times to the civilian population.

Anyone seen in that area would be regarded as CTs and liable to being shot on sight, and we were still carrying out our shooting into the caves and throwing in hand grenades. No we didn't use them all for fishing, and I am sure that we were only using up old Second World War stock that needed dispensing with anyway.

We had been on the patrol for about three hours, when we came across a cave at ground level, with the entrance sealed with an almost new wooden door, which was padlocked. We stood looking at the door for a minute or so while I decided what to do.

You must realise that it was still foreign to my nature and upbringing to just break down a door that was locked. Having decided that a door there was absolutely outside of the law, I told the lads to kick it down, but that proved to be impossible, so one of the lads shot the timber from around the lock, so the door then easily opened with just one kick. Once inside, we found that it was just a small cave about seven-feet high, ten-feet wide, and about twenty-feet in depth. The cave was being used for storing gardening tools. There was a wheelbarrow, spades and other equipment, and a pile of jars and wooden boxes. I contemplated moving everything in there over to the edge of the plantation, but instead we wrote 'NO ENTRY' on the wooden door.

The lads used their machetes to cut the message into the wooden door, as we had nothing else to write with. It did make me think twice though, about whether there could be some innocent individual inside one of the caves we were checking out, and also throwing grenades into, so with that in mind I carried on with the patrol, but with a little more concern.

The other item of note, was when we were patrolling on the cliff-tops high above. In this area there was only one steep valley, which started at ground level, and rapidly made its way up to the tops of the four-hundred feet high cliffs. The valley had been searched the first day by one of the other sections, and as I had done along all of the base of the cliffs, all we had left to patrol were the high hilltops, and I keep emphasising high for a reason.

We were up and on top of the cliffs, and well into our second day's patrol. I was heading to the North, and to what should be the end of the high rocky limestone area and back to the normal jungle. When I flew over the area in the helicopter a short time before, I had noticed that the land rose from the jungle edge to meet the back north-eastern corner of the rocky hilltops. I was heading the section in that direction, and with the intention of bringing the patrol back down to the jungle edge via the sloping ground. The jungle undergrowth at that northern end was unbelievably thick, and my leading scout was labouring at hacking away with his machete at the thick undergrowth, physically pushing his body through the thinner undergrowth.

Behind him was one of the lads who sometimes served as leading scout, and Sanden had moved to the back of the section for a break. Suddenly the leading scout, as he was pushing himself through a patch of thinner undergrowth, fell forwards and down. The lad who was fortunately close behind, and fully alert, grabbed hold of his belt and pulled him back. When we looked through the hole in the undergrowth, all we could see was the jungle two-hundred feet below, and straight down in the cleft that cut into the rocky limestone, and was not shown on the map. This was just another brush with the Loyals' luck and another talking point back in base camp.

# CHAPTER TWENTY
## *Difficult Operations - Difficult Ambush*

I was sat in my basha at Colombo Camp, building the model twin engine Mosquito, counting down my days to leaving Colombo Camp forever, and suffering the irritant of prickly heat, a condition that was caused by the heat and perspiration. The prickly heat was alleviated by plenty of cool showers and Johnsons baby powder; the NAAFI shop did a roaring trade in the baby powder, even though we could get a free issue of foot and body powder from the QMs store.

Prickly heat was another of the regular complaints that we got out there, along with athlete's foot and jungle sores, all of which got their share of the baby powder. We were due back into the jungle the following morning, and although I was totally content and fully at ease with Mr Rawstorne, Sergeant McGrattan and all of the lads in 4 Platoon, I couldn't but help having the extra worry about something going wrong with me being so close to leaving Colombo Camp and homeward bound. I found out later that all the national service lads suffered from the same anxiety, especially when their time to leave Malaya drew close.

I suppose that now, and in these more enlightened days, one would talk-out the concerns that caused the personal worries to all of us. But in those days, with not wanting to appear to be a softie, you kept such concerns to yourself. All around Colombo Camp you could see, on looking inside the various platoon bashas, the suitcases of the lads who were due to be going home next.

The suitcases were a display, just like flying a flag, which said to everyone, "I am going home next."

Many of the cases were painted and decorated, and many of them really were top class works of art. The most popular subject for the artwork were the cartoon characters, Andy Capp and Flo from out of one of the popular British daily newspapers. Each piece of artwork, would of course, be accompanied by some cryptic and appropriate comment coming out of the mouth of Andy Capp or Flo. But all of the cases, including mine, had boldly and brightly painted on them, Malaya to the UK.

Once again I found myself climbing onto the back of a three-tonner with that queer taste in my mouth. We were once again a good few miles to the North of Ipoh, and it was just coming daylight as we climbed down from the backs of the Bedford trucks. We were at the edge of a large rubber plantation, that we had to cross before coming to the jungle edge, and were then back under the green canopy and into surroundings that had almost become my own familiar back garden.

My section were bringing up the rear, and as we made our way through the plantation, my thoughts turned once again to home, and that this would probably be my next to last operation. I looked at the lads around me in the platoon, and it suddenly struck me that there was only one of them, a regular soldier, who had been a member of 4 Platoon before I had joined nearly eighteen months earlier.

The shrill cry of some nearby bird or monkey brought my thoughts back to the job in hand, and I told myself to stop thinking about home. If we ran into trouble, and my thoughts were elsewhere, then I may not get back home because I was too slow to respond to the problem.

We were going into the jungle for three days, and we were following a river up into the jungle for about four miles. This particular river had a lot of tributaries running into it, which gave us an indication that the area was full of valleys and gullies, with very little level ground, and that proved to be the case.

It made map reading more difficult, as you did rely on prominent streams and ridges to confirm your location, and this area had nothing prominent, except that it did hold a jumble of similar streams that just made matters worse. It was quite hard going, and very much up hill and down dale, and it was a relief to reach a piece of jungle that could be used for our base camp.

I took my section out on a reconnoitre patrol further up the stream to establish our exact position, while Mr Rawstorne took a section out and up the stream opposite to the base camp position for the same reason. We compared notes when we both returned, and disagreed on the exact map reference for the base camp, Mr Rawstorne was more than happy in the belief that he was correct, and radioed that position back to HQ Colombo Camp. I still think that I was correct, in that we were further upstream than the location given, but it was close enough not to worry about, and Mr Rawstorne was happy.

I took my section out the following day and we headed West and upstream. It was another hot day. Well I know that every day was hot in Malaya, but some days just seemed to be hotter than others! I always preferred it when we started in a Westerly direction with the early morning sun was behind us. That meant the strong beams of sunlight would be shining into the eyes, and illuminating anyone to the front of us, making it easier for us to see them before they saw us.

There were the sounds of monkeys shouting and screaming in the distance, and the insect world was creating its constant overriding hum. The night before we had seen the occasional firefly, which to me even after a year and a half, still hadn't lost their magic, as an impossible phenomenon. It was still all up hill and down dale, and we had been underway for two or three hours, when the leading scout and Sanden both went down on to one knee at the same time.

I was just going to follow suit when they both got back up, and my pulse rate went back down. Just in front of them, and to the side of the faint track we were following, was an attap shelter, which on inspection turned out to be an old CT sentry post. We realised that there could be the remains of a camp up-front, and even though we knew that it would be old, we still approached it with caution, and with a careful eye open for any bamboo punji bed traps.

Sure enough, fifty yards further on, the remains of the camp appeared through the jungle greenery. Sanden reckoned that it was about one and a half years old, which meant that the camp had been full of CTs when I arrived at Colombo Camp. We stayed inside the camp for a drink of water, barley-sugar sweet and cigarette break. As I looked around the camp, it was clear that they had left in a hurry, because there was a fair amount of equipment that had been left behind. There was nothing too important, but paraphernalia such as a water barrel, large pieces of waterproofing plastic sheeting and nylon cord still tying the old bashas together. Before we left, I made sure that there were no items that could be used again by Charlie.

We reckoned that the Australians must have been patrolling nearer to the jungle edge, and the CTs expected an imminent attack and left in a rush. The recurrent jungle patrols did work against Charlie, but you hardly ever found out if and when.

We left the camp and we had got two or three-hundred yards further West when one of the lads behind me gave out a cry of pain. He sat down on the ground, dropping his rifle and holding onto his foot.

I thought that something, possibly a snake had bitten him, but he screamed out that he had stood on something sharp.

He was thinking, as we were for a second, that it was an old CT punji trap, but it turned out that he had stood on a tree branch, that was full of long, hard, black-wood spikes. One of the spikes had penetrated through the thin rubber sole of his jungle boot, and well into his foot.

It was impossible to remove his boot, even with the lace completely removed, as the spike was pinning the boot to his foot. I could see only one course of action that could be taken, so I took out the razor blade.

One of the lads said to the injured party, " My God, he's going to cut your foot off."

Everyone laughed at that.

I said, "No, only the boot, and you lot keep your eyes on the jungle while I am doing it."

My Lance Corporal, who was Second-in-Command of the section, gave me a hand in cutting the top off the boot, so we could pull it straight down and off the foot, and all being well, along with the hard-wood spike.

Fortunately everything went to plan, and the boot came away, including the entire spike. I was worried about the end of the spike remaining in the lad's foot, because the foot would have been quickly poisoned. I decided that as it was nearly time to be returning to base, we should head back to the jungle camp immediately.

We had a rest break before setting off back to base, whilst everyone smoked a couple of cigarettes just to calm their nerves. The lads cut two convenient branches to act as crutches, and I took the injured lad's FN rifle and gave him my Patchet to hang around his neck, so as to leave his hands free.

We got back to camp in that manner and without further problems. When we went out on patrol the day but one after that event, the injured lad borrowed a jungle boot to wear on his injured foot, which was almost back to normal fitness, but it could have been far worse. We had no more excitement on that operation, much to my relief, and when we got back into Colombo Camp, there was good news waiting for me.

The dates for leaving Colombo Camp were in the Company Office, along with the sailing date from Singapore. We were catching the train at Ipoh, and then going down to Singapore docks where we would directly board the boat from the train, and we should be docking in Southampton on June 30th.

It all sounded good to me, and I wrote a quick airmail letter home to give Betty the good news and the dates, I could hardly believe that I had almost made it to the end of my service. We sorted out all our kit and got the washing ready for the Dhobi man. It worked out that we would be in camp for the weekend before we went out on the next jungle operation. I had also found out that the next operation was for seven days. I couldn't help but think that they were getting their money's-worth out of me.

One of the 'B' Company Lance Corporals, who if I remember correctly was L/Corporal Critchley, had finished my model Mosquito by fitting on the undercarriage. I had arranged for him to do that before I went into the jungle. That meant I would be able to test fly the aeroplane on Sunday morning at the Gurkha Camp on the North-West side of Ipoh, to where for some reason, we had moved our flying field.

I can well remember looking forward to flying the Mosquito, which really did look something special in the wartime camouflage colours. We arrived at the Gurkha camp in a specially provided Loyals three-tonner. I dismounted from the Bedford along with the rest of the Loyals Model Club members, and we all prepared our models ready for flying. It was decided that with my aeroplane not having flown before, I would go first, so that if any adjustments were required, I could carry them out, and then fly again later.

I stood in the centre of the circle while my much-admired Mosquito's engines were fired-up. At a signal, the plane was released and away it went. It flew perfectly and unbelievably fast, just like the real thing. Suddenly, and for no reason, the inboard engine cut out. With only the outer engine running, control was completely lost, and the model flew up in the air, over my head and powered nose first into the ground, and into a thousand pieces. Well it settled what to do with the plane when I left Colombo a few days later, and saved any arguing, as there were one or two of the lads who wanted to buy it from me.

That was the last time that I flew a model plane in Malaya, and two days later it was back to reality, and we were climbing down off the three-tonners by the side of a narrow and dusty Malayan road. This was my last jungle operation, just seven days to go and then I would see the last of the jungle. To the East the sun was just showing itself over the Cameroon Highland Mountains, and the sky was a brilliant light blue; while on the Western horizon it was still the dark Royal blue that would be gone in a few minutes.

The first leg of our operation was through about a mile and a half of basically flat terrain, which was overflowing with rough razor-edged scrub undergrowth, very similar to the area we had been travelling across when the Artillery opened fire over our heads. My section was doing the lead this time, and I kept thinking to myself, that if Charlie was going to stop me getting home, then this operation was his last chance. But we made the jungle edge okay, and without any artillery interruptions.

The jungle here was the thick, and what I used to call the friendly type, and a mile and a half into the jungle; we found a decent flat area next to a wide and good flowing stream. There was a waterfall that was about eighteen inches high, and was handy for separating the drinking water and washing areas.

While I was building my basha, I felt the first pangs of toothache, which got steadily worse as the day passed, and I had an uncomfortable night. I took my section out on patrol the following day, but I had great difficulty in concentrating on the job in hand, with the pain that I was suffering.

The following day we were picking up a two day's re-supply at the jungle edge, so that we could last out the seven days operation, so I made arrangements, via the radio, to visit the dentist and to return to Colombo Camp with the re-supply transport. The following morning I left the jungle camp, and also left behind all my equipment, that's apart from my personal needs, ammunition and Patchet. I got back to Colombo in the early afternoon, and was booked in to see the garrison dentist first thing the following morning.

I spent the rest of the day suffering with toothache, although the painkillers were beginning to work. That night I went to the new air-conditioned cinema, but I must admit that I felt guilty at being there, and not in the jungle with the lads. But also, not that guilty to be out of the jungle forever and away from the danger. I couldn't help but feel excited with the knowledge that in just over a week's time, I would be on my way home.

The following morning as I left my basha to go across the football field to the dentist, I saw three new faces in the 4 Platoon hut. I went into the basha to see what they were after, and found out that they were just out of jungle training and the new replacements for 4 Platoon. I told them that I would be back before long, and that I would sort them out then. It took me about ten minutes to walk across to the dentist, who was of course an army medical officer. Fifteen minutes later I was on my way back to my basha with no feeling in my mouth, and no toothache, and thinking that I would go and perform my last duty for the army by getting the new lads organised. Well you had to be an optimist to survive, and I should have known better after nearly two years of service.

I got the three lads sorted with places in one of the 4 Platoon bashas near to each other, and I also introduced them to the 'B' Company Arm's Cote and the Quartermaster stores. That afternoon I was sat reading in the Corporals' basha and on my own as all of the 'B' Company Platoons were out on jungle operations. One of the lads from the QMs stores came to the basha, and told me that the CSM wanted me urgently at the 'B' Company Office.

I didn't need telling that it would be bad news, and when I got to the Company office, it was. They had decided that as I was fit again and 4 Platoon still had three days left in the jungle, I would be able to take the new lads into 4 Platoon's base camp the following morning.

I was asked, "Would I have a problem with that?"

The only answer I could give to that one was, "No, providing that my platoon is informed via tonight's radio traffic, that I am coming back in."

I spent the rest of the afternoon sorting out the new lads with all their new equipment, including their own personal FN rifles, which they hadn't even had the chance to try out on the range. We were all sorted by teatime and ready for the off, first thing in the morning. The lads were very apprehensive at going into the jungle to join the platoon, especially when there were only the four of us, and with only myself fully experienced.

I explained to them, "I have been in there and come back out within the last three days, and there was absolutely nothing to worry about."

I eventually convinced them that there was no need to worry at all, and I was so good that I nearly convinced myself! The truth was that I was more worried than they were about making my way back through the jungle to 4 Platoon with three Joskins. One thing that one and a half years in the jungle had provided me with was experience, which had taught me that one of the biggest dangers we faced, was from nervous inexperienced newcomers. All the lads in the platoon and indeed throughout the Battalion, were first class at quickly showing any newcomer the ropes, and getting them settled into the platoon's jungle routine.

We were dropped off back at the same spot where I had been picked up two days before, when I had the tooth needing attention. With the lack of an experienced jungle fighter, I was thinking of doing the leading scout myself, but the thought of just three Joskins, and no one else behind made me think again. One of the lads was keen to do the leading scout bit, and as willingness was always a good sign, I gave him the job.

I put one of the other lads behind him, I went third, and the last lad did the tail end Charlie. So like that, off we went through the scrub and into the early morning sunshine. By the time we reached the jungle edge I realised that the three lads were still suffering from the training squad Corporals, and were more frightened of me than the jungle and Charlie.

It was a case of me having to tell them when they had heard or seen something, syndrome. We got about one-hundred yards into the jungle, and under the shade of the canopy, when I called a halt for a cigarette and drink break. It was also to give me the chance to have a few words with the Joskins, and to basically put them straight to the facts.

I told them, "I know that you are frightened of doing something wrong, but if you do, I will simply tell you how to do it right. When we get to the platoon, the lads will put you all straight on what to do."

I also told them that I would jump on them if they did something dangerous. That was basically putting their own and anyone else's life in danger, by such stupid little things as not having their safety catch on, their weapon pointing at someone or being loaded in the base camp. They were a lot better after that and friendlier. It was the start for them, of learning to be a top jungle fighter, and a process that would only be completed long after I had arrived back home in Blighty.

Three days later I was passing that resting place and on my way out of the jungle for the very last time, or so I thought then! There were only five days left, then I would be on the train to Singapore and the boat home. We got back into Colombo Camp and two days rest. I went swimming at the Kinta Swimming Pool for the last time. It occurred to me while I was there, that we hadn't had any invitations to the privately owned swimming pools for well over half a year. I wondered if it was a case of, now that we have chased Charlie off, the army aren't needed or welcomed anymore, but who knows? It just makes me wonder now; if any of the lads got invitations during the rest of the Loyals service in Malaya?

I got a call to attend the 'B' Company Office on the afternoon of the second rest day in Colombo Camp. I was told that I was in charge of a tricky ambush for two nights starting tomorrow. It was a shock to the system, as I had begun to relax completely, in the belief that my tour of duty in Malaya was over.

They were right about the ambush being difficult. It was next to a small village about twenty-miles to the North of Ipoh. The small back road ran through the village, and the policemen who manned the roadblock on the edge of the village, were believed to be sympathetic to Charlie. The ambush position was about two-hundred yards up a small track running into the jungle from the jungle edge, which bordered the edge of the road.

The major problems were that the position could not be reconnoitred in daylight because of the policemen. We had to dismount after nightfall from the three-tonner, while it was on the move, and to cap it all we had to climb up a very steep hill, starting from the edge of the road to get to the track.

I reconnoitred the road and the entrance to the track the following afternoon from the passenger seat of a one-tonner.

We just drove steadily past the track, and then past the police post and through the village. We stopped on the road a few miles to the North of the village and waited for half an hour, then drove slowly back and past everything again. There was another small problem, although I thought that in this case it was an advantage; the ambush position would only take four men in total.

We arrived at the drop-off point that night, and about fifteen minutes after dark on the back of a one-ton Bedford truck. There were three policemen visible on the road at the village edge, but the driver of the one-tonner had his headlights on full beam, so the policemen couldn't see when we jumped off the back of the still moving Bedford, and then scampered up the steep jungle track.

We found the ambush point that was on a bend in the track, and it was a peculiar feeling to make our way up the track to that point with the aid of torches. But we managed okay, including setting-up the flares. Everything went fine that night and early the following morning we lifted the ambush using the torches again, because we had to get back down to the road in the dark and then wait for the one-tonner to go past.

The driver then pretended to be having engine trouble and stopped on the roadside. This was to cover us while we got onto the lorry, and down in the back out of sight of the roadblock, but there was no sign of the police who were probably asleep.

The next night was a repeat performance of this, and once again we settled into the ambush position. I was tired that night, having spent a lot of the day getting ready for leaving Colombo, but as I lay in the ambush position thinking of home, I did something that I had never done before. I fell asleep!

That was the only time in Malaya that I ever did that during ambushing. The last time that I looked at my watch it had been just after midnight. I was woken by being nudged by the lad next to me on my right-hand side.

He whispered, "There's somebody coming down the track with a torch."

He had no need to say anything, because I had seen it as soon as my eyes opened, something was bobbing between the trees one-hundred yards or so up the track. My left hand reached out and touched the switch for the ground flares, and my right hand gripped the handle of my Patchet, with my thumb pushing off the safety catch, and my forefinger wrapped around the trigger. I caught a glance of my wrist-watch. It was 02:35hrs, but the watch only distracted me for a split second, before my eyes returned to the torch-light coming down the track.

The sweat was running down and under my chin, and I found that, with not wanting to cause any sound at all, it was difficult to breathe. The torch did not seem to be getting any nearer to us, and I wondered for a moment as to whether we had been seen?

I then realised what it was, and what had happened. I took my finger off the flares switch, and put my safety catch back on. I then knelt up.

"Stop panicking lads and put your safety catches back on." I knew that they had all been asleep, otherwise someone would have watched the moon coming up over the hilltop at the end of the track.

We remained sitting up, and also with the occasional flash of the torch up the track just to make sure that Charlie wasn't on his way down. I wasn't doing anything wrong in my actions, because I knew that if Charlie came down the track and we were just lying there, he would see us easily in the bright moonlight that was shining down the track and into our eyes. However we would not have seen him until the last second, and I was not willing to take that chance with our lives. We hadn't seen the moon on the previous night, so it had obviously been cloudy all through the hours of darkness. As the moon moved across and behind the thicker jungle canopy, the track was thrown back into the concealing darkness, so we settled back down once again into the ambush.

So that really was my last operation, and the final twist of the screw that the jungle held for me. The transport picked us up in daylight this time; we wanted the policemen who were manning the checkpoint to see us coming out of the jungle. It was just to send the little message to them, that they were not informed, or knew about everything that was happening around that area, and that they could be caught out.

When we got back to Colombo I was given the reality message when I went to hand in my sub-machine gun at the 'B' Company Arm's Cote.

Len who was in charge of the Arm's Cote said, "Well Fred you wont be needing that again."

"Don't tempt fate," was my reply to that. After all there were still twenty-four hours left to find something for me to do.

The rest of that day was spent packing my gear, doing deals with the QM on the equipment, giving my special Malaya gear to any of the lads who needed it, and saying my goodbyes, in and around Colombo Camp to a very, very special bunch of men.

I went to see Sanden to say thanks for all he did for me. I got his address in Sarawak, but unfortunately when I got home it had gone missing, so I was never able to write to him. Early the following morning we climbed onto the three-tonners and left the Loyal Battalion Motor Transport Park and Colombo Camp for the last time. We turned to the left and drove down the road towards Ipoh and the railway station.

I looked back for the last time at the camp situated on top of the low rise. From behind the mountains to the East, the large red sun was rising into the blue Malayan sky. The camp itself was just the same as when I first clapped eyes on the place one and a half years earlier. It was still a collection of dried grass native huts, but it had been home to us. I could see one or two of the lads moving around the Arm's Cote and walking over to the Company Offices.

As we drove past the guardroom and around the left hand bend, four lads were walking along the road to the main camp and busy chatting. Nobody gave us a wave, or even a second glance. I thought to myself that we had done our job and done it well, but we had already been relegated to a part of history. *The King is Dead, Long Live the King.*

# CHAPTER TWENTY-ONE
### *The Long Journey Home*

We boarded the train at Ipoh, and this time we were up towards the front. The armoured escort train was no longer used, and we didn't have a rifle or ammunition with us on this trip, which did seem to be a bit peculiar to us, as carrying weapons most of the time had become a part of our way of life. The reason for not carrying rifles was that the States of Malaya that we were travelling through, had all been declared 'white areas', which meant they were now free from the CTs.

Apart from the expedition to Hong Kong with the Battalion, this was the first time I had been back down and through the South of Malaya since I arrived one and a half years before. I had my last great meal in Malaya on the train, which was of course, Nasi Goreng.

"I wonder if they still serve the dish on the Malayan railway?"

We arrived at the Dockside, and next to The *S.S. Oxfordshire,* and in what seemed no time at all, we were on board with our gear stored, and pulling away from the dockside to the strains of *'Auld Lang Syne'* that was being played by a military band on the jetty.

We were all familiar with the *Oxfordshire* after the three-day Hong Kong trip, only this time we would be on board for over three weeks. As I have said before, Malaya was the other side of the world and a lifetime away, and now we had the frustration of a long and boring journey, but back to our world, and our life.

From Singapore, we sailed to the North between Malaya and Indonesia, up through the Straits of Malacca, and out into the Indian Ocean. We were heading for Ceylon (Now Sri Lanka) and the port of Colombo. The day before we were due to dock and go ashore for a few hours, a message came over the tannoy saying:-

**Due to a strike at the port, we would not be docking there and would continue on to Aden.**

We all had certain duties to do on the ship, and naturally all to do with cleaning on the vessel, the washroom, toilets and the mess deck, but there wasn't too much that could be done, and all the chores were finished by about 11:00hrs.

I did one Guard Commander on board. Yes you read that correctly. It was from 18:00hrs until 07:00hrs the following day, and consisted of spending most of the night in the guardroom, which was up in the bow of the ship and below the waterline. Built right into the bow were the cells that consisted of nothing more than iron railings, just like the cells in the Sheriff's Office in the Western cowboy movies. Inside the cells were several prisoners who were being taken back to the UK to serve whatever sentence they had been given. I had a Lance Corporal to act as Second in Command, and six Private soldiers for the guard. They were all strangers to me, and surprisingly none were out of the Loyals, but we all got on okay.

The rear of the boat was for Officers, females, civilians, Sergeant's quarters, and the hospital. One of the guard duties was to ensure that no one from the lower ranks passed through the doors to the rear of the boat without permission. I don't think that anyone bothered to try, and I certainly had no problems as the Guard Commander.

I can tell you that I absolutely hated being in the guardroom; down in the bow and below the waterline. You could hear the water constantly crashing against the bow of the boat, just like a sound track from a horror movie. I constantly left the guardroom to walk around the sentry points, and also to check that there was no trouble with drunks in the bars that were on board the ship. But everyone was on their way back home, and so not likely to be causing trouble for themselves at that stage of the game.

There was also quite a few things taking place each day on the boat, and that's apart from the bar that was selling English beer and Irish or Scotch whisky. There was also a film show each night, which was given on the upper deck and in the open air.

This took a bit of getting used to, because the boat was travelling at well over twenty knots an hour, so we had a fair old breeze blowing around us all the time. Also on board there were shops, so you could buy cigarettes, books, sweets and suchlike, and you still got paid weekly, so you did have money to buy what you wanted to suit your own requirements.

We sailed across the Arabian Sea and into the Gulf of Aden before docking at the port of Aden, which is situated in the South of the Arabian Peninsula. We had most of the day there, which we spent walking around the place, what there was of it to see, and in the NAAFI club for a meal and a drink, then back to the boat.

There was a lot of trouble in Aden, which fortunately started a few months after I had been there. Eventually the British pulled out. You could tell there was a bad feeling about the place, and I was glad to be back within the security of the ship. We set sail from Aden in the late afternoon and into the Red Sea, which led all the way up to port Suez and the Suez Canal.

One interesting moment in the Red Sea was one late afternoon, when we passed another British troopship that was full of national servicemen on its way to Aden, Singapore and Hong Kong. Both ships sounded their sirens in salute, and we were close enough for everyone on both ships to wave to each other. We gave the biggest wave, because we were going home and finished, but for those lads on the other boat, the story was just beginning.

It took us a couple of days to reach Port Suez where we anchored for the night in what was called 'The Roads.' It was peculiar sleeping on board the ship with no movement, nor the throb, throb, throb of the engines, but early next morning the movement and sounds were back, and we were underway and entering the Canal.

The Suez had not been reopened for very long, following the Suez War, and the British were only just tolerated and allowed to sail through; that was due to the Egyptians needing the money. The properties all along the Canal were still damaged after the war and in need of repair.

When we entered the Bitter Lakes in the middle of the Canal we could see a lot of the ships that were still under water, as they had been sunk to block the Canal. That all happened just over a year before I was called up into the army, and I couldn't help but think about my cousin Raymond. He was a national serviceman at that time, and very much involved in the Suez War while on board the Aircraft Carrier, *HMS Eagle.*

It was most peculiar to be sailing through a desert and on the Eastern side of the canal, that's all there was. On the West bank of the Canal there were scatterings of war-damaged houses, and a road that followed the Canal for the full length. The Canal is just over one-hundred miles long, and it took us the full day to sail to the other end and to Port Said.

That evening we sailed out into the Mediterranean, and into the late evening sunset, and that really was a bookmark, and the moment that we all felt, we were almost home.

The next stop was Gibraltar, and we had a good half-day there. It was great to be using British money again, and to see the good old British Bobby. It was even better to be back on the boat though, and underway for Blighty, any delay now that we were so near home, was regarded almost as a punishment. We made our way through the straits of Gibraltar and into the Atlantic.

We were in the Bay of Biscay on the 29th June 1959, and then we sailed into the English Channel, and docked at Southampton in the early morning sunshine on the 30th June.

"How do I remember the dates so easily? Well it was my 23rd birthday on the 29th, and I only remembered that it had been my birthday when we docked at Southampton, which was the day after? Doesn't that tell you how much getting back home meant to us?"

There were several trains waiting on the docks for us, and they were going to different destinations in the UK. Everyone who had come from Malaya was waved straight through Customs, and onto the various trains, but any lads from other postings had to endure the rigours of the Customs Officers' checks.

I said my goodbyes to Keith Hind, a lad I had met and got to know on the boat. He had been with the 13th/18th Hussars, and based in Ipoh at the Colombo Camp Garrison. He came from Belper in Derbyshire.

Three weeks later Keith and his wife came to Blackpool for a week's holiday, and Betty and I joined them for a night out on the town. Sad to say, we lost touch many years ago. I suppose it would be the appropriate saying, *'ships that pass in the night'.*

Nearly all the lads from the basic training days at Ladysmith Barracks were present at Southampton, and about to board the various trains, some for the Liverpool-bound train, and some for the train going to Manchester. I was going to climb aboard the Preston train, and then for the first time in my life, go on to Fulwood Barracks, the home of the Loyals.

We all said our goodbyes on the railway platforms by the docks, and without even thinking the impossible, that we would never meet again. We had all started this story together two years earlier at Ladysmith Barracks. What we had endured throughout the two years had created a bond, that not even time and distance could break.

Every so often, and for whatever reason, one of the lad's images, any one of them; will flicker into my mind's eye, taking me back to a darker moment that makes me fearful, even now! Or back, and without reason, to a moment that no matter where you are or what you are doing, brings a bright smile to your face.

The steam train pulled away from the platform with a shudder, and then picked up speed and headed North towards Preston. It was difficult to control our impatience, and most of the journey was spent looking out of the windows, or stood by one of the doors with the window fully down, and one's head stuck out in the slipstream of the train. It was just so good to be looking out on the peaceful green fields of the English countryside.

We were lucky to arrive back in England at the start of one of the precious heatwaves that we sometimes, but very rarely encounter. I remember that one well, for within a few short weeks, it had dried out most of the reservoirs. The first real shudder down the spine came in the late afternoon, when the train came to the brow of the hill at Charnock Richard, a few miles to the South of Preston.

Looking out of the window I could see across the Lancashire plains, and to the horizon, where I could see Blackpool Tower well over twenty-miles away, and standing proudly not too far from my home.

A few minutes later we crossed over the River Ribble, and pulled slowly into Preston Railway Station. Outside the railway station two Bedford three-tonners were parked up, and waiting to take us through Preston to Fulwood Barracks. We loaded our equipment and cases onto the back of the lorries, and climbed on board; then we were off, away from the station and up Fishergate, then down Church Street and past the Blue Bell Inn on the right, where we were all due to meet up the following year. On we travelled towards the prison, and then to the left, past Deepdale Football Ground and then on to Fulwood Barracks a few hundred yards further on.

When we got to the barracks, we were dropped off by the square, and ushered into one of the old barrack rooms. There we were told that we were just being kept long enough to be given a three week's leave pass, fully paid for the whole three weeks, and then we were free to make our way home.

We were told to return three weeks later, to hand in our kit, and to be discharged. I got the impression that with there being a new training squad in the barracks, they wanted any bad influence out of the way, meaning us old sweats. But that suited us all, and half an hour later we were waiting at the bus stop opposite the barracks for the next bus to Preston Bus Station. There I had a ten-minute wait for a bus that would take me to Wrea Green.

When I boarded the bus, and stored all my bags and case in the space provided underneath the stairs, I felt as though I was in a dream, and that any moment I would wake and be back in my jungle basha.

I went up the stairs, and sat on the front seat so that I could see everything in view on the bus journey home. As the bus passed through Kirkham and on up Ribby Road, I could see my Dad in the front garden busy hoeing the weeds around the rockery. I was ready to wave, when he looked up, and I was disappointed when the bus moved on past, without him actually seeing me. We arrived at the top of Ribby Road, and although we had passed quite a few of the homes of old friends and relatives, I didn't see any of them.

At the top of the road on the right stood my old school, and the place where as a Loyals' Army Cadet, I had first worn the Queen's uniform. Over four-hundred years of honourable tradition was held in place behind the old leaded light windows and brown sandstone walls, and all of it was standing defiant against the smothering green Ivy, and all the evils of the world.

My mind switched back to the times I had stood in the middle of the Communist camps deep in the Malayan jungle, the master of everyone and everything that I could see, and thinking of Kirkham Grammar School.

I couldn't help but reflect at that moment and to say to myself, "I didn't let you down."

The bus pulled out across the main road, turning right towards Blackpool, and two minutes later, with a squeal of brakes, it stopped at the Ribby Corner bus stop to let me off. Because they were always impatient to be on the move, and back underway even before the bus had stopped, the bus conductor, unusually helped me off with all my bags. As I stood with my pile of packs, kitbag and case by the side of the road, the conductor spoke to me.

"Good luck lad, it's good to be back home." and then he pressed the bell twice to tell the driver to move on.

I loaded the packs on to my back, and pulled the belt tight, swung the kitbag across my shoulders and picked up the case. The warm summer evening sun shone down from the clear blue sky, and I started to walk through the peaceful English countryside towards home and Betty. I was hoping that she would be at home, because I hadn't been able to say just what day I would be back home, never mind what time of day that I would be returning.

I should say that I walked proudly towards home. My uniform was pressed perfect; the strips on my arm gleaming white, and enhanced by the display of coloured badges, and my hard-earned medal ribbon was there for all to see.

I crossed over the road, so that I could see the house sooner as I walked around the bend in the road. I was walking on the road now, as there was no pavement on that side, just the low hawthorn hedge, and the beautiful green fields of the Fylde stretching all the way to Blackpool some eight-miles in the distance.

Over the gentle rise in the road the top of the house appeared in my view, and then I could see it clearly. Stood talking at the side gate were my brother-in-law Bob, and my old school friend, John Armour. I saw them both look up the road in my direction, and then Bob turned towards the back of the house and I heard him shout.

"He's here."

I saw Betty come running down the path by the side of the house, and then through the gate, running up the road and into my arms. I knew then that I was really home at last!

# ENDNOTES

I cannot believe that I have finally finished the book and arrived at the endnotes. It has taken me three years longer than I expected, as it has been surprising how many quirks have appeared in the formatting of the book. An example of one of the quirks is in the grammar. I have written in the English grammar of the 1950's, which is the time relative to the book. It did come as a surprise, just how much English grammar has changed in a fifty-year period, which also made me reflect on the enormous changes that have occurred within the last fifty years, and how much they had affected the way we live and how we live.

Amongst those changes is without doubt, how small the world has become now with modern easy fast travel and communications. This is especially so with the Internet, which I used to confirm some of the facts given within the book, which also led to me making contact once again with Johnny Morris, an old comrade and friend from the Somme Training Platoon. The last time I saw Johnny was on the platform in the Southampton dockyard. He and I were only two beds apart in the Somme Platoon barrack room at Ladysmith, and we endured all the twelve weeks pain and suffering together. Yet amazingly, we never met up in Colombo Camp, Ipoh. Doesn't that tell you that out in Malaya we really did fight a none stop battle with Charlie? John was with 'HQ' Company, and used to do a regular tail end Charlie, on re-supplies into the jungle for our jungle platoons.

He also vividly remembers it raining in Hong Kong. He was on guard duty when it started to rain in the middle of the night, and hundreds of snakes came out in the area he was patrolling within Fanling Camp. John emigrated to Canada along with his wife Anne and family in the 1960's, which is where they still live.

A special mention of thanks here to Susan, John's daughter, and the person responsible for putting a last hope message on the Internet for anyone who knew a Johnny Morris, ex Loyals Malayan Veteran.

Another ex-Malayan Veteran, ex-Loyal, who posted a message on the Internet, was Harry Barnes. Harry was in 2 Platoon 'A' Company, and he also emigrated to Canada in the 1960's, which is where he still lives. And yes they have been in touch with each other.

Another amazing meeting up with an old face from Malaya, was Major Tony Maher MBE. Slim, to his friends and Comrades out in Malaya. He is now heavily involved with the Regimental Museum in Fulwood Barracks. Slim was a regular soldier with the Loyals, and we were both Corporals together in 'B' Company. Slim, if he had a mind too, could quite easily write a couple of books on his, sometimes heart stopping, Malayan experiences.

In the course of writing this book, I have also found out how a sandwich made up with a tea-cake comes to be called a Banjo. Apparently it's a Liverpool expression, and from the days when the dock-workers used to have a fried egg on a tea-cake with their morning tea break. When they took a bite out of the sandwich, the egg yoke would run out and down the front of their clothing. They would hold the left hand with the tea-cake up and out of the way, while wiping the egg yoke away with their right hand. So from a distance it looked as if they were playing a Banjo. That explanation does make sense to me, remembering the number of Liverpool lads who were with the Loyals out in Malaya.

Other questions that I have been asked are:-

## Did we ever telephone home?

No, most of the lads didn't have a phone at home anyway in those days. The only phone was in the Company Office and for Company use, and the cost of a call to the UK was two weeks (national service) wages per minute. Phone calls had to be booked to the UK in advance, and it took half an hour or longer, to link the call through the various Telephone Exchanges.

## What was a free cigarettes issue?

With the Loyals being on active service in Malaya, it meant that each soldier was entitled to a free tin of 50 cigarettes every Thursday of each week, or pipe tobacco if you smoked a pipe. You had a choice of what brand of cigarettes you smoked, to suit your needs. Infrequently we were issued with additional free tins of cigarettes, that came from the Customs and Excise Officers in the UK. These were the cigarettes that had been seized from tobacco smugglers.

I remember on one occasion, when I got back into Colombo Camp from a long jungle operation, receiving 350 free cigarettes. It always amazed me, that we got the free issue on a Thursday afternoon, and by Friday night just about everyone was scrounging for cigarettes because they had run out.

***Were we paid in Pounds, Shillings and Pence?***

No, we were paid every Thursday if we were in Colombo Camp, and in Malayan Dollars and cents. The correct name was actually Ringgit and sen, and we were never paid in the jungle when we were out on an operation.

***What was the jungle operation about, where you had to sign the Secrecy Act?***

That is still clandestine! But I have started to write my next book?

# CASUALTY LIST

Casualties 1948/1960. During the LOYALS' Engagement **1957/1959.**

## COMMUNIST TERRORISTS.

| | | |
|---|---|---|
| KILLED | 6711. | **414.** |
| CAPTURED | 1289. | **62.** |
| SURRENDERED | 2704. | **797.** |
| WOUNDED | 3000.---- (Approximate number only).----- | **200.** |

## SECURITY FORCES.

| | | |
|---|---|---|
| KILLED | 1865. | **22.** |
| WOUNDED | 2560. | **61.** |

## CIVILIANS.

| | | |
|---|---|---|
| KILLED | 3283. | **33.** |
| WOUNDED | 1385. | **7.** |

Figures: Released and Published by Singapore University.